THE HANDBOOK OF COUPLE AND FAMILY ASSESSMENT

HANDBOOK OF COUPLE AND FAMILY ASSESSMENT

KARIN JORDAN
EDITOR

Nova Science Publishers, Inc.
New York

Senior Editors: Susan Boriotti and Donna Dennis
Coordinating Editor: Tatiana Shohov
Office Manager: Annette Hellinger
Graphics: Wanda Serrano
Editorial Production: Marius Andronie, Maya Columbus, Vladimir Klestov,
   Matthew Kozlowski and Thomas Moceri
Circulation: Ave Maria Gonzalez, Vera Popovic, Raymond Davis, Melissa Diaz,
   Magdalena Nuñez, Marlene Nuñez and Jeannie Pappas
Communications and Acquisitions: Serge P. Shohov
Marketing: Cathy DeGregory

Library of Congress Cataloging-in-Publication Data

Jordan, Karin.
   Handbook of couple and family assessment / Karin Jordan.
      p. cm.
   Includes index.
      ISBN: 1-59033-686-0 (hardcover)
      1. Family assessment—Handbooks, manuals, etc. 2. Marital psychotherapy—Handbooks, manuals, etc. I. Title.

RC488.53.K366 2003
616.89'156—dc21
                                                                                                2003004261

Copyright © 2003 by Nova Science Publishers, Inc.
   400 Oser Ave, Suite 1600
   Hauppauge, New York 11788-3619
   Tele. 631-231-7269   Fax 631-231-8175
   e-mail: Novascience@earthlink.net
   Web Site: http://www.novapublishers.com

All rights reserved. No part of this book may be reproduced, stored in a retrieval system or transmitted in any form or by any means: electronic, electrostatic, magnetic, tape, mechanical photocopying, recording or otherwise without permission from the publishers.

The publisher has taken reasonable care in the preparation of this book, but makes no expressed or implied warranty of any kind and assumes no responsibility for any errors or omissions. No liability is assumed for incidental or consequential damages in connection with or arising out of information contained in this book.

This publication is designed to provide accurate and authoritative information with regard to the subject matter covered herein. It is sold with the clear understanding that the publisher is not engaged in rendering legal or any other professional services. If legal or any other expert assistance is required, the services of a competent person should be sought. FROM A DECLARATION OF PARTICIPANTS JOINTLY ADOPTED BY A COMMITTEE OF THE AMERICAN BAR ASSOCIATION AND A COMMITTEE OF PUBLISHERS.

Printed in the United States of America

*Dedicated to my own family of origin,
and my husband Wayne Jordan.*

Contents

Preface		ix
Chapter 1	Couple and Family Assessment: An Overview *Karin Jordan*	1
Chapter 2	Managed Care and Assessment Instruments: Some Introductory Comments *Tracy Todd*	15
Chapter 3	Therapeutic Family Assessment: A Systems Approach *Robert W. Heffer, Mariella M. Lane and Douglas K. Snyder*	21
Chapter 4	Assessing Couples: Procedures, Tools, and Benefits *Mark Odell*	49
Chapter 5	A Developmental-Family Systems Approach to the Assessment of Adolescents *Robert W. Heffer and Danielle L. Oxman*	67
Chapter 6	Assessment of Older Adults and their Families *Sara H. Qualls and Daniel L. Segal*	109
Chapter 7	Assessment of Infidelity *Tina Pittman Wagers*	129
Chapter 8	Divorce Assessment Becomes Intervention *Pat Hudson*	147
Chapter 9	Assessing Parenting Capability *Chelsea T. Wolf and John J. Peregoy*	167
Chapter 10	Partner Violence Assessment *Sandra M. Stith, Carrie Penn, David Ward and Dari Tritt*	187
Chapter 11	Child Sexual Abuse Assessment: The Tri-Modal Interview Protocol *Linda E. Homeyer and Daniel S. Sweeney*	203

Chapter 12	Family Assessment of Drug and Alcohol Problems *Linda Chamberlain and Cynthia L. Jew*	**221**
Chapter 13	Multiculturally Sensitive and Aware Couple and Family Assessment and Testing *Karin Jordan and Jesse Brinson*	**241**
Chapter 14	Multiple Family Group Intervention and Assessment: Issues and Strategies *William H. Quinn*	**259**
Chapter 15	Ethical and Legal Issues in Marital and Family Assessment *Michael J. Strazi and Patricia W. Stevens*	**275**
Index		**291**

PREFACE

This book is intended to help systems practitioners keep abreast of how to do assessments of the couple, the family, the family sub-system and individual couple/family member(s). It is designed to assist both systemic practitioners and graduate students being trained in systems therapy. The chapters in this book will be most relevant to practitioners for their work with couples, families, (system as a whole, subsystems, and individual couple and family members) with a variety of presenting problems.

The chapter topics were chosen by surveying the field of systemic therapy and then focusing of those topics that are currently in the forefront. Couple and family assessment, certainly not a new topic, is important and foundational for dealing with couples and families, and the chapters in this book present effective responses for dealing with both traditional and more contemporary clinical topics, focusing on the structure, function, and interaction patterns of today's diverse families, in a systems context. The underlying philosophy of this book is that due to current demands for time and cost effective therapy, providing quality therapy for today's evolving diverse couples and families is no longer enough. Additionally, clients have become informed consumers who expect the same efficiency. Therefore, today's systems practitioners need to be knowledgeable about how to assess couples and families and guide the goal setting and treatment approach.

My thanks to all the authors and co-authors whose expertise and scholarship contributed to the development and final product – an assessment handbook for systemic mental health professionals working with couples and families.

Chapter 1

COUPLE AND FAMILY ASSESSMENT: AN OVERVIEW

Karin Jordan[*]
George Fox University

Over the past decade, the burgeoning family therapy field has sponsored a wide array of theories, goals, treatment processes, and techniques of family therapy, and the volume of these theories can be confusing for therapists. At the same time, therapists now find themselves dealing with ever-changing structures, forms, and compositions of couples and families, and these are inevitably here to stay. Problems addressed in therapy have become more complex and often are multi-problem systems. Clients today are consumers who are often sophisticated, verbal, and functional individuals desiring change in their lives.

OUTCOME ASSESSMENT

In addition to these challenges, therapists and clients are often faced with changes in the duration of treatment. Managed care has increasingly mandated careful assessment, using a brief treatment model that has been tailored to fit the family. Precise, efficient, and cost effective treatment, as well as accountability through empirical support data and evaluation by external reviews, are required to survive in the managed care environment.

In dealing with managed care and clients who have become informed consumers, being accountable means providing time and cost effective therapy, which can be achieved through careful assessment at the onset and throughout the process of therapy. Assessment results allow therapists to be focused in guiding the process of therapy. Additionally, doing outcome assessment can help the therapist and client(s) to discern whether change and growth have occurred, by highlighting the improvements made. Outcome assessment data are needed

---

[*] Karin Jordan, Ph.D., Associate Professor and Chair, Graduate Department of Counseling, George Fox University, Portland, Oregon.

today to verify to managed care providers that progress has been made in therapy. When dealing with outcome assessment, it is important that couple and/or family assessment focuses on the treatment's effect on relationship aspects, but also the impact that treatment has on the individualized problem.

Individual, couple and/or family members' goal achievement can be assessed using Goal Attainment Scaling (GAS) (Kiresuk, Smith & Cardillo, 1994). GAS is a way to identify and then assess a number of individual goals that are unique to each client, including clients seen in couple and family therapy. The goals are based on the presenting problems in the context of the family or couple system they live in that brought the individual, couple, or family to therapy and are the focus of therapy. Goal assessment should be a joint process between the therapist and the client(s) (individual, couple, or family) and is based on identifying the goals after the initial assessment process has been completed and periodically assessing if treatment goals have been met, if they are changing, and what else needs to be addressed in therapy to reach goal achievement. At the time of termination, as an outcome assessment, each goal achievement is measured according to the level of expectation: (a) somewhat more (than expected), (b) somewhat less (than expected), (c) much more (than expected), and (d) much less (than expected). "Each level of outcome is assigned a value on a five-point measurement scale that ranges from –2 for much less than expected level of outcome, to +2 for much more than expected level of outcome" (Widenfelt, Markman, Guerney, Beherns & Hosman, 1997, p. 682). Ongoing assessment has implications not only for the direction of therapy, but can also serve to assess client willingness and readiness to work on change and goal achievement. For example, a couple entering therapy might have one partner who is motivated and eager to work toward enhancing their couple relationship, but the other partner is not sure why s/he is even in therapy, and is unclear about what the goal of therapy should be. Careful assessment in those situations can help determine if the partner should be in therapy, and if couple or individual therapy might be most appropriate, and if so, serve as a springboard for the therapist to find ways to recruit the partner.

ASSESSMENT: A BRIEF OVERVIEW OF FAMILY AND COUPLE RELATIONSHIPS AND PROBLEM DEVELOPMENT

When we speak of the family or the couple system, we are talking about "… a more or less stable set of relationships, it functions in certain characteristic ways, it is continuously in the process of evolution as it seeks new steady states" (Goldenberg & Goldenberg, 1996, p.54). The family has multiple subsystems, and according to Minuchin, Rosman & Baker (1978) the most stable subsystems are the: "spousal", "parental" and "sibling" subsystems. The spousal subsystem (the couple) can be assessed separately or as part of the family system. It is important to remember that couple systems and family systems, regardless of structure and composition, go through certain markers that are predictable and viewed as developmental tasks that a family must move through. According to Zilbach (1989), there are three major developmental stages and seven secondary stages. The three primary stages are: (a) early stage: forming and nesting, (b) middle stage: family separation process and (c) late stage: finishing. The seven secondary stages are: (a) coupling, (b) becoming three, (c) entrance, (d) expansion, (e) exits, (g) becoming smaller/extended, and (f) endings (Zilbach, 1989). Zilbach calls these stages "family stage markers".

The basic premise that families move through stages which are orderly and developmental in nature was first described by Duvall and Hill (1948). They developed the family life cycle stages, believing that families had to deal with normal changes in family composition. Duvall and Miller (1985) reported that there are certain developmental stages that intact, middle-class, American families transition through: (a) married couple without children, (b) childbearing families (oldest child, birth-30 months), (c) family with preschool children (oldest child 30 months- 6 years) (d) families with children (oldest child 6-13 years), (e) families with teenagers (oldest child 13-20), (f) families as launching centers (first to last child leaves home), (g) middle-aged parents (empty nest to retirement), and (h) aging family members (retirement to death of both spouses). Of course most families do differ somewhat from this model, however it provides guidance and insight into stages and approximate times they are experienced. Each stage needs to be passed through successfully, to move into and through the next stage. The family's mastery of these different stages may be said to constitute the family's overall function or dysfunction. Families that are unable to master lifecycle changes need help to become more functional. Each of the stages that the family goes through requires change and adjustment. According to Satir and Bitter (1991), functional family's:

> ...process and personal maturation are characterized by many of the same aspects: an openness to change, flexibility of response, the generation of personal choices or system options, an awareness of resources, and appreciation for difference as well as similarity, equality in relationships, personal responsibility, reasonable risk, freedom of experience and expression, clarity, and congruent communication (p. 25).

These stages seem to be universal to families, according to Charles Fishman (1988). How couples and families, individually and as a whole, transition through these stages, characterizes them. Functional couple and family systems are flexible and adaptable, trying to deal with the changes that arise as the system moves through different developmental stages. Couples and families might differ in how they deal with these developmental transitions. They might range from very orderly and gradual, to chaotic and abrupt. Predictable changes such as getting married, the birth of a child, or retirement are generally better prepared for and dealt with by the system. Unpredictable changes such as the death of a family member, illness, or unexpected loss of a job generally create more stress. Reorganization and adjustment by the system is more difficult and can be experienced as trauma or a crisis. Additionally, it is important to remember that whenever a member is added or taken out of the system the system must reorganize and find ways to cope with the change. These are changes such as the birth of a child, adoption, children starting school, or children leaving home. These transitions can be experienced as a crisis by both the family and the couple system. How will the couple deal with the birth of their first child? Will it impact the couple's level of intimacy and care? Or, when the last child leaves home, the couple might wonder: What is left in our relationship? All of our focus has been on the children for so many years. What will we talk about? Will we be bored with each other? Or when an elderly parent moves in with a family, who takes care of the elderly parent? How is the couple relationship impacted when time, money, and other resources are stretched? All of these are just a few examples of how change can be disruptive to a couple and family system where the system needs to find new ways of how to transform the couple and/or family system.

Life-cycle changes need to be considered when working with families, couples, and individuals. Life-cycle transitions, or the lack of them, can impact the system's function at multiple levels. A dysfunctional system is generally characterized as maladjusted and rigid. The underlying problems of dysfunctional family systems are rules that can be rigid, fixed, and inconsistently applied when dealing with change and transitions, resulting in an inability to deal with necessary change, all in an attempt to maintain the status quo. Some families will say such things as: "We have always done it that way." Walsh (1980) wrote:

> The sequence begins with an incident between family members or between the family and the outside world. The incident causes stress in the unit and unbalances the delicate homeostasis that exists…An unhealthy family lacking effective communication methods will not resolve the incident in a functional way. Lacking this resolution they must then transmit the stress to the identified patient (IP). This individual will eventually develop symptoms, and he will carry the dysfunction for the entire family. The crucial point in this sequence of events is the attempted resolution of a problem using either good or faulty communication methods. Faulty methods lead directly to dysfunction, which is expressed in the IP. Therefore, the remediation of individual problem behavior is focused entirely on the family communication (p.12).

It is evident that it is not the stress that the couple or family system experience that is the problem, but rather how they try to communicate about it. Carter and McGoldrick (1988) discussed the impact of multiple stressors on the family, including developmental life-cycle transition challenges as well as the perhaps less predictable changes such as the sudden loss of a loved one or chronic or terminal illness. Additionally, they address the importance of how families relate and function with one another and how the family of origin's values, beliefs, myths, and stories are transmitted from one generation to the next. These multi-stressors can create developmental transitional challenges. Additionally, life-cycle developmental stages need to be transitioned through on the system (the family), subsystem (i.e. couple system or sibling system), and individual levels. Developmental transitions can lead to fixations in a particular stage, which generally means that the family as a whole, the sub-system within the family system, and individual family members are not ready to move to the next stage in their development. The level of anxiety experienced by the family is reflective of the family's ability or inability to deal with transitions. Barnhill & Longo (1978) pointed out that families, as they go through these different developmental stages, need to be able to negotiate, not getting fixated or arrested at a particular stage. When families enter therapy arrested in a particular stage of development, careful assessment is needed to understand the family's overall functioning and structure. More specifically, the assessment tools and techniques chosen should help clarify the structure and function of the family system as a whole, the couple or other subsystems, and individual family or couple members, determining if there are developmental fixations and generally accommodating anxieties.

ASSESSING FROM THE FIRST TO THE LAST SESSION

Assessment is and should be an ongoing process of the therapist and couple or family, from the first to the last therapy session, guiding the process of therapy, assessing client commitment to therapy and responding to managed care requirements to provide outcome data that shows that change has occurred as a result of therapy. Assessment can also provide motivation for how to modify existing treatment, including the theoretical orientation followed and specific techniques used.

The daunting challenge of the transformation of individuals, couples, and families in an evolving social context and a managed care environment requires a significant shift in therapeutic style, as well as family involvement. Today, couples and families who are entering therapy are expected to be active participants in the course of treatment. In addition, treatment no longer can be limited to the therapy session, but instead clients need to be actively engaged in working on creating change outside of the therapy room. Techniques such as programmed writing, journaling, and other homework assignments facilitate the process of change outside the therapy session and are both time and cost effective, serving to help assess the client's motivation and commitment to work on change. Therapists use couple and/or family self-reports in conjunction with assessment techniques and instruments in an attempt to be both cost and time effective by contributing to the understanding of the couple and/or family relationship, interaction patterns, difficulties, etc.

Assessments of couples and families are generally done in order to better understand their level of function, structure, boundaries, and developmental levels, as well as for the purpose of diagnosis and treatment planning, which has become increasingly important as HMOs, PPOs, and insurance companies demand time and cost effectiveness and problem-specific treatment. A formal assessment often includes (a) the individual's emotional well being, psychosocial history, affective range and management, possible abuse history, cognitive function, problem solving skills, strengths and difficulties, (b) the couple's overall function, cohesion, affect, consensus, communication, satisfaction, strengths and difficulties, and (c) the family's overall function, communication, problem-solving, role identity, consensus, satisfaction, transaction between family members, strengths and difficulties. Assessment also should include interpersonal relationships, work relationships, spiritual connections, social networks, and friends. Additionally, the larger, or eco-system should also be assessed for the impact of social forces (i.e. poverty, sexism, racism) on the individual client, couple and family.

ASSESSMENT PROCESS

Assessment generally starts with the intake interview, one of the most important components of assessment, since it is the time when the therapist and client(s) decide whether or not they want to engage in therapy. This decision is generally based on the information gathered, including presenting problem(s), the commitment to therapy of all (rather than some) of the couple or family system entering therapy, expectations, and hopes to resolve the problem. It is a time when the therapist assesses the client system for (Goldenberg & Goldenberg, 1990):

- Reasons and events leading to the decision to seek help now
- Who is the symptom bearer
- Is the symptom chronic or acute?
- When did the problem first start, and who is most bothered by it?
- What is the function of the symptom? How does it serve as a system stabilizer?
- Attitudes, beliefs and values of the system

- Previous therapy experiences (What was helpful? What was not helpful?)
- Overall couple and family function and boundaries
- Is the system enmeshed or disengaged?
- How is the system functioning?
- Are there any other stressors?
- Expectations about the intake and future therapy
- What is their commitment to therapy?

If the client system or part of the system are immigrants or of multi-cultural heritage, issues of oppression, racism, bilingualism, and ethnic identity conflicts should be assessed for as well. The intake session is designed to get an understanding of the couple and family structure and function, but also to determine if therapy is appropriate. Additionally, it is a time to assess if the therapist conducting the intake assessment should be doing the therapy, or if a referral would be most beneficial. Therefore the intake assessment needs to be completed thoroughly and completely, to obtain as much information as possible. This means doing an assessment as part of the intake session, by way of:

- Interviewing
- Individual, couple, and family psychometric instruments
- Observing behavior and assessing for congruence of verbal and non-verbal communication

A comprehensive intake assessment provides an opportunity to gather important information about the individual's, couple's, and family's, function, structure, background, problem solving ability, insight into the situation, as well as their desire to be in therapy. It is important to assess whether the client is a "window shopper" (one who comes primarily at the behest of another and is generally not invested in making any changes in the complaint) or a "customer" (one who is invested in making changes in the complaint) (Fish, et al, 1989). A thorough initial assessment is critical in the decision making process (Reiss, 1980):

- Should the couple or family seek therapy (now)?
- Should the focus be on observable behavior, or on underlying family and/or family of origin themes?
- Should therapy be crisis or issue based?
- How much focus (if any) should be based on the family and/or the environment?
- Should therapy be developmental or cross-sectional?
- Should therapy focus on the system's pathology or competence?
- Does the therapist have the skills and experience to work with this couple or family, or individual couple or family members?
- Can the therapist and the couple or family mutually agree on the goal for therapy?

This data gathering process serves as a preliminary assessment that guides in formulating the initial hypothesis and goal-setting process and promotes healthier functioning. Therapists who do not pursue a systematic assessment can easily be misguided and ineffective. It is therefore important to remember that a single couple and/or family assessment generally does not provide adequate insight into the cause of the problem or the treatment needs (Baucom & Epstein, 1990). Instead, it provides an opportunity for therapists to develop a working hypothesis, guide clinical judgment, and test causal models, always keeping the treatment goal(s) in mind (Cone, 1988; Haynes, et al., 1993). Therapists should systematically assess the couple or family while recognizing that the presenting problem within a system (couple as well as family) can involve cognitive, emotional, psychological, behavioral, and biological components within the context of being part of multiple systems. Additionally, while couples and families entering therapy might share a perception of the problem, they most likely will present it from their own experience, which is often negative, focusing on the difficulties they experience and challenges they face without reporting the positive, such as strengths and abilities (e.g. degree of success to resolve this or other problems in the past), or support systems. So it is important that therapists gather information from multiple viewpoints, because there is a possibility of measurement error in multiple and idiosyncratic sources of couple and family assessment. It is recommended that a multi-method, multi-mode approach be used (Halford & Markman, 1997). La Greca (1990) pointed out the importance of therapists remembering that particularly with self-report measures issues such as memory problems, response bias, misinterpretation of questions, and social desirability, all need to be considered when looking at self-report measures. Additionally, when choosing assessment tools, therapists should consider using a variety of tools to measure the same construct, recognizing that a self-report instrument versus a family interview and an observational system will provide a deeper understanding for both the couple and/or family system seeking therapy, but also for the therapist, since this kind of assessment evaluates different components within the construct, at different levels and depths (Weiss & Heyman, 1990).

INSTRUMENT SELECTION PROCEDURE IN ASSESSMENT

Couple and family assessment serves as a cornerstone for therapeutic intervention and prevention. Instruments chosen need to stress the relevance of the individual, and at the same time not deny the interconnectiveness of couple and family members. It is important that the instrument is appropriate for the system the therapist is working with, i.e. traditional family, single parent family, adopted children, or cohabitating or married couples with children. Considering that systems therapists are generally not interested in finding an explanation of "why", but rather "how", the instrument(s) need to be chosen accordingly. It is important that the instruments are standardized (administration and interpretation), and have good reliability and validity. When dealing with immigrants and cultural and ethnic minority clients, assessment tools should have been normed with the population tested. Only when these things are considered will the information gained be meaningful and accurate.

The administration of couple and family, as well as individual assessment instruments might vary greatly. Therefore it is important that each instrument is administered under standardized conditions (which extends to oral and written instructions, material used, preliminary demonstration, time limits, and all other aspects of the testing situation), and standardized instructions (which extend to the tone of voice, voice infraction, pauses, hesitations, and facial expressions as well as individual's, couple's and family member's queries and discussion during the assessment). Instruments that are standardized (sample, selection, age and gender norms, local and national norms) must be administered to a large representative sample for which this test was originally designed. This kind of standardization not only serves as a way to establish the norm/average but assists in determining how far away a couple, family or individual might be from the norm.

Before choosing a standardized instrument, the therapist should evaluate the instrument's reliability and validity. Reliability testing of an instrument is important because it evaluates if instrument scores are consistent over time (time-retest reliability), across instrument subsections (split-half reliability), across instrument items (Kuder-Richardson reliability) and across therapists or scorers (interrated reliability). Validity testing is important, since it evaluates to what degree the instrument samples an entire domain of interest (content validity), to what degree this instrument agrees with other measures of the construct (criterion-related validity) and to what degree the instrument construct is related to other theoretical constructs (construct validity). Individual, couple and family assessment instruments should be chosen carefully, with well documented standardization, reliability, and validity. Only then can the therapist be sure that the results are accurate and not tentative.

Assessment tools also need to be chosen carefully regarding the appropriateness of each person's taking the instruments. For example, is the assessment tool chosen to adequately assess each member in the system? In family assessment, can the self-report tool be used with children and/or adolescents? Is the language such that a child might understand it? Has it been normed for that age group, or only for adults? Additionally, it needs to be asked if the assessment tool is sensitive to and has been normed to the client's race, gender, and ethnicity. The issue of culturally sensitive assessment requires that the therapist is aware of culturally specific behavior, identity, or acculturation. Issues of English language proficiencies, length of stay in the United States, and acculturation need to be assessed before administering an assessment tool (Sue, 1998). Although knowing the client's level of acculturation is essential, it is generally not enough to accurately assess the couple, family, and individuals within these systems. The assessment instruments chosen must have been normed on the population the instrument is being administered to. Unfortunately, many assessment instruments have not been normed on a multiculturally and ethnically diverse population.

When dealing with self report assessment tools, it is important to remember that clients might (a) misinterpret the questions, (b) overanalyze the questions, (c) have response bias, (d) answer according to social desirability, and (e) misinterpret items (La Greca, 1990). On observational assessment data, the therapist needs to remember that there is a possibility of social desirability and since the client(s) are observed in an artificial environment, their usual behavior might not be demonstrated. In situations of interviews being used as an assessment tool, therapists need to be aware that the client(s) might have difficulty with recall.

Additionally, the therapist needs to address any kind of disabilities, such as physical and learning disabilities, assessing what kind of accommodations need to be provided for the disabled person, and ultimately get the most accurate assessment results. Accommodations might include administering the assessment instrument in two parts over a two week time span or reading the questions and answers for the client(s) instead of having the client read the instrument questions alone. The therapist needs to assess carefully for disabilities that one or more couple or family members might have. Only then can proper accommodations be provided and accurate assessment results obtained.

MULTI SYSTEM, MULTI METHOD ASSESSMENT

Assessment today focuses on the couple, the family and the larger system. No longer do we focus exclusively on intra-personal assessment, but rather on the larger systems that clients function in. Therefore, assessment strategies should be more formalized and might include, but not be limited to such things as projective tests (Elbert, Rosman, Minuchin & Guerney, 1964), self-report instruments, behavior rating forms (Orton, 1996), focused and/or structured interviews (Watzlawick, 1966), unstructured clinical interviews (Fitzgerald, 1973), informal assessment techniques (Frey, 1986; Irwin, 1993), genograms, timelines, or standardized tests such as the Dyadic Adjustment Scale (DAS) (Spanier, 1976), the Commitment Inventory (CI) (Stanley & Markman, 1992), the Circumplex Model (Olson, Russel & Sprenkle, 1989), the McMaster Model of Family Competence (Beavers & Boeller, 1983) or the McMaster Model of Family Coping Skills (Westley & Epstein, 1969). This list is in no way exhaustive, as there are other methods and instruments directed specifically at individual, couple and/or family domains. The list provided serves as an example of the many different assessment strategies available. For instance, a therapist might choose to administer a self-report family function inventory to a family prior to the first therapy session and encourage family self and family member monitoring in the first few therapy sessions. This will help the therapist gain a better understanding of the family function and provide direction regarding other assessments needed and what the goals for therapy should be. Additionally, this kind of assessment also raises consciousness for family members about their own and other family member's functioning, which encourages families to think about other possible problem areas.

Since clients' distress, or presenting problems generally are constructed by multiple emotional, cognitive, behavioral, physiological, and relational/interpersonal components, assessments should be chosen carefully for each of these components. For example, the therapist might assess the family's conflict resolution skills both on an individual and larger systems level. This can be achieved through interviewing, observation, or self-report assessment instruments. For families, this might include looking at issues of the family transitioning through developmental stages, or parenting skills, and children leaving home, to list just a few. The underlying assumption of a multi-method assessment is that it enhances the probability that therapy will focus on important variables that underlie the problem(s). This could include a combination of physical, emotional, and behavioral based problems.

Comprehensive assessment of couples and families should consist of a variety of assessment tools and techniques, including a clinical interview, in order to answer questions about structure and function and get a more complete picture of the wholeness of the individual, couple, and family, and it is a way to assess the hierarchical qualities of the couple and family system. This helps to untangle the present and temporary situation, as well as the family history, over multiple generations, as well as the function of the presenting problem (Reiss, 1980). Finally, it is also believed that the use of multiple assessment gets therapy "off to the right start", since the therapist makes therapeutic decisions based on not only impressions, but on a multi-system, multi-method assessment process. The assessment should include a variety of different assessment techniques and tools and should focus on cognition, behavior, affective, and physiological factors (Floyd, Haynes & Kelly, 1997). Additional assessment targets should include: (a) life cycle transitions, (b) support systems such as family, friends, etc., (c) problem representation across time and situation, and (d) problems that might be co-varied and/or co-morbid, with distress, such as major mental illness, substance abuse, etc.

The assessment process does not stop after the first or second therapy session, but is an ongoing process. L'Abate (1994) supported the need for doing family and individual assessment to see how the problem is maintained. Comprehensive assessment can help identify (a) the client's problem(s), (b) client's goal for therapy, and (c) causal variables. L'Abate (1994) wrote:

> A traditional systems perspective stresses the subjective nature of the therapist's understanding of the family, whereas a psychological perspective finds an additional need for the objective understanding of the family and therefore uses both the subjective (interview) and objective (questionnaires, rating sheets, tests). (p. 4)

When doing a multi-method assessment, some of the assessment tools chosen may provide only limited information regarding the presenting problem. Additionally, some of the assessment results might be similar, since they validly tap into the same dimensions, where others measure different components, as well as variance of dimensions within the component(s). It is important to remember that both similarity and variance of assessment results are all valid, and can contribute to a better understanding of the current presenting problem, and provide some prediction for potential problem resolution (short and long term) (Gottman & Krokoff, 1989). Doing a multi-method assessment not only contributes to obtaining valid assessment results, but also is clinically valuable for guiding goal setting and process of therapy (Weiss & Heyman, 1990).

In summary, the philosophy behind doing multiple assessment is that it guides the acquisition of valid data when working with a couple, family or individual member of the subsystem. Self-ratings through standardized assessment tools, interviews, and therapist observations, although they measure various response modes across various aspects of individual, couple, and family function and structure, can all be valid in providing a more comprehensive understanding of the couple or family system, as well as the individuals within these systems. This should not imply that therapists should err by measuring unfocused multiple aspects of the couple and/or family system or individuals within these systems. Additionally, using instruments that have low reliability and validity scores can reduce the reliability and validity of the assessment, resulting in a treatment method, strategy, and direction error. Clearly, developing an accurate understanding of the couple and family system or individuals within each of these systems should be a multi-system, multi-method process.

SUMMARY AND CONCLUSION

This chapter is designed to serve as a global overview of how couple and family systems, and individuals within each of these systems, should be assessed carefully and purposefully. Assessment should use various tools and techniques, from a formal interview, to a genogram, to standardized couple and family assessment instruments. It is important to choose assessment tools that assess the structure and function of the system, standardized instruments that have adequate reliability and validity, and are culturally and ethnically sensitive. It is also important to use assessment tools that are appropriate for clients of different ages, socioeconomic status, and ethnicities, and appropriate for minority as well as immigrant clients. Finally, the roots of the presenting problems are related to life-cycle transitions that contribute to anxiety and reorganization of the couple and family system as well as other subsystems, but also individual couple and family members. Additional stressors are unpredictable, such as the death of a loved ones or chronic or terminal illness. These can create additional stress and anxiety, and demand reorganization and potential hierarchical change(s). It is important to purposefully choose the assessment tools and techniques that together provide a more accurate and comprehensive view of the couple and family system, and individual members of these systems. Assessment that is random can be problematic in that it might provide error information and mis-guide the therapist to use techniques that are not meeting the client's needs or goals for therapy. Comprehensive multi-system, multi-method assessment is a valuable tool in providing top quality, time- and cost-effective individual, couple, and family therapy.

REFERENCES

Barnhill, L.R. & Longo, D. (1978). Fixation and regression in the family life cycle. *Family Process, 17*(4), 469-478.

Baucom, D.H., & Epstein, N. (1990). *Cognitive-Behavioral Marital Therapy*. New York, NY: Brunner/Mazel.

Beavers, W.R. & Boeller, M.N. (1983). Family models: Comparing and contrasting the Olson Circumplex with the Beavers Model. *Family Process, 22*, 85-98.

Carter, E.A. & McGoldrick, M. (Eds.) (1999). *The extended family life cycle: Individual, family & social perspectives*. Boston, MA: Allyn & Bacon.

Carter, E.A., & McGoldrick, M. (1988). Overview: The changing family life cycle: A framework for family therapy. In E.A. Carter & McGoldrick (Eds.), *The changing family life cycle, A framework for family therapy (2nd ed)*. New York: Gardner Press.

Cone, J.D. (1988). Psychometric considerations and the multiple models of behavioral assessment. In A.S. Bellack & M. Hersen (Eds.), *Behavioral Assessment: A practical handbook (3rd ed.)*, (pp. 42-66). New York, NY: Pergamon.

Duvall, E.M., & Hill, R. (1948). *Report to the committee on the dynamics of family interaction*. Washington, DC: National Conference on Family Life.

Duvall, E.M., & Miller, B.C. (1985). *Marriage and family development (6th ed.)*. New York, NY: Harper & Row.

Elbert, S., Rosman, B., Minuchin, S. & Guerney, B. (1964), A method for the clinical study of family interaction. *American Journal of Orthopsychiatry, 34*(5), 885-894.

Fish, R. Weakland, J.H. & Segal, L. (1989). *The tactics of change: Doing therapy briefly*. San Francisco: Jossey-Bass Publishers.

Fishman, H.C. (1988). Structural family therapy and the family life cycle: A four-dimensional model for family assessment. In C.J. Falicov (Ed.), *Family transitions: Continuity and change over the life cycle*. New York, NY: Guilford Press.

Fitzgerald, L.E. (1973). Women's changing expectations: New insights, new demands, *Counseling Psychologist, 4*(1), 90-95.

Floyd, F.J., Haynes, S.N., & Kelly, S. (1997). Marital assessment: A dynamic functional-analytic approach. In W. K. Halford and H. J. Markman (Eds.), *Clinical handbook of marriage and couples intervention*. New York, NY: John Wiley & Sons.

Frey, M.J. (1986), Person perception in children: An investigation of prior expectations, sex-role stereotyping and cognitive maturity on the perceptual process. *Disertation Abstracts International, 46*(8-B). University Microfilms International

Goldenberg, H. & Goldenberg, I. (1990). *Counseling today's families*. Pacific Grove, CA: Brooks/Cole.

Goldenberg, I., & Goldenberg, H. (1996), *Family therapy: An over view (4th ed.)*. Pacific Grove, CA: Brooks/Cole Publishing Company.

Gottman, J.M. & Krokoff, L.J., (1989) A valid procedure for obtaining self-report of affect in marital interaction. *Journal of Counseling and Clinical Psychology, 53*, 151-160.

Halford, W.K. & Markman, H.J. (1997), *Clinical Handbook of Marriage and Couples Intervention*. New York: Wiley.

Haynes, S.N., Uchigakiuchi, P., Meyer, K., Orimoto, B., Blaine, D. & O'Brien, W.O. (1993). Functional analysis causal models and the design of treatment programs: Concepts and clinical applications with childhood behavior problems. *European Journal of Psychological Assessment, 9*, 189-205.

Irwin, E.C. (1993). Using puppets for assessment. In C.E. Shaefer and D.M. Cangelosi: *Play therapy techniques*. Northvale, NJ: Jason Aronson, Inc.

Kiresuk, T.J., Smith, A. & Cardillo, J.E. (1994). *Goal attainment scaling: Applications, theory, and measurement*. Hillsboro, NJ: Lawrence Earlbaum Associates

L'Abate, L. (1994). *Family evaluation: A psychological approach*. Thousand Oaks. CA: Sage Publications.

La Greca, A.M. (1990). *Through the eyes of the child*. New York, NY: Allyn & Bacon.

Minuchin, S., Rosman, B., & Baker, L. (1978). *Psychosomatic families: Anorexia nervosa in context*. Cambridge, MA: Harvard University Press.

Olson, D., Russell, C.S., Sprenkle, D.H. (Eds.) (1989). *Circumplex model: Systematic assessment and treatment of families*. New York: Haworth.

Orton, P.Z. (1996). Effects of perceived choice and narrative elements on interest in and liking of story. *Dissertation Abstracts International, A, 56*(10-A), University Microfilms International.

Reiss, D. (1980). Pathways to assessing the family: Some choice points and a sample route. In C.K. Hofling & J.M. Lewis (Eds.), *The family: Evaluation and treatment*. New York: Brunner/Mazel.

Satir, V.M. & Bitter, J.R. (1991). Human validation process model. In A.M. Horne & J.L. Passmore (Eds.), *Family Counseling and Therapy (2nd ed)*. Itasac, IL: F.E. Peacock.

Spanier, G.B. (1976). Measuring dyadic adjustment: New scales for assessing the quality of marriage and similar dyads. *Journal of Marriage and Family, 38*, 15-28.

Stanley, S.M., & Markman, H.J. (1992). Assessing commitment in personal relationships. *Journal of Marriage and Family Therapy, 54*, 595-608.

Walsh, F. (1980). *A primer of family therapy*. Springfield, IL: Charles C Thomas.

Watzlawick, P. (1966). A structured family interview. *Family Process, 5*(2), 256-271.

Weiss, R.L. & Heyman, R.E., (1990). Observation of marital interaction. In F.D. Fincham & T.N. Brandury (Eds.), *Behavioral Change: Methodology, Concepts and Practice*. Champaign, IL: Research Project.

Weiss, R.L., & Heyman. R.E. (1990). A clinical-research overview of couple interactions. In W. K. Halford and H. J. Markman (Ed.), *Clinical handbook of marriage and couples intervention*. New York, NY: John Wiley & Sons.

Westley, W.A. & Epstein, N.B. (1969). *The silent majority*. San Francisco: Jossey-Bass.

Widenfelt, B.V., Markman, H.J, Guerney, B., Beherns B.C.& Hosman, C. (1997) Prevention of relationship problems. In W.K. Halford & H.J Markman (Eds.), *Handbook of Marriage and Couple Intervention*, New York, NY: John Wiley & Sons.

Zilbach, J.J. (1989). The family life cycle: A framework for understanding children in family therapy. In L. Combrinck-Graham (Ed.), *Children in family context: Perspectives on treatment*. New York, NY: Guilford Press.

Chapter 2

MANAGED CARE AND ASSESSMENT INSTRUMENTS: SOME INTRODUCTORY COMMENTS

Tracy Todd[*]
Brief Therapy Institute of Denver, Inc.

ABSTRACT

Specialized assessment tools are important additions in the area of family and couples therapy. These tools assist clinicians in their treatment decisions. Special considerations need attention when implementing assessment tools into service delivery systems operating under a managed behavioral health care umbrella. Clinical outliers and clinical checkpoints are two of these important considerations. Discussion and clinical examples demonstrate these important variables.

MANAGED CARE AND ASSESSMENT INSTRUMENTS: SOME INTRODUCTORY COMMENTS

Managed mental health care continues to be a hotly debated topic. Typically, the arguments against manage care involve confidentiality, clinical intrusion, paperwork, and payment. Managed care typically argues it saves corporations money and helps "clean up" treatment services. As psychotherapists, we understand that managed care can offer excellent referral streams provided we can tolerate payment and practice intrusion.

Despite many fictional and nonfictional cases involving confidentiality breaches, kickbacks, and premature terminations, managed behavioral health care continues. However, managed behavioral health organizations (MBHO's) have had some significant positive

---

[*] Tracy Todd, Ph.D., LMFT, is a licensed marriage and family therapist in the state of Colorado and a clinical member of the American Association for Marriage and Family Therapy. He is President of the Brief Therapy Institute of Denver, Inc. and Children of Aging Parents Consulting Group, Inc. Tracy has consulted and provided workshops throughout the country on managed behavioral health care. Send all correspondence to 8120 Sheridan Blvd., C-112, Westminster, CO 80003 or to ttodd@btid.com.

impacts on psychotherapy. Before managed care, many service providers engaged in activities just as outlandish as those MBHO's are criticized for: "wave therapy" in psychiatric hospitals, "genetic regression therapy," and in outpatient settings, the need for EVERY client to explore EVERY historical issue that may be influencing a EVERY current negative emotion (Todd, 1994). Most managed behavioral health care clinicians have heard the argument over the last 10 years from MBHO's that focused mental health treatment results in better psychotherapy services leading to cost containment. Although this logic appears sound, the idea that ALWAYS accomplishing "focused treatment" without tools, such as assessment instruments, is naïve. At times, an assessment instrument near the beginning of treatment would save money and heighten clinical effectiveness.

It is not my intent to argue the pros and cons of managed care or assessment tools. Rather, it is my intent to emphasize that PROVIDERS are responsible for the care of patients. Quality assessment instruments should help providers deliver better care by helping give clinical direction and keep providers from straying into questionable clinical practices. Furthermore, these assessment instruments can help therapists diminish any MBHO pressure to reduce or discontinue care. Yet, the question remains, "What clinical population and at what time in treatment should these assessment tools be utilized?"

CLINICAL OUTLIERS

Clinical outliers are the one population that every assessment instrument in this book may be appropriate. Simply put, clinical outliers are those clients that are not getting better with a standard length or course of treatment. The outlier population presents many challenges to both MBHO's and providers. Every managed behavioral health care system has a method of identifying clinical outliers. The main point is that clinical outliers (inpatient, outpatient, substance abuse, day treatment) are unpredictable in clinical outcomes, costly because of this unpredictability, and remain symptomatic despite quality care. Outliers have atypical treatment lengths, are frequent users of services, often use crisis services, may or may not follow through with treatment suggestions, and generally create frustration among service providers because they lack responsiveness to treatment interventions.

The opportunity to clinically help clients that have a history of nonresponsive treatment is present with clinical outliers. From a clinical perspective, these clients are extremely frustrated with lack of progress and often terminate care. At work, they can compromise the environment, safety, attendance and quality. At home, they may jeopardize all close relationships. To the clinicians, burnout, frustration, and resentment set in. Finally, to a funding source, increased costs will result in raising costs to all the other members covered under this plan.

Clinical outliers and assessment tools are a natural combination. Clinicians are searching for clues to improve the quality of care via the assessment tool. Additionally, clinical outliers place service providers in a vulnerable legal position because of the lack of improvement and often crisis nature of their clinical complaints. Specialized assessment tools can help clinicians account for unknown treatment variables that may be compromising treatment.

CLINICAL CHECKPOINTS

Episodic care is delivering care in "bunches" and each "bunch" has a specific purpose. A clinical checkpoint is an evaluation time during treatment for effectiveness and need for treatment alterations. Assessment tools give insight and direction to treatment and both are critically important with the clinical outlier population. However, questions' involving *when* to use the assessment instrument and *how* to use results are necessary to answer. Episodic care combined with clinical checkpoints is a possible method of determining the timing and implementation of results from the assessment tool.

For example, if a child falls and breaks a leg, the first episode of care is the trip to the emergency room. In the emergency room, they diagnose the problem and immediately try to fix it (set the broken bone). The second episode of care involves follow up by the child's physician or a designated specialist. This episode may include monitoring of the broken bone. However, after two weeks the bone is not setting appropriately. Now what? A third episode of treatment commences. It is likely that the orthopedic specialist will assess the situation, create a plan of action, and execute this plan. The fourth episode is following up on the child's leg. Fortunately for our fictitious child, the leg is mending correctly. The fifth episode is removing the cast and beginning physical therapy. Our sixth episode may occur after physical therapy and our fictitious child "checks in" for a few months with the physician until a clean bill of health is granted.

In this example, our child had a normative course beginning to treatment but the third episode of care became atypical (correcting the situation). In the emergency room, the physicians may have conducted routine procedures for the medical situation (broken leg). However, due to individual circumstances, physician error, or any unknown reason, the procedure did not work correctly. The checkpoint quickly corrected the situation. Thus, our child was able to get back on an appropriate treatment path.

Assessment instruments are excellent tools to help correct and improve care. Service providers, especially under a managed care service delivery system, need to insure care is most effective and efficient. Some tension will exist however. Managed care systems are not inclined to immediately approve assessments when routine care may be sufficient (Todd, 1994). In our broken leg example, routine procedures in the emergency room are routine because they are effective for the vast majority of broken legs. Yet, the clinical checkpoint built into the routine helps to monitor variances and lack of effectiveness. The checkpoint also provides justification for additional services so that our child can begin normative healing.

Clinical example. An adolescent diagnosed with Bipolar I Disorder, and discharged from a psychiatric hospital has entered outpatient treatment. The precipitant for admission included suicidal ideations with a plan and method identified. He has a highly escalative mother and uninvolved father. His sister is a "superstar" at school.

Episode one, provided there was no outpatient care prior to the hospitalization, was the hospital stay. The focus was on crisis stabilization, getting a psychotropic medication evaluation, a family meeting, and outpatient services coordinated.

Episode two involved weekly family meetings for approximately four months (16 sessions). The clinician, feeling frustrated and defeated, requested a clinical staffing. The clinician and the agency typically see good improvement in these types of clinical situations within 15-18 sessions. However, there is no noticeable improvement as the mother is continuously escalative, father still avoids conflict, and our teenager has had continued suicidal ideations but of less severity than when admitted to the hospital.

Episode three involved the clinical team recommending that the family receive the following assessments to help give treatment new direction: Family, Couple, Adolescent Assessment and Testing. Based on the results of the assessments, a new clinical treatment plan was established.

Episode four commenced with a new treatment plan and after a few meetings there is noticeable improvement in the clinical situation. The clinician continues with the treatment plan until termination.

In this example, the treatment team had a checkpoint to insure that treatment was effective. When concluding that treatment was ineffective, a case staffing resulted in recommending use of the assessment instruments. The instruments assisted the clinical direction and eventually contributed to the successful completion of therapy.

Within a managed care treatment model, this clinical team would have solid justification to request payment for these assessments. A quality managed care organization would give strong consideration to such a request and may recommend additional assessments to help the client family.

Too much, too soon. The error, however, that many treatment providers make when using assessment instruments is assuming the assessment process will benefit ALL clinical situations. In our clinical example, this treatment agency knew that approximately 80% of their clients with a similar clinical presentation experience notable gains within 15 sessions and do not receive specialized assessments.[1] Therefore, there is no justification for using specialized assessment tools in every clinical situation. Our fictitious agency used the benchmark of 15-18 sessions as a clinical checkpoint and to identify clinical outliers. All agencies and providers need to have such checkpoints to insure treatment is effective and justify additional costs in conducting such assessments.

Considering clinical outliers, legal issues, and assessment/testing, it is vitally important for clinicians to understand and develop clinical checkpoints. Meaning, there needs to be points in treatment (e.g. number of sessions, length of treatment) matched against treatment effectiveness evaluation, to determine when these assessments and tests should be administered. Every agency and therapist is different. Yet, using a simple clinical checkpoint, costs can be contained, effectiveness can be heightened, and legal matters reduced. These are positive outcomes for all parties.

REDUCING PREMATURE TERMINATION PRESSURES

Another area that assessment tools will aid managed behavioral health care clinicians involves the potential to under serve a clinical population. Even high quality MBHO's can inadvertently send messages to clinicians that a case is costing too much, involving too many services or the clients are noncompliant and terminating treatment is indicated.

Caudill (2001) maintains that clinicians need to demonstrate a community standard of service of average, or C grade. When treatment is considered overall less than a C grade, the

---

[1] Please note, our fictitious agency knew this statistic and chose it for its checkpoint. It is vitally important that service providers understand and have research about their own choice of checkpoints.

clinician is probably in an area where questioning the standard of care is reasonable. Using a clinical checkpoint, particularly at a time whereby a MBHO is suggesting termination of care, a treatment provider is demonstrating an attempt to maintain quality of care standards.

From our hypothetical clinical example, we can examine how an assessment tool used at the checkpoint helps demonstrate the treatment agency was comprehensive and not under serving the client family. After 16 sessions, and no noticeable improvements, the agency administered the Family, Couple, and Adolescent Assessments. The results provided information about areas of therapy that needed addressing to enhance treatment effectiveness. The treating agency alters treatment direction insuring services that are more effective and result in the satisfactory completion of the episode of care. Not administering the assessment tools, and the family decompensating and physically harming one another, could be grounds that the treating agency was neglectful regarding a treatment issue. In this example, the assessment assists the client family in improving their situation and demonstrates the agency did not under serve the client family.

The managed behavioral health care provider needs to balance costs with treatment effectiveness. At the same time, it is critical not to compromise care because of financial considerations. If the HMO denies a request, that is a completely different issue. It is important that the provider had a system to make a clinical request. Requesting the assessments provides strong argument that the provider did not compromise care due to financial considerations.

At this point, a word of caution is needed. Using specialized assessments, without appropriate integration into treatment, can demonstrate lack of clinical follow through. Personally, when consulting with agencies using psychological tests, measurements or assessments, I have found providers ignoring the assessment information after its administration. Providers look for specific pieces of information while ignoring others. Furthermore, when asking an agency or provider about the use of the instrument, comments about how it *might* have given insight were frequent but this insight did not alter the treatment course. It is important to fully account for the results or a clinician might be considered negligent. Remember, the assessment tool provides documentation of the clinical situation. Using this documentation would be appropriate regarding the service delivery, or lack thereof.

SUMMARY

From every perspective, outliers are in desperate need of help. It is the outliers that these assessment tools can be extremely helpful. Under a managed care umbrella, clinicians can use these tools to increase their clinical effectiveness and help with any managed behavioral health care pressures.

It is imperative that service providers determine checkpoints, episodes of care, and what they consider a clinical outlier. In so doing, they can confidently make requests to MBHO's for payment to administer assessment tools. Without this process, MBHO's will find it difficult to authorize payment for services. Furthermore, providers need to be careful of the mentality that every client should receive a reimbursable assessment. Finally, the results of an assessment should validate or alter the course of treatment. These steps will also help in demonstrating that financial consideration did not exclusively alter all clinical decisions.

REFERENCES

Caudill, B. (Speaker). (2001). *Legal risk management.* (Cassette Recording No. 111) Palm Desert, CA: Convention Cassettes Unlimited.

Todd, T. (1994). *Surviving and Prospering in the Managed Mental Health Care Marketplace.* Sarasota, FL: Professional Resource Press.

Chapter 3

THERAPEUTIC FAMILY ASSESSMENT: A SYSTEMS APPROACH

Robert W. Heffer, Mariella M. Lane and Douglas K. Snyder[*,†]
Texas A&M University

THERAPEUTIC FAMILY ASSESSMENT: A SYSTEMS APPROACH

Family assessment is *therapeutic* when: (a) it involves a collaborative process between the therapist and family members, (b) both the process and content of the assessment are linked to intervention strategies grounded in contemporary theory and empirical findings regarding family dysfunction and treatment, and (c) the assessment outcome renders both the family and clinician with an enriched understanding of family strengths, weaknesses, and goals that promotes effective change efforts both in and outside the therapy session. In its broadest context, family assessment implies a systematic information-gathering process that may include clinical interviews, behavioral observations, and self-reports regarding family members' beliefs, affect, perceptions, values, and desired outcomes (Heffer & Snyder, 1998; L'Abate, 1994). The assessment process becomes *therapeutic* only after a meaningful formulation is shared with the family in a collaborative process that invites their own evaluation of its accuracy and relevance for suggesting specific change strategies.

In this chapter we articulate principles underlying family assessment and describe a multifaceted, multilevel assessment model. We address practical issues of whom to include in family assessment and how to tailor an assessment strategy that satisfies criteria of both comprehensiveness and parsimony. Specific assessment techniques are proposed, including observational and self-report measures to complement the clinical interview. Integrative family assessment systems are summarized as a means for integrating assessment findings

---

[*] *Authors' note*. The authors thank Luciano L'Abate for his collegial encouragement in the process of preparing this manuscript.
[†] Robert W. Heffer, Ph.D. is Clinical Associate Professor and Clinic Director, Douglas K. Snyder, Ph.D., is Professor and Director of Clinical Training, Mareilla M. Lane, M.S. is a Clinical Psychology Graduate Student, all at Texas A&M University, College Station, Texas.

and potentially providing a conceptual linkage between the initial assessment and subsequent interventions. Finally, we present a case study illustrating key components of therapeutic family assessment.

A COMPREHENSIVE CONCEPTUAL MODEL FOR FAMILY ASSESSMENT

Assessment and intervention processes are an iterative, recursive blend of evaluation, hypothesis formulation, intervention, observation of effects, and intervention adjustments. The process often begins with a review of referral information or presenting concerns, and a list of questions or hypotheses to be addressed by obtaining and evaluating relevant observations. Knowing where to target assessment efforts can be critical to achieving both an efficacious and parsimonious process. Obtaining relevant data typically includes some combination of a clinical interview with family members, observation of family interactions in structured as well as informal exchanges, self- and other-reports using paper-pencil techniques and, where relevant, eliciting information from individuals outside the family such as a teacher, physician, or social service personnel. Integrating data across diverse domains from diverse sources requires an overarching theoretical or conceptual framework that, ideally, offers a developmental and systemic perspective on how emotional or behavioral concerns evolved, how they're presently being maintained, and what interventions would need to be undertaken by family members to bring about their improvement.

We have previously proposed a comprehensive conceptual model for assessing couples and families (Heffer & Snyder, 1998; Snyder, Cavell, Heffer, & Mangrum, 1995). The model proposes five construct domains similar to those identified in previous family assessment models: (a) cognition, (b) affect, (c) interpersonal communication, (d) structure and development, and (e) behavior control and sanctions domains (see Figure 1). Constructs relevant to each of these domains can be assessed at each of the multiple levels comprising the psychosocial system in which the couple or family functions. The model posits five distinct levels of this system: (a) individuals, (b) dyads, (c) the nuclear family, (d) the extended family and related social systems, and (e) the community and cultural systems. Each of the five target domains may be assessed with varying degrees of relevance and specificity across each of the five system levels using both formal and informal assessment approaches to self-report and observational techniques.

Several aspects of this model merit elaboration. With respect to construct domains, the model emphasizes the fluid nature of individual as well as system structure by linking structural with developmental processes. Assessment findings at any system level are best understood within a broader temporal context. Second, our model presumes that individual members of a couple or family recursively influence, and are influenced by, the broader social system. Whereas early psychodynamic approaches to couples and family therapy emphasized individual psychopathology to the neglect of dyadic and family processes, subsequent systemic approaches initially emphasized broader social influences to the neglect of individual factors. Such elements as capacity for self-observation, emotional empathy, and inhibition of aggressive impulses all comprise critical components contributing to the well being of the couple or family system.

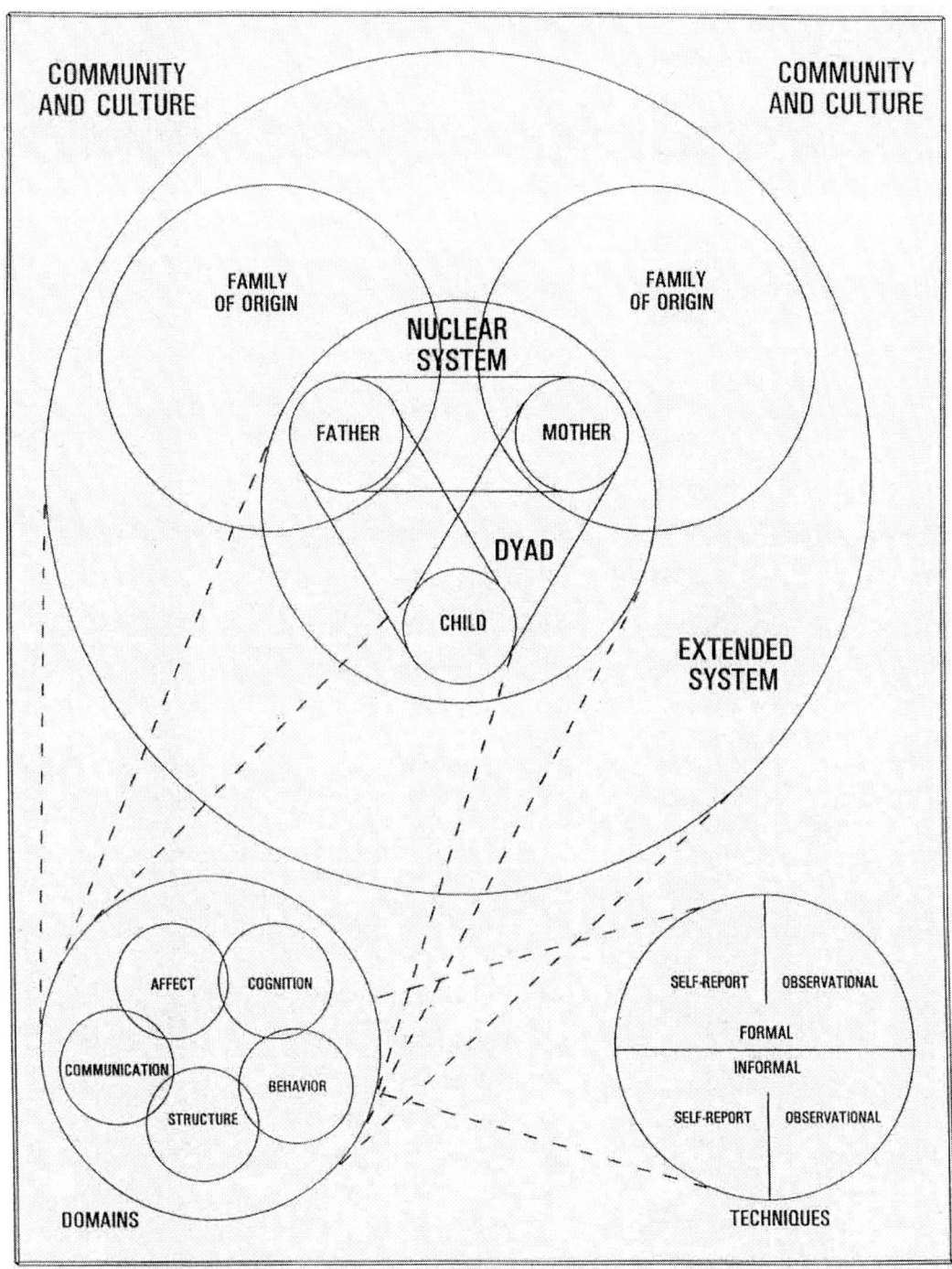

Figure 1

Figure 1. A comprehensive conceptual model for assessing families from a systems perspective. The model presents five system levels including: (a) individuals, (b) dyads, (c) the nuclear family, (d) the extended family system, and (e) the community and cultural systems. Each system level may be assessed across five overlapping domains including: (a) cognitive, (b) affective, (c) behavioral, (d) structural/developmental, and (e) communication and interpersonal. Information across domains may be gathered using multiple assessment strategies, including both formal and informal self-report and observational techniques. From *Integrating Family Therapy: Handbook of Family Psychology and Systems Theory* by R. H. Mikesell, D. D. Lusterman, and S. H. McDaniel (Eds.). Copyright © 1995 by the American Psychological Association. Reprinted with permission.

Most if not all of the constructs identified as relevant to dyads also apply to assessing nuclear systems. Differences at the family level include the following: (a) the number and complexity of dyadic relationships increase in nonlinear fashion as a function of the number of individuals comprising the family system, (b) each individual directly impacts (and is impacted by) two or more others in the system, so that the potential for conflict increases commensurately, (c) the range in developmental stages of individual members can expand dramatically, increasing the potential for interpersonal differences in values, expectations, and ability to engage in system-enhancing behaviors, and (d) the structure of relationships within the family requires analysis beyond dyads involving simultaneous observation of all members comprising the nuclear system. Finally, our model distinguishes between extended systems in which family members interact on an affective basis with individuals outside the nuclear family versus broader social systems at the community or cultural levels.

PRACTICAL ISSUES IN FAMILY ASSESSMENT

Although conceptual models such as the one described here are integral to systematic evaluation of family functioning, they may not explicitly address practical issues in assessment. For example, how should decisions be made regarding which family members to have present during, and for what portions of, the assessment? What specific information should be gathered from specific family members using which assessment strategies? Under what circumstances should certain family members not be included in direct inquiries and what is the rationale for such exclusion?

From the outset, a family therapist and assessor must explicitly define not only the professional model that guides the evaluation process, but also the personal model that is the foundation for decision-making. Barnett and Zucker (1990) postulate that therapists "are guided by personal theories regarding their own behavior and the behavior of clients" (p. 128). One family evaluator may routinely include both members of a couple or all family members regardless of age throughout the clinical interview. Another family evaluator may conclude that age or cognitive capacity of the family member, content of the specific issues discussed, intensity or configuration of the family relationships, and family perceptions of the evaluator suggest that certain family members be excluded from portions of the interview. Although theory or "best practice" guidelines may partially drive these decisions, we contend that one's personal model (i.e., the *person* within the professional) steers the process as well.

Generally family evaluators should gather information through multiple strategies from multiple sources. Therefore, including all family members with the cognitive capacity to express their impressions in informal assessment strategies, such as the clinical interview, is advised. Further, family members who may be unable to verbally report their perceptions of family functioning can be observed regarding patterns of family interactions via structured observation tasks. However, we believe that some topics, based on family members' ages and intensity or configuration of family relationships, should be assessed without certain family members present. For example, clearly, children are not served well if they are included in a discussion between parents regarding marital infidelities.

A good rule-of-thumb is to gather as much information as one can, from as many persons as is appropriate, through as many methods as are available, within current time and resource constraints. This approach may be reminiscent of the Goldilock's porridge test – that is, " …

not too cold, not too hot, but just right!" Family evaluators must invoke their personal and professional models to make tactical decisions about how best to pursue a thorough but parsimonious assessment process with families. In addition when assessment instruments are used for research, attention is required to ensure that constructs to be studied and time resources available are conceptually and practically congruent with a given measure (Dashiff, 1994). Some basic methods for effective information gathering are provided next.

BASIC FAMILY ASSESSMENT STRATEGIES

Clinical Interview

The clinical interview remains the cornerstone of family assessment. In therapeutic family assessment, a desirable goal of the initial interview is not to simply gather assessment information but rather to set the stage for therapeutic change by building positive expectancies and trust among family members and by providing them with actual benefit. Because families come to an initial interview primed to talk about their problems and often explain why one or another family member is primarily at fault, it is useful to begin the interview with a few questions aimed at getting to know each individual separate from the family's concerns. For example, what kinds of responsibilities do they have inside and outside the home (e.g., work or school)? What do they do for fun? Who are their best friends? What are their best individual and family memories? How do they wish their life to be in five years, and how likely do they believe this will be?

Once rapport has been established with each participant in the interview, information should be gathered that clarifies the structure and organization of the family. For example, who is considered a member of the family, and who is not (e.g., a child from a previous marriage living out-of-state with an ex-spouse)? Who does what in the family? Have there been recent role changes? Who is close to whom? Who is in conflict with whom? Who makes the decisions in various areas of their family life? Then, a general question can be used to invite important information not yet disclosed: "What do I need to know about your family that I don't know yet to understand better the kinds of difficulties you're having?"

We advocate next stating, "Tell my why you're here and how you'd like me to help" to indicate a clear shift from building a general understanding of family dynamics to a solution-focused description of presenting concerns and desired outcomes. Additional questions are typically needed to delineate the precise nature of family concerns, their development, and previous efforts to address these difficulties. For example, how does the family define their primary difficulties? Who has defined the problem? Is one family member more involved in or more distressed by the problem than another and, if so, why? What does each person identify as the primary contributing factors to the family's current struggles? How do family members agree or disagree on their definition and understanding of their difficulties? What experiences and discussions lead them to define their concerns in this way? What solutions have they tried in the past, and how did they decide to seek outside assistance at this time? What does each individual believe would be required from him- or herself to promote positive change in the family?

Additional dynamics relevant to family evaluation include the following (L'Abate, 1994):

- To what degree do intergenerational ties exist? How open is the family to input from outside the system? To what extent do outside influences function as a resource or a stressor?

- What types of communication-relational patterns exist among family members? To what extent do redundant, cyclical interactional patterns prevent the family from setting goals, solving problems, negotiating conflict, overcoming crises, and achieving family tasks?

- To what extent have family members been able to negotiate mutually acceptable patterns of separateness and connectedness? To what extent are members emotionally supportive of each other?

- What are the recurrent themes in the extended family? What are the personal, conjugal, and family myths that prevent family members from setting goals and solving problems effectively?

Family Genogram

The family genogram comprises a graphic means of depicting transgenerational family structures, dynamics, and critical family events potentially influencing family members' interactions with one another (McGoldrick, Gerson, & Shellenberger, 1999). The genogram reflects a family systems perspective positing that relationship patterns in previous generations may provide implicit models for family functioning in the next generation. The genogram is constructed from information derived from an extended clinical interview regarding family history--and it both directs the interview content and evolves in response to new information gleaned during the course of therapy. On a single sheet of paper, each member of the extended family system is denoted by a symbol that reflects their gender along with information about their current status as living or deceased, age, occupation, and salient physical or emotional/behavioral concerns. Structural organization as well as functional dynamics are viewed both horizontally across the family context and vertically through the generations. For example, individuals' generational status is reflected by their hierarchical organization vertically within the genogram. Parents' previous marriages, and their offspring's relationships to one another as step- or half-siblings are reflected by their horizontal organization along with connecting lines that can be varied to depict not only biological relationships but the degree of emotional closeness or conflict. Additional information can be noted on the genogram reflecting patterns of conflict engagement and resolution, emotional expressiveness, individual and relationship strengths and liabilities, core values, or similar themes having special relevance to this family. As such, the genogram provides a subjective, interpretive tool helping the therapist to delineate contrasts and consistencies throughout the extended families of origin.

Observational Assessment: A Clinical Approach

Equally important to attending to the content of what family members disclose is observing the process of their interactions. Virtually all theories of family dysfunction and intervention emphasize communication deficits as a common pathway to family problems. Thus, family therapists typically use a variety of both formal and informal observational techniques that range from: (a) observing characteristics of family members' emotional expressiveness and problem-solving behaviors during the initial interview and subsequent treatment sessions, to (b) directing the family to discuss a specific conflict in a clinical setting while the therapist refrains from intervention and takes notes to provide subsequent feedback, or (c) videotaping structured problem-solving tasks in research settings and subjecting participants' interactions to elaborate systems of coding verbal and nonverbal behavior.

Similar to empirical findings for distressed couples (Heyman, 2001), our clinical impressions of distressed families are that, compared to nondistressed families, distressed families: (a) are more negative in their interactions, (b) start their conversations with greater negativity and maintain more negativity during the course of conversation, (c) are more likely to reciprocate and escalate one another's negativity within distressed relationships (e.g., a parent-adolescent exchange), (d) are less likely to edit their behavior during conflict, resulting in longer negative reciprocity loops, (e) emit less positive behavior, and (f) particularly in parent-youngster interactions, are more likely to show "demand → withdraw" patterns in which one member (e.g., the parent) engages in negative interaction (such as demanding, blaming, or accusing) while the other (e.g., a youngster) avoids and withdraws from the interaction.

In helping families recognize dysfunctional interaction patterns as a prelude to promoting change, the therapist should first attend to the following questions: How do conversations start? Does the level of anger escalate, and what happens when it does? Do family members enter repetitive negative loops? Are their communication patterns consistent across different dyads and across different domains of conflict? Do their behaviors differ when it is a topic initiated by one of the parents, versus an issue identified by one of the youngsters? A key premise in therapeutic assessment is that the clinician works to reduce the level of negativity and hostile withdrawal early in the therapy. Specific techniques for disrupting negative escalations, getting back on track, or resuming discussions at a later time are essential. Equally important to disrupting negative communication patterns is promoting positive communication behaviors including emotional expressiveness, validation, and problem-solving skills.

Structured Interaction Tasks, Coding Systems, and Clinician Rating Scales

A variety of structured techniques also have been developed for observing and analyzing family interactions. Direct observation of family interaction supplements self-report data by allowing clinicians to directly observe the actual dynamics of family interaction and draw personal conclusions, rather than solely relying on client descriptions of their communication processes (Margolin et al., 1998; Snyder & Abbott, 2000). These data permit the clinician to observe how behavior fluctuates as a function of context and how behavioral sequences develop across time, as well as gather information about particular behavioral sequences including the antecedents, nature, and resolution of conflict.

Structured interaction tasks. Multiple tasks have been developed to allow for the observation of marital and family interaction, with variations on activity type, amount of therapist direction, family unit observed, and setting. Task selection should be driven by the type of interactional process and range of affect the clinician is seeking to observe, as well as which family members are to participate (Margolin et al., 1998). Structured interactions designed for observations of parent-child interaction include problem-solving discussions, unrevealed difference discussions, structured play tasks, parent-child clean-up tasks, and teaching tasks. Structured tasks for couple observations typically involve discussing identified areas of conflict, revealed differences, unrevealed differences on predetermined topics, or discussion of daily events. After selecting a task, the clinician must structure the task appropriately, as variations in specificity and direction can greatly impact the nature of the interaction and thus its generalizability and clinical utility (Margolin et al., 1998; Snyder & Abbott, 2000).

Observational coding systems. Multiple coding systems have been developed for recording observational data. A thorough review of the coding systems available for use with families and their relevant dyads is beyond the scope of this chapter, but a brief description of two observational coding systems of family interaction is provided.

An extensive observational coding system for home observations, now termed the Henry Ittleson Center Family Interaction Scales, was developed by Behrens and Goldfarb in 1958 and refined with other colleagues in 1969. In its revised form the system includes 41 scales of family interaction grouped into seven categories: (a) family members' investment of selves in the home, (b) family group patterns of interactions, (c) interaction of husband and wife as marital partners, (d) interaction of husband and wife as parents, (e) parent-child interaction, (f) child-parent interaction and (g) child-child interaction. The system allows for coding of dyadic interactions in addition to the global family system (L'Abate & Bagarozzi, 1993a).

The Home Observation Assessment Method (HOAM) was developed by Steinglass in 1979 to study family interactions as they unfold over time. A 2-person team codes in 40-minute time blocks over a 2- to 4-hour observation period. These 40-minute blocks are further subdivided into twenty 2-minute coding segments. Within each 2-minute segment the initial interaction is coded for context, behavioral characteristics, whom-to-whom speech, and interaction (L'Abate & Bagarozzi, 1993a).

Clinician rating scales. Clinician rating scales provide an alternative to observational coding systems and can be used to focus on constructs of systems theory spanning marital, parent-child, and sibling interaction (Margolin et al., 1998; Sajatovic & Ramirez, 2001). Beavers and colleagues developed the Beavers Interactional Competence Scale and the Beavers Interactional Style Scale, designed for observing a 10-minute family discussion based on the prompt, "What would you like to see changed in your family?" (Beavers & Hampson, 2000). The Beavers Interactional Competence Scale assesses overall level of family health and competence. The Beavers Interactional Style Scale assesses family style and can range from centrifugal (most relationship satisfaction derived outside the family) to centripetal (most relationship satisfaction derived within the family). Olson developed the Clinical Rating Scale (CRS) to assess the cohesion, adaptability, and communication dimensions of the Circumplex Model. This scale is based on observation during a clinical interview or family interaction tasks (Olson, 2000; Thomas & Lewis, 1999). Miller and colleagues developed the McMaster Clinical Rating Scale (MCRS) to assess overall health and six dimensions of the McMaster Model of Family Functioning (Problem-Solving, Communication, Roles, Affective Responsiveness, Affective Involvement, and Behavioral Control). The MCRS can be used by a clinician or independent rater following a comprehensive family interview (Miller, Ryan, Keitner, Bishop, & Epstein, 2000).

The Darlington Family Rating Scale (Wilkinson, 2000) accompanies a structured interview based on the Darlington Family Assessment System and summarizes the main features of a case along 18 problem dimensions within domains of family functioning (i.e., child-centered problems, parent-centered problems, parent-child interaction, and whole family functioning). The Family Health Scales (FHS) developed by Kinston and colleagues consist of 18 subscale items tapping six dimensions (i.e., affective life, communication, boundaries, alliances, adaptability and stability, and family competence) of family functioning (Thomas & Lewis, 1999). Raters use the six scales to generate an overall rating of family functioning.

Self-Report Techniques

Paper-and-pencil techniques can form an important component of clinical assessments. Several self-report instruments of family functioning are commonly used in practice and in research. A brief summary of selected measures for family assessment is provided in Table 1 and expanded below.

The Family Adaptability and Cohesion Evaluation Scale (FACES-IV)

The FACES-IV operationalizes the two primary constructs of the Circumplex Model of family functioning, adaptability and cohesion (Halvorsen, 1991). Tielsel and Olson (1997) developed the most recent version of the FACES in response to controversy over the curvilinear hypothesis and in attempt to better capture the dysfunctional extremes of the two constructs. Rather than hypothesizing Adaptability and Cohesion scales to be curvilinearly related to family functioning as in previous versions, four separate scales were developed to represent the two extremes of cohesion (Disengagement and Enmeshment) and the two extremes of adaptability (Rigid and Chaotic). Thus, balance is no longer located at the midpoint of cohesion and adaptability, but instead at the low end of each of the four extreme dimensions; a linear relationship is predicted between increasing scores on the four dimensions and family dysfunction.

Reliability and validity of the FACES-IV have been assessed but remain unpublished at this time (Teilsel & Olsen, 1997). The instrument appears to have acceptable internal consistency and temporal stability. Craddock (2001) reported results from an undergraduate sample supporting a strong link between dimensions of the Circumplex Model as assessed by FACES-IV and family quality; however more research is needed on this newest version of the instrument.

Table 1. Self-Report Measures for Family Assessment

Scale / Developers	Response Format	Scales	Forms/ Respondent	Norms	Scoring	Reliability	Validity	Clinical Utility
Family Adaptability & Cohesion Evaluation Scale-IV Olson, Tiesel, & Gorall	24 items, 6-point Likert scale	4 scales: Disengagement, Enmeshment, Rigidity, & Chaos	Single form, no minimum age indicated	Adults & adolescents	Hand-scored	Internal consistency: Disengagement .82, Enmeshment .81, Rigidity .81, & Chaos .93 Test-retest: .83 to .96	Discriminant: distressed families scored significantly higher on a total system extremity score (summation of the 4 scale scores) & on all subscales	Useful in clinical settings to identify characteristics of troubled families & to facilitate family discussion concerning family quality; further research needed on this version
Family APGAR Smilkstein	5 items, 3-point Likert scale	A total score & 5 scales: Adaptation, Partnership, Growth, Affection, & Resolve	Single form, no minimum age indicated	No	Hand-scoring, cutoffs subjectively defined by Smilkstein	Internal consistency: .80 to .86 Split-half: .93 Test-retest: (2 weeks) .83	Concurrent: correlated .80 with Family Functioning Index Discriminant: significantly discriminated clinical & normal families, sensitivity of 68% & specificity of 62% for classifying those with & without psychological problems Construct: .64 correlation with therapist rating	Screening instrument, developed for use by physicians
Family Assessment Device Epstein, Baldwin, & Bishop	60 items, 4-point Likert scale	A General Functioning score & 6 scales: Problem Solving, Communication, Roles, Affective Responsiveness, Affective Involvement, & Behavior Control	Single form, appropriate for family members over age 12	Nonclinical, primarily middle-class Caucasian families	Hand- or computer-scoring	Internal consistency: .72 to .92 Test-retest: (7-day) .66 to .76	Concurrent: equivocal research concerning correlation with FACES, significant mother/father agreement but only moderate coefficients, McMaster CRS ratings significantly related to parental ratings on all 7 scales, significantly correlated with Dyadic Adjustment Scale on all but Behavior Control, correlated .47 with Dyadic Adjustment Scale, correlated .59 with Locke-Wallace Marital Satisfaction Scale, correlated .40-.60 with the McMaster CRS Discriminant: discriminated normal & clinical families on 6 of 7 scales, distinguished between families rated as healthy or unhealthy on each domain of the McMaster model, correctly predicted 67% of nonclinical group & 64% of clinical group, sensitivity of .57 to .81, specificity of .60 to .79 Construct: GF scale correlated as predicted with family variables from the Ontario Child Health Study, over 90% of items loaded on factors as hypothesized	Parallels the McMaster Structured Interview of Family Functioning (McSIFF); specifically designed as a screening instrument; 12-item General Functioning Scale has good psychometric properties & is useful as a research or screening measure of global functioning; can be used to target areas of intervention & assess change after treatment

Scale / Developers	Response Format	Scales	Forms/ Respondent	Norms	Scoring	Reliability	Validity	Clinical Utility
Family Assessment Measure-III Skinner, Steinhauer, & Santa-Barbara	General Scale: 50 items, Dyadic Relation-ship Scale & Self-Rating Scale: 42 items each, brief versions: 14 items each; 4-point Likert scale	An overall index of functioning is included for all scales but only constitutes a formal subscale for the General Scale. All 3 Scales include 7 subscales: Task Accomplish-ment, Role Performance, Communication, Affective Expression, Involvement, Control, & Values and Norms. The General Scale also contains an additional subscale, Social Desirability and Defensiveness, totaling nine subscales.	3 Forms: General Scale Form, Dyadic Relationship Scale Form, Self-Rating Scale Form, appropriate for children with a 5th grade reading level (age 10 & up)	Adults & adolescents from a community sample, other special population means & standard deviations in manual	Hand- or computer-scoring	Internal consistency: General Scale (adults): Overall Rating .93, subscales ranged .65 to .87; (children): Overall Rating .94, subscales ranged .60 to .87 Dyadic Relationships Scale (adults): Overall Rating .95, subscales ranged .59 to .82; (children): Overall Rating .94, subscales ranged .55 to .77 Self-Rating Scale (adults): Overall Rating .89, subscales ranged .39 to .67; (children): Overall Rating .86, subscales ranged .27 to .58 Test-retest: (12-day) General Scale (mothers): .64, (fathers) .71, (children) .75	Concurrent: strongly related to MMPI special family scales; significantly correlated with FACES Cohesion, FES, FAD, & Parental Stress Index Discriminant: discriminated clinical from nonclinical families, including families seeking professional help for psychiatric or emotional problems, those with an alcoholic father, a depressed father, a bipolar parent, in a distressed relationship, with a bulimic or anorexic member, & with children with various . psychological & emotional problems Construct: elevated mean ratings of fathers, mothers, & children on the General Scale for families with an alcoholic or clinically depressed father; mothers of anorexic children showed elevated scores	May be used as a diagnostic tool or research instrument; useful for facilitating family discussion; can be used to gain a comprehensive picture using all 3 scales to assess different family subsystems; may be used in brief form as screening; includes a Profile of Family Perceptions for comparing family members' scores on a single form; is useful for presenting results to clients; provides forms designed to analyze functioning over multiple administrations for outcome assessment
Family Concept Inventory Van der Veen	80 items, 9-point Likert scale	3 scales: Family Congruence, Family Satisfaction, & Family Effectiveness	Single form, but can be used to rate Real Family Concept, Ideal Family Concept, or Family of Origin; no minimum age indicated	No	Hand-scored	Test-retest: Real Family Concept .63 to .80, Ideal Family Concept .87	Concurrent: significant positive correlation with Locke Marital Adjustment Questionnaire, correlated with California Psychological Inventory Discriminant: discriminated parents of runaways versus non-runaways, families of disturbed versus non-disturbed children, & healthy versus disturbed adolescent siblings	Considerable use but much research unpublished
Family Crisis Oriented Personal Evaluation Scales McCubbin, Olson, & Larsen	30 items, 5-point Likert scale	5 subscales: Reframing, Passive Appraisal (internal coping scales), Acquiring Social Support, Seeking Spiritual Support, & Mobilizing Family to Acquire and Accept Help (external coping scales)	Single form, no minimum age indicated	Sample characteris-tics are unclear	Hand-scored	Internal consistency: overall .86, subscales ranged .63 to .83 Test-retest: (4-week) overall .81, subscales ranged .61 to .95.	Concurrent: reportedly adequate	Specific assessment of family coping responses to crises

Scale / Developers	Response Format	Scales	Forms/ Respondent	Norms	Scoring	Reliability	Validity	Clinical Utility
Family Distress Index McCubbin, Thompson, & Elver	8 items, 4-point Likert scale	Total score reflecting family dysfunction	Single form, no minimum age indicated	Sample characteristics unknown	Hand-scored	Internal consistency: .87	Construct: strongly correlated with intense family pressures & lack of social support in a Hawaiian sample	Useful as a brief measure to quickly identify dysfunction; needs further psychometric evaluation
Family Environment Scale Moos & Moos	90 items, true-false format	3 underlying construct dimensions measured by 10 subscales: 1) Relationship Dimension: Cohesion, Expressiveness, Conflict 2) Personal Growth Dimension: Independence, Achievement Orientation, Intellectual-Cultural Orientation, Active-Recreational Orientation, Moral-Religious Emphasis 3) System-Maintenance Dimension: Organization & Control	3 Forms: Form R (the Real Form), Form I (the Ideal Form), & Form E (the Expectation form); no minimum age specified, but the Children's FES can be used with those ages 5-11	A national sample of normal & distressed families for Forms R & I; no norms for Form E. Form R subscale means are available for families of various characteristics	Hand-scored	Internal consistency: .61 to .78 Test-retest: Form R (2-month) .73 to .86, (4-month) .54 to .91, (12-month) .52- to 89	Concurrent: correlated with Social Support Appraisals, Dyadic Adjustment Scale, Locke-Wallace Marital Adjustment Scale, the Parental Bonding Instrument, the FAD, the FACES, & MMPI Family Scales; also correlated with clinician ratings Discriminant: little association between FES Cohesion & various measures of cohesion (Family Sculpture Test, Bowerman & Bahr Identification Scale) Construct: FES subscales related to family & social functioning, Moral-Religious Emphasis scale highly related to religious participation, Conflict scale associated with an index of family arguments	Useful for evaluating family change as a result of treatment; extensive research has been conducted using the FES in diverse subgroups
Family Evaluation Form Emery, Weintraub, & Neale	136 items, 7-point Likert scale	18 content-relevant scales: Conflict/Tension, Open Communications, Emotional Closeness, Extra-Familial Support, Community Involvement, Children's Relations, Children's Adjustment, Inconsistent Discipline, Mother/Father Dominance, Marital Satisfaction, Financial Problems, Nurturance, Independence Training, Behavioral Control, Explanation of Rules, Strict Discipline, Homemaker Role, & Worker Role. 7 additional scales are also included, totaling 25 subscales	Single form, only appropriate for parent-rating	132 Caucasian individuals in New York	Hand-scored	Internal consistency: overall .69, with 21 of 25 scales higher than .70 Test-retest: .40 to .94, with 19 subscales exceeding .75	None reported	Assesses broad areas of family functioning & applicable to broad range of family structures & sizes; validation research lacking

Scale / Developers	Response Format	Scales	Forms/ Respondent	Norms	Scoring	Reliability	Validity	Clinical Utility
Family Functioning Index Pless & Satterwhite	19 items with some subitems; response format includes short answer, Likert scales, & ordinal format	A Total Index Score; Factor analysis has yielded 6 factors: Marital Satisfaction, Frequency of Disagreements, Happiness, Communication, Weekends Together, & Problem Solving	Parent forms only with a parallel form for each spouse, no child-report	No	Hand-scored, criticized for lack of clarity	Internal consistency: (husbands) .07 to .96, (wives) .21 to .95 Test-retest: (5-year) .83 Inter-spouse correlation: .65 to .72	Concurrent: correlated .80 with F-APGAR, total index score correlated .39 with professional ratings Discriminant: discriminated clinical & normal families Construct: correlated .48 with therapist rating for husbands, .39 for wives	Intended to be a screening for families needing further assessment & assistance in coping with stressful events
Family Functioning Scale Tavitian, Lubiner, Green, Grebstein, & Velicer	40 items, 7-point Likert scale	A total score & 5 subscales: Positive Family Affect, Family Communication, Family Conflicts, Family Worries, & Family Rituals/Supports	Single form, no minimum age indicated	No	Hand-scored	Internal consistency: .74 to .90	Concurrent: correlated as predicted with FACES-III Discriminant: discriminated clinical & nonclinical groups	Used in both research & treatment, research has attempted to develop family profiles of different problem populations
Family Functioning Questionnaire Linder-Pelz, Levy, Tamir, Spenser, & Epstein	8 items, 5-point Likert scale	Evaluates a single general construct, with an item each concerning 8 areas: esteem, open-talk, help from family, expression of love, time spent together, decision making, contacts outside family, & feeling close	Single form, no minimum age indicated	No	Hand-scored	Internal consistency: (both partners) .85, (men only) .89, (women only) .28 Inter-spouse correlation: .75	None reported	Very brief screening measure; requires more psychometric evaluation
Self-Report Family Inventory-II Beavers & Hampson	36 items, 5-point Likert scale	5 scales: Health/ Competence, Conflict, Cohesion, Leadership, & Emotional Expressiveness	Single form, appropriate for all family members 11 & older	No	Hand-scored	Internal consistency: total scale .84 to .88, subscales ranged .84 to .93 Test-retest: (1-month) .88, (3-month) .80	Concurrent: correlated -.39 to .02 with FACES-III Adaptability scale; -.18 to -.78 with Cohesion scale; correlated .07 to .77 with FAD scales; Health/Competence subscale correlated .77 with FAD general functioning subscale, .17 to .73 with FES, moderate correlations with FAS; canonical correlation with Beavers Interactional Competence Scale at .62 or better Discriminant: discriminated between groups of psychiatric patients with differing diagnoses	Useful for identifying high-risk families in need of intervention, can evaluate results of intervention, can be used for treatment-matching on variables of power differential, disclosure of strategy, & partnership with members

Scale / Developers	Response Format	Scales	Forms/ Respondent	Norms	Scoring	Reliability	Validity	Clinical Utility
Structural Family Interaction Scale Perosa & Perosa	83 items, 4-point Likert scale	8 scales: Enmeshment/ Disengagement, Spouse Conflict Resolved/ Unresolved, Mother-Child Cohesion/ Estrangement, Father-Child Cohesion/ Estrangement, Flexibility/ Rigidity, Parental Coalition/Cross-Generational Triads, Family Conflict Avoidance/ Expression, & Overprotection/ Autonomy	Single form, no minimum age specified	No	Hand-scored	Internal consistency: ranged .71 to .93 Test-retest: (4-week) .81 to .92	Concurrent: significant correlations between cohesion scales of the SFIS-R & those of the FES, FAD, & FACES-III; the Enmeshment/Disengagement scale correlated .89 with FES Cohesion; significant correlations between the adaptability scales of the SFIS-R & those of the FACES-III & FES; Flexibility/Rigidity scale correlated -.59 with FES Control & .40 with FACES III Adaptability Discriminant: discriminated incest families from a clinical control group & a nonclinical control group	Psychometrics for the original SFIS were poor; use of the revised instrument is recommended instead.

Family APGAR (FAPGAR)

The FAPGAR (Smilkstein, 1978) was designed as a brief screening questionnaire for physicians to elicit a patient's view of the functional state of his or her family. The Family APGAR is based on five components: Adaptation (utilization of resources for problem-solving during crisis), Partnership (sharing of decision-making and nurturing responsibilities), Growth (physical and emotional maturation), Affection (the caring and loving relationship between members), and Resolve (commitment of other members to physical and emotional nurturing). The FAPGAR has adequate internal consistency and test-retest reliability. Support for its concurrent and discriminant validity also exist. Overall the FAPGAR is easy to use but most likely is more useful as an initial step in a more comprehensive assessment strategy (Halvorsen, 1991).

Family Assessment Device (FAD)

Epstein, Baldwin, and Bishop (1983) developed the FAD as a screening measure to efficiently identify problems in family functioning. The FAD is a self-report instrument based on the McMaster Model that provides scores on the 6 individual domains of the model as well as a General Functioning score (Hayden et al., 1998)

Psychometric evaluation of the FAD has supported its internal consistency and test-retest reliability (Halvorsen, 1991). Research has also supported its discriminant validity and, to a lesser extent, its concurrent validity (Epstein et al., 1983; Halvorsen, 1991; Hayden et al., 1998; Miller et al., 2000). Factor analyses suggest that the FAD should possibly be reorganized or that only the General Functioning score should be used due to substantial scale overlap (Ridenour, Daley, & Reich, 1999).

Family Assessment Measure-III (FAM-III)

The FAM-III is derived from the Process Model of Family Functioning (Skinner, Steinhauer, & Santa-Barbara, 1995) and is intended to assess family strengths and weaknesses. It may be used as a diagnostic tool, a measure of therapeutic outcome, or as a research instrument. The FAM includes a General Scale reflecting the family as a system, a Dyadic Relationships Scale examining relationship pairs, and a Self-Rating Scale assessing an individual's perception of his or her functioning in the family. These three scales each yield seven subscales corresponding to the Process Model. Brief (14-items) FAMs also have been developed for each scale version (Skinner et al., 1995).

Directionality is not a component of the FAM. For example, a high score on the involvement scale could indicate that an individual feels excluded or rejected, that he or she feels that boundaries are violated, or both. Thus, the clinician must further clarify the nature and direction of a problem detected by the FAM (Skinner, Steinhauer, & Sitarenios, 2000). The manual reports adequate internal consistency for most scales, especially for the Overall Rating scale, but less so for the child Self-Report scales. Research has supported discriminant validity of the instrument (Skinner et al., 1995). Factor analyses indicate a large general factor underlying the subscales.

Family Concept Inventory (FCI)

The FCI (van der Veen, 1960) is based on the Family Concept Assessment Method (FCAM) that assesses an individual's perception of his/her family and its cognitive, social, and emotional structures. The FCI can be used to elicit perceptions of the family as it currently exists, the ideal family concept, or the family of origin. Scales derived from the FCI include Family Congruence (degree of agreement between the real and ideal family concepts for family pairs or the whole unit), Family Satisfaction (correlation between an individual's real and ideal scores), and Family Effectiveness (a summary score of adjustment based on 48 items). Reliability appears adequate, and some evidence exists for concurrent and discriminant validity. An alternative technique, the Family Concept Q-Sort (FCQS) is also based on the FCAM model and requires individuals to sort 80 cards into piles corresponding to a 9-point continuum of similarity to the family (Forman & Hagan, 1984).

Family Crisis Oriented Personal Evaluation Scales (F-COPES)

The F-COPES (McCubbin & Thompson, 1991) assesses problem-solving and behavioral strategies implemented by a family in difficult situations. The five subscales include: Acquiring Social Support, Reframing (redefining stressful events as more manageable), Seeking Spiritual Support, Mobilizing Family to Acquire and Accept Help, and Passive Appraisal (ability to accept problems). Adequate internal consistency and test-retest reliability, and good concurrent and factorial validity has been demonstrated for the F-COPES (Corcoran & Fischer, 2000; L'Abate & Bagarozzi, 1993b).

Family Distress Index (FDI)

The FDI (McCubbin, Thompson, & Elver, 1996) is an 8-item instrument designed to quickly identify family dysfunction. Specifically, it elicits self-reports of family hardships and challenges that reflect ongoing family conflict and difficulties including emotional problems, substance use, and conflict over various issues. Thus, scores are intended to indicate the degree to which the family is in continuous disharmony or imbalance. The FDI provides norms and has preliminary support for its reliability and validity (Corcoran & Fischer, 2000).

Family Environment Scale

The FES (Moos & Moos, 1994) is one of 10 Social Climate Scales developed to assess family functioning. Dimensions of the family are Relationships, Personal Growth, and System Maintenance, and a set of subscales was constructed for each of these dimensions (Halvorsen, 1991; Moos & Moos, 1994). The FES has three forms: Form R (the Real Form) measures a family member's perception of his or her current family environment, Form I (the Ideal Form) measures conception of the ideal family environment, and Form E (the Expectation Form) assesses expectations of a family climate. A Children's Version is also available and involves a 30-item pictorial adaptation of the adult form used for children between 5 and 11 years of age. A Family Incongruence Score can be calculated to indicate the level of disagreement in a family. Test-retest reliability is moderate and appears to decrease over time (Halvorsen, 1991; Moos & Moos, 1994). The FES is one of the most widely used measures of family functioning and has been studied with a wide variety of populations including families with psychiatric disturbances and medical problems (Moos & Moos, 1994).

Family Evaluation Form (FEF)

The FEF (Emery, Weintraub, & Neale, 1980) was developed as a measure of family life using both rational and empirical procedures and has 25 subscales in all (e.g., Conflict/Tension, Children's Adjustment, and Marital Satisfaction) rated once for oneself and again for one's spouse. Test-retest reliability varies greatly across scales, but internal consistency appears adequate; little research has addressed the FEF's validity (Forman & Hagan, 1984).

Family Functioning Index (FFI)

The FFI (Pless & Satterwhite, 1973) was designed to identify families needing help in coping with stressful events. In its current form, the FFI includes 19 items administered to parents only, with a form for each spouse. Response format varies across items, including short answer, Likert scale, and ordinal format. Psychometric evaluation has indicated adequate test-retest reliability and high inter-spouse correlation (Forman & Hagan, 1984; Halvorsen, 1991). The FFI has correlated highly with the Family APGAR and moderately with therapist ratings (Halvorsen, 1991).

Family Functioning Scale (FFS)

The FFS (Tavitian, Lubiner, Green, Grebstein, & Velicer, 1987) is a 40-item measure used to assess five general dimensions of family functioning: Positive Family Affect, Family Communication, Family Conflicts, Family Worries, and Family Rituals/Supports. Internal consistency is adequate and concurrent validity and discriminant validity have been demonstrated (Corcoran & Fischer, 2000).

Family Functioning Questionnaire (FFQ)

The FFQ (Linder-Pelz, Levy, Tamir, Spenser, & Epstein, 1984) includes eight Likert-scale items evaluating families in areas of self-esteem, open talk, help from family, expression of love, time spent together, decision making, contacts outside family, and feeling close. The FFQ is easy to administer and has demonstrated internal consistency and high inter-spouse correlation, but lacks validation research (Halvorsen, 1991).

Self-Report Family Inventory (SFI)

Beavers and colleagues (Beavers & Hampson, 2000) developed the SFI to assess family perceptions about two major dimensions of the Beavers Systems Model: Health/Competence and Style (Halvorsen, 1991). The authors' intent was to identify high-risk families for researchers and to evaluate change following intervention. The SFI consists of five scales – Health/Competence, Conflict, Cohesion, Leadership, and Emotional Expressiveness – that can be plotted on axes of the Beavers Systems Model (Halvorsen, 1991). The SFI appears to have adequate internal consistency and test-retest reliability. Concurrent validation studies have been equivocal, but the SFI is reported to correspond well with other measures of family functioning (Beavers & Hampson, 2000; Halvorsen, 1991).

Structural Family Interaction Scale - Revised (SFIS-R)

The SFIS-R (Perosa & Perosa, 1990) was developed to operationalize Minuchin's structural model emphasizing boundaries, cohesion, and adaptability (Forman & Hagar, 1984; L'Abate & Bagarozzi, 1993b). The revised instrument (Perosa, 1996; Perosa & Perosa, 1990) consists of eight scales assessing elements of cohesion (e.g., Enmeshment/Disengagement) and adaptability (e.g., Flexibility/Rigidity). Internal consistency and test-retest reliability of the revised instrument are acceptable to good (Perosa, 1996; Perosa & Perosa, 1990). Modest evidence for concurrent and construct validity have been offered. The SFIS-R has been used to identify family characteristics associated with identity achievement in adolescents and has been used to differentiate family variables associated with clinical groups from those related to nonclinical control groups (Perosa & Perosa, 1990).

INTEGRATIVE MODELS FOR FAMILY ASSESSMENT METHODS

Some of the self-report techniques, structured interaction tasks, coding systems, and clinician rating scales described earlier in this chapter have been derived from integrative models for family assessment. Five of the major integrative family assessment systems are outlined in Table 2. Although these assessment models differ in their number of dimensions used to conceptualize family functioning and their degree of focus on family subsystems, all emphasize focus on family strength and competence (Carr, 2000). All five models have spawned assessment instruments to operationalize and quantify their constructs, and these instruments are routinely used in clinical practice to aid in case conceptualization, treatment planning, and outcome evaluation.

Beavers Systems Model of Family Functioning

The Beavers Systems Model (BSM) of family functioning is driven by a clinical family systems approach. The two dimensions of the BSM are Family Competence and Family Style. The Self-Report Family Inventory, the Beavers-Timberlawn Family Evaluation Scale, and the Beavers Interactional Scales are based on the Beavers Model (Beavers & Hampson, 2000). On the horizontal axis is the Competence dimension related to the structure, available information, and adaptive flexibility of the family system. Although flexible and adaptable systems manage stressful situations more effectively, competent families must also have structure (Halvorsen, 1991). The Competence dimension ranges from optimal to severely dysfunctional. On the vertical axis is the Stylistic dimension ranging from centripetal to centrifugal family styles. Centripetal style describes families who believe that relationship satisfaction comes from within the family, and centrifugal style characterizes those believing that most satisfaction will be derived from outside the family. Mid-range families are more adept at changing their style to meet family members' needs and are considered more competent; both the centrifugal and centripetal extremes are associated with poorer functioning (Beavers & Hampson, 2000).

Based on this 2-dimensional grid, nine distinct family groups are postulated by the BSM Model: (a) optimal, (b) adequate, (c) midrange centripetal, (d) midrange centrifugal, (e) midrange mixed, (f) borderline centripetal, (g) borderline centrifugal, (h) severely disturbed centripetal, and (i) severely disturbed centrifugal families (Beavers & Hampson, 2000).

Table 2. Integrative Models of Family Assessment Methods

Model	Developers/ Authors	Domains of Family Functioning/Assessment	Advocated Assessment Techniques	Model-Specific Measures	Clinical Utility
Beavers Systems Model of Family Functioning	Beavers & Hampson	Family Competence & Family Style	Emphasis on direct observation but also uses self-report	Self-Report Family Inventory, Beavers-Timberlawn Family Evaluation Scale, Beavers Interactional Scales	Helps provide assessment structure and a systems perspective to novices in family therapy; can be used for treatment-matching
Circumplex Model of Marital and Family Systems	Olson	Cohesion, Adaptability, & Communication	Advocates multi-method, multi-person, multi-trait, multi-system assessment primarily using self-report and clinician rating	Family Adaptability and Cohesion Evaluation Scales, Circumplex Assessment Package, Clinical Rating Scale, Georgia Family Q-sort	Can assist in specifying goals of therapy and is useful in assessment-based treatment planning
Darlington Family Assessment System	Wilkinson	Child-Centered Problems, Parent-Centered Problems, Parent-Child Interaction, & Whole Family Functioning	Focus on Structured Interview & Observation	Darlington Family Interview Schedule, Darlington Family Rating Scale	Useful as a training device, repeating measures can provide evaluation of treatment outcome
McMaster Model of Family Functioning	Miller & Colleagues	Problem-Solving, Communication, Roles, Affective Responsiveness, Affective Involvement, & Behavior Control	Clinical Interview, Self-report, & Observation	The McMaster Structured Interview of Family Functioning, The McMaster Clinical Rating Scale, Family Assessment Device, Mealtime Interaction Coding System	Comprehensive model including theoretical, assessment and treatment approaches; developed as a clinical model useful for clinical practice
Process Model of Family Functioning	Skinner & Colleagues	Task Accomplishment, Role Performance, Communication, Affective Expression, Involvement, Control, & Values and Norms	Not explicitly specified	Family Assessment Measure	Integrates intra-psychic, interpersonal, and family systems levels; includes the effect of the larger social system; predicts ways in which constructs interrelate

Circumplex Model of Marital and Family Systems

The Circumplex Model of Marital and Family Systems was designed to guide clinical assessment, treatment planning, and research on treatment efficacy (Olson, 2000). The Circumplex Model consists of three dimensions: Cohesion, Adaptability, and Communication (Craddock, 2001; Olson, 2000). Several assessment tools have been developed to correspond with the Circumplex Model including the FACES, Circumplex Assessment Package (CAP), the Clinical Rating Scale, and the Georgia Family Q-sort (Comunian, 1996; Olson, 2000).

Cohesion is defined as the emotional bonding among family members and the degree to which they are separated or connected (Craddock, 2001). In the original 2-dimensional model, four levels of Cohesion were espoused: disengaged (very low), separated (low to moderate), connected (moderate to high), and enmeshed (very high); separated and connected levels represented more balanced functioning (Olson, 2000). Adaptability is considered to be the family's ability to change leadership, role relationships, and relationship rules in response to situational and developmental stress (Craddock, 2001; Olson, 2000). In the original model families could be categorized into four levels of Adaptability: rigid (very low), structured (low to moderate), flexible (moderate to high), and chaotic (very high); those with balanced levels of Adaptability were considered to function more adequately than those at the extremes (Olson, 2000). The third dimension, Communication, is considered to be a facilitating dimension critical to movement on the other two (Olson, 2000). Communication is described in terms of positive features (empathy, reflection, and support) and negative features (double messages, double binds, and criticism) (Craddock, 2001).

In accordance with the structure of the original model, Olson and colleagues hypothesized a curvilinear relationship between both the constructs of cohesion and adaptability and family functioning. To reconcile the model with research indicating linear relationships, Olson and his colleagues redesigned the structure of the model from a 2-dimensional circular matrix to a 3-dimensional model (Craddock, 2001). The two dimensions were divided into their four extremes of disengagement, enmeshment, rigidity, and chaos. Thus, instead of balance being at the mid-point of the two dimensions, it now falls at the low end of the four extreme dimensions.

Darlington Family Assessment System (DFAS)

The Darlington Family Assessment System (DFAS) was designed by Wilkinson (2000) as a multisystem, multimethod family assessment model. The DFAS is based on four family system levels: the child perspective, the parental perspective, the parent-child perspective, and the whole family level. For each of these perspectives, a set of problem dimensions were derived to provide clear distinction among the different problems within each system level. The Darlington Family Interview Schedule and the Darlington Family Rating Scale are assessment methods that have been developed to correspond with the DFAS (Wilkinson, 2000).

The problem dimensions for Child-Centered Problems are Child Health (Physical), Child Development, Emotional Disturbance, Relationships, Conduct, and Negative Life Events. Parent-Centered Problems consist of Parental Health (Physical), Parental Health (Psychological), Marital Partnership, Parenting History, and Parents Social Support. The

Parent-Child Interaction domain includes Care and Control. A global dimension of Whole Family Functioning includes Closeness and Distance, Power Hierarchies, Emotional Atmosphere and Rules, Contextual Stresses, and Summary of Family Development.

Wilkinson (2000) indicated that the DFAS framework is helpful in generating hypotheses about causal links between problems across system levels. Primary strengths of the DFAS include four clinical guidelines to use integrative assessment, obtain family members' views of the problems, formulate the problem, and communicate the formulation to the family. The DFAS incorporates concepts from multiple therapeutic traditions, is an example of theoretical integration as applied to assessment, and is well-suited for those practitioners using an eclectic or integrated approach (Wilkinson, 2000).

McMaster Model of Family Functioning

The McMaster Model of Family Functioning incorporates a multidimensional theory of family functioning, assessment instruments to measure the constructs, and a method of family treatment (Miller et al., 2000). Based on systems theory, the McMaster Model emphasizes determining whether families are able to accomplish basic tasks of daily life (Hayden et al., 1998). The McMaster Model postulates six dimensions thought to be important in treating families in a clinical setting: (a) Problem-Solving, (b) Communication, (c) Roles, (d) Affective Responsiveness, (e) Affective Involvement, and (f) Behavior Control. A global construct–Overall Family Functioning–reflects the family's ability to accomplish basic daily tasks across domains.

The McMaster Model includes several assessment instruments designed to operationalize the above constructs. These include the McMaster Structured Interview of Family Functioning (MCSIFF), the McMaster Clinical Rating Scale (MCRS), the Family Assessment Device (FAD), and the Mealtime Interaction Coding System (MICS). The Problem Centered Systems Therapy of the Family (PCSFT) was developed as a structured, systems-oriented, short-term intervention based on the McMaster Model (Miller et al., 2000).

Process Model of Family Functioning

The Process Model of Family Functioning is a conceptual framework emphasizing family dynamics and processes that encourages formulation at both the individual and systemic levels (Skinner, et al., 2000). The Process Model also emphasizes the ways in which its basic constructs are interrelated. The seven dimensions of the Process Model are Task Accomplishment, Role Performance, Communication, Affective Expression, Involvement, Control, and Values and Norms. The primary goal of the family is conceptualized as the successful mastery of various developmental and crisis tasks. Task Accomplishment is central to the achievement of the central family objectives of development, security, cohesion, and effective functioning and requires the allocation, assumption, and enactment of various family member roles, termed Role Performance. Communication is central to Role Performance. Affective Expression is an important communication element that can impede or facilitate both Task Accomplishment and Role Performance. Involvement, or the degree and quality of family members' interest in each other, can also help or hinder Task Accomplishment.

Control is the process by which family members influence each other, and management styles can vary on the constructs of constructive versus destructive, and responsible versus irresponsible. Values and Norms of the individual family or culture can affect the definition of tasks and process of accomplishing them. The Family Assessment Measure (FAM), described earlier, was based on the Process Model and assesses its seven basic constructs.

CASE STUDY

Sandra and Carl had been married for 20 years. Both were college educated, from a primarily European-American ethnic background, and active in a Protestant church. They lived in a Southern city of 350,000 in the United States with their children Kayley (age 13), Jennifer (age 6), and Martin (age 4). Carl worked as a mid-level executive in a service business. Sandra was employed at a university human resources department until the birth of Jennifer, when she began caring for the children full-time. All their extended family lived several states away. Jennifer had multiple developmental and physical disabilities that required a great deal of daily care. Kayley was starting junior high school and Jennifer was beginning Kindergarten in a special education classroom. Martin had just started attending a preschool morning program two days per week. Carl and Sandra requested family services to address: (a) differences in parenting styles, (b) recent oppositionality of Martin, (c) changes in Kayley's "attitude," (d) stressors and grief over Jennifer's disabilities and their impact on the family.

The process of the therapeutic assessment was guided by the comprehensive conceptual model described in this chapter (Heffer & Snyder, 1998; Snyder et al., 1995). Therapeutic assessment methods were drawn from the McMaster Model of Family Functioning (see Hayden et al., 1998; Miller et al., 2000) due to its functional approach to evaluating how families accomplish the basic tasks of daily life. The initial clinical interview was conducted with only Sandra and Carl to discuss practical issues (e.g., consent for services), obtain the adults' history and perspective on family functioning, and allow for discussing marital issues. Paper-and-pencil measures were not obtained from Jennifer or Martin due to their ages and cognitive levels. All the children were present for the structured interview and behavioral observations.

During the initial clinical interview, issues such as the couple's families of origin, marital relationship, family history, adult and child roles and role changes in the family, agreements and disagreements as partners and parents, critical incidents in the family's development, support systems, patterns of managing and coping with conflict, family interaction patterns, personal formulation of their circumstances, and hopes and expectations for improved family functioning were addressed. Based on data from this interview, an initial family genogram and plans for on-going assessment were generated in collaboration with Sandra and Carl.

The entire family was present for the second assessment session in which the McSIFF, a 2-hour structured interview, was conducted. An adjacent playroom, with an open door connecting to the interview room, was available for the younger children to move in and out of during the interview. Before beginning, an overview of the purpose of this session was discussed with the family, and Kayley's assent to participate was obtained. Then, Carl, Sandra, and Kayley completed the FAD (Epstein et al., 1983). The anchors on the original FAD were reversed (i.e., 1=unhealthy to 4=healthy) to better correspond to anchors used later in the clinician ratings. After introducing the general structure and process of the interview, the family was asked to generate a list of problem areas. A dry erase board was used to display the family's responses. The family then was directed to delineate steps they had taken to resolve these problems. Queries continued to gather family perceptions of functioning across seven areas of the McSIFF. After the family left the session, the MCRS (Epstein et al., 1982) was used, with modifications from Hayden et al. (1994), to quantify data from the McSIFF through clinician ratings. Specifically, ratings from 1=very unhealthy to 7=superior functioning were produced for each of the seven dimensions of family functioning.

At the close of the structured family interview, plans were made for the family to record interactions during two family meals within the following week. Specifically, Sandra and Carl agreed to use their video camera to videotape a weekday and a weekend dinner when all family members were present. The camera was placed on a tripod in the dining room for the entire week to acclimate the family to its presence. For the two videotaped meals, Carl, Sandra, and Jennifer rated (1=not at all typical to 4=very typical) the extent to which they judged the mealtime interactions to be representative of common family dinner experiences. Tapes were returned at the next assessment session and later were evaluated using definitions of the seven McMaster dimensions of family functioning described in Hayden et al. (1998).

The third assessment session was dedicated to evaluating parent-child interaction patterns between both parents and both younger children and to conduct an informal interview with Kayley. The Dyadic Parent-Child Interaction Coding System-II (DPICS-II; Eyberg, Bessmer, Newcomb, Edwards, & Robinson, 1994), as described and adapted in Hembree-Kigin and McNeil (1995) was applied to the observations of parent-child interaction patterns. Specifically, Sandra and Martin were videotaped in the playroom for three distinct 5-minute situations. In the Child Directed Interaction (CDI) situation, Michael was allowed to choose the play activities, and Sandra was instructed to follow his lead and provide undivided attention to him. During the next situation, Parent Directed Interaction (PDI), Sandra was instructed to begin choosing play activities and requiring Michael to follow her lead. Cleanup was the last situation, in which Sandra was instructed to tell Michael to put the toys away and to require him to do so without her help. These series of situations and instructions were discussed with Sandra in advance, and a brief, written script for each set of instructions was given for her to use as a prompt during the interaction. The CDI situation typically elicits optimal play interactions, the PDI situation often provides on opportunity for observing parent direction-giving and the child's responses, and the Cleanup situation often evokes conflictual interactions, especially for dyads with behavior management problems. This observational procedure was repeated for each of the other parent-child dyads (i.e., Sandra-Jennifer, Carl-Martin, and Carl-Jennifer).

Following the session, specific behaviors associated with positive and negative parent-child interactions were coded from the videotape. Parent behaviors included descriptive statements, reflective statements, ignoring, praise, questions, critical statements, commands, "no opportunity" (i.e., inadequate chance given to child to comply), and responding (i.e., verbal or nonverbal reaction following disruptive child behavior). Disruptive behavior (e.g., complaining, disrespectful speech, crying/yelling, damaging toys, and physical aggression toward parent), compliance, and noncompliance were the child behaviors coded. [An alternative procedure we have also used is to conduct live, immediate observations and coding of parent-child interaction using the DPICS system.] The parent not involved in the structured task at a given time took the other young child on a walk outside the office, allowing informal observations of transition interactions among parents and the younger children as they returned to the office.

Given her age and position in the family, a clinical interview was conducted with Kayley alone while the parents and younger children were cycling through the playroom. Kayley was told that the purpose of the interview was to get "her ideas," as the oldest daughter in the family, and that these views would be shared with the whole family. If she thought that some of her impressions would be difficult to report to the family, she was assured that she and the interviewer would negotiate how best to communicate this information to the family. The content of this interview was similar to that of the initial interview with the parents. Emphasis was placed on gathering Kayley's perceptions of changes in the family, family strengths and weaknesses, and her own issues of early adolescence. Talking while playing age-appropriate board games was used to increase her comfort level with the interview.

Data from the McMaster measures provided an overview of family functioning. Although fairly effective in problem solving and appropriately cohesive, central issues affecting family functioning included discrepancies among family members in affective responsiveness/emotional expressiveness, inflexible roles and limited communication among the couple, substantial family stress due to Jennifer's physical and developmental needs, limited meaningful social support, and developmental transitions for all children. Information from the clinical interviews with Sandra and Carl and with Kayley further elaborated on family stressors and family members' coping styles. The DPICS data indicated differential parent-child interaction patterns for Sandra and Carl, such that interactions between Carl and Martin were especially conflictual.

Many of the problematic family patterns seemed rooted in different grief and loss reactions between Sandra and Carl. Only a few months earlier, medical and developmental evaluations indicated the likely life-long sequelae of Jennifer's disabilities. Sandra was saddened, but also somewhat relieved to have clarity on Jennifer's developmental trajectory. In contrast, Carl was grief-stricken, but stoic overtly, regarding how his daughter's life would progress at such an altered pace from typical expectations. The couple slowly became less able to meet the other's emotional needs. In addition, Carl began to devote himself almost exclusively to caring for Jennifer and to resenting the other children for their health in contrast to their sister and Sandra for her apparent contentment with Jennifer's plight. These patterns amplified when transitions such as Kayley's advancement to junior high and Jennifer and Michael's start, respectively, in a special education class and in preschool further stretched the family system. Further, feeling overwhelmed and beleaguered the couple described some "crises of faith" and a sense of isolation from church members who had "normal" lives.

The family genogram and a summary of the assessment findings were presented to Carl and Sandra (and later to Kayley, with information about marital functioning excluded) as a vehicle to convey the assessment data. The formulation of the case was fine-tuned and amended based on a collaborative process with the family. Similarly, establishing specific treatment goals emerged from such a *therapeutic* assessment process. Family therapy was recommended including some sessions for the couple only, and others for the entire family, or for Kayley and her parents. Couple-focused therapy goals were addressed first, then Kayley-parent therapy goals along with general family goals. Components of parent-child interaction therapy (Hembree-Kigin & McNeil, 1995) were introduced to enhance the relationships among parents and the younger children and to ameliorate Michael's oppositionality. Sandra and Carl were encouraged to conference with their pastor about spiritual issues and building better support within the church. They also were informed about a local support group for Parents of Children with Disabilities. An abbreviated assessment (i.e., McSIFF, FAD, and DPICS observations) was readministered after 12 sessions to assess changes and adjust goals for therapy.

CONCLUSIONS

Competent family assessment is theory-driven, guided by a conceptual model, and implemented in a multi-method manner. When it also is completed using sound measurement techniques chosen to answer specific assessment questions, then a parsimonious and comprehensive evaluation process is possible. The assessment itself becomes *therapeutic* when both evaluator and family collaboratively formulate family functioning issues and create and prioritize therapy goals.

REFERENCES

Barnett, D.W., & Zucker, K.B. (1990). *The personal and social assessment of children: An analysis of current status and professional practice issues*. Boston: Allyn & Bacon.

Beavers, R., & Hampson, R. B. (2000). The Beavers Systems Model of Family Functioning. *Journal of Family Therapy, 22*, 128-143.

Carr, A. (2000). Editorial: Empirical approaches to family assessment. *Journal of Family Therapy, 22*, 121-127.

Comunian, A. L. (1996). The relation between observed and perceived family structures: An integrative model. *Psychological Reports, 78*, 67-75.

Corcoran, K., & Fischer, J. (2000). *Measures for clinical practice: A sourcebook* (Vol. 1). New York: The Free Press.

Craddock, A. E. (2001). Family system and family functioning: Circumplex model and FACES IV. *Journal of Family Studies, 7*, 29-39.

Dashiff, C. J. (1994). Decision points in choosing family self-report scales in research. *Journal of Nursing Scholarship, 26*, 283-288.

Emery, R. E., Weintraub, S., & Neale, J. M. (1980). *The Family Evaluation Form: Construction and normative data.* Presented at the meeting of the American Psychological Association, Montreal, Canada.

Epstein, N. B., Baldwin, L. M., & Bishop, D. S. (1983). The McMaster Family Assessment Device. *Journal of Marital and Family Therapy, 9*, 171-180.

Eyberg, S. M., Bessmer, J., Newcomb, K., Edwards, D., & Robinson, E. (1994). *Dyadic Parent-Child Interaction Coding System-II: A manual.* Unpublished mansucript. Gainesville, FL.

Forman, B. D., & Hagan, B. J. (1984). Measures for evaluating total family functioning. *Family Therapy, 11*, 1-36.

Halvorsen, J. (1991). Self-report family assessment instruments: An evaluative review. *Family Practice Research Journal, 11*, 21-55.

Hayden, L. C., Schiller, M., Dickstein, S., Seifer, R., Sameroff, A. J., Miller, I., Keitner, G., & Rasmussen, S. (1998). Levels of family assessment: I. Family, marital, and parent-child interaction. *Journal of Family Psychology, 12*, 7-22.

Heffer, R. W., & Snyder, D. K. (1998). Comprehensive assessment of family functioning. In L. L'Abate (Ed.), *Handbook of family psychopathology* (pp. 207-233). New York, NY: Guilford Press.

Hembree-Kigin, T. L., & McNeil, C.B. (1995). *Parent-Child Interaction Therapy*. New York: Plenum Press.

Heyman, R. E. (2001). Observation of couple conflicts: Clinical assessment applications, stubborn truths, and shaky foundations. *Psychological Assessment, 31*, 5-35.

L'Abate, L. (1994). *Family evaluation: A psychological approach*. Thousand Oaks, CA: Sage.

L'Abate, L., & Bagarozzi, D. A. (1993a). Atheoretical and eclectic approaches. In *Sourcebook of Marriage and Family Evaluation* (pp. 202-226). New York: Brunner/Mazel, Inc.

L'Abate, L., & Bagarozzi, D. A. (1993b). Self-report of family functioning. In *Sourcebook of Marriage and Family Evaluation* (pp. 167-201). New York: Brunner/Mazel, Inc.

Linder-Pelz, S., Levy, S., Tamir, A., Spenser, T., Epstein, L. M. (1984). A measure of family functioning for health care practice and research in Isreal. *Journal of Comparative Family Studies, 15*, 211-230.

Margolin, G., Oliver, P., Gordis, E. B., O'Hearn, H. G., Medina, A. M., Ghosh, C. M., & Morland, L. (1998). The nuts and bolds of behavioral observation of marital and family interaction. *Clinical Child and Family Psychology Review, 1*, 195-213.

McCubbin, H. I., & Thompson, A. I. (1991). *Family assessment inventories for research and practice*. Madison, WI: University of Wisconsin.

McCubbin, H. I., Thompson, A. I. & Elver, K. M. (1996). Family Distress Index (FDI). In H. I. McCubbin, A. I. Thompson, & M. A. McCubbin, *Family assessment: Resiliency, coping, and adaptation inventories for research and practice*. Madison, WI: University of Wisconsin.

McGoldrick, M., Gerson, R., & Shellenberger, S. (1999). *Genograms: Assessment and intervention* (2nd ed.). New York: Norton.

Miller, I. W., Ryan, C. E., Keitner, G. I., Bishop, D. S., & Epstein, N. B. (2000). The McMaster approach to families: Theory, assessment, treatment and research. *Journal of Family Therapy, 22*, 168-189.

Moos, R, H., & Moos, B. S. (1994). *Family Environment Scale manual*. Palo Alto, CA: Consulting Psychologists Press, Inc.

Olson, D. (2000). Circumplex Model of Marital and Family Systems. *Journal of Family Therapy, 22*, 144-167.

Perosa, L. (1996). Relations between Minuchin's structural family model and Kohut's self-psychology constructs. *Journal of Counseling & Development, 74*, 385-392.

Perosa, L. M., & Perosa, S. L. (1990). Convergent and discriminant validity for family self-report measures. *Educational and Psychological Measurement, 50*, 855-868.

Pless, I. B., & Satterwhite, B. B. (1973). A measure of family functioning and its application. *Social Science and Medicine, 7*, 613-621.

Ridenour, T. A., Daley, J. G., & Reich, W. (1999). Factor analyses of the Family Assessment Device. *Family Process, 38*, 497-510.

Sajatovic, M., & Ramirez, L.F. (2001). *Rating scales in mental health*. Hudson, OH: Lexi-Comp, Inc.

Skinner, H. A., Steinhauer, P. D., & Santa-Barbara, J. (1995). *FAM-III manual.* New York: Multi-Health Systems, Inc.

Skinner, H., Steinhauer, P., & Sitarenios, G. (2000). Family Assessment Measure (FAM) and Process Model of Family Functioning. *Journal of Family Therapy, 22*, 190-210.

Smilkstein, G. (1978). The Family APGAR: A proposal for a family function test and its use by physicians. *Journal of Family Practice, 6*, 1231-1239.

Snyder, D. K., & Abbott, B. V. (2001). Couple distress. In M. M. Antony & D. H. Barlow (Eds.), *Handbook of Assessment and Treatment Planning* (pp. 341-374). New York, NY: Guilford Press.

Snyder, D. K., Cavell, T. A., Heffer, R. W., & Mangrum, L. F. (1995). Marital and family assessment: A multifaceted, multilevel approach. In R. H. Mikesell, D. D. Lusterman, & S. H. McDaniel (Eds.), *Integrating family therapy: Handbook of family psychology and systems theory* (pp. 163-182). Washington, DC: American Psychological Association.

Tavitian, M. L., Lubiner, J. L., Green, L., Grebstein, L. C., & Velicer, W. F. (1987). Dimensions of family functioning. *Journal of Social Behavior and Personality, 2*, 191-204.

Thomas, V., & Lewis, R. A. (1999). Observational couple assessment: A cross-model comparison. *Journal of Family Therapy, 21*, 78-95.

Tielsel, J., & Olson, D. H. (1997). FACES IV: Reliability and validity. Unpublished manuscript, University of Minnesota at Minneapolis.

van der Veen, F. (1960). *Family Concept Inventory.* Unpublished manuscript.

Wilkinson, I. (2000). The Darlington Family Assessment System: Clinical guidelines for practitioners. *Journal of Family Therapy, 22*, 211-224.

Chapter 4

ASSESSING COUPLES: PROCEDURES, TOOLS, AND BENEFITS

Mark Odell[*]
University of Nevada, Las Vegas

Recent texts on couple therapy present a consensus that a crucial aspect of starting off couple work well is formulating an assessment of the couple, from which a treatment plan is generated (e.g., Weeks & Treat, 2001; Young & Long, 1998). In this chapter, the practical aspects of conducting an assessment with a couple will be discussed. These include determining who should be present and when, and some of the particular areas in which assessment may provide the most useful information. Specific descriptions of major assessment tools and techniques, including their rationales, will be presented. Finally, an illustrative case study will be presented to demonstrate the benefits conferred by assessing couples well.

WHEN IS ASSESSMENT DONE?

Assessment is often conceptualized and discussed as an activity with a determinate starting and ending point. For instance, traditional evaluations of mental status and the generation of *DSM* diagnoses with individuals are performed and finished within the first few sessions of therapy (and there is usually the implication that such activities are not revisited unless specific information or client behavior compels a subsequent evaluation). These evaluations may begin with a statement to the client orienting him/her to the activity about to commence: "I'm going to ask you a few questions that may not seem very relevant to what brings you here today, but I need to get an overall sense of how you're doing. What day is today? Who is the current president of the United States?" Or "Please count backward from one hundred by threes." These and other similar questions provide data by which the clinician

---
[*] Mark Odell, Ph.D. is Associate Professor, Department of Counseling, University of Nevada, Las Vegas.

makes an evaluation of the client's mental functioning. Similarly, the client's manner of presentation, dress, speech, etc., are all considered. This is all a valid part of developing a good assessment.

However, as an evaluative and planning strategy, assessment de facto begins at the outset of contact with a prospective client. The therapist listens to the content of the client's presentation, often on the telephone or in an intake session, as well as the manner in which that content is articulated. In addition, the client is often asked a number of questions for the purposes of gathering factual information: "Who lives with you? How long has this been going on? What steps have you taken to try to solve this thus far?" The therapist, particularly one who has been trained systemically, attempts to contextualize the client's presentation, all in an effort to begin to craft a treatment approach.

A second underlying assumption regarding assessment is that it is a theoretically driven process. The information sought and the constructs investigated are dictated by the theoretical framework the clinician prefers. Theory tells the therapist what functionality and health are, so the therapist moves to address the issues that theory holds up as central to health. For example, a Bowenian therapist views health as a matter of differentiation of self from the emotional gravities of the family of origin. For an experiential therapist, health and functionality are found in being able to experience and express fully the existential realities that comprise living in relationships where a tension exists between intimacy and autonomy. The narrative therapist is interested in the story the clients tells about their lives and both the tyrannies of living with the externalized problem and the "sparkling events" that have overcome it, at least from time to time. Each family therapy model posits a set of foci delineating healthy functional living. The integrative or eclectic family therapist routinely is able to move between various theoretical frameworks to choose an approach that is believed to be most likely to be successful.

Further, assessing a couple adds a large amount of complexity not typically found in individual assessment. First, there are two individuals, each with their own "issues," histories, and individual biopsychosocial makeup that contribute to the relationship under therapeutic consideration. Secondly, from a systemic perspective, a recursive dynamic is always at play in both adaptive and maladaptive relationship patterns, and so the therapist must acknowledge that any description of the couple's relationship struggles represents one particular way of punctuating an ongoing circular reality. This is true regardless of who is doing the punctuating, whether it is the two members of the couple (which is typically what happens at the outset) or the therapist. Thirdly, the couple's relationship itself must be contextualized within its larger social setting, including such things as extended family and in-law relationships (and ex-law relationships), life cycle stage of the family, neighborhood, social class, ethnicity, religion, and the like. Each of these levels presents targets for potential intervention, and choosing among them well is essential if therapy is to progress.

So, in answering the question of when assessment is done, the conclusion is that it is both a specific structured activity at the outset of treatment, and an ongoing more or less unstructured activity conducted at all points of contact in the therapy system. Practically, assessment is continuous, and, as mentioned, it begins from the first moment of contact with a prospective client. In this chapter, the emphasis will be on assessment as a more formalized, though ongoing, activity, although some attention will be given to less formalized aspects of it. One final aspect of assessment that must be noted is that it can also be simultaneously interventive. Questions and homework assignments, and even some paper measures, by their very nature can implicitly suggest changes that may have a significant impact on the couple and on therapy. The most efficient assessment process will make maximal use of these potentially interventive moments, and assessment should be developed with an eye on intervention.

WHO TO INCLUDE IN ASSESSMENT

From a systemic perspective, it is especially informative to place the persons seeking treatment within their context. This is true even when working with an individual. When considering couple therapy, the default position is to assume that both partners should be included because the relationship to be treated is both an entity and a context in itself. It is most likely the single most important relational context that the partners have.

Part of the difficulty in assessing couples lies in the fact that not all initial contacts are explicitly for the purpose of couple therapy. In fact, it is often the case that another problem or issue is the presenting one for which help is being sought. However, the astute therapist recognizes that, at least for some clients bringing in individual and/or family issues, a couple approach may actually be warranted. Structural theory from the 1970s made the somewhat cliched claim that very often "family therapy eventually becomes marital therapy," and while this is no longer held doctrinally, it is still quite often applicable.

Let us assume couple therapy is being sought explicitly. Nichols (1988) discusses the importance of paying close attention to even the initial telephone contact with a client investigating making an appointment as a means of assessment. He suggests that the therapist, whenever possible, take on the task of managing the initial telephone interview so that a number of important questions may be answered. Specifically, the telephone conversation can provide the clinician with information relating to the caller's perceptions of the problem requiring treatment, any prior therapy or other attempts to solve the problem, and whether the client's stated situation is appropriate for counseling or referral. Things like tone of voice, pace and intensity of speech, manner and amount of disclosure (are things volunteered freely or does the therapist have to inquire frequently?), presentation of "facts," and the like may be very telling about the caller and the situation, from which a plan can be germinated.

The caller's identity is also important. Borrowing from Solution Focused theory, it is useful to determine if the person calling for help is a "customer" for change (de Shazer, 1988). The customer sees him/herself as having a role in the problem and its solution and an investment in change, and thus is the best kind of client with whom to work. However, many callers may turn out to be "complainants," who do not see their own participation in the solution of the problem and whose agenda requires primarily that someone else change. Discriminating between a customer and a complainant will allow the therapist to identify clients who are motivated for change even before they attend a session, and ordinarily, the therapist can develop a sense of where the caller stands via the initial phone contact. Persons who come to treatment as something other than a customer, which is quite common when working with couples, need to be helped toward becoming a customer, and there is a body of literature that the reader can pursue to develop greater expertise in this regard (e.g., Brothers, 1997).

Discriminating between the caller's status as complainant or customer also is informative about the relationship. Women tend to be the custodians of intimate relationships and are more likely to seek therapy for couple-related issues than are men. When women are customers, they will generally be able to note their own participation in their relationship's struggles. This is even more the case for men because men are less likely to seek therapy, and so when they call they usually are aware that they have a problem in which they participate. When women are complainants, however, they may not see the need for their own participation to be examined, and may be bringing in the partner to get him "fixed," which most men fail to appreciate. A complainant male may be interested in having the therapist get his partner "off his back," and so a token effort at counseling is hoped to be sufficient. Neither of these complainants is likely interested in making genuine systemic change.

A woman calling for couple treatment may indicate that the relational dynamics are stereotypical, such that she is the pursuer or initiator of relationship and he is the distancer or withdrawer. This may contribute significantly to the problem(s) that bring them in, or in fact may be the overarching issue itself. In contrast, a male caller is more likely to be in a position of last resort (i.e., he has just been threatened that a divorce is imminent or something of that nature) or calling as a result of an immediate crisis, such as the discovery of an affair.

The foregoing has examined couple assessment via the information gathered from one member of a couple relationship. While this strategy may be fairly common from a practical standpoint in that the initial effort to obtain treatment is made by one person, it is a mistake to assume that this information contains all of the essential substance of what the therapist needs to know to proceed well.

Although having both partners present during assessment may be preferred and normative, there are some issues for which such an approach is somewhat controversial. The two that are most significant are domestic violence and substance abuse. There is some ongoing debate among scholars and practitioners alike about how to best assess and treat both of these issues.

Unfortunately, as an aside, there is not necessarily complete consensus on whom to include in assessment (and treatment) when examining issues of less obvious controversy. In some of my own ongoing research (Odell, in progress), therapists presented with clinical scenarios depicting a variety of fairly typical couple issues approached them initially from quite divergent points of origin. For some therapists, separating the couple and seeing each person individually was the first action, whereas for others, separating them at the outset was to be avoided. Understanding that even in fairly "benign" couple situations there is a lack of agreement about whom to include in the assessment process, it should come as no surprise that there is considerable debate about the merits of each position when it comes to domestic violence and substance abuse. Let us consider both briefly.

Domestic violence is of grave concern to the couple therapist for several reasons, the most obvious of which is client safety. If there is reason to believe that a legitimate threat exists to the safety of either party from their partner, proceeding into couple therapy directly is contraindicated (Weeks & Treat, 2001). Unfortunately, defining terms like "legitimate threat" and "safety" is not as easy as it may sound. Feminist thinkers have criticized family therapy theory in general for colluding with male power and privilege to subtly sanction violence against women and children (Avis, 1996), and while this has led to increasing recognition and intervention in family violence, it has also resulted in a degree of "political correctness" being introduced into clinical work with couples. One therapist's view of abuse may be much broader than another's and thus their clinical work with the same highly conflictual couple would look vastly different, to the point where one therapist may choose to *not* work with them as a couple at all. Such differences notwithstanding, it is recommended for safety's sake that assessment not include both partners if violence is an issue in the relationship. This holds regardless of whether violence is a primary or secondary issue in the couple's presentation, i.e., whether they perceive it to be a concern.

Similarly, substance abuse calls for discernment. It is generally acknowledged in the family therapy field, with a few notable exceptions (e.g., Berg & Miller, 1992), that substance abuse issues require collaborative methods that combine systemic and substance specific treatment, such as 12 step programs. So, in determining who should be present during couple assessment when addressing substance abuse issues, the short answer is: It depends.

One of the major concerns in treating alcohol and substance abuse, whether in individual or other kinds of therapy, is overcoming denial (Treadway, 1989), wherever it may be found in the system. Having both partners present during the initial assessment is a good way to determine the degree to which the couple (or family) system is supporting the substance abuse, and in these circumstances, it generally is the case that substance abuse will not be presented as a primary concern. The seriousness of the abuse will only begin to become apparent after couple therapy has begun, sometimes after several sessions. In contrast, when substance abuse is mentioned from the outset as a problem in the relationship, it is wise to be prepared to separate the partners, at least temporarily, if it turns out that the substance abuse issues are serious enough to warrant suspending couple treatment until individual therapies for the user and the partner can be secured. Once this is accomplished and some progress made, couple therapy can be resumed purposively, and ideally simultaneously with ongoing individualized work. Indeed, there is a rich and growing literature supporting systemic therapy's utility for working with substance abusing persons and their families (Piercy, Fontes, Bischof, & Chang, 1996).

On the whole, it is consistent with systemic thinking that both members of the couple attend the initial session or sessions of therapy. This allows the therapist not only to acquire the narratives of both partners, but also to observe their interactional patterns as they listen to each other and talk between themselves. For example, consistent interruptions wherein either partner corrects, questions, or flatly argues the points made by the other during their invited description of their situation are quite telling. Such couples may be highly conflictual in their day to day interaction and are given to combat over even the smallest of points, and they demonstrate this dynamic spontaneously in the therapy room. Blame is apparently inexhaustible. Obviously, working with a couple like this requires certain skills and abilities that less "exciting" couples may not require.

WHAT TO ASSESS, AND HOW—TOOLS AND TECHNIQUES

To this point, when to assess couples and whom to include in assessment (one or both partners; having neither partner present is not particularly fruitful, but after a long day in the office...) have been examined. However, the questions of *what* to assess and *how* to assess it have not been. Before we examine tools and techniques explicitly, an understanding of the *what* of assessment is necessary. More specifically, the question really is this: Along what criteria do we evaluate the functioning of a given couple and the health, or quality, of their relationship? While pointing this question out explicitly may seem like stating the obvious, its significance would be hard to actually overstate. Identifying the criteria for evaluation is far more important than one might think at first glance because the standard to which a relationship is compared is what generates the evaluation.

It is beyond the scope of this chapter to discuss in any substantive detail the underpinnings of contemporary public philosophy regarding intimate relationships in Western society, but it is useful to examine them at least briefly. As has been noted elsewhere (e.g., Fowers, 1993), present conceptualizations of intimate relationships put tremendous pressure on them, making them both increasingly valuable and increasingly fragile. This is because the expectations for the benefits intimate relationships confer on participants are extraordinarily high while at the same time the expectations for the effort and skills necessary to obtain the benefits are largely overlooked. In short, people are buying into a mythology about intimate relationships, including and perhaps especially marriage, that leads them to expect a nearly unattainable vision of bliss without significant effort or struggle.

Developments in Western society placing increasing primacy on the companionate relationship have led to an ever rising standard of quality to which ordinary couple relationships are routinely compared (Odell, 2000). These relationships are expected to bring companionship, "soul-mate"-ness, and a host of other goods that seem to be transcendent of ordinary life, and this is simply expected as a function of having the relationship; effort toward that end is believed largely unnecessary. If the expected benefits are not forthcoming, individuals often make the dubious conclusion that the partner is lacking or that there is an "inevitable" incompatibility, and thus they set off to find a better partner and more compatibility, never really examining the assumptions and expectations they hold for intimate relationships nor their participation in them. This is particularly apparent in persons who appear in the therapist's office having had multiple failed relationships.

The significance of recognizing this reality lies in the fact that marital and couple therapists (and researchers) have often unwittingly contributed to the perpetuation of this problematic mythology, fueling a stronger and consumer mentality about intimate relationships in society (Doherty, 2001). By encouraging the creation and maintenance of these expectations without adequate emphasis on the skills and work, and sacrifices, necessary to increase the chances of actually obtaining the goal, therapists have helped couples to fail. Our culture influences people to develop unrealistic visions of relational living as a matter of course, but if clients have been in treatment before, checking to see if such expectations have been examined and challenged as needed is a good idea. If prior therapy experience has perpetuated unworkable expectations, the initial effort at developing a good working alliance may be a bit more difficult because clients may not want to hear that some of their ideas validated in previous counseling need adjusting.

Returning to the issue of assessment with couples, it is readily apparent that the criteria along which a relationship is evaluated is itself a bit tricky. Assessment with an individual client is a fairly straightforward affair, wherein the clinician can literally make good use of the manual depicting non-health, the *Diagnostic and Statistical Manual of Mental Disorders* (DSM) (American Psychiatric Association, 1995). No such relationship manual exists, so clinicians likely make use of a template drawn largely from cultural descriptions of "healthy" relationships and their own personal experiences. The limitations of such an approach must be acknowledged and appreciated. An obvious example is Gottman's empirically based contention that not all functional couples communicate in the stereotypical validating style usually preferred and taught by therapists (Gottman, 1994).

That truth notwithstanding, the foundation along which an assessment of a given couple can be generated can be developed from a combination of the therapist's experience with "functional" relationships, the couple's stated desires for what they want their relationship to be, and a familiarity with the empirical literature on characteristics of good relationships. Practically, assessing a client couple requires that their expectations of their relationships, themselves, and their partners be examined in as much detail as possible. Once it can be established that their expectations are reasonably attainable, i.e., that the degree to which they subscribe to cultural mythology is fairly limited and balanced by a more judicious system of thinking (which can be a significant task in itself; individual partners must both be decent candidates for the demands of a relationship), the therapist is free to move into evaluating major aspects of their relationship. Accepting that nearly all couples presenting for therapy hold as an ideal the companionate marriage or intimate relationship, tying an assessment to the empirical literature pertaining to what is often called "successful" or "functional" relationships affords a good foundation.

Fortunately, there is no shortage of empirical literature available discussing nearly every component of intimate relationships, including their functional aspects. In reviewing this literature, one can categorize in four domains the major elements that functional couples seem to have in common: 1) Individual personal characteristics and traits, including prior relationship history and family of origin factors; 2) Compatibility factors; 3) Relational skills and habits; 4) Situational variables impacting the relationship. Obviously, there is considerable overlap among these categories. Relationships that have strength in each of these areas are more likely to thrive, and so holding out a generic model of relational health based on these factors can provide a solid template useful for guiding both assessment and treatment.

In my clinical work, I have been very successful in putting this into actual practice by having couples think in terms of preparing a marital or relational resume'. They are asked to consider how they would go about comporting themselves so as to convince their partner that they are indeed the best candidate with which to develop an intimate relationship, in a way analogous to landing a job. They are to highlight explicitly their strengths and qualifications, including examples of them in actual practice as much as possible, as well as acknowledge their areas of weakness. In addition, they are asked to discuss how they would go about improving themselves and what deliberate steps they would take to accomplish the requirements of being in an intimate relationship, in particular with their partner. Put this way, many clients come to recognize with some embarrassment or chagrin that they are not very well prepared, either by fortunate circumstance or purposive effort, to participate well in an intimate couple dyad. This often has the effect of helping them to see how cultural mythology and their family of origin experience shape their mental models of marriage and intimacy. Then they are more receptive to examining their expectations as well as particular traits and habits that have obvious implications for relational life.

One instrument that offers data pertaining to the degree to which individuals subscribe to unrealistic expectations and beliefs about intimate relationships is the Relationship Belief Inventory (Eidelson & Epstein, 1987). It is a 40 item measure with good reliability and validity assessing belief systems about intimate relationships in general, and it has been used with both clinical and non-clinical samples. Because it examines intimate relationships in general rather than the relationship under present consideration, it offers a particularly good view of why some of the struggles a couple is experiencing may be occurring.

Individual Personal Characteristics. Some individuals seem to do very well in relationships of many kinds, and they are likely to be successful with a wide variety of intimate partners, whereas there are other people who are not nearly as well suited for most kinds of relationships, particularly intimate ones. Part of what contributes to their capacity to participate in relationships well is beyond their control, but nonetheless significant. For example, there is ample evidence documenting that individuals whose parents divorced are more likely to divorce themselves and that persons from single parent homes have more difficulty in intimate relationships (Amato, 1996). Similarly, an individual raised in a violent home may have rarely witnessed a number of important social and relational skills and yet be unaware of that fact in itself. There may be nothing that can be done about these descriptors, but being aware of them helps partners develop a more realistic approach to what weaknesses or liabilities they must overcome in their relationships. A thorough couple assessment should include elements of each partner's family of origin experience.

Specific questions to be answered may include: Who raised you and with whom were you raised? How were things like love, anger, affection, conflict, discipline, hurt, and support shown in your family, especially between the adults? How stable of a relational environment did you live in? What do you believe you learned about intimate relationships from your family of origin experience? What do you want to replicate from that experience in your current relationship and what do you want to discard?

A standardized instrument/technique that has a long history of use in family therapy that addresses these kinds of questions, and more, readily is the genogram. Developing a genogram on both members of the couple is strongly recommended, and there are several texts available that guide the clinician in performing genogram interviews. One very recent book worth making use of is Demaria, Weeks, and Hof's *Focused Genograms*(1999).

The Family of Origin Scale (Hovestadt, Anderson, Piercy, Cochran, & Fine, 1985) is a self-report inventory that has been used to assess individual perceptions of the healthiness of one's family of origin on a number of dimensions. It has been used clinically and consists of 40 items getting at communication clarity, expression of feeling, emotional warmth, personal responsibility, and the like. Higher scores reflect greater health. It would be logical to assume that two individuals with relatively high scores would have more going for them as they attempt to create and maintain a good relationship.

Although much about one's family of origin experience may be out of one's control, there are also many individual personal characteristics that can be chosen that have serious implications for a couple relationship. Personal traits such as honesty, patience, loyalty, etc., and personal choices such recreational pursuits, eating habits, and the like play a major role in relational functioning and can be purposely affected to a large degree by the individual. Questions that are raised in this area have to do with how easily relationship facilitating attitudes and behaviors are practiced, regardless of the relationship context in which they show up. For instance, a person who fails to show much empathy in ordinary social situations or who does not possess enough self-confidence to accept a little good natured teasing from friends or colleagues is likely going to have difficulty managing the more complex and nuanced world of an intimate relationship (Davis & Oathout, 1992). Being aware of strengths and limitations in this regard can often be the first step in developing such necessary character traits, independent of any given intimate relationship.

An instrument that has been used with some regularity in assessing individual's empathic capacities, specifically in the context of particular dyadic relationships (although not clinical samples), is the Dyadic Perspective Taking Scale (Long, 1990). It is actually two scales; the first assesses an individual's perspective taking ability (i.e., their ability to see their partner's point of view) with 13 items, and the second uses 20 items to assess the individual's perceptions of the perspective taking of their partner. Acceptable estimates of validity and reliability using factor analysis and item analysis have been reported (Long & Andrews, 1990). In short, higher scores indicate a greater degree of perspective taking, which suggests greater empathy.

A second aspect of personal characteristics is the relationship history that each individual has. Questions are raised pertaining to the relationships the partners have had prior to this relationship, what they have learned from them, and again, what they wish to bring forward and what they wish to leave behind. The patterns of relating and habits of maintaining an intimate relationship that each partner has developed that either work or lead to trouble are important to understand.

The literature on cohabitation, for example, strongly emphasizes that it is not a practice leading to the kinds of outcomes most people want (Nock, 1995). Cohabitors choose cohabitation because they typically believe it to be a good way to test out a given relationship, and although there is evidence that a gender disparity exists here (Popenoe & Whitehead, 2000), it has become increasingly normative in the development of couple relationships. In any event, because couples tend to enter into cohabitating relationship with a "wait and see how it goes" attitude, they often end up aborting the relationship when inevitable conflict surfaces as they prematurely conclude that the relationship is not viable and/or the partner is flawed. Consequently, they reduce the likelihood that they will develop the skills necessary for intimate relationships and become increasingly cautious in subsequent relationships, more insistently choosing cohabitation to "test things out." This vicious cycle is very hard to interrupt and either partner with this kind of history may be bringing a worrisome lack of skill into this relationship, as well as a tendency to bail out at the first sign of genuine struggle. Neither of these characteristics is associated with success in couple relationships.

What is most significant in relationship success that individuals bring on their own and also create as a function of their relationship is commitment. The importance of both partners to making a relationship work is extremely important (Nock, 1995). Asking couples about their commitment to each other and to the relationship has been somewhat controversial in terms of timing, but there is general consensus that doing so makes sense at some point in treatment if there is any question about it in the therapist's mind. It is usually the case that couples who are willing to come to counseling have at least some degree of commitment, although on occasion a couple (or one partner in a couple) will come to treatment to obtain a professional therapist's "rubber stamp" of approval for effort and/or a death certificate for the relationship.

Compatibility. Obviously, the degree of fit between a pair of individuals intent on forming a satisfying intimate relationship is critical in determining their success. Rather than explicate the rather voluminous literature examining various characteristics as they affect relational health, it is sufficient to say that the general rule of homogamy offers useful guidelines. Homogamy refers to the process of selection governing relationships based on similarities of the partners, with a trajectory of greater homogamy being predictive of relational success. Although homogamy can be examined with regard to virtually any aspect of a relationship, homogamy in foundational areas of the relationship is most important. Specifically, couples whose values, philosophies of life, and worldviews are similar are much more likely to be successful. Any good textbook on marriage and the family can delineate a host of other factors about which homogamy plays a significant role. Couples with limited compatibility may be able to use the areas they do share as anchoring points from which to move forward, while couples with much compatibility enjoy many advantages that make relational life easier.

The area of compatibility that has received the lion's share of attention is the perception of satisfaction in a given relationship. Although the issue of compatibility is not explicitly raised by inventories assessing relational satisfaction, it underlies such instruments' utility. This is because couples who agree (i.e., are compatible) in their perception of the relationship's quality are easier to work with than couples whose perceptions are widely disparate.

There are many measures available for assessing perceived relationship quality. Both the Marital Adjustment Test (Locke & Wallace, 1959), and the Dyadic Adjustment Scale (Spanier, 1976) have long use histories, but as they are somewhat dated, the Revised Dyadic Adjustment Scale (Busby, Christensen, Crane, & Larson, 1995) may be a better choice. The RDAS is highly correlated with the DAS, but shorter. It is a 14 item scale with excellent psychometric properties assessing the perception of a relationship's cohesion, consensus, and satisfaction, all critical dimensions of relationship functioning.

Relational Skills. The behaviors that couples actually engage in is what either maintains satisfaction or dysfunction, and so they may be assessed with regard to what they actually do that works and does not work. Well functioning couples, i.e., couples whose relationships are likely to be permanent and satisfying, tend to operate differently than couples whose relationships are in trouble. The most important area in which skills and good habits are needed is conflict.

All couples have conflict, but what makes the critical difference is what they do with it. John Gottman's work on couple interaction vis-à-vis conflict has been most illuminating, as has the work of several of his protégés, such as Howard Markman and Clifford Notarius. According to Gottman and his colleagues (1998), there are a number of significant patterns that are predictive of divorce among married couples. Among those that they note are problematic are husband's unwillingness to accept influence from the wife, the wife's negative start up in conflict situations, the failure of the husband to deescalate the wife's low-level negative affect, and the wife's failure to physiologically sooth the husband. To paraphrase (loosely), husbands who are unwilling to consider and value what their spouses say to them are at risk, as are wives who begin conversations with their spouses with criticism and blaming, husbands who ignore wive's persistent but subtle irritation with them, and wives who do not make efforts to calm their husbands with touch and gentle words.

Conflict, and communication in general, can be measured by several reasonably short instruments, such as the Marital Communication Inventory (MCI) (Bienvenu, 1970), and the Marital Problem-Solving Scale (MPSS) (Baugh, Avery, & Sheets-Haworth, 1982). Both of these measures have been used regularly and have good psychometric properties, with the former assessing perceptions of each partner regarding the quality of communication and the latter a couple's ability to solve problems. The MPSS is particularly interesting in that it has been shown to be as useful as more expensive and time consuming observational coding systems for evaluating problem solving (L'Abate & Bagarozzi, 1993).

While managing conflict effectively is essential in couple relationships, there are other areas where skill development is important. Couples who are able to consistently prioritize their partners and relationships in the face of multiple competing demands will likely do well over time. Specific examples of doing this include being able to set aside times for conversation, activities, and intimacy in the midst of busy schedules, choosing battles to fight wisely, making deliberate efforts to speak the "love language" of the partner, and offering grace and forgiveness regularly. I call this the cultivation of mutual good faith and good will.

One other skill that is quite important is the ability of at least one partner, preferably both, to develop patience and flexibility to accommodate unexpected situations as well as the mundane stresses of daily living. Rigidity has long been noted in the family therapy literature as being related to a host of problems, and this readily applies to couples. Couples who cultivate an adaptive mentality and practice flexibility, even insisting on *not* getting their individual ways may be in better shape in the long run.

Skills in use over time by couples result in accomplishments that they both can recognize and celebrate, as well as concrete strengths upon which they can build further. Couples who are in better shape relationally usually are able to recall times when they overcame difficult obstacles or challenges, whether they were external to the relationship (e.g., job loss) or internal (e.g., conflict over household chores). There are few measures of relational accomplishments and skills beyond those addressing communication and problem solving. However, a relational time-line may access the couple's history in a way that can highlight those times and situations where they showed the ability to overcome trouble. Asking them about solutions they have generated to problems in the past, including problems unrelated to why they are in treatment now, can help the therapist identify and highlight some of their latent strengths. This is analogous to Solution Focused therapy's exception question, which itself can get at skills and accomplishments the couple has.

Getting a narrative of their history also has some assessment value in other ways. Kayser's work (1993) on relationship disaffection suggests that the way in which couples present their history is quite telling in terms of how they are at present. It is virtually always the case that a couple enters into a relationship on a positive trajectory, based on the fact that "courting" has moved to "committed." They usually view their coming together as romantic and exciting at that time, and they view their decision to commit to each other as a good one. Over time, couples whose relationships move into distress find that their evaluation of their coming together changes, such that they view their history as regrettable or worse. Couples recounting their history in primarily negative terms are in much worse condition than couples whose stories reflect a generally positive bent.

Situational variables. Although there are a number of situational and contextual factors subject to at least some degree of the couple's control or influence, there are also some that are not that are important to acknowledge. Among the former are choice of living arrangement, in-law relationships, friendships, occupation and income, educational level, children, and involvement in community life, such as church and social organizations, and recreational activities. Couples that are largely satisfied or positive about each of these areas will likely find them helpful in their relationships. Situational factors that are typically beyond the couple's control are health concerns, economic cycles, governmental policies and realities that affect daily life, neighborhood life and participants, and aspects of their community, such as schools, and crime and safety. Again, as these areas are perceived positively by both members of the couple, they are a source of strength.

Most intake forms include at least some information of a situational nature that can serve as a launching point for inquiry and assessment, and asking broadly about any areas not already addressed in the paperwork is also a good idea. It is curious that clients often take their situational contexts for granted without perceiving the degree to which those contexts influence them. Pointing these influences out and helping clients contend well with them can be very helpful in terms of increasing therapy's effectiveness.

Case Study

Following is an illustrative case study of a couple in therapy, with an emphasis on the assessment process by which treatment moved forward. Much clinically relevant information is omitted for reasons of space, and so the focus is primarily on what was assessed, how, why, and what effect it had on therapy's course. Identifying information about the couple has been changed to protect their confidentiality.

First Contact

Gina called my office and requested an appointment for marriage counseling with her husband, Paul. Speaking briefly with the office manager, she said they had "communication problems" and needed help. Using the standard telephone intake form, the office manager obtained some basic data about them. They were Caucasian, solidly middle class in terms of income, and living in a small semi-rural town not far from a large city. Paul, 41, ran a family business with his brother, and Gina, 37, was a senior flight attendant for a major airline. They had no children, and this was the first marriage for both of them; they had been married for twelve years. That was all I knew going into our first meeting, and quickly reviewing that beforehand was helpful.

The First Session

Because the request had been for couple counseling, and because there was no obvious reason from the initial call to not see them together (and there rarely is in that first call), Paul and Gina were set for an initial session of couple therapy. As Gina had been the caller, I wondered if she was the stereotypical custodian of the relationship, so I made a mental note to ask about how they decided to seek help as a means to investigate that more fully. The fact that they came to therapy together indicated that they had some degree of belief that theirs was a relational problem, or at least they were willing to start out that way. They filled out initial paperwork prior to our session that included the informed consent form and the Dyadic Adjustment Scale, as well as an open-ended question asking them to describe why they were coming to therapy. Although I couldn't have the DAS scored before we met, a quick inspection let me estimate their score to be indicative of relational distress. Their description of why they were seeking counseling reiterated "communication problems."

In the first interview, I asked them to tell me about themselves, their problem, how they decided to seek therapy, and what they wanted to accomplish therein. It was quickly apparent that Gina had an agenda and Paul was somewhat puzzled about the problem; he acknowledged its existence but seemed to have a hard time understanding Gina's point of view. She spoke rather eloquently about her frustrations with feeling as though she was an afterthought to Paul, and she was able to catalog several attempted solutions that she had tried to no avail to make him prioritize her more highly (curiously, they all ended up becoming the same class of action, criticism in some form). Along the way, she had mentioned frustrations with his devotion to his work and by extension his family of origin, and she also stated that she wanted to make a final decision about whether to have a child, a conversation that she claimed he avoided. She had reached the point of insisting that they see a counselor, and he had agreed (though she took the responsibility for making it happen). Paul made almost no effort to disagree or defend himself, and I had to ask him explicitly to comment on what he thought and felt about what his wife said and what his views were. Based on their behavior, I hypothesized that they clearly did not fight well, with Gina as the pursuer and Paul as the withdrawer. Paul did say that he did not like Gina's anger and what he defined as her nagging bothered him greatly.

As individuals, both of them were likable, even amidst the tension between them and Gina's overt anger. They reported no alcohol, drug abuse, or violence issues, and they both stated that they wanted things to get better. They also seemed to believe that their issues were not trivial, and they said they were motivated to take whatever steps were necessary, although Paul was less vocal, nodding agreement to Gina's assertion.

Expectations. I asked them about what they wanted from counseling as a means to check their expectations for treatment and for the desired relationship. Unlike many couples, they seemed to have fairly realistic expectations in that they both understood that conflict and sacrifices are relational realities and that feelings should not be the only criteria for success. An area of concern regarding their expectations showed up in that they both implicitly expected their partner to meet most if not all of their intimacy needs; neither mentioned anything about supportive friendships or participation in a community of intimates. They were putting considerable pressure on each other in this way.

Genogram. A basic genogram was constructed to round out the first session that revealed some interesting information. Paul's family of origin lived within a few miles of them, and in fact, they were living in the house previously owned by his parents. At work, he saw his brother daily, and his father, though officially retired from the business, came in nearly every day and was integrally involved in its operations. Paul's family maintained a large amount of contact with him even outside of work. As he talked about it, he stated that he sometimes felt as though he was torn between being with his family, which he reported he enjoyed for the most part, and being with Gina, who said she felt it was time they developed more of their own lives together alone. I did not attempt to delve further into that area in the first session, but I knew we would need to come back to it at some point, and we ultimately did.

Gina's father and mother had divorced when she was a teenager, and she had lived with her mother until she turned 20 when she moved out on her own. Her father had died about two years ago. She reported that they had not been as close as she wished, but added that much of that was because he did not seem very interested in keeping up a relationship with her, even after she had left home. Her widowed mother lived in the major city nearby, and as an only child, she kept a close eye on her, often spending the night at her mother's when she had a short turnaround between assignments. Gina stated toward the end of the session that she found herself staying with her mother more often to avoid Paul than to take care of her. Both of them stated this was not good, and partly what prompted them to get into therapy.

Evaluating them on *individual characteristics*, there were several positives and some negatives. They had not cohabited prior to marriage and neither had been married before.

However, Gina's parents had divorced and she did not see a well functioning couple relationship modeled for her. She reported that she did not have a lot of relationship experience prior to meeting Paul, which was both a positive and a negative. Paul's parents' marriage was traditional, and though they did not express love verbally very often, they were reported to have been constant companions, starting an agricultural supply company together prior to raising their children. Paul observed commitment but not much overt intimacy in his family of origin.

I ended the first session by asking them to pay attention specifically to their conflicts—how they start, how they end, who says what to whom, and how—and to compare them to when they were getting along better. I also asked them to think about what skills they both felt they brought to the marriage, using a brief description of the marital resume' idea mentioned above. Both of these assignments were designed to assess while at the same time potentially intervene and promote change. With the former, if they began to pay closer attention to the behaviors they engaged in when in conflict and compared them to when they are doing well, they may bring new behaviors to bear that will change their conflict pattern. At the same time, such observation assesses several areas, such as motivation (clients who do not do "easy" assignments may not be customers or very motivated for change), self-awareness and self-control, and their ability to take a meta-position to their own processes. The latter assignment offered a window into their thinking about what their expectations of themselves in an intimate relationship are and what their expectations are for how such relationships function. The briefer an answer to the marital resume' question, the more likely it is the respondent has a view that relationships run automatically with little or no personal effort. Such thinking is problematic.

Between the first and second session, the DAS was scored. Paul's overall score was 94, while Gina's was 81, both of which categorize their marriage as distressed. The subscales indicated that a relative strength in their marriage was cohesion, whereas their satisfaction and affectional expression scores were low and their consensus was higher, though still marginal. That instrument offered a picture of a couple that was clearly disappointed with each other and not as close as either would like, yet who wanted to get better and had little interest in quitting the marriage. The foundation of the marriage appeared to be intact. That information was very useful in allowing me to highlight and commend them for their perseverance as well as giving them a relative place to understand the status of their relationship in the second session. The DAS' clinical cutoff score is 100, and they were not too far from that, which they seemed pleased to hear.

Subsequent Sessions

Marital Resume'. Their responses to the marital resume' assignment were quite illuminating. Paul came prepared with a couple of pages of thoughts written down, which surprised Gina and me. He put a lot of effort into the question, which suggested his motivation for change was higher than either she or I thought. It also suggested he may do better with a very specific request than a more general one. He presented himself as a good candidate for a marriage in terms of his work ethic and his ability to provide a secure income in an uncertain business. He laughed a little as he reiterated the cliched "I don't drink, I don't smoke, and I don't run around." He thought of himself as sensible and levelheaded, and mentioned that Gina's more outgoing nature was appealing to him precisely because he tended to be too introverted. He also volunteered his insight that he had moved away from appreciating that quality in his wife, and needed to recover it. He also said that he was "mystified" by communication as Gina tried to relate it to him. Talking about "stuff" seemed somehow trivial, and yet he realized that he was failing in this area. He stated he needed to learn to talk more and include his wife in his daily life. He added that his family of origin had not modeled that kind of communication, which led him to discuss with just a hint of defensiveness that he did not want to feel like he must choose his family or his wife; he wanted both.

Gina was able to listen to him without interruption, but we ran out of time before she could offer her own resume'. She did say how much she appreciated that he had put so much effort into the assignment, which suggested to me how starved she was for his attention. As we were unable to address the assignment to observe their interaction, I simply reiterated it.

Relational Dynamics in Session. Our third session was cancelled. Gina called, obviously irritated, that Paul had an emergency at work, and we rescheduled for two days later. When they came in, they immediately moved into a conflict cycle about the cancellation. Gina lashed out at Paul, saying how hurt and angry she was, especially given that the week before he had said so many good things in therapy and had seemed more attentive to her at home. She said she felt like it was a "bait and switch." Paul sat silently, head down, while she attacked, and I interrupted her when she began to pull in disappointments and hurts from the past. I asked Paul what he was thinking at that moment. He said quietly, "Dealing with work is so much easier. When I make a mistake there, I can at least fix it. I feel like I keep blowing it with her, and I can never catch up. I said I was sorry a dozen times, but it never seems enough and she just doesn't understand what I have to do at the job. It's always me choosing something else over her." As he spoke, he seemed to become more expressive, and his voice took on an angry undertone.

This interchange was helpful in giving me a look at their conflict processes, so I asked them how this compared to their conflicts at home. Gina stated that he usually just "clams up," and if I had not asked him to talk, he would have sat there until she exhausted herself. Paul nodded. I wondered aloud if Paul might be afraid to fight with her overtly. He said he did not think he would ever be able to win. Gina threw in a comment that he could not win because he was in the wrong most of the time. That was interesting in terms of explaining their conflict dynamic.

Over the course of the next several sessions, we were able to get to Gina's marital resume', which included several strengths as well as a few obvious weaknesses. We were able to highlight how the degree of *compatibility* between them was actually fairly high. They had many things in common in terms of goals, hobbies, and recreational pursuits. They had a similar philosophy of life and valued many of the same things. The assessment of their compatibility offered us several points of strength and stability as well as underscoring where their struggles were.

Relationship History. We also spent a couple of sessions recounting their relationship's history. Their narrative was largely similar, and mostly positive, indicating again a more favorable state currently in their marriage. I pointed out to them the importance of their history as something worth both holding on to and learning from. They seemed a bit surprised that they had so many positives already in place. This led naturally to a number of discussions about their *skills and accomplishments*—ways that they had already shown they could work together to overcome obstacles.

One of the most significant was how they worked through Gina's father's death two years earlier. They reported that she was powerfully impacted by his death; on the one hand, she reported she felt devastated, as if her "last chance for a relationship was ripped away," leaving her empty, while at the same time, she felt strangely disconnected from it. She reported that Paul had been wonderfully supportive, and he stated that he could tell she really needed him and he was committed to making himself available to her. This was a great example of his skill in prioritizing her, and I asked him how he accomplished that. He said that "it was the right thing to do—I hate to see her in pain," and he became misty at that point, which allowed a real connecting moment to occur between them. I gently prodded him to try to articulate his feelings, and he was able to express verbally how important Gina is to him. That moment became another accomplishment for them to bank.

Unlike some couples, their *situational context* was playing a significant and obvious role in their problems. Paul's involvement with his work and family of origin seemed to provoke jealousy on Gina's part, which further distanced him into his work and family. Fortunately, both acknowledged their ability to choose these contexts, and they were able to generate some specific ways they could draw a boundary around their marriage without damaging their relationship with Paul's family. One way that this became explicit was on the decision to have a baby. Paul's family had been explicitly encouraging them to give them another grandchild, while simultaneously saying how important is was that Paul keep a close watch on the company's helm. Paul and Gina became aware that they were receiving mixed messages, and decided together to point that bind out to his family. This helped Paul and Gina create the situation in which they could decide for themselves what they wanted to do, how, and when. Paul became aware of how his loyalty to his family and the family's business had compromised their family planning, and that he had been unable to break free of their inappropriate pull.

Therapy progressed with this couple for a total of 14 sessions over the course of four months. At the end of treatment, their DAS scores had risen to 118 for Paul and 113 for Gina. Both of them acknowledged that they had improved, and they still saw room to continue improving outside of therapy. Gina was still more extroverted and pursuing, but Paul had come a long way toward matching her, and there was much less discomfort and pressure in their relationship.

Ongoing and interventively designed assessment played a crucial role in this case. When it is done well, as this case illustrates, therapy is greatly improved. Written measures, conversational and observational techniques, and conceptual tools such as the genogram and marital resume' all played vital roles in assessment, and ultimately, in treatment.

REFERENCES

Amato, P.R. (1996). Explaining the intergenerational transmission of divorce. *Journal of Marriage and the Family, 58,* 628-640.

American Psychiatric Association. (1995). *Diagnostic and statistical manual of mental disorders* (4th ed.). Washington, DC: Author

Avis, J.M. (1996). Deconstructing gender in family therapy. In F. Piercy, D. Sprenkle, J. Wetchler, and Associates (eds.), *Family therapy sourcebook* (2nd ed.) (pp. 220-255). New York: Guilford.

Baugh, C.W., Avery, A.W., & Sheets-Haworth, K.L. (1982). Marital Problem-Solving Scale: A measure to assess relationship conflict negotiation ability. *Family Therapy, 9*, 43-51.

Berg, I.K. & Miller, S.D. (1992). *Working with the problem drinker*. New York: Norton.

Bienvenu, M.J. (1970). Measurement of marital communication. *The Family Coordinator, 19*, 26-31.

Brothers, B.J. (Ed.) (1997). *When one partner is willing and the other is not*. New York: Haworth.

Busby, D.M., Christensen, C., Crane, D.R., & Larson, J.H. (1995). A revision of the Dyadic Adjustment Scale for use with distressed and nondistressed couples: Construct hierarchy and multidimensional scales. *Journal of Marital and Family Therapy, 21*, 289-308.

Demaria, R., Weeks, G.R., & Hof, L. (1999). *Focused genograms*. New York: Brunner/Mazel.

Davis, M.H. & Oathout, H.A. (1992). The effect of dispositional empathy on romantic relationship behaviors: Heterosocial anxiety as a moderating influence. *Personality and Social Psychology Bulletin, 18*, 76-83.

de Shazer, S. (1988). *Clues: Investigating solutions in brief therapy*. New York: Norton.

Doherty, W. (2001). *Take back your marriage*. New York: Guilford.

Eidelson, R.J., & Epstein, N. (1987). Relationship Belief Inventory. In K.D. O'Leary (ed.), *Assessment of Marital Discord: An Integration for Research and Clinical Practice* (pp. 330-333). Hillsdale, NJ: Lawrence Erlbaum.

Fowers, B. (1993). Psychology as public philosophy: An illustration of the moral dimension of psychology with marital research. *Theoretical and Philosophical Psychology, 13*, 124-136.

Gottman, J.M. (1994). *Why marriages succeed or fail*. New York: Simon & Shuster.

Gottman, J.M., Coan, J., Carerre, S., & Swanson, C. (1998). Predicting marital happiness and stability from newlywed interactions. *Journal of Marriage and the Family, 60*, 5-22.

Hovestadt, A.J., Anderson, W.T., Piercy, F.P., Cochran, S.W., & Fine, M. (1985). A family of origin scale. *Journal of Marital and Family Therapy, 11*, 287-297.

Kayser, K. (1993). *When love dies: The process of marital disaffection*. NY: Guilford.

L'Abate, L., & Bagarozzi, D.A. (1993). *Sourcebook of marital and family evaluation*. New York: Brunner/Mazel.

Locke, H., & Wallace, K. (1959). Short marital adjustment and prediction tests: Their reliability and validity. *Marriage and Family Living, 21*, 251-255.

Long, E. (1990). Measuring dyadic perspective-taking: Two scales for assessing perspective-taking in marriage and similar dyads. *Educational and Psychological Measurement, 50*, 91-103.

Long, E., & Andrews, D. (1990). Perspective taking as a predictor of marital adjustment. *Journal of Personality and Social Psychology, 59*, 126-131.

Nichols, W.C. (1988). *Marital therapy: An integrative approach*. New York: Guilford.

Nock, S.L. (1995). Commitment and dependency in marriage. *Journal of Marriage and the Family, 57*, 503-514.

Odell, M. (2001). Unpublished raw data.

Odell, M. (2000). *Psychotherapy and Marriage: How Compatible Are They?* Paper presented at the Revitalizing the Institution of Marriage for the 21st Century Conference, Provo, UT.

Piercy, F.P., Fontes, L.A., Bischof, G.H., & Chang, Y.H. (1996). Family therapy with several specific presenting problems. In F. Piercy, D. Sprenkle, J. Wetchler, and Associates (eds.), *Family therapy sourcebook* (2nd ed.) (pp. 319-349). New York: Guilford.

Popenoe, D. & Whitehead, B.D. (2000). *The state of our unions, 2000: The social health of marriage in America.* Rutgers, NJ: National Marriage Project.

Spanier, G. (1976). Measuring dyadic adjustment: New scales for assessing the quality of marriage and similar dyads. *Journal of Marriage and the Family, 38*, 15-28.

Treadway, D.C. (1989). *Before It's Too Late: Working with Substance Abuse in the Family.* New York: Norton.

Weeks, G.R., & Treat, S.R. (2001). *Couples in treatment* (2nd ed.). Philadelphia: Brunner/Routledge.

Young, M.E., & Long, L.L. (1998). *Counseling and Therapy for Couples.* Pacific Grove, CA: Brooks/Cole.

Chapter 5

A DEVELOPMENTAL-FAMILY SYSTEMS APPROACH TO THE ASSESSMENT OF ADOLESCENTS[*]

Robert W. Heffer and Danielle L. Oxman[‡]
Texas A&M University

Adolescents have much to accomplish in 10 short years. "During adolescence, children are expected to consolidate and apply their knowledge about their roles and rules in adult society, to begin to achieve emotional and economic independence from parents, and to complete the biological and physical changes that began in the preadolescent period." (Lamb, Hwang, Ketterlinus, & Fracasso, 1999, p. 421). So much to do in such a compressed time period! One can easily understand the rationale behind Anna Freud's description of the adolescent developmental period as "normal psychosis" (Freud, 1958). Folklore and anecdote project the notion that teenagers in most industrial, Western societies struggle with the challenges of their developmental transition and engulf their parents and siblings in the tempest along the way. Family therapists and researchers understand that, although many families ride the waves along with their teen surfers, others seem to backstroke somewhat effortlessly with their adolescent into young adulthood.

This chapter will offer a theoretical framework for assessing and assisting families with teenagers. Specifically, developmental and behavioral-family systems issues will be discussed to provide the socio-ecological theoretical context for assessment. Practical, ethical, and legal issues unique to assessing adolescents and their families will then be raised to sharpen the application of assessment skills. A description of selected major measures used to assess adolescents' socio-emotional functioning will then be offered as the centerpiece of this chapter. A case example and summary conclusions will complete the chapter.

---

[*] The authors thank Nancy Baker, Erin Collins, Clarissa Escobar, Elsa Hernandez, Ryan Loss, Laurel Mangrum, Barbara Meehan, and Mike Stefanov for assistance in gathering materials to prepare this manuscript.
[‡] Robert W. Heffer, Ph.D. is Clinical Associate Professor and Clinic Director, Danielle L. Oxman, M.S. is a Clinical Psychology Graduate Student, both at Texas A&M University, College Station, Texas.

THEORETICAL FRAMEWORK FOR ADOLESCENT ASSESSMENT

Developmental Issues

We agree with Yule (1993) that a developmental perspective on the assessment of adolescents promotes an appreciation for interactions among the ecobehavioral context of the domains of functioning being evaluated, characteristics of the individual, and developmental variables such as chronological age and maturation. Further, a flexible developmental perspective gathers useful applications from a wide range of developmental theorists.

Developmental theorists historically have focused on continuities and discontinuities of ontogeny in childhood. However, the adolescent developmental period has received considerable attention from many researchers and theorists, including G. Stanley Hall, the father of adolescent psychology (Berzonsky, 2000). Hall (1904) originated the concept of *Sturm and Drang* (i.e., storm and stress) as typical of the adolescent years, during which time a teenager wrestles with the intense tug between self-interest and social responsibility (Arnett, 1999). Later theorists (Benedict, 1938; Mead, 1970) accentuated how a teenager's cultural context influences whether or not the adolescent period is navigated through stormy waters or is experienced as relatively smooth sailing. Greater pressures during adolescence tend to be normative in cultures in which childhood activities and expectations are clearly demarcated from adult roles and responsibilities and in which technological and social change are brisk, such as in industrial, Western societies. Further, Anna Freud (1972) distinguished that some turmoil during adolescence may motivate an adaptive transformation into adulthood and that calm seas through adolescence may prevent the breeze that can fill the sails of a teenager who is developing her own unique sense of self. For Erickson (1968), the "crisis" that must be resolved during adolescence, "identity vs. identity diffusion," serves as the fulcrum on which pivots the other seven life span stages of development. The extent to which a teenager formulates a clear sense of who she is, where she has been, and where she is going plots the trajectory for future integration and synthesis of past and present experiences.

Although focusing more on cognitive development than psychosocial development, Jean Piaget articulated the thinking style that starts in adolescence and lays a foundation for the cognitive and metacognitive processes that carry an individual into adulthood (Simeonsson, Huntington, Brent, & Balant, 2001). According to Piaget (1970, 1971), children develop through the mechanisms of assimilation and accommodation, creating new schemas or modifying existing schemas to make sense of their world. As a result, individuals' worldview forms as they mature. The adolescent years mark the onset of formal operational thought, which allows for introspection, perspective taking, abstract thinking, metacognition, idealism, and hypothetical-deductive logical reasoning (Inhelder & Piaget, 1958).

Of course, some might question the association of the term "logical" and adolescent thinking! The cognitive and social problem solving approaches of teenagers truly are distinct from the approaches of children and adults. In the process of honing formal operational thinking, for example, adolescents develop a sense of conceptual egocentrism (Shaffer, 2002). According to Elkind (1978), conceptual egocentrism is the belief that others are just as preoccupied with an adolescent's appearance and behavior as the adolescent is himself. Imaginary audience and personal fable are the two primary constructs underlying adolescent conceptual egocentrism. Imaginary audience is the belief that others are as admiring or critical of the adolescent as the adolescent is of himself and that he is the focus of attention form others. Personal fable is an adolescent's belief that his feelings are special and unique and, perhaps, that he is invulnerable to the negative consequences of risky behavior. These constructs are integral to adolescents' typical preoccupation with appearance, press to live "outside the box," and identification with specific peer groups and cultural experiences.

The sociocultural context of development is precisely the emphasis of Vygotsky's theory of cognitive development (Burk, 2002). Vygotsky's (1962) term, "zone of proximal development," underscores the dynamic, social influences on learning and refers to the range of tasks too difficult to be mastered alone but that can be mastered with the guidance of adults or more skilled peers. As applied to adolescents, this concept can elucidate the experience in adolescence of using interpersonal contexts (e.g., family, social network, religious or cultural organizations) to develop skills at understanding, interpreting, and relating to the world and to others. Of course, the family system is an invaluable compass for teenagers who begin to plot course for their journey toward the horizon (Holmbeck, Colder, Shapera, Westhoven, Kenealy, & Updegrove, 2000).

Family Systems Issues

Our approach to adolescent assessment in a family systems context is strongly influenced by the related areas of ecobehavioral assessment (Simeonsson & Boyles, 2001) and behavioral-systems assessment (Mash & Terdal, 1997). Both areas emphasize empiricism, ideographic methods, low inference conceptualizations, and the functional, transactional interplay between the person (physical features, behavior, thoughts, feelings) and her environment. Our family systems oriented approach "...is directed at describing and understanding (a) characteristics of the [adolescent] and family; (b) the contexts in which such characteristics are expressed; and (c) the structural organizations and functional relationships that exist among situations, behaviors, thoughts, and emotions." (Mash & Terdal, 1997, p. 10).

Further, we strive to integrate developmental and family systems approaches by taking into account not only the developmental status of the adolescent, but also the developmental status of the family as a unit (Witt, Heffer, & Pfeiffer, 1990). The structure, tasks, and roles of a family, for example, are influenced by how the family develops over time across pre-marriage, marriage, first-child parenthood, young child parenthood, school aged child parenthood, teenager parenthood, and "empty nest." Hill and Mattessich (1979) postulated that predictable family stages exist and that family development is punctuated by the emergence and alteration of norms, roles, and other family characteristics necessary for continuity of the family as a social system. Gerson (1995) specifically identified three family life phases, each divided into two stages: (a) coupling phase in which individuals progress from the unattached young adult stage to the family formation stage; (b) expansion phase, in which families progress from the family with young children stage to the family with adolescents stage; and (c) contraction phase, in which families progress from the stage of launching adolescents into life on their own to the stage of "moving on" in later life without children at home. When a family struggles during a specific life stage or during transition to the next stage, the "crisis" may result in either discord or collaboration among family members.

As the reader might suspect, we endorse the comprehensive conceptual model for assessing couples and families (Heffer & Snyder, 1998; Snyder, Cavell, Heffer, & Mangrum, 1995) described in chapter 3 of this book. This comprehensive conceptual model encompasses the theoretical issues previously outlined here and provides methodologies for assessing individuals, dyads, nuclear family, extended family and social networks, and community and cultural systems. Specifically relevant to the discussion here is that this model asserts that "…the range in developmental stages of individual members can expand dramatically, increasing the potential for interpersonal differences in values, expectations, and ability to engage in system-enhancing behaviors…" (Heffer, Lane, & Snyder, 2002, p. xxx). Life span developmental issues of teenaged family members, other family members, and the nuclear family itself are interwoven into how experiences are perceived, interpreted, and responded to in the family. The specific methods suggested by this model certainly can be applied to assessing families with adolescents. This chapter will highlight practical and ethical/legal issues in family therapy in which an adolescent is the focus of the referral. Further, global and problem-specific measures designed to assess common socio-emotional problems of adolescents will then be presented.

PRACTICAL ISSUES IN ASSESSING ADOLESCENTS AND THEIR FAMILIES

Initial Interview Issues

Although some therapists may work in individual therapy with an adolescent, the problems to be addressed almost always ultimately entail a parent-adolescent issue that involves some combination of parental concern, teenager behavioral or emotional difficulty, and/or parent-adolescent discord (Rae, 1999). We, therefore, utilize a flexible approach to interviewing, and using other assessment methods with, adolescents and their families. For example, we typically meet with parents and teenager together for the first part of an initial interview, then meet with the teenager alone, and then with the parents alone. This allows the purpose of the session and the "ground rules" for communication to be established with all parties present and then each party's perspective on the problem to be obtained. In addition, the parents can complete paper-and-pencil assessment measures while the adolescent is being interviewed and *vice versa*. Depending on the circumstances, parents may be interviewed first or may meet for an initial assessment session without the adolescent present (e.g., if the adolescent is a young teenager or if marital or parent problems are severe). Reuniting the parents and adolescent to conclude the session provides a forum to recap the session, and includes all family members in case formulation and planning and sets the stage for family interventions.

A flexible approach to the logistics of assessment also enhances an evaluator's ability to become aware of any relevant issues regarding serving families who are linguistically and cultural different from the evaluator (Gopaul-McNicol & Thomas-Presswood, 1998). Awareness and sensitivity to language, religion, or culture based family issues are vital to effective family assessment and therapy, but perhaps especially so when working with an adolescent who often has not requested services and may be reluctant to actively participate in the process. The role of culture in the acceptance of psychological services, family attributional style, roles and expectations of family members, developmental tasks of adolescence, and therapist's interpretations of the family's experiences must be factored into the assessment process with adolescents and their families (Canino & Spurlock, 2000; Johnson-Powell, Yamamoto, Wyatt, & Arroyo, 1997). For example, although adolescent depression and comorbid social, academic, and family discord problems occur across all cultural and socioeconomic groups (Hammen, Rudolph, Weisz, Rao, & Burge, 1998), ethnicity appears to play an important role in the experience of depression and suicidal behavior among adolescents (Roberts, 2000).

Many family therapists eschew interviews with adolescents, who can express their unhappiness and displeasure about being brought to a stranger's office to discuss private matters by acting surly, aloof, withdrawn, or even hostile. Of course, some adolescents seek services and are open to disclosure, entering the therapeutic assessment process fairly readily. Whether or not the teenager is shy, fearful, gruff, hesitant, or eager, rapport building skills are essential to successful interviewing and therapy (Micucci, 1998). Of course the evaluator must balance on a tight rope with most teenagers, not teetering either too much toward being an authoritative adult "helper" or toward being a want-to-be-peer pal. House (2002) offered,

> "Specifically, I believe the essential elements of success in forming working relationships with adolescents are our tolerance of differences in motives, our own and the client's honesty, and our respect for those in a weaker position than ourselves. Although these may be valuable or important clinician attributes for work with many or all clients, for work with teens I believe they are vital" (p. 16).

The reader is referred to both House (2002) and Morrison and Anders (1999) for excellent applied information about conducting initial diagnostic interviews with adolescents and children. Two Sattler (1998; 2002), also, are replete with scholarly and practical information regarding interviewing family members, as well as extensive compilations of brief checklists and semistructured interview questions for a host of referral concerns.

Ethical and Legal Issues

Chief ethical and legal issues when including adolescents in family assessment and therapy include: (a) informed consent for services, (b) confidentiality of communications and records, and (c) abuse reporting laws. Currently, an abundance of texts exist that expound upon the ethical practice of psychological assessment and therapy. Of course, the savvy evaluator will be familiar with the most recent version of the *Standards for Educational and Psychological Tests* (American Educational Research Association, 1999). In addition, Koocher and Keith-Spiegel (1998), Nagy (2000), and Pope and Vesquez (1998) are excellent resources for the ethical practice of mental health services.

Informed consent for services and the other practical issues discussed here have therapeutic, ethical, and legal implications. Legally in most US States, consent for psychological services may be provided voluntarily by a person who has full knowledge of the services being consented to, is competent to make such judgements, and has legal authority to do so. This right and responsibility typically is extended to adolescents' (ages 18 years and younger) parents or legal guardians, with only a few exceptions. For example, an adolescent who has been legally emancipated (e.g., member of the armed services, is married, and/or lives separately and financially independent from parents) or has been declared an "mature minor" by a court may consent to services independently and expect confidentiality from parents (Melton, Ehrenreich, & Lyons, 2001). In addition, some States allow minors to independently consent to services for substance abuse, pregnancy, sexually transmitted disease, or even mental health. Of course, mental health professionals are ethically obligated to obtain informed consent or assent from those they serve who are competent to do so, which includes most adolescents involved in family assessment and therapy.

Therapeutically, offering a sense of mutual respect and collaboration with adolescent family members is vital to successful inclusion in the evaluation and therapy process. Since most adolescents do not request services and yet their parents have the legal right to include them in services (or refuse services), we work to strike a balance among the ethical, legal, and therapeutic issues. For example, we do not directly ask an adolescent whether or not she consents to treatment when the parents, who have the legal right to do so, expect their participation. Why ask a question of an adolescent when you cannot deftly deal with a "NO" answer? Rather, we describe the evaluation process, create at milieu of mutual respect and cooperation, obtain informed consent from the parents, and request assent from the adolescent—assent to *understanding* what the parents have consented to already. Typically, this approach "buys time" to build rapport with the adolescent and to more fully describe how the evaluation process may benefit her and her family so that assent to services is less affectively driven.

Confidentiality of communication and records regarding family assessment and therapy is a well established ethical principle and legal protection. The therapeutic benefit of maintaining confidentiality is quite apparent. When family members, including an adolescent, are confident that private and often distressing personal information is not disclosed by the evaluator/therapist to anyone outside the family unless authorized to do so, they will be more likley to seek appropriate services, to provide all the information essential for effective services, and to remain in services as necessary. Of course, the process of fully informed consent for services requires a discussion of the legal limits of confidentiality (e.g., threat of injury to self or others, abuse or neglect of a minor or developmentally disabled or elder adult, certain court proceedings, filing claims with third party payers, and when compelled to do so by a judge).

The central issue with adolescents in therapy, typically is less focused on keeping information private from persons or entities outside the family and more focused on how information is shared among therapist and other family members (Rae & Fournier, 1999). Since the emphasis here is on *family* assessment and therapy, in which an expectation of shared information among therapist and family members is made explicit, adolescents should be given an opportunity to discuss these issues in unambiguous terms at the outset of services. In fact, even in individual assessment or therapy sessions, we overtly do not give an adolescent under the age of 18 years any expectation of legal protection for confidentiality. We do not want to mislead or be untruthful with adolescents. In Texas, for example, either parent (or legal guardian) has a right to receive both oral communication and written records regarding psychological services to their minor child until the minor is 18 years old, unless a court has terminated all parental rights or in specific situations as ordered by a judge (Shuman, 1997).

Therapeutically, we often establish agreements within the family about what information will not be discussed with all family members (e.g., details of marital strife, adults' history of criminal or sexual behavior) and what information may be *delayed* in disclosing to family members at the discretion of the therapist. For example, an adolescent may privately disclose substance use or sexual behavior with peers that the therapist, based on an *a priori* agreement with the parents, delays disclosure to the parents until the adolescent, in concert with the therapist, can discuss this openly himself. Of course, we make clear to all participants that the goal of the assessment process is to gather and share relevant information so that recommendations for diagnosis and interventions can be formulated.

Ethics codes and State and Federal laws have established exceptions to confidentiality and privacy of information disclosed in the delivery of psychological services (Koocher & Keith-Speigel, 1990). In fact in most States, mental health professionals, categorized as "mandated reporters," have a legal obligation to report a reasonable suspicion of abuse or neglect of a minor or a developmentally disabled or elder adult. In addition, some States have established "dangerous persons" reporting laws, in which situations are codified regarding when confidentiality may be broken when immanent threats of injury or loss of life to self or others are disclosed to a mental health professional (DeKraai, Sales, & Hall, 1998). The actual application of these reporting laws varies by State. For example, some State laws are based on a "duty to warn" principle, such that a mental health is mandated to warn the intended victim when a client discloses threats to physically harm or kill a person. In Texas, the acceptable reasonable action of a psychologist (when informed by a client that he intends to immanently injure or end the life of someone) follows a "duty to protect" principle. Specifically, a psychologist may break confidentiality to inform the appropriate law enforcement or health professionals to prevent the harm threatened by a client (Shuman, 1997). A legal protection in Texas is not necessarily extended to the psychologist who may decide, based on ethical or moral obligations, to directly contact the intended victim in these circumstances. Therapeutically, we deal with these potentially serious scenarios by informing the family and adolescent together the legal limits to confidentiality within the first few minutes of the initial contact. Our informed consent form includes this information and a copy if given to the parents immediately after it is signed. In addition, to the extent possible, we inform the appropriate family members of our requirement and intention to report before contacting the relevant agency, so as to engage their cooperation.

MAJOR MEASURES USED TO ASSESS ADOLESCENT'S SOCIO-EMOTIONAL FUNCTIONING

Adolescent socio-emotional functioning may be assessed by an array of available measures. Measures may be self- or other-report, may aim to measure either broad or global functioning, or may have a more narrow or specific focus on a particular problem area. A selection of measures frequently used in adolescent assessment will be discussed in the sections that follow. Substance abuse, delinquency/criminal behavior, and forensic evaluations are somewhat specialized areas of assessment with adolescents and, therefore, the reader is referred to other citations on these topics (Brown, Aarons, & Abrantes, 2001; Johnson & Shaw, 2001; Scaht, 2001; Schaffer, 2001; Vik, Brown, & Myers, 1997). In addition, evaluators may access a plethora of published and unpublished measures for use with adolescents from resources such as Science Directorate of the American Psychological Association (2002), Corcoran and Fisher (2000), and Rush (2000). Based on the Heffer and Snyder (1998) comprehensive conceptual model, we will limit the following discussion to self- and other-report paper-and-pencil techniques that assess individual (i.e., adolescent) behavioral and affective functioning. Selected paper-and-pencil measures of the parent-adolescent relationship will also be described.

Self-Report Measures of Global Psychological Functioning

Self-report measures of global psychological functioning in adolescents aim to obtain a picture of how adolescents view their overall functioning in daily life. Global self-report measures offer an opportunity to compare an adolescent's responses with reports from others, such as parents or teachers. A selection of frequently used global self-report measures will be described briefly here and in Table 1.

As outlined in Table 1, the Personality Inventory for Youth (PIY; Lachar & Gruber, 1995a, 1995b) measures emotional and behavioral adjustment in adolescents, as well as issues concerning academic and family functioning. The PIY is composed of 270 true/false questions, and generates scores on nine clinical scales indicating internalizing and externalizing symptoms, as well as school performance and cognitive limitations. Use of the PIY also includes the options of using a parallel parent inventory and a teacher problem checklist and of using an audiotape of the items for respondents with reading problems.

The Millon Adolescent Personality Inventory (MAPI; Millon, Green, & Meagher, 1982), which was developed based on Millon's theory of personality, contains eight personality scales yielded from 150 true/false questions. Scores on these eight scales may facilitate initial intervention planning, especially the Expressed Concerns scale, which targets areas the adolescent finds problematic (Millon, Green, & Meagher, 1982). This component of the MAPI allows disclosure in a less personal manner and may be particularly helpful with adolescents that are initially unwilling to respond to an examiner's questions.

The Adolescent Psychopathology Scale (APS; Reynolds, 1998a, 1998b) consists of 346 items and utilizes a multiple-response item format. Scores on the APS form 20 clinical disorder scales that correspond to DSM-IV Axis I disorders, five personality disorder scales, eleven psychosocial problem content scales, and four response style indicator scales. A 115-item short form (APS-SF; Reynolds, 2000) is available and takes 15-20 minutes to complete. In addition, the Reynolds Adolescent Adjustment Screening Inventory (RAASI; Reynolds, 2001) consists of 32 items from the APS, uses a 3-point Likert scale, takes 5 minutes to complete, and provides a Total Adjustment score and four factorially derived scale scores (Antisocial Behavior, Anger Control Problems, Emotional Distress, and Positive Self).

Table 1. Self-Report Measures of Global Psychological Functioning and Behavior Checklists

Scale/ Developers	Response Format	Scales	Forms/ Respondent	Norms	Scoring	Reliability	Validity	Clinical Utility
Self-Report Personality Measures								
Personality Inventory for Youth (PIY) *Lachar & Gruber*	270 true-false items	9 clinical scales; Each clinical scale is broken into 2 or 3 homogeneous subscales.	Self-report paper & pencil measure designed to measure emotional & behavioral adjustment, family character & interaction, & school adjustment & academic ability in children/ adolescents aged 9 to 18 years. Statements are written at a third-grade reading level.	Standardized using 2 samples ranging in age from 9 to 18 years. Both regular education students & clinically referred children were utilized from diverse sites and states. Representativeness for gender, ethnicity, & SES was adequate.	Hand or computer scored. Raw scores are transformed to T-scores via the use of gender-based tables and transferred to a Scoring Profile form.	Regular education sample: internal consistency for 9 clinical scales, .71 to .89, for 24 subscales: .40 to .79. Test-retest: .81 to .91 for clinical scales, .66 to .89 for subscales. Clinically referred sample: clinical scales, .74 to .92; subscales, .44 to .84. Test-retest: .76 to .91 for clinical scales, .58 to .88 for subscales.	Content: majority of items were adapted from PIC-R items, so most have already "demonstrated diagnostic utility in a variety of clinical & educational contexts over the course of many years in actual clinical application and research reports". Criterion-Related: scales of the PIY have been shown to be statistically correlated with appropriate scales on other measures, such as the MMPI-A, PIC-R, Reynolds Adolescent Depression Scale, Suicidal Ideation Questionnaire, Social Support Scale, Adolescent Hassles Scales, & the State-Trait Anxiety Inventory. Construct-Related: factor analyses (maximum likelihood with Varimax rotations) resulted in 4-factor solutions within both the male & female samples. The 4 factors are: (1) internalizing behaviors, (2) externalizing behaviors, (3) social adjustment, peer adjustment & depression, & (4) family. A discriminant classification analysis correctly classified 82.5% of adolescents diagnosed as conduct disordered or with major depressive disorder.	The PIY gathers information regarding emotional & behavioral adjustment of adolescents, generating scores indicating internalizing & externalizing symptoms, cognitive limitations, & poor school performance.

Scale/ Developers	Response Format	Scales	Forms/ Respondent	Norms	Scoring	Reliability	Validity	Clinical Utility
Millon Adolescent Personality Inventory (MAPI) *Millon, Green, & Meagher*	150-items, self-report measure. Respondents answer "True" or "False".	The MAPI has 20 scales: 8 Personality Scales: (1) Introversive, (2) Inhibited, (3) Cooperative, (4) Sociable, (5) Confident, (6) Forceful, (7) Respectful, & (8) Sensitive. 8 Expressed Concerns Scales: (1) Self-Concept, (2) Personal Esteem, (3) Body Comfort, (4) Sexual Acceptance, (5) Peer Security, (6) Social Tolerance, (7) Family Rapport, & (8) Academic Confidence. 4 Behavior Correlates Scales: (1) Impulse Control, (2) Societal Conformity, (3) Scholastic Achievement, & (4) Attendance Consistency.	Designed to be used with adolescents with at least a 6th grade reading level. 2 forms: (1) clinical form for use in mental health settings, & (2) a guidance form appropriate for use in academic settings. May be administered in either a group format or individually.	Norms are provided for both the "normal" & the "clinical" populations. The MAPI utilizes base rate scores to determine cutoff scores.	Hand scoring templates are not available for the MAPI, as the process is described as "complicated & time consuming" by the authors. Additionally, minor refinements in calculation of scores and norm refinements are continually being made. The best way to use up to date scoring procedures is to use the computer scoring through National Computer systems, Inc.	Test-Retest: reliability coefficients reported in the mid-seventies for a 5-month interval in a clinical group.	Convergent: correlational data comparing the MAPI with other commonly used measures (e.g., California Personality Inventory, 16 Personal Factor Questionnaire) yielded correlations from .30 to .80.	The MAPI's personality style information may be useful in initial assessments & in intervention selection. Furthermore, the Expressed Concerns scales may be helpful in targeting what areas the adolescent is finding problematic.

Scale/ Developers	Response Format	Scales	Forms/ Respondent	Norms	Scoring	Reliability	Validity	Clinical Utility
Adolescent Psycho-pathology Scale (APS) & APS – Short Form *Reynolds*	346 multiple-response items	40 scales that measure 4 broad content domains: 20 clinical disorder scales that correspond to DSM-IV Axis I disorders, 5 personality disorder scales, 11 psychosocial problem content scales, & 4 response style indicator scales.	Designed for use with adolescents between 12 & 19 years of age. Items are written at a 3rd-grade reading level. It uses a multiple response, paper & pencil format.	Samples used to develop the APS were geographically diverse (public junior & senior high schools in 8 states & inpatient & outpatient treatment sites in 21 states). Norms were based on gender, age, and gender by age groups for the entire standardization sample of school-based adolescents	Automated scoring program generates a clinical report: Clinical Score Report, which includes a summary of the APS scale elevations, score summary table, score profile compared to norm group selected, summary of critical items, & an item response summary table.	No test-retest reliability coefficients available. Internal consistency: Major Depression subscale: .95 for both normal & clinical samples. Dysthymic Disorder subscale: .89 for clinical sample & .88 for the school sample.	Studies have yielded evidence of content validity, contrasted groups validity (involving groups of 'normal adolescents' & those with a diagnosis of major depression), as well as criterion related validity (which was noted by correlations with other self-report measures like the RADS).	The APS is designed to measure a wide range of mental health problems experienced by adolescents. It specifically evaluates DSM-IV symptoms to psychiatric disorders found in adolescents, & aims to provide more applicable clinical utility due to the close match between DSM-IV criteria & APS scores. It also assesses other psychological problems that intercede with pathology, such as psychosocial variables & personal proficiency. Scores on the APS denote severity of symptomology across different time periods.

Scale/ Developers	Response Format	Scales	Forms/ Respondent	Norms	Scoring	Reliability	Validity	Clinical Utility
MMPI-A *Butcher, Williams, Graham, Archer, Tellegren, Ben-Porath, & Kraemmer*	478 true-false items. All items on basic scales appear in the 1st 350 items. May be administered in either a group format or individually.	10 Clinical Scales: (1) Hypochondriasis, (2) Depression, (3) Hysteria, (4) Psychopathic Deviate, (5) Masculinity-Femininity, (6) Paranoia, (7) Psychasthenia, (8) Schizophrenia, (9) Hypomania, & (0) Social Introversion. 6 Additional Scales: (1) Lie Scale, (2) Infrequency, (3) Defensiveness, (4) Variable Response Inconsistency, (5) True Response Inconsistency, & (6) Cannot Say.	Respondents must have approximately a 5th grade reading level. The MMPI-A may be administered with test booklets, audiocassettes, or by computer.	The normative sample included both "normal" & "clinical" samples.	The MMPI-A may be scores either by hand, or by a computer program.	Test-Retest: .65 to .84 for the clinical scales.	Many items that comprise the MMPI-A were selected through criterion keying. A list of scale correlates is provided in the manual in Tables D-1 through D-15. Furthermore, Table 23 of the Appendix provides validity data for the content scales.	MMPI-A is a useful measure yielding a broad band measure of psychopathology in adolescents. It is easily administered, scored, & interpreted, and may add valuable initial assessment information and facilitate treatment planning.

Scale/ Developers	Response Format	Scales	Forms/ Respondent	Norms	Scoring	Reliability	Validity	Clinical Utility
Self-Report Behavior Checklists								
Youth Self Report (YSR) *Achenbach*	113 items, 3-point Likert scale; Questions concerning competencies	2 competence/ adaptive functioning scales: activities & social. 8 syndrome scales: withdrawn, somatic complaints, anxious/ depressed, social problems, thought problems, attention problems, delinquent behavior, & aggressive behavior. 3 syndrome groupings were formed: Internalizing, Externalizing, & Other Problems	Single form, to be completed by children/ adolescents with at least 5th grade reading skills and a mental age of at least 10 years. The YSR is appropriate for use with children ages 11-18.	Normed on children/ adolescents in the eastern United States.	Hand-scored on a profile designed for the YSR. Raw scores can be converted to both T scores and percentiles based on the normative data.	Test-retest: (1 week interval) .77 to .89	Content: demonstrated by ability of 10 of the 17 competence items & 89 of the 102 problem items to discriminate between referred & nonreferred adolescents; 2 of the competence items were scored in the opposite direction of what was expected for referred adolescents, thus competence scores should not be used in determining clinical status. Criterion-related: all YSR problem scales, social scale, & school performance discriminated between referred & nonreferred adolescents.	Useful in a variety of clinical and medical settings to identify competencies and problem areas of children & adolescents. Part of a multiaxial assessment system, it can be used in conjunction with other Achenbach measures such as the CBCL & TRF to guide further interviewing and assessment. Useful as an aid in making formal DSM diagnoses & diagnostic formulations. May also be used for program evaluation by helping in needs assessment & aiding with documentation of cases receiving services.

Scale/ Developers	Response Format	Scales	Forms/ Respondent	Norms	Scoring	Reliability	Validity	Clinical Utility
Behavior Assessment System for Children (BASC) – Self Report of Personality (SRP) *Reynolds & Kamphaus*	186 True/ False self-report items.	14 scales: (1) Attitude to School, (2) Attitude to Teachers, (3) Sensation Seeking, (4) Atypicality, (5) Locus of Control, (6) Somatization, (7) Social Stress, (8) Anxiety, (9) Depression, (10) Sense of Inadequacy, (11) Relations with Parents, (12) Interpersonal Relations, (13) Self-Esteem, & (14) Self-Reliance. 3 Composites: (1) School Maladjustment Composite, (2) Clinical Maladjustment Composite, & (3) Personal Adjustment Composite.	2 forms (one for children & one for adolescents ages 12-18). There is also a audiotape available to facilitate administration for children who have trouble reading or for those children for whom English is a 2nd language.	Separate norms available for General, Male, Female, & Clinical normative populations.	Once the SRP form is completed, it may be separated to reveal the necessary scoring page, table, & profile. Item scores are summed horizontally, & then scale totals are yielded by adding all numbers in each scale column. Normative scores are then obtained by finding raw scores in appropriate norm tables. Composite scores & the Emotional Systems index may then be found.	Internal Consistency: approximately .80 for both males and females at the adolescent age group. Test-Retest: .76 to mid-80's over a 1-month interval.	Structure of the Composite scores was developed through the use of factor analyses of the scale intercorrelations in the General norm sample. There was also a comparison with scales based on expert judgment. The SRP was compared with 4 other measures, (MMPI, YSR, Behavior Rating Profile, & the Children's Personality Questionnaire). Although some of these measures tap different domains, on those domains that were shared, the SRP correlated moderately to highly with those domains.	The BASC-SRP is part of a multimethod, multidimensional approach to evaluating the behavior & self-perceptions of children & adolescents aged 2-18 years. The SRP is a personality inventory that can facilitate initial assessment & treatment planning.

Scale/ Developers	Response Format	Scales	Forms/ Respondent	Norms	Scoring	Reliability	Validity	Clinical Utility
Other-Report Behavior Checklists								
Child Behavior Checklist (CBCL) – Parent Report Form (PRF) Versions: CBCL/4-18 & CBCL/2-3 *Achenbach*	CBCL/4-18: 118 items, 3-point Likert scale; Additional questions concerning competencies. CBCL/2-3: 100 items, 3-point Likert scale	3 competence/ adaptive functioning scales: activities, social, & school. 9 syndrome scales: withdrawn, somatic complaints, anxious/ depressed, social problems, thought problems, attention problems, delinquent behavior, sex problems, & aggressive behavior. 3 syndrome groupings were formed: Internalizing, Externalizing, & Other Problems	Single form to be used by either parents or parental figures with at least a 5th grade reading level; Questions ask for ratings of behaviors over the past 6 months.	Children & adolescents aged 4-18, drawn from a subset of non-handicapped subjects from a national sample chosen to be representative of SES, ethnicity, & geographical location.	Hand-scored on a profile designed for the CBCL. Raw scores can be converted to both T scores and percentiles based on the normative data.	Internal consistency: .90 and above Test-retest: .56 to .89	Content: almost all CBCL items discriminated between referred and non-referred children Construct: significant correlations found between CBCL scales and many analogous scales, such as the Conners. Criterion-related: ability of CBCL's quantitative scale scores to discriminate between referred and non-referred children after the effects of demographics was partialled out.	Useful in a variety of clinical and medical settings to identify competencies and problem areas of children & adolescents. Can be used in combination with other Achenbach measures such as the YSR & TRF to guide further interviewing and assessment. Useful as an aid in making formal DSM diagnoses & diagnostic formulations. May also be used for program evaluation by helping in needs assessment & aiding with documentation of cases receiving services.

Scale/ Developers	Response Format	Scales	Forms/ Respondent	Norms	Scoring	Reliability	Validity	Clinical Utility
Teacher Report Form (TRF) *Achenbach*	118 items, 3-point Likert scale; Questions concerning competencies and 4 adaptive characteristics	Adaptive functioning scales include a scale for the mean rating of the child's performance in academic subjects; a scale reflecting each of the 4 adaptive characteristics; and a scale reflecting the sum of these 4 adaptive characteristics. 8 syndrome scales: withdrawn, somatic complaints, anxious/ depressed, social problems, thought problems, attention problems, delinquent behavior, & aggressive behavior. 3 syndrome groupings were formed: Internalizing, Externalizing, & Other Problems	Single form, appropriate for teachers; Questions ask for ratings of behaviors over the past 2 months.	Teachers of children both referred and non-referred for mental health services, special school services, & behavioral/ social-emotional problems from both public & parochial schools throughout the United States.	Hand-scored on a profile designed for the TRF. Raw scores can be converted to both T scores and percentiles based on the normative data.	Test-retest: (15-day) .84 - .92. Agreement was calculated between teachers and aides who worked in the same classrooms, the median was .57, with teachers rating students slightly less favorably than aides.	Content: all but 1 problem item & all adaptive functioning items were significantly associated with referral status. Construct: correlations between the TRF & corresponding scales on the Conners' Revised Teacher Rating Scale ranging between .62 to .90. Criterion-related: most effects associated with referral status demonstrated in significant differences between referred and nonreferred subjects on TRF scores accounted for a medium to large percentage of the variance in the scores when the effects of SES, race, and age were partialled out.	Useful in a variety of clinical settings to identify competencies and problem areas of children & adolescents. Can be used in combination with other Achenbach measures such as the CBCL & YSR to guide further interviewing and assessment. Useful as an aid in making formal DSM diagnoses & diagnostic formulations. May also be used for program evaluation by helping in needs assessment & aiding with documentation of cases receiving services. Can be useful to help specify and clarify teachers' concerns about their students' behaviors.

Scale/ Developers	Response Format	Scales	Forms/ Respondent	Norms	Scoring	Reliability	Validity	Clinical Utility
Behavior Assessment System for Children (BASC) – Parent Rating Scales (PRS) *Reynolds & Kamphaus*	126 items rated on a 4-point Likert scale.	14 scales: (1) Hyperactivity, (2) Aggression, (3) Conduct Problems, (4) Anxiety, (5) Depression, (6) Somatization, (7) Attention Problems, (8) Learning Problems, (9) Atypicality, (10) Withdrawal, (11) Adaptability, (12) Social Skills, (13) Leadership, (14) Study Skills. 5 Composites: (1) Externalizing Problems Composite, (2) Internalizing Problems Composite, (3) School Problems Composite, (4) Behavioral Symptoms Index, & (5) Adaptive Skills Composite.	2 forms (English & Spanish) There is also an audiotape available to facilitate administration for parents who understand English better that they read English.	Separate norms available for General, Male, Female, & Clinical normative populations.	Once the PRS form is completed, it may be separated to reveal the necessary scoring page, table, & profile. Item scores are summed horizontally, & then scale totals are yielded by adding all numbers in each scale column. Normative scores are then obtained by finding raw scores in appropriate norm tables. Composite scores & the Behavioral Symptoms index may then be found.	Internal Consistency: approximately .80 to low .90's for both males and females at the adolescent age group. Reliabilities for the BSI were also high (.88 to .94) Test-Retest: .70's to .90's. Interrater reliability: both parents rated their children, with correlations ranging from .46 to .67.	3 types of evidence of the validity of the PRS are reviewed: support for factor analysis for grouping the scales into composites, the correlations of PRS scales & composites, & the PRS score profiles for groups of children having received a particular clinical diagnosis. The PRS was compared with 4 other measures, (CBCL, Personality Inventory for Children-Revised, Conners' Parent Rating Scales, & the Behavior Rating Profile). Although some of these measures tap different domains, on those domains that were shared, the PRS correlated moderately with those domains.	The BASC-PRS is part of a multimethod, multidimensional approach to evaluating the behavior & self-perceptions of children & adolescents aged 2-18 years. The PRS is a behavior inventory that can facilitate initial assessment & treatment planning.

Scale/ Developers	Response Format	Scales	Forms/ Respondent	Norms	Scoring	Reliability	Validity	Clinical Utility
Behavior Assessment System for Children (BASC) – Teacher Rating Scales (TRS) *Reynolds & Kamphaus*	138 items rated on a 4-point Likert scale.	14 scales: (1) Hyperactivity, (2) Aggression, (3) Conduct Problems, (4) Anxiety, (5) Depression, (6) Somatization, (7) Attention Problems, (8) Learning Problems, (9) Atypicality, (10) Withdrawal, (11) Adaptability, (12) Social Skills, (13) Leadership, (14) Study Skills. 5 Composites: (1) Externalizing Problems Composite, (2) Internalizing Problems Composite, (3) School Problems Composite, (4) Behavioral Symptoms Index, & (5) Adaptive Skills Composite.	2 forms (English & Spanish) There is also an audiotape available to facilitate administration for parents who understand English better that they read English.	Separate norms available for General, Male, Female, & Clinical normative populations.	Once the TRS form is completed, it may be separated to reveal the necessary scoring page, table, & profile. Item scores are summed horizontally, & then scale totals are yielded by adding all numbers in each scale column. Normative scores are then obtained by finding raw scores in appropriate norm tables. Composite scores & the Behavioral Symptoms index may then be found.	Internal Consistency: approximately .80 for both males and females at the adolescent age group. The range of the composite scale reliabilities was .89 to .97. Test-Retest: .82 to .91. Interrater reliabilities: .63 to .83.	3 types of evidence of the validity of the TRS are reviewed: support for factor analysis for grouping the scales into composites, the correlations of TRS scales & composites, & the TRS score profiles for groups of children having received a particular clinical diagnosis. Moderate to high correlation shave been reported between the TRS & other teacher report measures (TRF, Revised Behavior Problem Checklist, Conners' Teacher Rating Scales, Behavior Rating Profile, & Burks' Behavior Rating Scales).	The BASC-TRS is part of a multimethod, multidimensional approach to evaluating the behavior & self-perceptions of children & adolescents aged 2-18 years. The PRS is a behavior inventory that can facilitate initial assessment & treatment planning.

The MMPI-A (Butcher et al., 1992) consists of 478 true-false items. Respondents require a 5th-grade reading level to complete the MMPI-A. The MMPI-A generates scores across 16 scales, is easily administered, scored, and interpreted, and can also serve to facilitate initial assessment and treatment planning. Clinicians familiar with the MMPI should be certain to consult resources such as Archer (1997) to apply relevant developmental psychopathology literature to the interpretation of MMPI-A profiles.

Behavior Checklist Self-Report Measures

Behavior checklist self-report measures provide an opportunity to gain information on a variety of behaviors in a relatively parsimonious manner. Adolescents are typically instructed to indicate how often they engage in various behaviors. This information may then be used in conjunction with other reports (such as parent or teacher) of the same or similar behaviors to provide convergent or divergent assessment information. The behavior checklist measures described here are outlined in Table 1.

The Youth Self-Report (YSR; Achenbach & Rescorla, 2001) consists of 113 items on a Likert-scale format, as well as separate questions concerning social competencies and activities. Two functioning scales are formed for competence in activities and social functioning. Eight syndrome scales are also formed, yielding three broad-band grouping scores (Internalizing Problems, Externalizing Problems, and Other Problems) and a Total Problems score. The YSR is part of a multiaxial assessment system, and may be used in conjunction with other Achenbach measures such as the Teacher Report Form (TRF) and the Child Behavior Checklist (CBCL), parent report, to guide assessment, interviewing, and intervention planning.

The Behavior Assessment System for Children-Self-Report of Personality (BASC-SRP) is part of a multimethod, multidimensional approach to assessment (Reynolds & Kamphaus, 1998). The BASC-SRP is a personality inventory composed of 186 true/false items. Responses on these items form three composite scores (School Maladjustment, Clinical Maladjustment, and Personal Adjustment) as well 14 scales. Parent-report (BASC-Parent Rating Scale) and the and teacher-report (BASC-Teacher Rating Scale) forms are available, as well as self-report versions for respondents in age groups 8 to 11 years and 12 to 18 years. An audiotape is also available for use with adolescents who have difficulty reading or for which English is a second language.

Problem-Specific Self-Report Measures

While global measures provide estimates of functioning across a broad range of domains, specific measures of an adolescent's functioning with a given domain are often crucial to effective evaluation and treatment planning. This section will focus on four problem-specific areas in which adolescents often experience problems (i.e., depression, anxiety, self-concept, and the parent-adolescent relationship). Obviously, this review will not be exhaustive; much of the relevant measure information is contained in Table 2.

Table 2. Self-Report Measures of Specific Problems

Scale/ Developers	Response Format	Scales	Forms/ Respondent	Norms	Scoring	Reliability	Validity	Clinical Utility
Depression								
Child Depression Inventory (CDI) & CDI-Short *Kovacs*	CDI: 27-self-report items; respondent selects 1 of 3 sentences that best describes their experience in the past 2 weeks. CDI-Short Form: 10-items	Yields a total depression score as well as 5 factors: negative mood, interpersonal problems, ineffectiveness, anhedonia, & negative self-esteem	Respondent must have a 1st-grade reading level & be 7 to 17 years of age; respondent may record answers on a scoring sheet, or they may complete the CDI on an IBM-compatible microcomputer.	Respondents ages 7-17 were included in the normative sample.	The CDI form may be separated at the perforation, revealing the scoring key underneath the answer sheet. Responses from scoring sheet are totaled for each scale & subscale and plotted onto a profile form. Conversion of raw scores to standardized scores is built into the profile form. The scoring procedure is similar for the CDI-Short Form. The CDI may also be computer scored (the CDI may either be administered on the computer, or results from an administration may be entered to be scored.	Internal Consistency: .71 to .89 Test-Retest: .38 to .87 for varying samples and intervals. (e.g., .82 for normal youths over a 2-week interval).	Concurrent: the CDI was reported to be correlated with other similar measures of depressive symptoms, such as the Coopersmith Inventory & the Piers-Harris Self-Concept Scale.	Quick way to obtain information pertaining to an adolescents depressive symptoms & may be used for treatment planning &/or routine screening. The CDI-Short Form may be useful for quick screenings.
Beck Depression Inventory-II (BDI-II) *Beck, Steer, & Brown*	21 self-report items, each item composed of 4 statements listed in order of severity about a certain symptom of depression	1 scale yielding a score of total depressive symptoms.	2 forms: both English & Spanish	Samples from 4 psychiatric outpatient clinics & 1 college-student group were used.	Scored by summing ratings of the 21 questions. If respondent has circled more than 1 answer for a particular question, the one with the highest rating is used. Total scores are then grouped to yield 4 classifications, minimal, mild, moderate, & severe.	Internal Consistency: .92 for the outpatient population, .93 for the college-students Test-Retest: .93 for a 1-week interval.	Content: BDI-II was developed especially for the purpose of assessing symptoms of depression as outlined in DSM-IV. Convergent: BDI-II has been found to be positively related to the Beck Hopelessness Scale, the Scale for Suicide Ideation, & the Hamilton Rating Scale for Depression.	Assesses depression level in clinical & normal populations. Changes in BDI-II reflect current DSM-IV guidelines.

Scale/ Developers	Response Format	Scales	Forms/ Respondent	Norms	Scoring	Reliability	Validity	Clinical Utility
Beck Hopelessness Scale (BHS) *Beck & Steer*	20 true/false self-report items	1 scale yielding negative attitudes about the future.	1 form. Scale is reported to be most appropriate for respondents age 17 & over, but has been used with adolescents 13 & over.	Normed with adult clinical populations, it should be used cautiously with normal adult & adolescent respondents.	Scored by placing the scoring key over the response form & adding responses of hopelessness for each item. Response sets may then be given a descriptive label (normal, mild, moderate, & severe) & interpreted.	Internal Consistency: with all of the separate normative samples (e.g., Major Depressive Disorder, alcoholics), reliabilities range from .82 to .93. It is suggested that reliability may be lower with college students. Test-Retest: .66 for a 6-week interval.	Concurrent: relationship between clinical ratings of hopelessness & BHS scores ranged from .62 to .74. Discriminant: BHS was not developed to discriminate between respondents with different diagnoses. The manual reports different discriminant validities for very specific group comparisons. Construct: Hopelessness has been found to be a good predictor of suicidal intent, & has been reported as being a better predictor than depression (.47 vs. .26).	The BHS should be used cautiously for screening purposes with adolescents. It was designed to measure degree of negative attitudes about the future, & has been described in the manual as an "indirect indicator of suicidal risk in depressed examinees or individuals who have made suicide attempts".
Reynolds Adolescent Depression Scale (RADS) *Reynolds*	30-item self-report, respondent answers on a 4-point Likert scale how frequently they feel what is described by each question.	Only total score	Respondents may be 13-18-years-of-age. 3 forms are available: Form HS (hand scored), Form I (individual), & Form G (group)	Percentile norms for the standardization sample and sex are included; Percentile Rank Conversion Totals are also provided by grade	Hand-scorable answer sheets are used to facilitate easy scoring, as well as the use of a scoring key for the HS version. Mail-in scoring service is available for Forms I & G.	Internal Consistency: ranged from .91 to .94. Test-retest: .80 for a 6-week period; .63 over a 1-year time period.	Content: 19 of the 30 items yielded correlation coefficients above .50; 4 items have coefficients below .30. Concurrent: a strong relationship between scores on the RADS & the Hamilton Rating Scale were reported (.83) Convergent: the RADS was found to be highly correlated with other self-report measures of depression, such as the BDI, CES-D, & the CDI.	A quick screening tool to evaluate depressive symptoms in adolescents, the RADS may also be used to evaluate treatment outcomes.

Scale/ Developers	Response Format	Scales	Forms/ Respondent	Norms	Scoring	Reliability	Validity	Clinical Utility
Suicide Ideation Questionnaire (Including Junior version) (SIQ & SIQ-JR) *Reynolds*	SIQ: 30 self-report questions on a 7-point scale, assessing frequency with which the cognition occurs. SIQ-JR: 15 self-report items.	Assesses individual's level of current suicidal ideation.	2 forms: SIQ assesses thought about suicide in adolescents' grades 10-12; SIQ-JR can be used for grades 7-9. Both forms come in hand scoring format (HS), & an optical recognition answer sheet (OCR), which can be machine-scored once sent in to a scoring service provided by the publisher.	Cutoff scores are provided for both age groups (grades 7 through 9 & 10 through 12).	Hand- & machine-scoring yields a cutoff score indicating a clinically important level of suicidal ideation. The HS form may be scored by placing the scoring key over the items & summing the scores for each item. The scoring key indicates critical items. Form G sheet may be mailed in for computer scoring.	Internal Consistency: .94 for the SIQ-JR & .97 for the SIQ. Test-Retest: .72 over a 1-month interval.	Content: Reynolds states that "suicidal ideation is not a disorder for which the domain of symptoms has been formally delineated..." stating that evidence of content validity may be seen in item congruence with specified suicidal cognitions, as well as item-total scale correlations. Construct: suicidal ideation correlated to varying degrees to different measures of depression, hopelessness, self-esteem, anxiety, & learned helplessness. Some of the measures that the SIQ was found to be correlated with are the CDI, BDI, RADS, & BHS	Provides a quick administration time, and administration may be in a group or individually. The SIQ & SIQ-JR may be used as a supplement to other measures, such as the RADS.
Anxiety								
Revised Children's Manifest Anxiety Scale (RCMAS) *Reynolds & Richmond*	37-items, rated by respondent as either "Yes" or "No".	4 Subscales: (1) Physiological Anxiety, (2) Worry/Over-sensitivity, (3) Social Concerns/ Concentration, & (4) Lie	Instrument instructions are printed on the front of the sheet, with questions printed on the back. The RCMAS was designed for use with respondents ages 6 to 19 years, with approximately a 3rd grade reading level.	Norms are given for the normative sample at 1-year intervals, as well as for ethnic & gender combinations.	5 scores make up the RCMAS, the 4 subscales & the Total Anxiety score. Raw scores for each subscale are calculated by adding the number of items circled "Yes" for that subscale. Tables in the appendix convert raw scores to scales scores & percentiles.	Internal Consistency: Total Anxiety score: .79 to .85. Test-Retest: Total Anxiety score: .68 for a 9-month interval. Much of the test-retest reliability data has been conducted using children younger than the 7th grade.	Construct: a large correlation was found between the RCMAS & the STAIC (r=.85), providing support for the construct validity of the RCMAS as a measure of chronic manifest anxiety (Reynolds & Richmond, 1985).	The RCMAS is a useful tool for assessing both the degree & nature of anxiety in adolescents. Results yielded from use of the RCMAS may help guide therapeutic interventions.

Scale/ Developers	Response Format	Scales	Forms/ Respondent	Norms	Scoring	Reliability	Validity	Clinical Utility
State-Trait Anxiety Inventory (STAI) *Spielberger*	40 items on a 3-point scale (20 State items & 20 Trait items). The STAI may be self-administered in either a group or individual format.	2 scales: State & Trait Anxiety (S-anxiety & T-anxiety)	13 years and above. There is also the State-Trait Anxiety Inventory for Children (STAIC), which may be used in elementary school-aged children.	Normative data for the STAI is provided in the manual for a few different groups, including working adults, students, & military recruits.	Each item is assigned a weighted score of 1 to 4, with some items being reversed scored. Template keys are available to facilitate hand scoring.	Test-Retest: correlations varied for T-anxiety & S-anxiety, with higher correlations found for T-anxiety. This finding was to be expected, as a valid measure of state anxiety should reflect the factors present at the time of testing.	Construct: Previous research has provided evidence that the STAI discriminates between normal subjects and psychiatric patients. Similarly, the STAI yielded much higher scores for military recruits about to begin a stressful training than same age students tested under nonstressful situations. Concurrent: Relatively high correlations were found between the STAI and other measures of trait anxiety, such as the Manifest Anxiety Scale & the Affect Adjective Checklist.	The STAI assesses both state & trait anxiety with a quick & easy one page test form. Furthermore, the STAI is an instrument that may be used with a variety of various clients, as it has been adapted in over thirty languages. Over 2,000 studies and reviews have been compiled in a bibliography that is available from Consulting Psychologists Press. The STAIC is also available to use with children.
39-items, can be completed quickly. The MASC utilizes a 4-point Likert-scale format ranging from "never true about me" to "often true about me", with all items phrased in a positive direction.		4 scales: physical symptoms, social anxiety, harm avoidance, & separation/ panic. 3 indices: Anxiety Disorders Index, Total Anxiety Index, & Inconsistency Index	Respondent ages 8-19 completes a MHS QuikScore™ form. 4th-grade reading level is needed	The MASC Profile form displays the respondent's scores and allows for a comparison with the appropriate normative group. Normative data is based on large sample (N=2,698), with separate norms provided for males and females. Data are provided in 4-year increments for ages 8 – 19.	Results are scored and then transferred to a Profile Form, which automatically converts raw scores to T-scores. The MASC was developed such that higher scores indicate increasing emotional problems for the respondent. The MASC may also be scored using the MASC Computer Program.	Internal reliability coefficients are provided by age, gender, and are provided for each scale. Overall, they range from approximately .602 to .869. Test-retest reliability coefficients are reported to be excellent, ranging from approximately the .70's to the .90's.	Confirmatory factor analysis was conducted, finding an excellent fit for the four-factor structure of the MASC. Low to moderate intercorrelations of the four MASC scales lends support to the theory that the MASC assesses different dimensions of anxiety in adolescents. Results from a discriminate-function analysis suggested that the MASC can be used to identify those	Simple & quick to administer & score, the MASC is useful in situations valuing a quick assessment of an adolescent's anxiety symptoms. The manual states that the MASC may be administered and scored within approximately 25 minutes. There is also available the MASC-10, which is useful in situations requiring repeated

Scale/ Developers	Response Format	Scales	Forms/ Respondent	Norms	Scoring	Reliability	Validity	Clinical Utility
							adolescents that may need a more thorough assessment. Responses from individuals completing the MASC were also compared with their responses on the CDI-S and the RCMAS. Moderate to high correlations were found with the MASC and scales of the RCMAS in which there was overlap, while low to moderate correlations were found for scales in which there was little symptom overlap. Similarly, the MASC and the CDI-S were found to be more greatly correlated on the Physical Symptoms Scale.	assessment or a very quick screening.
						The Standard Error of Measurement for the Total MASC is reported to be 5.788 for females aged 12 to 15. Tables in the manual describe the Standard Error of Measurement and the Standard Error of Prediction for both the M<ASC and the MASC-10 for age and gender.		
Self-Concept								
Piers-Harris Self-Concept Scale *Piers*	80-item self-report, may be administered either individually or in a group format. Respondents indicate whether statements apply to them by choosing either "yes" or "no".	6 "cluster scales": Behavior, intellectual & school status, physical appearance & attributes, anxiety, popularity, happiness & satisfaction.	To be used by children/ adolescents ages 8 to 18 years of age. 3 ways of administration: (1) 4-page booklet (2) scannable answer sheet (3) microcomputer diskette for online administration	Normative sample consisted of children from a small town in Pennsylvania. All children were from a public school system. Finally, this data was obtained in the early 1960's. Due to these limitations, norms should be interpreted with caution, as there may be limited generalizability to other populations.	Responses may be either hand or computer scored, yielding 3 summary scores: total raw score, percentile score, & an overall stanine score. If hand-scored, a scoring template is used, with the total raw score reflecting the total number of responses marked in the positive direction (indicating positive self-concept).	Test-Retest: .42 for an 8-month interval, .96 for a 3-4 week interval. Internal Consistency: coefficients ranged from .88 to .93.	Examples of relationship to other self-concept measures: Coopersmith Self-Esteem Inventory, .85. Personal Attribute Inventory for Children (O Factor), .32-.67.	Easy to administer & score, it assesses how children & adolescents feel about themselves. It may be used as a screening instrument, to assist in assessment, help generate hypotheses, in intervention selection, & to monitor changes in self-concept over time.

Scale/ Developers	Response Format	Scales	Forms/ Respondent	Norms	Scoring	Reliability	Validity	Clinical Utility
Offer Self-Image Questionnaire - Revised (OSIQ-R) *Offer, Ostrov, Howard, & Dolan*	129 items; 6-point Likert scale (responses range from "describes me very well" to "does not describe me at all". The OSIQ-R may be administered either individually or in a group setting.	12 subscales: (1) Emotional Tone (2) Impulse Control (3) Mental Health (4) Social Functioning (5) Family Functioning (6) Vocational Attitudes (7) Self-Confidence (8) Self-Reliance (9) Body Image (10) Sexuality (11) Ethical Values (12) Idealism	13-18 years; items are worded at a 5th grade reading level. The OSIQ-R may be administered either by paper-and-pencil, or by microcomputer disk.	Norms for the OSIQ-R are based on a sample of 964 adolescents, made up of individuals from 13 different samples in various geographic regions. These participants varied in ethnicity, parental education, & gender.	The OSIQ-R is scored by computer, & WPS Test Report provides interpretive reports comparing the respondent to other same-age & same-sex respondents from the normative sample. Both raw scores as well as T-scores are provided.	Internal Consistency: Scales with greater numbers of items tended to demonstrate greater reliability. The range for the 12 scales & the Total Self-Image scale was .45 - .90.	There are 3 validity checks included in the OSIQ-R: (1) R-check, which is a check of response bias and completeness (2) I-check, which examines the tendency of a respondent to endorse little-used or infrequent responses For example, there are a few critical items that if endorsed, may give reason to question the validity of the results. (3) C-check, which examines consistency of responses. Moderate inter-correlations were found between the 12 scales, with most ranging from .3 to .7. Similarly, moderate stability correlations (ranging from .46 to .63) were found in a study in which adolescents were administered the OSIQ-R after a 2-year time period. Studies have also demonstrated correlations between the OSIQ & various other measures, such as the Beck Depression Inventory & the Piers-Harris Self-Concept Scale.	The OSIQ-R is a convenient measure of an adolescents' self-image in a variety of areas, including areas in which an adolescent may be hesitant to verbally discuss during the initial assessment period.

Scale/ Developers	Response Format	Scales	Forms/ Respondent	Norms	Scoring	Reliability	Validity	Clinical Utility
Self-Perception Profile for Adolescents (SPPA) *Harter*	The respondent is first asked to read two statements & decide which kind of person she/he is most like. Then, the respondent decides if that description is "really true for me" or "sort of true for me".	9 subscales: Scholastic Competence, Social Acceptance, Athletic Competence, Physical Appearance, Job Competence, Romantic Appeal, Behavioral Conduct, Close Friendship, & Global Self-Worth.	No particular age range was stated, giving the examiner the freedom to decide if the scales in the instrument will be appropriate for a particular respondent. There is also a parallel Teacher Rating Scale, which may be completed by either teachers or other adult raters such as parents or counselors.	Data from samples including males & females from the 8th through the 11th grades were discussed in the manual. It is reported that these subjects were all from Colorado, with approximately 90% of respondents being Caucasian. Socioeconomic status of these respondents ranged from lower middle class to upper middle class. The author noted that another large sample was also being collected.	Items are scored using the numbers 1 through 4, with higher numbers representing more adequate self-judgments. The Appendix of the manual includes a scoring key as well as a data-coding sheet. Scores can be transferred to the data coding sheet, where items from each subscale are grouped together, yielding the mean of each subscale. Nine subscale means then make up a respondent's profile.	Internal consistency reliabilities were reported in the manual, & typically ranged from approximately mid-.70's through the mid-.90's across different samples and subscales. Subscale means & standard deviations are also reported in the manual, noting subscale differences across gender & samples. For example, girls were found to consistently rate their athletic competence lower than do boys, while girls tend to rate themselves as more adequate than do boys on the subscale of close friendships.	The eight domains were factor-analyzed, and the manual states that "given the clarity and replicability of this factor pattern, across samples representing grades 8 through 11, we can conclude that these domains define distinct factors that provide a differentiated and meaningful profile of self-perceptions for adolescents" (pg. 15). Intercorrelations among the 8 subscales is also included in the manual, as are correlations among specific subscales and Self-worth.	The SPPA is an extension of the Self-Perception Profile for Children, including additional scales that are appropriate to various aspects of an adolescent's life. As the content in the SPPA is largely parallel to that of the Self-Perception Profile for Children, subscale scores may be compared across version.
Coopersmith Self-Esteem Inventories (SEI) *Coopersmith*	The SEI may be administered either individually of in a group setting, however, the Adult Form is typically administered individually.	School Form: 4 subscales (1) General Self (2) Social Self-Peers (3) Home-Parents (4) School-Academic	3 forms: (1) School Form, 58-items, to be used with respondents ages 8-15. (2) School Short Form, consisting of items 1-25 of the School Form; it does not include the Lie Scale items & does not yield subscale scores. & (3) Adult Form, to be used with respondents ages 16	Coopersmith (1989) encourages the development of local norms whenever possible. Coopersmith (1989) encourages users to develop local norms when using the SEI. Results using the School Form & and School Short Form were not found to be significantly different,	The SEI may be scored with the scoring keys that correspond to the form that was given. The SEI may also be scored without the keys by scoring the negative items correct if they have been answered "unlike me" & scoring the positive items correct if they have been answered	Internal consistency: coefficients obtained from various studies ranged from .80 to .92. Test-retest: A 3-year interval yielded results ranging from .42 to .70. A 1-year interval reported a coefficient of .64. Correlation between	Construct: several studies have been reported as supporting the construct validity of the subscales in the SEI.	In addition to it's many uses in the school setting, in self-esteem programs, & in research, the SEI may be useful in conducting Individual assessment, especially in assessing particular areas to target self-esteem building.

Scale/ Developers	Response Format	Scales	Forms/ Respondent	Norms	Scoring	Reliability	Validity	Clinical Utility
			and older. It is 25 items that were adapted from the School Short Form. Correlations of scores from the School Short Form & the Adult Form exceeded .80 for 3 samples of high school & college students.	thus, normative samples presented in the manual are for the School Form. School Form: normative samples consisted of children of various socioeconomic and ethnic backgrounds from different areas of the United States. Individuals from both urban & rural areas were included. Adult Form: the SEI was administered to 226 college students with a mean age of 21.5 years. Reliabilities ranged from .78 to .85.	"like me". The School Form includes the Lie Scale, which consists of 8 items that are scored separately, giving 1 point for each item answered "like me". Four subscales of the School Form can be scored individually if desired. Coopersmith (1989) states that a Total Self Score is yielded by summing the number of self-esteem items answered correctly. Higher scores on the SEI are associated with higher self-esteem. A service to score & report SEI results by computer is also available.	the School Form & the School Short Form is .86.		
Self Description Questionnaire II (SDQ-II) *Marsh*	102-items; respondents answer simple statements such as "I worry a lot" with one of six Likert-scale responses ranging from False to True. The SDQ-II may be administered individually or in a group format.	The SDQ-II is composed of 11 scales, which are summed to yield a Total Self-Concept Score. The 11 scales are: Physical Abilities, Physical Appearance, Opposite-Sex Relations, Same-Sex Relations, Parent Relations, Honesty-Trust-worthiness, Emotional Stability, Math, Verbal, General School, & General	The SDQ-II was developed to be used by adolescents in grades 7 through 12, although it may also be used with older adolescents & young adults. However, the SDQ-III is typically used with college-aged students.	Normative data on a large sample of Australian students is presented in the manual for each of the scales, as well as for the Total Self-Concept score. This sample included students from diverse backgrounds, and included individuals from both public & private schools, as well as students from single-sex & coeducational	The SDQ-II may be scored using the Score Calculation and Summary page that is part of the Scoring and Profile Booklet, which facilitates the calculation of the 11 scales raw scores as well as a raw score for the Total Self-Concept. Raw scores for both the scales and for the Total Self-Concept score may then be converted into percentile-rank scores	Internal Consistency: Total Self-Concept score: .94 Coefficient alphas for the 11 scales ranged from .83-.91. Test-Retest: Pre- and post-intervention data yielded short-term stability coefficients ranging from .72-.79 for the 11 scales.	Construct: The SDQ-II was developed from previous research utilizing the SDQ-I as well as the SDQ-III & has items from both of these measures; support for the validity of the SDQ-II is inferred from research conducted using these two related measures. Furthermore, validity research described in detail in the SDQ-II manual demonstrate support that responses to the SDQ-II	Designed to measure self-concept in adolescents, the SDQ-II is a useful measure that may be administered and scored easily. The SDQ-II yields important information of a variety of scales, as well as an overall Total Self-Concept score that may be helpful in initial assessment as well

Scale/ Developers	Response Format	Scales	Forms/ Respondent	Norms	Scoring	Reliability	Validity	Clinical Utility
		Self.		schools. Both percentiles & nonnormalized T-scores, are presented in the manual, as well as separate norms tables for gender.	& nonnormalized T-scores that have a mean of 50 & a standard deviation of 10. Explicit directions are provided in the SDQ-II manual for users. It is important that the respondent attempt to answer each item, as questionnaires with 6 or more missing responses may not be scored.		are related to other self-concept measures as well as other variables, such as age, gender, & academic achievement.	as treatment planning. Due to the existence of related measures (SDQ-I & SDQ-III), changes over extended time intervals may also be tracked if so desired
Parent-Child Relationship								
Issues Checklist *Robin & Foster*	44 self-report items, which reflect issues that adolescents & parents may argue about.	Three scores yielded: (1) Quantity of issues, (2) mean anger-intensity level of endorsed issues, & (3) weighted average of the frequency & & anger-intensity of endorsed issues.	1 form, which may be used by both parents & adolescents.	Although preliminary norms are available (Robin & Foster, 1984), Barkley, Edwards, & Robin (1999) note that the use of a broader normative sample would be helpful.	Three scores are yielded for each respondent: the quantity of issues indicated, the estimated intensity of anger associated with each issue, and the weighted average of the frequency & the anger-intensity for each issue.	Test-retest: Adolescent: quantity of issues: .49-.87 anger-intensity score: .37-.49 weighted frequency by anger-intensity score: .15-.24 Parent: Quantity of issues: .65 for mothers & .55 for fathers Anger-intensity scores: .81 for mothers, .66 for fathers Weighted frequency by anger-intensity scores: .90 for mothers & .40 for fathers The agreement reliability between	Discriminant: Barkley, Edwards, & Robin (1999) note that "distressed family members reported significantly more frequent, angrier disputes than nondistressed family members". Treatment studies utilizing male & female adolescents ages 10-18 revealed: Maternal anger-intensity scores: 48% of the variance in distressed/nondistressed status Paternal quantity of issues scores: 36% of the variance. Adolescent effects: 3-19% of the variance	The Issues Checklist may be helpful when identifying issues that tend to be sources of conflict in a particular family, as well as assessing the degree of anger associated with those conflicts. The Issues Checklist assesses issues that may have occurred within the past two weeks, and may be useful in identifying any discrepancies noted by family members.

Scale/ Developers	Response Format	Scales	Forms/ Respondent	Norms	Scoring	Reliability	Validity	Clinical Utility
						mothers & adolescents was also assesses, and was found to range from 38-86%. When these results were examined using correlations, the range was .10-.64. These results raise the issue of how different members within the family are perceiving and/or remembering specific events.		
Family Environment Scale (FES) *Moos & Moos Moos & Moos*	90 items, true-false format.	Each form has 10 subscales: cohesion, expressiveness, conflict, independence, achievement orientation, intellectual-cultural orientation, active-recreational orientation, moral-religious emphasis, organization, & control.	3 forms; the Real Form (Form R), Ideal Forms (Form I) & the Expectations Form (Form E). Items are printed in reusable booklets with separate answer sheets which respondents mark their answers on. Instructions are read aloud to respondents.	For Form R, data from both normal & distressed families was obtained, with families from various sources & differing family compositions & ages. Normative sample for Form I also sampled individuals from both normal & distressed families. No separate norms were obtained for Form E; it is recommended that one compare scores to Form R for normal families.	A template is available to facilitate hand scoring. A table converts an individual's subscale raw score or a family's mean raw score to a standard score. Profiles may be plotted graphically. A self-scorable answer sheet is also available. Results may also be sent to the publisher to obtain a narrative report.	Internal consistency: for the 10n subscales on Form R, ranged from .61 to .78. Test-retest reliabilities on subscales: 2-month, .54 to .91; 1-year, .53 to .84. The moral-religious orientation and organization subscales tended to remain the most consistent over time.	Concurrent: correlated with Social Support Appraisals, Dyadic Adjustment Scale, Locke-Wallace Marital Adjustment Scale, the Parental Bonding Instrument, the FAD, the FACES, & the MMPI Family Scales; also correlated with clinician ratings. Discriminant: little association between FES Cohesion & various measures of cohesion (Family Sculpture Test, Bowerman & Bahr Identification Scale) Construct: FES subscales related to family & social functioning, Moral-Religious Emphasis scale highly related to religious participation, Conflict scale associated with an index of family arguments.	Useful in describing family social environments, as well as comparing perceptions of different family members and comparing actual & preferred family climates. The FES may be helpful in gaining information regarding an individual or the family system, and can be used in formulating cases, facilitating family therapy, or measuring treatment outcome.

Scale/ Developers	Response Format	Scales	Forms/ Respondent	Norms	Scoring	Reliability	Validity	Clinical Utility
Family Adaptability & Cohesion Evaluation Scale-IV (FACES-IV) *Olson, Tiesel, & Gorall*	24-items on a 6-point Likert scale.	4 scales: Disengagement, Enmeshment, Rigidity, & Chaos.	2 versions (couple and family). May be administered in either a group or individual format. No minimum age required.	Items were normed based on results of factor analysis & reliability analysis of scores of a large sample of respondents, with both adults & adolescents included.	Measure is hand scored by adding particular scale items & other addition & subtraction calculations to yield scale scores.	Internal consistency: Disengagement .82, Enmeshment .81, Rigidity .81, & Chaos .93 Test-Retest: .83 to .96.	Discriminant: distressed families scored significantly higher on a total system extremity score (summation of the 4 scale scores) & on all subscales.	Useful in clinical settings to identify characteristics of troubled families & to facilitate family discussion concerning family quality; further research needed on this version.
Conflict Behavior Questionnaire (CBQ) *Prinz, Foster, Kent, & O'Leary*	20-item questionnaire Respondents are asked to decide if each item is "mostly true" of "mostly false", as pertaining to their relationship over the past 2 weeks.	Only total score	Parallel forms for parents & adolescents.		The CBQ is scored by adding all items the respondent endorsed in a negative direction, thus, the higher the score, the more negative the perceptions. Raw scores may then be converted into T-scores, which are available in tables (Barkley, 1991). Significant family conflict is associated with T-scores over 65.	Internal consistency: .90	The CBQ has been found to be a "valid indicator of conflict and negative interaction, which discriminates well between families with and without conflict and which correlates moderately with observations of parent-teen interactions" (Robin & Foster, 1989)	The CBQ may be useful in assessing weaknesses in problem solving between parents & their adolescent, as well as examining the degree of perceived negative communication in the relationship.
Parent-Adolescent Relationship Questionnaire (PARQ) *Robin, Koepke, & Moye*	True/false items; 250 for parents & 258 for adolescents.	16 scales designed to assess 3 broad dimensions of family functioning: (1) skill deficits/overt conflict (2) faulty belief systems/distorted cognitions (3) family structure problems	Two forms, one for parents and one for adolescents. Parents & adolescents may complete their forms individually. Furthermore, the entire PARQ may be administered, or only specific scales if so desired by the clinician.	When using the microcomputer-scoring program, T-scores based on a normative sample of adolescents are yielded, with T-scores over 60 considered significantly elevated.	The PARQ may be hand-scored if only specific scales are of interest. However, computer scoring is more appropriate when scoring the entire measure. A microcomputer-scoring program is available, which provides T-scores and profiles of family functioning for both parents & adolescents.	Internal consistency: .80 and above for most scales.	Robin, Koepke, & Moye (1990) states that the PARQ has been found to "discriminate well between families with externalizing behavior disorders & no psychiatric problems". Furthermore, the PARQ has been found to have good construct validity (Koepke, 1986; Koepke, Robin, Nayar, & Hillman, 1987; Webb, 1987)	The PARQ is a useful measure when assessing family structure & belief systems, as well as assessing problem-solving communication skills between parents & adolescents.

Depression

Depression in adolescents can be assessed using a variety of different measures. The Child Depression Inventory (CDI; Kovacs, 1992) is a measure in which the respondent selects one of three sentences that best describes their experience in the past two weeks. Similarly, the Beck Depression Inventory-II (BDI-II; Beck, Steer, & Brown, 1996) is another inventory in which the respondent chooses which of four statements best describes the severity of a certain symptom of depression. The BDI-II has recently made changes to reflect current DSM-IV guidelines. The Reynolds Adolescent Depression Scale (RADS; Reynolds, 1987), a third measure of depression in adolescence, has an extensive normative sample and is frequently used in group administration to screen for depressive symptoms. All measures serve as useful tools to assess depressive symptoms and facilitate treatment planning. The Beck Hopelessness Scale (BHS; Beck & Steer, 1988) useful primarily as a screening tool to measure the degree of negative attitudes about the future, a common correlate of depressive symptomatology and suicidal ideation. Hopelessness, as a construct, has been described as an "indirect" measure of suicidal risk in individuals who have made previous suicide attempts (Beck & Steer, 1988). The Suicide Ideation Questionnaire (SIQ; Reynolds, 1987) assesses an individual's current level of suicidal ideation by asking respondents to indicate how frequently certain cognitions occur. Both the BHS and the SIQ may serve as a useful follow-up instrument to paper-and-pencil measures that screen for depression.

Anxiety

Anxiety is another area of socio-emotional functioning that frequently assessed when working with adolescents. The Revised Children's Manifest Anxiety Scale (RCMAS; Reynolds & Richmond, 1985) asks respondents to answer either "Yes" or "No" to questions representative of three subscales concerning anxiety (Physiological Anxiety, Worry/Oversensitivity, and Social Concerns/Concentration). The Multidimensional Anxiety Scale for Children (MASC; March, 1997) is a more recently developed measure of anxiety in adolescents. The MASC provides a quick assessment of anxiety as it relates to four scales: Physical Symptoms, Harm Avoidance, Social Anxiety, and Separation/Panic. Completion of the MASC also yields a Total Anxiety scale, as well as an Inconsistencies index and an Anxiety Disorders index. The State-Trait Anxiety Inventory for Children (STAIC; Spielberger, 1973), as well as the State-Trait Anxiety Inventory (STAI; Spielberger, 1983), are both commonly used measures of anxiety, examining both state and trait anxiety on two separate scales. No version specifically for use with adolescents has been developed. The STAIC includes normative data through sixth grade; and normative data for the STAI begins at age 13 years.

Self-concept

Adolescence marks a period of development in which individuals often struggle with issues of self-concept. Self-report assessment measures facilitate further understanding of this construct in adolescents presenting in therapy. The Piers-Harris Self-Concept Scale (Piers, 1984) allows respondents to indicate if statements apply to them by responding either "Yes" or "No". Responses yield six scales: Behavior, Intellectual and School Status, Physical Appearance and Attributes, Anxiety, Popularity, Happiness and Satisfaction. The Piers-Harris Self-Concept Scale provides an overview of how individuals perceive themselves and facilitates intervention selection and monitoring changes in self-concept over time.

The Offer Self-Image Questionnaire for Adolescents-Revised (OSIQ-R; Offer, Ostrov, Howard, & Dolan, 1992) asks respondents to answer items on a 6-point Likert scale, with options ranging from "describes me very well" to "does not describe me at all". This 129-item questionnaire is appropriate for use with individuals' ages 13 to 19 years and is designed to measure how adolescents describe themselves. The OSIQ-R yields 12 subscales within five categories, including Psychological Self, Sexual Self, Social Self, Familial Self, and Coping Self, as well as a Total Social Behavior score.

Harter's Self-Perception Profile for Adolescents (SPPA; Harter, 1988) measures perceived social acceptance in adolescents. The SPPA contains eight subscales (Scholastic Competence, Social Acceptance, Athletic Competence, Physical Appearance, Job Competence, Romantic Appeal, Behavioral Conduct, Close Friendship, and Global Self-Worth), with higher scores reflecting a higher degree of an adolescents' perceived social acceptance (Harter, 1990).

The Coopersmith Self-Esteem Inventories (SEI; Coopersmith, 1989) include three forms, the School Form, the School Short Form, and the Adult Form. The School Form is to be used with individuals' ages 8 to 15 years, while the Adult Form may be administered to individuals' ages 16 years and older. Respondents answer whether or not statements are "like me" or "unlike me." Since the School Form yields four subscales that may be scored separately, the SEI is a helpful tool when assessment of particular areas of self-esteem is desired, and is a useful measure of attitudes about the self in social, academic, family, and personal areas of experience.

The Self-Description Questionnaire II (SDQ-II; Marsh, 1990) was developed to measure self-concept of adolescents in grades 7 through 12. This 102-item questionnaire is easily administered and scored, yielding important information on 11 scales, including Parent Relations and Emotional Stability. These eleven scales may be summed to provide a Total Self-Concept score.

Parent-adolescent Relationship

Given that parent-adolescent interactions are often part of a referral problem, several measures can aid in assessing the parent-adolescent relationship. For example, the Issues Checklist (Robin & Foster, 1989) is composed of 44 self-report items that reflect issues about which parents and adolescents may argue. The Issues Checklist has been nicely adapted by Barkley (1991) and may be used by both parents and adolescents, yielding three scores for each respondent: (a) the quantity of issues indicated, (b) the estimated intensity of anger associated with each issue, and (c) the weighted average of the frequency and the anger-intensity for each issue (Robin, 1998).

The Parent-Adolescent Relationship Questionnaire (PARQ; Robin, Koepke, & Moye, 1990) consists of 250 true/false items for parents and 258 true/false items for adolescents. These items form 16 scales that are designed to assess three broad dimensions of family functioning: skill deficits/overt conflict, faulty belief systems/distorted cognitions, and family structure problems (Foster & Robin, 1997). Also available for use with the PARQ is the Parent-Adolescent Interaction Coding System (PAIC; Foster & Robin, 1989), which contains 14 problematic speaker behaviors and six problematic listener behaviors, with alternate appropriate behaviors for each. The PAIS can be used as both an observational assessment and a teaching tool. The PAIC has been adapted and updated nicely by Foster and Robin (1998).

The Conflict Behavior Questionnaire (CBQ; Prinz, Foster, Kent, O'Leary, 1979) is a 20-item questionnaire in which respondents judge if items are "mostly true" or "mostly false" as pertaining to their relationship over the past two weeks. There are parallel forms for both parents and adolescents. The CBQ may be helpful in assessing perceived negative communication in a relationship, as well as weak areas in family problem solving (Robin, 1998).

The Family Environment Scale (FES; Moos & Moos, 1994) asks the respondent true/false questions concerning the social environment of the family. Ten subscales are formed, providing information that allows comparison of different perceptions within the family, case formulation, and facilitation of family therapy (Moos & Moos, 1994).

The Family Adaptability and Cohesion Evaluation Scale-IV (FACES-IV; Tiesel & Olson, 1997) attempts to identify characteristics of troubled families and to engage families in discussions concerning family quality. Respondents select one of six responses that best describe their family. Answers to these questions yield four scales (Disengagement, Enmeshment, Rigidity, and Chaos) that add valuable information when engaging in family therapy.

Integrative Assessment Systems

Integrative assessment systems can offer a useful way to gather rich information concerning an adolescent's functioning in a variety of settings and from various reporters. These assessment systems allow for information to be gathered and compared from parents and teachers. Due to the differing nature of the home and school environments, it is often helpful to have measures of an adolescent's functioning from multiple informants who interacts with them in multiple settings. Two such integrative assessment systems will be described here and in Table 1.

The frequently used Achenbach System of Empirically Based Assessment (ASEBA), when used with adolescents, includes the Achenbach Teacher Report Form (TRF) and, parent report, Child Behavior Checklist (CBCL; Achenbach & Rescorla, 2001). These measures typically are used in conjunction with the YSR, which was discussed previously. The CBCL asks parents questions concerning their adolescent's competencies, which yield three competence/adaptive functioning scale scores. Parents also complete a variety of Likert-scale questions that best describe their adolescents' behaviors over the past six months. These questions form nine syndrome scales, which in turn form three main composite scores (Internalizing, Externalizing, and Other Problems) and a Total Problems score. The CBCL is useful in guiding interviewing and assessment, as well as facilitating diagnostic formulations, as it is often an easy and relatively quick way to identify competencies and problem areas in adolescents (Bérubé & Achenbach, 2001). The TRF is very similar to the CBCL, but slight alterations have been made to facilitate use with teachers in an academic setting. The TRF asks teachers to rate behaviors over the past two months. Like the CBCL, adaptive functioning is measured, but in the TRF academic functioning is included. Responses on the TRF yield eight syndrome scales and same composite scores as does the CBCL. In addition, the system includes a standardized Semistructured Interview for Children and Adolescents (SICA; McConaughy & Achenbach, 2001).

A second frequently used assessment system is the Behavior Assessment System for Children (BASC), which includes parent and teacher forms, in addition to the BASC-SRP previously discussed. The BASC-Parent Rating Scale (BASC-PRS) and the BASC-Teacher Rating Scale (BASC-TRS; Reynolds & Kamphaus, 1998) are both behavior inventories useful in initial assessment and treatment planning and monitoring. The BASC-PRS consists of 126 items, while the BASC-TRS consists of 138 items. Responses, using a Likert-scale, on the BASC-PRS yield 14 scale scores and four composite scores (Externalizing Problems, Internalizing Problems, Behavioral Symptoms Index, and the Adaptive Skills Composite). Responses on the BASC-TRS yield the same scale and composite scores, with the addition on a fifth composite score, the School Problems Composite. Both measures have English and Spanish translations. An audiotape is available for both the BASC-TRS and the BASC-PRS to facilitate administration for respondents who understand English better than they read it (Reynolds & Kamphaus, 1998; Reynolds & Kamphaus, 2002). This assessment system also includes the Student Observation System (SOS), the Structured Developmental History (SDH) form, and a companion measure, the BASC Monitor for ADHD Rating Scales, a tool for outcome measurement of ADHD treatments (Kamphaus & Reynolds, 1998)

CASE STUDY

Tess (age 39) and Rinaldo (age 40) were concerned about their only child, Tomás, a 15-year-old, whose grades began suffering during his 9th grade school year. Changes in their son's typically open communication with them and resistance to their efforts to monitor and supervise his activities were particularly troubling to this couple, who had been married for 18 years. Rinaldo's family was Mexican-American and Tess' family of origin was European-American. English was the primary language and Spanish was the secondary language spoken in the home. Both sets of extended family lived in the same community as the family, a major city in the Southwestern United States. The couple were married just prior to their senior year at the university were they met each other. Tess' career was in marketing, and Rinaldo owned his own landscape architecture business. The family was active in a nondemoninational Protestant church, in youth sports leagues (baseball and soccer), and in community service organizations. Tomás had a history of being a strong student and a gifted athlete. Until recently he had enjoyed a relatively small, but supportive peer group and positive relationships with teachers and coaches. He had become somewhat aloof from and moderately disrespectful to his parents. His interests in sports and in applying himself at school waned significantly after about mid-way through the Fall semester. The couple reported disagreement between themselves about how best to respond to changes they saw in Tomás. They were self-referred for family therapy.

The assessment process was guided by the comprehensive conceptual model described in 3 of this book (Heffer, Lane, & Snyder, 2002; Heffer & Snyder, 1998; Snyder et al., 1995). The entire family met with the evaluator for the first assessment session. The purposes of the session, consent and assent for services, limits to confidentiality, issues of mandated reporting of abuse and intent to injure self or others, and each family member's expectations for the assessment process were elaborated. The evaluator emphasized her role in working with the family to better understand relationships and patterns that served the family well and to generate ideas on how to improve relationships and patterns that were not working well for the family. The evaluator then interviewed Tomás alone while his parents each completed an Achenbach Child Behavior Checklist (CBCL) and both completed together a background and developmental form (Sattler, 2002). An Achenbach Teacher Report Form (TRF) was given to the parents to request completion by Tomás' school counselor after they signed an authorization to exchange information form.

The evaluator interviewed Tomás following guidelines in Sattler (1998). Care was given to establish rapport with Tomás and to portray sincere appreciation for his views on his life at home, school, and the community. Tomás warmed to the interview process within approximately 10 minutes and began offering more than only a few word responses to the evaluator's direct questions. He voiced frustrations about his parents not understanding what it was like for him to always have to do well in school and sports, to adjust to the transition from junior high school to a large high school, and to be "his own person." Tomás expressed pride and satisfaction with his family's mixed cultural heritage, but also voiced confusion about what identity he was supposed to convey (i.e., Hispanic or non-Hispanic). Further, he reported great solace from his friends and experiences at church, but was feeling pulled by peers at school in a different direction. He seemed to think that few or no other of his friends from church, most of whom attended other high schools in the city, felt torn between "two worlds" the way he did. He said he loved his parents, but just wished they would let him "grow up." During interview and on paper-and-pencil measures, Tomás denied experimentation with drugs, sexual behavior, criminal behavior, or suicidal ideation or intent. The evaluator explained to Tomás the Achenbach Youth Self Report Form (YSR), the Reynolds Adolescent Depression Scale (RADS), and the Self Description Questionnaire-II (SDQ-II) and ask him to complete these measures during the parent interview.

The parents, during interview following guidelines in Sattler (1998), revealed that they had benefited from marital therapy early in their marriage and felt they had a "solid" relationship as a couple. Over the past three months, however, they had increasing disagreements about setting limits with Tomás. Rinaldo was in favor of maintaining a similar approach that had worked in the past (i.e., supportive, authoritative, warm parenting), whereas, Tess believed they should substantially increase their monitoring and supervision of Tomás' activities. Although Tomás had showed no evidence of substance use or delinquent behavior, Tess, in particular, was worried that he might make some of these "bad choices" if they did not "nip this bad attitude in the bud." Tess also fought tears as she expressed a sense of personal hurt that her son on longer shared what was happening in his life with her, as she had been accustomed. Rinaldo was intent on continuing to guide his son toward healthy and opportunity creating life decisions, but attributed attitudinal changes in Tomás to a "typical teenaged boy" aloofness and a shift in priority to his peer group. Both parents reported displeasure with Tomás' grades falling from As and Bs to Cs and Ds this semester and from his choice in school friends, who seemed not to value succeeding academically. They also were confused by Tomás' languishing interest in community soccer and baseball teams. Both parents reported that Tomás did not seem to be happy lately.

The family was reunited to sum up the first session and to plan for a second assessment session. Each family member was given a copy of the Issues Checklist and asked to complete it independently before the next session. Before ending the session, the evaluator scanned Tomás' responses on the YSR, RADS, and SDQ-II to screen for serious issues (e.g., reports of intent to self-injure) that might need to be discussed. Finding none, the family was dismissed.

A brief telephone interview with Tomás' school counselor indicated that group administered aptitude and achievement testing predicted that Tomás was capable of A and high B level work across all academic areas. The school counselor (who had know Tomás in the 8th grade) also noted that he thought Tomás was "trying on a new identity" by realigning with less academically oriented peers and that Tomás seemed somewhat despondent compared to last year and even to the first few weeks of the current school year. The TRF completed by the school counselor showed elevations for Tomás on the Withdrawn/Depressed and Anxious/Depressed scales. Tomás' YSR indicated significant elevations on the Withdrawn/Depressed, Anxious/Depressed, Somatic Complaints, and Social Problems scales. Both parent's CBCL reports demonstrated significant elevations for Tomás on the Withdrawn/Depressed, Social Problems, and Rule-Breaking Behavior scales, with Tess' report being relatively higher (more problems reported) than Rinaldo's report. On the RADS, Tomás' total score was just at the cut-off for significant depressive symptomatology for 9th grade boys in the normative sample. Based on scores on the SDQ-II, Tomás reported significant dissatisfaction with his perceptions of himself as reflected by elevations on the Parent-Relationships, Same-Sex Relationships, Honesty-Trustworthiness, and General School.

At the second assessment session, Tomás completed the Multidimensional Anxiety Scale for Children (MASC), while the evaluator followed up with the parents about some of the information they provided on the background and developmental form. A quick scoring of the MASC revealed only moderately elevated scores for Tomás on the Physical Symptoms and Social Anxiety scales. The evaluator met with the entire family and reviewed their independent responses to the Issues Checklist. This provided ample opportunity to assess communication style, interaction patterns, family problem solving, and conflict resolution among family members. Frequent sources of conflict in the family over the past two weeks included Tomás' household chores, friend selections, grades, going places without parents, talking back, and being bothered by parents when he wanted to be left alone.

During the last 20 minutes of the session, the evaluator formulated her clinical impressions with the family. She pointed out that not only was Tomás experiencing quite unsettling developmental changes, but also that the family itself was being transformed into a family with a teenager, who would likely leave home for college or career in four years. She accentuated the history of positive communication that the family had enjoyed until recently and their common feelings of love and respect for each other. The evaluator reviewed the information gathered from multiple sources (adolescent, parents, and school counselor) and multiple methods (interview, paper-and-pencil measures—global and problem-specific—and in session observations of family interactions). With the evaluator's assistance, Tomás was able to express directly to his parents that he was apprehensive and despondent about who he wanted to "become." He did not want to continue with soccer and baseball community teams and wanted to focus only on baseball, if any organized sports, for now. He said that "it hit him" after the first few weeks of school that he was going to have to make decisions about college and career now that he was in high school. The parents echoed their desire to support and assist him during this confusing time, but felt helpless to do so when Tomás' kept them "at arms' length." The evaluator described to the family that Tomás was, in fact, reporting substantial depressive and somewhat anxious symptoms presumably as a function of the stress of starting high school and the conflicts in the family that ensued. The family agreed to meet for six sessions of behavioral-family systems therapy before re-evaluating progress and deciding how best to proceed.

CONCLUSIONS

Adolescents in family therapy can provide the evaluator/therapist with both some of the greatest challenges and the most exhilarating successes. Equipped with a developmental-family systems approach, the evaluator can tailor an assessment of adolescents to be thorough, yet distinct to the specific referral questions. The ebb and flow of the "adolescent tide" can be navigated by a family through the competent piloting of an evaluator familiar with adolescent and family developmental issues and instruments commonly used to assess teenagers.

REFERENCES

Achenbach, T. M., & Rescorla, L. A. (2001). *Manual for ASEBA School-Age Forms & Profiles*. Burlington, VT: University of Vermont, Research Center for Children, Youth, & Families.

American Educational Research Association (1999*). Standards for educational and psychological testing*. Washington, D.C.: American Educational Research Association, American Psychological Association, and National Council on Measurement in Education.

Archer, R.P. (1997). *MMPI-A: Assessing adolescent psychopathology* (2nd ed.). Mahwah, NJ: Lawrence Erlbaum Associates, Publishers.

Arnett, J.J. (1999). Adolescent storm and stress, reconsidered. *American Psychologist, 54,* 317-326.

Bérubé, R. L., & Achenbach, T. M. (2001). *Bibliography of published studies using ASEBA instruments: 2001 edition*. Burlington, VT: University of Vermont, Research Center for Children, Youth, & Families.

Barkley, R. A. (1991). *Attention-deficit hyperactivity disorder: A clinical workbook*. New York: Guilford Press.

Barkley, R. A., Edwards, G.H. & RobinA.L. (1999). *Defiant teens: A Clinician's manual for assessment and family intervention*. New York: Guilford Press.

Beck, A. T. & Steer, R. A., (1988). *Beck Hopelessness Scale manual*. San Antonio, TX: Psychological Corporation.

Beck, A. T., Steer, R. A., & Brown, G. K. (1996). *Beck Depression Inventory, Second Edition, manual*. San Antonio, TX: Psychological Corporation.

Berk, L.E. (2002). *Infants, children, and adolescents* (4th ed.). Boston: Allyn and Bacon.

Brown, S.A., Aarons, G.A., & Abrantes, A.M. (2001). Adolescent alcohol and drug use. In C.E. Walker & M.C. Roberts (Eds.), *Handbook of clinical child psychology* (3rd ed., pp. 257-775). New York: John Wiley and Sons.

Butcher, J. N., Williams, C., Graham, J. R., Tellegren, A. M., Ben-Porath, Y. S., & Kraemmer, B. (1992). *MMPI-A: Manual for Administration, Scoring, and Interpretation.* Minneapolis: University of Minnesota Press.

Canino, I.A., & Spurlockm J. (2000). *Culturally diverse children and adolescents: Assessment, diagnosis, and treatment* (2nd ed). New York: Guilford Press.

Coopersmith, S. (1989). *Manual for the Self-Esteem Inventories.* Palo Alto, CA: Consulting Psychologists Press, Inc.

Corcoran, K. & Fischer, J. (2000). *Measures for clinical practice, volume 1: Couples, families, & children* (3rd ed.). New York, NY: The Free Press.

DeKraai, M.B., Sales, B., & Hall, S.R. (1989). Informed consent, confidentiality, and duty to report laws in the conduct of child therapy. In R.J. Morris & T.R. Kratochwill (Eds.), *Child therapy* (3rd ed., pp. 540-559). Boston : Allyn and Bacon.

Elkind, D. (1978). Understanding the young adolescent. *Adolesence, 13,* 127-134.

Elkind, D. (1984). *All grown up and no place to go: Teenagers in crisis.* Reading, MA: Addison-Wesley.

Erickson, E.H. (1968). *Identity: Youth and crisis.* New York: W.W. Norton.

Farrell, M.P., & Barnes, G.M. (2000). Family stress and adolescent substance abuse. In P.C. McKenry & S.J. Price (Eds.), *Families and change: Coping with stressful events and transitions.* (pp. 208-228). Thousands Oaks, CA: Sage Publications.

Foster, S.L., & Robin, A.L. (1997). Family conflict and communication in adolescence. In E.J. Mash & L.G. Terdal (Eds.), *Assessment of childhood disorders* (3rd ed., pp. 627-682). New York: Guilford Press.

Foster, S.L., & Robin, A.L. (1998). Parent-adolescent conflict and relationship. In E.J. Mash & R.A. Barkley (Eds.), *Treatment of childhood disorders* (2nd ed., pp. 601-646). New York: Guilford Press.

Freud, A. (1958). Adolescence. *Psychoanalytic Study of the Child, 13,* 255-278.

Freud, A. (1972). Adolescence. In J.F. Rosenblith, W. Allinsmith, & J.P. Williams (Eds.), *The causes of behvavior* (3rd ed.). Boston: Allyn and Bacon.

Gopaul-McNicol, S., & Thomas-Presswood, T. (1998). *Working with linguistically and culturally different children: Innovative clinical and educational approaches.* Boston: Allyn and Bacon.

Gerson, R. (1995). The family life cycle: Phases, stages and crises. In R. H. Mikesell, D. D. Lusterman, & S. H. McDaniel (Eds.), *Integrating family therapy: Handbook of family psychology and systems theory* (pp. 91-111). Washington, DC: American Psychological Association.

Hammen, C., Rudolph, K., Weisz, J., Rao, U., & Burge, D. (1999). The context of depression in clinic referred youth: Neglected areas in treatment. *Journal of the American Academy of Child and Adolescent Psychiatry, 38(1),* 64-71.

Harter, S. (1988). *Manual for the Self-Perception Profile for Adolescents.* Denver, CO: Author

Harter, S. (1990). Issues in the assessment of the self-concept of children and adolescents. In A.M. LaGreca (Ed.), *Through the eyes of the child: Obtaining self-reports from children and adolescents* (pp. 292-325). Boston: Allyn and Bacon.

Heffer, R.W., Lane, M., & Snyder, D.K. (2002). Therapeutic family assessment: A systems approach. In K. Jordan (Ed.), *Handbook of Couple and Family Assessment* (pp. xxx-xxx). New York: Prentice-Hall.

Heffer, R. W., & Snyder, D. K. (1998). Comprehensive assessment of family functioning. In L. L'Abate (Ed.), *Handbook of family psychopathology* (pp. 207-233). New York, NY: Guilford Press.

Hill, R., & Mattessich, P. (1979). Family development theory and life-span development. In P. B. Baltes & O. G. Brim (Eds.), *Life-span development and behavior* (Vol. 2) (pp. 161-204). New York: Plenum Press.

Holmbeck, G.N., Colder, C., Shapera, W., Westhoven, V., Kenealy, L., & Updegrove, A. (2000). Working with adolescents: Guides from developmental psychology. In P.C. Kendall (Ed.), *Child and adolescent therapy: Cognitive-behavioral procedures* (2nd ed., pp. 334-385). New York: Guilford Press.

House, A.E. (2002). *The first session with children and adolescents: Conducting a comprehensive mental health evaluation.* New York: Guilford Press.

Inhelder, B., & Piaget, J. (1958). *The growth of logical thinking.* New York: Basic Books.

Johnson, M.J., & Shaw, W.J. (2001). Delinquency and criminal behavior. In C.E. Walker & M.C. Roberts (Eds.), *Handbook of clinical child psychology* (3rd ed., pp. 776-803). New York: John Wiley and Sons.

Johnson-Powell, G., Yamamoto, J., Wyatt, G.E., and Arroyo, W. (1997). *Transcultural child development: Psychological assessment and treatment.* New York: John Wiley & Sons.

Kamphaus, R.W., & Reynolds, C.R. (1998). *BASC Monitor for ADHD: Manual and software guide.* Circle Pines, MN: American Guidance Service.

Koocher, G.P., & Keith-Spiegel, P.C. (1998). *Ethics in psychology: Professional standards and cases* (2nd ed.). New York: Oxford University Press.

Koocher, G.P., & Keith-Spiegel, P.C. (1990). *Children, ethics, and the law: Professional issues and cases.* Lincoln, NB: University of Nebraska Press.

Kovacs, M. (1992). *Children's Depression Inventory manual.* New York: Multi-Health Systems.

Lachar, D. & Gruber, C. P. (1995a). *Personality Inventory for Youth (PIY) manual: Technical guide.* Los Angeles: Western Psychological Services.

Lachar, D. & Gruber, C. P. (1995b). *Personality Inventory for Youth (PIY) manual: Administration and interpretation guide.* Los Angeles: Western Psychological Services.

March, J.S. (1997). *Multidimensional Anxiety Scale for Children.* Ontario: Multi-Health Systems.

Marsh, H.W. (1990). *Self-Description Questionnaire-II manual.* Sydney: University of Western Sydney at Macarthur.

Mash, E.J., & Terdal, L.G. (1997). Assessment of child and family disturbance: A behavioral-systems approach. In E.J. Nash & L.G. Terdal (Eds.), *Assessment of childhood disorders* (3rd ed., pp. 3-68). New York: Guilford.

McConaughy, S.H., & Achenbach, T.M. (2001). *Manual for the Semistructured Clinical Interview for Children and Adolescents* (2nd ed.). Burlington, VT: University of Vermont, Center for Children, Youth, & Families.

Micucci, J.A. (1998). *The adolescent in family therapy.* New York: Guilford.

Melton, G.B., Ehrenreich, N.S., & Lyons, P.M. (2001). Ethical and legal issues in mental health services to children. In C.E. Walker & M.C. Roberts (Eds.), *Handbook of clinical child psychology* (3rd ed., pp. 1074-1093). New York: John Wiley and Sons.

Millon, T., Green, C.J., & Meagher, R.B. (1982). *Millon Adolescent Personality Inventory manual.* Minneapolis: National Computer Systems.

Morrison, J., & Anders, T.F. (1999). *Interviewing children and adolescents: Skills and strategies for effective DSM-IV diagnosis.* New York: Guilford Press.

Moos, R.H. & Moos, B.S. (1994). *Family Environment Scale manual.* Palo Alto, CA: Consulting Psychologists Press.

Nagy, T. (2000). *Ethics in plain English: An illustrative casebook for psychologists.* New York: American Psychological Association.

Offer, D., Ostrov, E., Howard, K. I., & Dolan, S. (1992). *Manual for the Offer Self-Image Questionnaire, Revised.* Los Angeles: Western Psychological Services.

Piaget, J. (1970). Piaget's theory. In P.H. Mussen (Ed.), *Manual of child psychology* (3rd ed., Vol. 1). New York: John Wiley and Sons.

Piaget, J. (1971). *The construction of reality in the child.* New York: Ballantine.

Piers, E. V. (1984). *Piers-Harris Children's Self-Concept Scale.* Los Angeles: Western Psychological Services.

Pope, K.S., & Vasquez, M.J.T. (1998). *Ethics in psychotherapy and counseling: A practical guide* (2nd ed.). San Francisco, CA: Jossey-Bass Publishers.

Prinz, R.J., Foster, S.L., Kent, R.N., & O'Leary, K.D. (1979). Multivariate assessment of conflict in distressed and non-distressed mother-adolescent dyads. *Journal of Applied Behavior Analysis, 12,* 691-700.

Rae, W.A. (2001). Common teen-parent problems. In C.E. Walker & M.C. Roberts (Eds.), *Handbook of clinical child psychology* (3rd ed., pp. 621-637). New York: John Wiley and Sons.

Rae, W.A., & Founrier, C.J. (1999). Ethical and legal issues in the treatment of children and families. In S.W. Russ & T.H. Ollendick (Eds.), *Handbook of psychotherapies with children and families.* (pp. 67-83). New York: Kluwer Academic/Plenum Publishers.

Reynolds, C. R. & Kamphaus, R. W. (1998). *Behavior Assessment System for Children manual.* Circle Pines, MN: American Guidance Service.

Reynolds, C.R. & Kamphaus, R.W. (2002). *The clinicians guide to the Behavior Assessment System for Children.* Circle Pines, MN: American Guidance Service.

Reynolds, C.R. & Richmond, B.O. (1985). *Revised Children's Manifest Anxiety Scale manual.* Los Angeles, CA: Western Psychological Services.

Reynolds, W.M. (1987). *Reynolds Adolescent Depression Scale professional manual.* Lutz, FL: Psychological Assessment Resources.

Reynolds, W.M. (1987). *Suicidal Ideation Questionnaire professional manual.* Lutz, FL: Psychological Assessment Resources.

Reynolds, W.M. (1998a). *Adolescent Psychopathology Scale: Administration and interpretation manual.* Lutz, FL: Psychological Assessment Resources.

Reynolds, W.M. (1998b). *Adolescent Psychopathology Scale: Psychometric and technical manual.* Lutz, FL: Psychological Assessment Resources.

Reynolds, W.M. (2000). *Adolescent Psychopathology Scale-Short Form professional manual.* Lutz, FL: Psychological Assessment Resources.

Reynolds, W.M. (2001). *Reynolds Adolescent Adjustment Screening Inventory professional manual.* Lutz, FL: Psychological Assessment Resources.

Roberts, R.E. (2000). Depression and suicidal behaviors among adolescents: The role of ethnicity. In I. Cuéllar & F.A. Paniagua (Eds.), *Handbook of multicultural mental health: Assessment and treatment of diverse populations* (pp. 359-388). San Diego: Academic Press.

Robin, A.L. (1998). *ADHD in adolescents: Diagnosis and treatment.* New York: Guilford Press.

Robin, A.L., & Foster, S.L. (1989). *Negotiating parent-adolescent conflict: A behavioral-family systems approach.* New York: Guilford Press.

Robin, A. L., Koepke, T., & Moye, A. (1990). Multidimensional assessment of parent-adolescent relations. *Psychological Assessment: A Journal of Consulting and Clinical Psychology, 2,* 451-459.

Rush, A.J., Pincus, H.A., First, M.B., Blacker, D., Endicott, J., Keith, S.J., Phillips, K.A., Ryan, N.D., Smith, G.R., Tsuang, M.T., Widiger, T.A., & Zarin, D.A., (2000). *Handbook of psychiatric measures.* Washington, DC: American Psychiatric Association.

Sattler, J.M. (2002). *Assessment of children: Behavioral and clinical applications* (4th ed.). San Diego: Jerome M. Sattler, Publisher.

Sattler, J.M. (1998). *Clinical and forensic interviewing of children and families: Guidelines for the mental health, education, pediatric, child maltreatment fields.* San Diego: Jerome M. Sattler, Publisher.

Schacht, T.E. (2001). Issues in the forensic evaluation of children and youth. In Vance, H.B., & Pumariega, A.J. (Eds.), *Clinical assessment of child and adolescent behavior* (pp. 98-119). New York: John Wiley and Sons.

Schaffer, A.B. (2001). Forensic evaluations of children and expert witness testimony. In C.E. Walker & M.C. Roberts (Eds.), *Handbook of clinical child psychology* (3rd ed., pp. 1094-1119). New York: John Wiley and Sons.

Simeonsson, R.J., & Boyles, E.K. (2001). An ecobehavioral approach in clinical assessement. In R.J. Simeonsson & S.L. Rosenthal (Eds), *Psychological and developmental assessment: Children with disabilities and chronic conditions* (pp. 120-140). New York: Guilford Press.

Simeonsson, R.J., Huntington, G.S., Brent, J.L., & Balant, C. (2001). Qualitative developmental approach to assessement. In R.J. Simeonsson & S.L. Rosenthal (Eds), *Psychological and developmental assessment: Children with disabilities and chronic conditions* (pp. 83-119). New York: Guilford Press.

Science Directorate of the American Psychological Association. (2002). *FAQ/Finding information about psychological tests.* New York: American Psychological Association (located at *http://www.apa.org/science/faq-findtests.html*).

Shaffer, D.R. (2002). *Developmental psychology: Childhood and adolescence* (6th ed.). Belmont, CA: Wadsworth Thompson Learning.

Shuman, D.W. (1997). *Law and mental health professionals: Texas* (2nd ed.). Washington, DC: American Psychological Association.

Snyder, D.K., Cavell, T.A., Heffer, R.W., & Mangrum, L.F. (1995). Marital and family assessment: A multifaceted, multilevel approach. In R.H. Mikesell, D.D. Lusterman, & S.H. McDaniel (Eds.), *Integrating family therapy: Handbook of family psychology and systems theory* (pp. 163-182). Washington, DC: American Psychological Association.

Spielberger, C.D. (1973). *Manual for the State-Trait Anxiety Inventory for Children.* Palo Alto, CA: Consulting Psychologists Press.

Spielberger, C.D. (1983). *Manual for the State-Trait Anxiety Inventory (Revised).* Palo Alto, CA: Consulting Psychologists Press.

Tiesel, J., & Olson, D.H. (1997). *FACES IV: Reliability and validity.* Unpublished manuscript, University of Minnesota at Minneapolis.

Vik, P.W., Brown, S.A., & Myers. (1997). In E.J. Mash & L.G. Terdal (Eds.), *Assessment of childhood disorders* (3rd ed., pp. 717-748). New York: Guilford Press.

Vygotsky, L.S. (1962). *Thought and language.* Cambridge, MA: Massachusetts Institute of Technology Press.

Witt, J.C., Heffer, R. W., & Pfeiffer, J. (1990). Structured rating scales: A review of self-report and informant rating processes, procedures, and issues. In C. R. Reynolds & R. W. Kamphaus (Eds.), *Handbook of psychological and educational assessment of children: Personality, behavior, and context* (pp. 364-394). New York: Guilford Press.

Chapter 6

ASSESSMENT OF OLDER ADULTS AND THEIR FAMILIES

Sara H. Qualls and Daniel L. Segal[†]
University of Colorado at Colorado Springs

ASSESSMENT OF OLDER ADULTS AND THEIR FAMILIES

Assessment pervades nearly every aspect of psychotherapeutic work with older adults and their families. Thorough evaluation of the psychological status and functioning of an older person and the aging family system is an important but complex process, even for experienced clinicians. A few of the major challenges include choosing appropriate tools for the assessment, engaging the right persons in the process, assessing the full range of necessary domains at both the individual and family levels of analysis, and presenting usefully the results of assessment. The purpose of this chapter is to educate practitioners and researchers about unique characteristics of the assessment process during work with later life families. First we begin by reminding readers that most practitioners will work with older adults at some point, given the rapidly changing demographic patterns. We then review the key components of a multidimensional assessment, suggest specific tools and strategies for conducting an assessment, and finally we discuss pragmatic aspects of implementing an assessment.

THE DEMOGRAPHICS OF AGING

It is abundantly clear from Census data that the older adult population of America is booming, and this trend is expected to continue. According to U.S. Census data, there were

---

[†] The corresponding author Sara Honn Qualls, Ph.D. is Professor, Psychology Department and Center on Aging, University of Colorado at Colorado Springs, P.O. Box 7150, Colorado Springs, Colorado 80933-7150; Phone: 719-262-4151; Fax: 719-262-4166; Email: squalls@mail.uccs.edu; Daniel L. Segal, Ph.D. is Associate Professor, Department of Psychology, University of Colorado at Colorado Springs.

only 3.1 million older adults (defined as 65 years old and older) in 1900 (4% of the total population). In contrast, as of 2001, there are 35 million older adults (almost 13% of the total population). Furthermore, even larger increases are expected to occur in the next 30 years: by 2030, it is estimated that older adults will comprise over 20% of the total population, a staggering 70 million older persons. The most rapidly growing sub-group of older adults is people over age 85, commonly called the oldest-old, who are also the frailest of the older adult population. The oldest-old group is projected to increase from the current 4.4 million to 8.9 million by 2030 (U.S. Bureau of Census, 2000). Notably, these populations trends are mirrored in most of the world's other industrialized countries.

The aging of the population is experienced profoundly within families. The extended life expectancy combined with declining fertility rates has produced "beanpole families" consisting of long vertical lineages due to multiple generations living simultaneously and fewer members of each generation (Hagestad, 1988). Thus, most westerners have family members who are elderly, and most midlife adult couples have more aging parents than children. Despite popular mythology, families of older adults are intensively involved with them, even if from a geographic distance. Family support is a key variable predicting well-being in older adults, and thus warrants attention when an older adult is evaluated, even if the presenting problem is not specifically a family problem.

RAPIDLY GROWING GERIATRIC SERVICES NEED TO INCLUDE FAMILIES

The "graying" of America affects all aspects of healthcare, in that there are simply more older persons seeking diverse health services. Specifically, mental health care has been affected by this population boom as there has been a concurrent increase in the number of mentally ill older persons, although their mental health problems are often not appropriately recognized or treated. Approximately 20% of community-dwelling older persons have a *diagnosable* mental disorder (Jeste et al., 1999), and an even higher percentage experience significant signs of a mental disorder, although the symptoms fall below the diagnostic threshold. Medical illness is a significant risk factor for mental illness: prevalence rates range from 40-50% in hospitals and from 65-90% in nursing homes (Burns et al., 1993). The occurrence of mental disorder is expected to increase as baby boomers age because they are more likely than earlier-born cohorts to have lifelong histories of mental disorder (Jeste et al., 1999).

Despite high rates of mental illness, access to mental health services among the current cohort of older persons is lower than its rate of need, and has grown only modestly in recent years (Jeste et al., 1999). In long term care facilities, as many as 76% of older adults who need services do not get them (Burns & Taube, 1990) and only one-fourth to one-third of facilities use psychologists' services for patient care (DeRyke, Wieland, Wendland, & Helgeson, 1991). Other data are more encouraging: utilization among older persons of outpatient mental health services has increased appreciably in recent years (Knight & Kaskie, 1995). An upward trend in the number of older mental health clients is likely to occur in the near future as younger cohorts of adults who are educated about and experienced with the benefits of mental health treatment age. With a rising number of older persons seeking psychological services, assessment of older couples and families will surely increase as well.

Routinely including families in the physical and mental health assessments of older adults is important for several reasons. First, families often seek involvement and they are key components of the care system. Families provide the bulk of care required by older adults living in the community (Stone, Cafferata, & Sangl, 1987). One remarkable example of this point comes from data on family involvement that continues even after nursing home placement of a frail elder. High and Rowles (1995) document the very high rate of family involvement in decisions related to care of the older resident over a two year period post-placement: Families were involved in 90% of crisis decisions, 82% of financial decisions, 73% of daily living decisions, and 61% of physical environment decisions. This profile of high rates of involvement occurs while the person's basic daily needs are provided by a formal institution. Thus, family involvement in evaluation makes sense because they are clearly key players in the lives of older persons.

An additional reason for engaging families in any assessment of older adults is that older adults have a profound impact on the families. Certainly, elder care extracts a cost from family members who provide care. Adverse effects of long term caregiving on the physical and mental health of the caregiver are well documented (Schulz, O'Brien, Bookwala, & Fleissner, 1995). Family counseling interventions can ameliorate these effects and delay institutionalization (Mittelman et al., 1993), a finding that also points to the value of evaluating the family's needs when an older person is being evaluated. In contrast to a focus on older family members as sources of burden, national data also remind us that the majority of families receive benefits from older members that may be lost if the older adult's physical or mental health deteriorates (Cohler, 1988). Thus, evaluation of the ripple effects of changes in individual lives are prudent (Pruchno, Blow, & Smyer, 1984).

Finally, families may become involved in assessment because family problems are the reason for the evaluation. Family conflicts, stresses, and dysfunctions may be the identifying factor that brings the older adult and his or her family into an assessment process. More is said below about how and why families become the focus of assessment, but for now the key point is that disruptions in family interaction patterns may be the tip of an iceberg of aging-related problems in individuals as well as the family system. For example, deteriorating cognitive functioning may impair a person's ability to regulate emotion, thus leading to an increased rate of marital or family conflict. Families that have remained stable throughout middle adulthood may experience significant changes when age-related losses and compensatory efforts kick in.

ASSESSING AGING FAMILY SYSTEMS BEGINS WITH THE INDIVIDUALS

When considering assessment of older adult couples and families, a necessary beginning point is to consider issues related to assessment of the individuals involved. Although a systemic perspective discourages focus on individuals in favor of interpersonal analysis, later life families are often changing interpersonally because of changes in individuals. For example, a common risk factor for family level systems change is cognitive impairment. In order to understand the shifts in family structure and function that generated the immediate problem, a clear picture is needed of the members' functioning. Because older adults are at high risk of declining capacities due to physical disorders or cognitive impairment, it is especially critical to get an accurate picture of older individuals' functioning, with a special focus on recent changes. In other words, an "identified patient" may truly be a patient, and family problems may arise because they are not responding to, or adapting to, the needs and changing capacities of that person. Changes in basic capacity may occur in multiple family members from multiple generations, and thus, the guidelines in this next section can be viewed as applicable to all relevant family members linked to the problem.

The unique psychosocial contexts of later life, combined with biological aspects of the aging process, require that assessment of family problems in later life involve multidimensional evaluations of relevant members of the family system. Just as the contexts in which children live and function (e.g., schools and neighborhoods) are relevant to child-rearing families, the housing, finances, social relationships, and physical health contexts are vitally important to understand before working with an aging family system. A wide array of housing choices is now available to older adults in our society, each of which has unique characteristics that influence daily functioning. Financial resources often serve as the gatekeeper for formal services, including those funded by entitlement programs such as the Older Americans Act (e.g., transportation, Meals-on-Wheels), Medicare, and Medicaid. Important aspects of the social contexts of later life include the high rate of social loss (Rook, 2000) or social selection (Carstensen, 1991) that influences the way the social support system functions. For example, understanding the distinct roles of family and friends is relevant to the assessment of a family system. Finally, physical health changes that are characteristically negative in later life are key to determining capacity to function independently.

Multidimensional and Multidisciplinary

Given the complexity of the contexts of aging, a multidimensional, multidisciplinary approach to assessment is needed. Typically, a key piece is a medical evaluation, including a detailed review of medications (prescribed and over-the-counter). The evaluation should produce a clear picture of medical illnesses; pharmacological risk factors for behavior problems, interpersonal problems, or functional limitations; and positive characteristics of physical well-being. Another piece of the assessment is a functional evaluation that identifies the level of independence in accomplishing Activities of Daily Living (ADL's; e.g., bathing, dressing, self-feeding) and Instrumental Activities of Daily Living (IADL'S; e.g., managing finances, arranging transportation; managing medications). Family members often become involved in new ways when older adults lose functional capacity, thus potentially triggering family systems problems. A careful social history that includes family structures and transitions as well as financial and occupational history provides other critical information. Psychological assessment includes an evaluation of cognitive functioning, emotional well-being or distress, adaptational or coping styles, and personality functioning.

The multiple pieces of the evaluations need to be viewed not only as a "snapshot" of the immediate moment, but as a moment in a video so the evaluator considers how much change has occurred as well. Evaluations of older adults require careful review of historical information as well as current functioning because often the family system is responding to *changes* in functional capacity secondary to contextual or biological aspects of aging.

Unique Challenges for Psychological Assessment

Couples and families seeking assistance are often dealing with unrecognized cognitive impairment or mental disorders, requiring an in-depth psychological assessment. Interestingly, the Diagnostic and Statistical Manual of Mental Disorders, 4th edition (DSM-IV; American Psychiatric Association, 1994) has separate sections for childhood and adult disorders, but there is no specific section on, or criteria for, mental disorders in later life, although the typical course over the lifespan for some disorders is described. Although limited information on age-related manifestations of mental disorders is provided in the DSM-IV, the lack of unique categories or criteria that accurately reflect the presentation of disorders in older adults is a weakness of the manual. Because older adults may not present with classic signs of some mental disorders including depression, personality disorders, and substance abuse, the current classification system may encourage under-identification. Cultural, social, physical, and cognitive factors are among some of the variables that may affect the way some psychiatric disorders appear in older adults.

A key issue in psychological assessments with older adults is to select tests that have been demonstrated to be reliable and valid with older adult samples, and for which there are appropriate norms. Reliability and validity can vary across populations, as has been demonstrated with widely used instruments such as the Center for Epidemiological Studies-Depression Scale (CES-D; Radloff, 1977) that varies in validity and factor structure according to factors such as gender (Stommel et al., 1993), ethnicity (Manson, Ackerson, Wiegman, Baron, & Fleming, 1990), and language (Roberts, Rhoades, & Vernon, 1990). Ideally, reliability and validity data for specific older adult populations should be available for the assessment tools selected in clinical work with older adults and families.

The use of age-appropriate norms is also a significant concern in assessment of older individuals. Tests developed specifically for older adults (e.g., Geriatric Depression Scale) have excellent norms. Likewise, standard intelligence tests now have extensive age norms. Many other psychological and neuropsychological tests did not initially furnish norms for older adults, but researchers have since provided age-norms for many of them (Lezak, 1995; Mitrushina, Boone, & D'Elia, 1999; Spreen & Strauss, 1998). Unfortunately, some psychological tests are still inadequately normed by age, or by other relevant characteristics (e.g., gender, ethnicity) for older adults or older families (Segal, Coolidge, & Hersen, 1998). If age-appropriate norms are not available, be cautious in interpreting scores since they may be significantly biased or inaccurate.

All psychosocial data must be viewed within the context of physical health. Information about medical illnesses is important because some problems (e.g., thyroid dysfunction, multiple sclerosis, hypoglycemia) can cause psychiatric conditions (APA, 1994). Likewise, many medications commonly taken by older adults are known to cause psychological symptoms. For example, some antihypertensive drugs and steroids can induce depressive symptoms, some stimulants and steroids can cause manic-like symptoms, and some analgesics, bronchodilators, and anticonvulsants can cause anxiety symptoms (APA, 1994).

Due to age-related increases in the frequency of many chronic medical conditions (e.g., arthritis, poor circulation, osteoporosis), older adults consume a disproportionate amount of prescribed and over the counter (OTC) medications. With increased medication use, older persons are at increased risk for adverse drug effects because of harmful drug interactions and the build-up of medication in the body because older persons metabolize many drugs at a slower rate than when they were younger. Diverse drug interactions can cause memory problems that mimic a dementing illness such as Alzheimer's disease. Older adults are encouraged to bring a complete listing of medications to the testing session, or preferably a bag full of current medications from which the evaluator can compile a listing. Referral for a thorough medical work-up is always indicated if the person has not recently been medically evaluated.

Sensory impairments (e.g., hearing and vision) that are also common among older adults complicate assessment. Difficulties perceiving instructions or testing stimuli can have obvious adverse effects on performance. Sensory deterioration is considered a primary cause of reduced performance on cognitive tasks (Lindenberger, Scherer, & Baltes, 2001) and even certain psychiatric disorders such as late-onset paranoia (Almeida, Forstl, Howard, & David, 1993). Certainly, interpersonal interactions are heavily impacted by sensory impairments making it imperative that careful assessment of the range and intensity of sensory impairment be identified.

Physical disabilities similarly complicate assessment by limiting response options (e.g., hand movement or writing), constraining reaction time on speeded tasks, limiting access to test stimuli (e.g., standing to engage in a balance task), or limiting stamina for long test procedures. Evaluation tools or scoring strategies may need to be altered to accommodate physical disabilities.

ASSESSMENT TECHNIQUES AND TOOLS

Due to the complex nature of assessment with older persons and older families, multiple strategies are often used in combination to elicit the most comprehensive and meaningful description.

Clinical Interview

The clinical interview is perhaps the most important and informative strategy during an evaluation of an older family or individual. During the interview, the clinician gathers information about the individuals' current difficulties including a history of the problem. Other topics include an in-depth personal history, mental health history (including interventions), marital and family history, mental status examination, and social functioning. Obviously, older clients have a longer, often more complex history due to their longevity, and thus, patience and perseverance are valuable clinical skills.

As with any adult, rapport must be developed with the older person in order to allow him or her to disclose intensely personal information about their current experience. Family interviews also require rapport, but with all participants simultaneously. Boszormenyi-Nagy and Sparks (1984) refer to this as "multidirectional partiality" in which each participant experiences the interviewer attempting to establish empathy with their unique perspective. The unique aspect of this work with later life families is that the participants are all legal, equally autonomous adults, yet they experience their relationships as having a generational, hierarchical component. Thus, joining the family and even eliciting information about the family is a process of discovering the relative importance of hierarchies and roles among adults who are technically mutually autonomous.

Clinicians should explain clearly the purposes and procedures of the assessment (Segal et al., 1998). When the assessment is to investigate the effects of limited capacity on the family (e.g., cognitive impairment), the clinician needs to be particularly careful to model how to tell the truth about limitations while showing respect for the older person. Address any concerns the participant(s) may have about the evaluation, since many older adults associate mental health services with shame and negative stigma. Family members may have very different levels of information about the reason or strategy of the evaluation, depending upon the dynamics within the family. Often, a key piece of the evaluation is coming to agreement on its purpose, scope, and possible outcomes. The process of getting everyone on the same page may be a meaningful intervention in itself. Lack of consensus often reflects structural or dynamic problems within the family (e.g., information has been withheld from some members because of conflicts or cutoffs).

Interviewers need to be flexible when engaging older persons and their family members (Segal et al., 1998). The environment should be adjusted to reduce the impact of any sensory or physical limitations (e.g., brightly lit and quiet testing room; use of big print versions of tests). Traditional time constraints should be adjusted to not fatigue the older person(s). Family interventions may require flexibility in communication modalities (e.g., using speakerphones to include geographically distant relatives) and meeting times (e.g., a longer meeting on a holiday weekend when everyone is home may be more useful than weekly meetings with part of the family).

Multidimensional Assessment Tools

Although most clinicians put together the multidimensional picture through interviews and written reports from other disciplines, several multidimensional assessment tools have emerged in recent decades for the purpose of systematically tapping the broad array of social, cultural, financial, psychological, and physical functioning of older adults. Commonly used instruments are the Comprehensive Assessment and Referral Evaluation (Gurland & Wilder, 1984), Older Americans Resources and Services (OARS; Fillenbaum & Smyer, 1981) and the Multilevel Assessment Instrument (MAI; Lawton, Moss, Fulcomer, & Kleban, 1982). Norms are available for all of these tools, as are findings from many research studies which have relied upon them to gather multidimensional data.

Symptom Checklists

Several elder-specific checklists are available and they have excellent psychometric properties. Some interesting examples include the Geriatric Depression Scale (GDS; Yesavage et al., 1983), the Geriatric Hopelessness Scale (GHS; Fry, 1986), the Michigan Alcoholism Screening Test - Geriatric Version (MAST-G; Blow et al., 1992), and the Worry Scale for Older Adults – Revised (WSOA-R; Wisocki, 1994). The GDS, a widely used screening measure for depression in older adults, consists of 30 items presented in a simple Yes/No format. Items focus on cognitive and behavioral aspects of depression, and somatic items (that generally bias depression tests for older populations) are excluded. A short form is also available. The scale is in the public domain, and thus is available on the GDS website at www.stanford.edu/~yesavage/GDS.html. The GHS is a 30 item Yes/No self-report scale that assesses pessimism and hopelessness in older adults, which are related to suicide. The MAST-G is used for substance abuse assessment, which is a significant problem among older persons and is linked to depression and suicide. The MAST-G contains 24 Yes/No items unique to older problem drinkers. In all cases, "yes" is the pathological response, and a cutoff of 5 positive responses indicates an alcohol problem. The WSOA-R contains 88 items and measures six categories of worry: financial, social, health, personal, world, and family concerns.

Cognitive Functioning

Assessment of cognitive functioning is an important part of any thorough geriatric assessment, because cognitive impairment (e.g., dementia) is an age-related problem (i.e., rates of dementia increase with age). Notably, other test results may not be valid if the respondent has significant cognitive impairment. Early detection of cognitive problems is crucial because symptoms are sometimes reversible. The primary DSM-IV categories for cognitive disorders are delirium and dementia. Delirium refers to a clouding of consciousness with impaired concentration, disorientation, and perceptual disturbances that develop over a short period of time (hours to days). Since delirium is often obvious and acute, there are no specific cognitive tests for it. If delirium is suspected in an older person, they should be quickly referred for medical treatment since delirium is typically reversible but can be deadly if the underlying cause (e.g., infections, malnutrition, dehydration) is not corrected.

Dementia is a chronic syndrome of multiple cognitive deficits, including impairment of memory and executive function that deteriorates over time, but without impairment in consciousness. Dementia affects about 5 to 7% of those over age 65 and at least 30% of those over age 85 (APA Working Group on the Older Adult, 1998). The most common type of dementia is Alzheimer's disease which accounts for 50-60% of demented persons.

Clinicians should *screen* for dementia in all older clients during any psychological or family assessment. Several brief, standardized, and easily administered screening tools are available. The Folstein Mini Mental State Exam (Folstein, Folstein, & McHugh, 1975) takes 5 to 10 minutes to administer and is well-validated. Items tap orientation, concentration, memory, language, and gross motor skills. Scores range from 0 to 30, with scores under 25 indicating a need for further testing and evaluation. The Dementia Rating Scale-2 (Mattis, Jurica, & Leitten, 2001) is a psychometrically sound, quantitative, and multifaceted interviewer administered test designed for dementia evaluation. It consists of 36 tasks and takes about 30 minutes to complete, and the new version contains extensive age- and education-corrected normative data. Evaluations of cognitive functioning need to include input from a collateral information source, usually a family member, to ask about problems in daily living.

Should concern about cognitive impairment result from a screening test, more thorough neuropsychological testing is warranted. Such testing assesses brain-behavior relationships in multiple domains and behavioral disturbances that are caused by brain dysfunction, and helps to quantify and localize brain damage. One approach is for the examiner to use a standard and fixed battery (e.g., the Halstead-Reitan Battery), whereas another strategy is to carefully choose a variety of different tests to assess particular neuropsychological domains of interest. Finally, laboratory tests (e.g., electrolyte panel, urinalysis, electroencephalography) and high-tech brain-imaging procedures (e.g., CAT scan, MRI scan) are often used to complement neuropsychological assessment.

ASSESSMENT OF MARITAL AND FAMILY FUNCTIONING IN LATER LIFE

Typical Referrals

Two typical referral categories are families caring for an older member and families caring for a disabled younger member. The former category typically includes spouses and adult children seeking assistance with problem behavior in an older person. They may need assistance identifying the cause of recent changes in behavior or functioning, strategies for handling behavior problems or physical health problems, or strategies for self-care while they are providing care for others. The other category is aging parents who are caring for an adult child with a lifelong history of mental illness or cognitive disability. These parents are often concerned about long term planning for the well-being of their child after they become incapacitated or die. Although they are often grieving the loss of their ability to provide direct care, they are also concerned that a plan be developed for how practical matters (e.g., legal, housing, finances) will be handled after their death. Rarely does a couple or family come to therapy solely from a growth-based motivation (i.e., to become a "better" family). The rule is that there is some kind of recent change in a practical aspect of life that is making the marital or family problem salient.

Sources of Problems

Many families are woefully unprepared for the transitions of later life. Previous generations in their lineage may not have lived into later adulthood. Even if the family has experience with old age, the current contexts of aging are unique, challenging families in unique ways. Financial, social, and health contexts of aging influence the dynamics of the family. For example, the mythically happy three generation household of the past century had unique power dynamics internally due to the control the eldest generation usually held over the economic well-being of the family through ownership of farms or other assets. Financial independence due to retirement funds and pensions removes economic power as a strong force in intergenerational contact, leaving the family more reliant on emotional ties.

Some transitions in later life can be genuinely confusing. Older adults are sometimes faced with the challenges of creating meaningful social roles post-retirement, meeting intimacy needs during widowhood from an irreplaceable 50 year marriage, or making difficult end of life health decisions (e.g., whether to use a feeding tube in a loved one with a severe chronic illness or watch him/her starve to death).

Families do not always anticipate the intensive ripple effect of the "life event web" (Pruchno et al., 1984). Changes in the lives of other family members, even from other generations, can have a profound impact on the well-being or life context of an older person, or vice versa. Life events often require interpersonal adjustments in the dimensions of time structure, roles, communication, power balance, or nurturance (Qualls, 1995).Thus, family restructuring following a daughter's divorce, a son's death, or a parent's chronic illness may challenge the adaptive capacity of the family.

Some families have not functioned well at any stage of the family life cycle, and cannot be anticipated to magically become effective in later life. Chronically poorly functioning families have not met members' needs at previous stages of the family life cycle with the consequence that adults bring low interpersonal skills, stunted individual and family development, and a general lack of maturity to later life. Many of these families have structural problems that impair functioning. For example, families with significant cut-offs of parts of the family, poor boundaries around subsystems, chronic intrusions on roles, and abdication of parenting can be expected to face the tasks of later life with a serious handicap.

Assessment of Later Life Families

A key question when evaluating a later life family is why they are seeking assistance now. The obviously long history of the family, whether highly functional or not, makes salient the question of what would provoke an effort to seek assistance at the present time. Key places to look for the answer to this question are: 1) what current developmental tasks are not being accomplished by one or more members, 2) how is the family stuck on these tasks, and 3) what solutions have they attempted previously (Herr & Weakland, 1979). As is true at any age, later life families often have identified one member of the family whose functioning or behavior is in question. This "identified patient" (IP) often is a patient in the sense that some aspect of their functioning has changed and some kind of medical treatment is in progress. Other problems that might characterize the IP include mental disorders (e.g., depression), poor adjustment to a geographic move, or changes in cognitive capacity.

As noted earlier, a unique aspect of family assessment with later life families is the importance of obtaining an accurate picture of the IP's status. The necessary multidimensional picture is rarely painted because typically no one else has pulled all of the pieces together. Thus, family work with later life families requires significant individual as well as systemic evaluation, using the approach outlined above. An important additional piece to the picture of the IP's individual function is to ask whether there are any prostheses that could be used to improve the person's autonomous function. Small interventions such as hearing aids, walkers, memory aids, handrails, or a chairlift to the upstairs bedrooms may be sufficient to reverse the negative effects of a recent health change.

Whom to include in the assessment is a practical concern that warrants some thought. Geographic dispersion establishes a practical problem of getting people into the same room. A conceptual problem precedes the practical, however. Who *should* be included? If the concern is an aging adult, should all members of the second generation be included, and does that list include in-laws? What about other members of the first generation, such as siblings or cousins? For some older adults, a non-relative such as a neighbor serves the function of a family member by overseeing daily well-being.

Participation is dictated by purpose. A broadly inclusive gathering might be appropriate for sharing feedback of assessment results and considering options for providing adequate support for a member to remain in his or her home. Typically, the people who are likely candidates to participate in the decision-making subsystem need to be included. The therapist may not know initially who that is, and may need to investigate a bit before suggesting a starting set of participants that the most key family members can modify. Often, this includes the IP, his or her spouse, and their children. The participation of in-laws, siblings, and other family members (e.g., grandchildren) is an internal decision that the most involved family members must make unless it is evident that power or responsibility will reside with the in-laws.

A genogram is a particularly useful tool when working with later life families since they typically have multiple generations and complex relationship structures. The genogram may be constructed by the therapist as he or she hears the story or by family member(s). The linkage of the structure with the story is, of course, a key characteristic of the use of the genogram as an assessment tool. Dynamics can be mapped onto the structural graphic in order to build a picture of transitional points in the family lineage, and patterns in such transitions (e.g., geographic moves or migration patterns, significant economic gains/losses). The transitions required by developmental tasks also can be added to the genogram in order to clarify intergenerational patterns that might be influencing the immediate problem. For example, noting the patterns in each generation's process of launching or mate-selection may be key to understanding the emotional lineage that is influencing a current family system problem. Mapping major historical events (e.g., war, economic depression, regional flood) onto the genogram often helps explain structural changes as well. Historical events also can help clarify differences in the values and options between generations because birth cohort effects have such powerful influence on the structures of early adulthood in particular (Baltes, Reese, & Lipsitt, 1980).

Another type of family information that is useful relates to generational boundaries. Each family has unique rules about the roles and obligations of the generations. The roles can be conceptualized at the level of individuals. What does it mean in a particular family to be the oldest member? What does it mean to be a midlife daughter or a young son/grandson/great-grandson? The generational boundaries also have an interpersonal component because they determine who is included in key decisions for whom. For example, a marital subsystem is usually presumed to have a boundary around their decisions about sex and finances. However, the onset of cognitive impairment in an aging father may place a midlife daughter in the role of sharing decisions with her mother about these domains. Similarly, families vary in the information that aging parents have about the details of a midlife couple's life. Weak or rigid intergenerational boundaries may impair a family's ability to meet needs when significant transitions occur (e.g., a midlife son divorces, a midlife daughter is imprisoned).

Comparison and contrast questions are useful to families who may have trouble articulating the inner dynamics of their family. For example, is your sister or sister-in-law more likely to host the holiday meals after your mother dies? Would your mother or your father be more likely to include you in conversations about their finances? Which siblings are likely to view your mother's choice to move into a nursing home as a problem (implicit comparison)? Which members of this generation seemed to launch themselves into adulthood with a rocket launcher and which used a leash? How do those different launchings influence parent care motivations, skills, and styles? Recent structural transitions are often key precipitants of the current problem and warrant particularly careful evaluation. Who has entered or exited the family recently? What subsystems have reorganized? Whose relationship ties have grown stronger or weaker? A full assessment in this area may be highly informative for treatment planning.

Another area for assessment is how a particular family actually accomplishes the typical functions of families in our culture. Most families attempt to meet at least some social needs, mark life events with rituals, provide care to the oldest and youngest generations, maintain a kind of lineage identity, provide financial support and safety nets, remind members of life's beginnings and endings, and provide the context for developmental tasks. Families vary in how many of these tasks are done solely or primarily within the family, and in how skilled they are in accomplishing the tasks. Information about how and how well the basic family functions are met provides a backdrop for work on the specific precipitating problem for which the family sought assistance. In particular, information about attachments within the family are key to determining whether the family has sufficient emotional nurturance to survive the conflicts inherent in solving problems interpersonally (Shields, King & Wynne, 1995).

A family life review provides another specific mechanism for gathering information about family transitions over time. Although the genogram provides a static image to which transitional details can be added, a life review process requires a focus on change. Transition points, new directions, and disrupted functioning are the key focal points of a family life review. The clinician can note not only the nature (content) of key transitions, but also the process by which the family experienced the transitions. Were transitions welcomed or resisted? Were transitions a crisis or a smooth developmental process? Did family members implode or explode under stress?

The in-depth information suggested in this section cannot be obtained quickly, often does not emerge in a sequential manner, and may not even be needed in all cases. Families usually seek help with a specific task or problem, and the assessment needs to center around that problem. The in-depth approach outlined above is the informational context in which specific tasks or situations become problematic for families, however. Thus, the assessment process typically moves back and forth between the evaluation of a narrow problem and an effort to figure out how the family's structure and dynamics turned this task or situation into a problem for which they need assistance. How is it that the family could not gather and share information effectively to make decisions about a chronic health problem? How is it that aging parents could not set boundaries on the intrusion of a poorly functioning adult child on their financial well-being?

Summary and Conclusion

Assessment of later life families and couples requires a broad understanding of the biological and psychosocial contexts of later life within a particular cohort of a particular culture. Often, the person identified by the family as a problem actually has experienced a recent change in functioning that is requiring significant family adaptation in structure or dynamics. The process of evaluation, therefore, often begins with careful evaluation of the Identified Patient to gather a clear multidimensional picture of current functioning as well as recent changes in functioning. This may require the clinician to gather and organize existing information from multiple formal care providers or the clinician may initiate a complex evaluation process for the first time. Once the information about functioning is organized into a clear snapshot of current functioning and into a video that depicts change over time, the clinician can work with the family to identify strategies for restructuring themselves as needed in order to meet *all* members' needs, including those of the IP.

The process of gathering the information is a rich opportunity for observing the family in action, so it in itself constitutes part of the family assessment. The family becomes the focus of more in-depth assessment when members do not spontaneously restructure their relationship dynamics to adapt to the needs of the IP. Evaluation of the family can include assessment of problem-solving strategies or structures and functions (e.g., using a genogram and developmental life review). In essence, the family assessment identifies the important structural, historical, and developmental characteristics of the family. This information can be used to help the family identify the relationship between their current task and the longer-term family challenges that may be impairing their ability to address the current task or problem.

The process of the family evaluation often requires flexibility in frequency of meetings, who is included in the process, and the big versus small picture focus (family structure and dynamics or immediate problem). The fact that all participants have equal status as adults in the family is moderated by the family's rules about roles and hierarchies in ways that shape their participation in the assessment.

CASE STUDY

Marsha's psychologist referred her, her sister Jill and brother-in-law Brian, and her mother Genevieve for a family consultation. The psychologist suspected that Marsha's stress and depressive symptoms were exacerbated by the family's struggle to make decisions about Genevieve's care and safety. The request for consultation initiated a family meeting during which an assessment process similar to that described above was launched.

Marsha, age 54, had been in individual psychotherapy for two years, since she moved cross-country to live with her mother who was showing early signs of dementia. The move resolved Marsha's need for financial stability and shelter as well as both daughters' concerns about their mother's safety living alone. Marsha was an unhappy woman who appeared psychologically less mature than her age. Her adulthood had been characterized by unsuccessful attempts to accomplish developmental tasks and a lifelong struggle with depression. Marsha currently worked at a blue collar job that was stressful to her but matched the skills that she had from a lifetime of disjointed employment. Her only marriage ended in divorce, and her two children were marginally functioning young adults who intermittently needed assistance that Marsha lacked the resources to provide. She reported having no friends locally nor any strong relationships from previous places she lived. Although committed to caring for her mother, Marsha was clearly very stressed by the challenges of interacting with a woman whose functioning was declining.

Jill, age 60, lived nearby with her husband, Brian. Jill and Brian have been closely involved in their mother's life throughout their marriage. After Genevieve's husband died, Jill and Brian made it a point to have dinner regularly with her and to handle any financial or home maintenance tasks she asked them to do. A growing tension between Marsha and Jill over sharing responsibilities for Genevieve is complicated by Marsha's long history of resentment of Jill's status as the "older, successful sister." Marsha feels like she is stuck with the frustrating parts of daily contact with their mother while Jill enjoys the greater respect and trust from their mother.

The first family meeting assessed the daughters' shared concerns about their mother's memory. Initially, both daughters and Brian were unsure if what they were seeing was serious or a normal part of aging. Marsha was very anxious, timid, and tearful as she tried to articulate to her mother the evidence she saw of impaired memory functioning. Jill was somewhat more forceful although very kind. Genevieve appeared to be anxious and defensive about the reason for the meeting. The therapist asked some pointed questions that often help to discern the presence of cognitive impairment in daily life (e.g., handling of finances, repeated stories, forgetfulness of appointments). Genevieve acknowledged some problems but vehemently denied that they were serious.

Based on evidence of likely cognitive impairment, the therapist offered the family a framework for further evaluation. In order to reduce Genevieve's fears, the therapist framed neuropsychological testing as an experimental investigation of whether there is anything seriously wrong, or just a concerned family wanting what is best for their mother. Genevieve found that a tolerable framework, and agreed to try her best to show how capable she was when she was evaluated by a neuropsychologist. She also agreed to have a thorough physical to look for any medical causes of her difficulties. Marsha asked Jill if she would set the appointments for all of the necessary evaluations.

The assessments of Genevieve's physical and mental health showed that while she was in good physical health for an 82 year old woman, she was in fact demonstrating significant cognitive impairments caused by a dementing illness. Specifically, her memory and executive function test performances were in the 10-25th percentile range, far below what would be expected of someone of her previous education and occupational status.

A second family session, including Genevieve, Marsha, Jill, and Brian, was scheduled to provide feedback from the evaluations. The therapist provided a simplified list of problems identified in the assessment, along with descriptions of how those problems might affect daily life. Marsha, Jill, and Brian acknowledged that the profile matched their observations, but Genevieve denied that most of the problem areas were in fact problems for her. She could not give an alternative explanation for her low performance, and became increasingly agitated at the idea that she was perceived to have these deficits. In order to keep Genevieve willingly engaged in the evaluation, the therapist directed the family members to reaffirm their warmth and support of her, regardless of what lie ahead. Genevieve was then relieved of her position as the focus of attention when the therapist invited her to return to the waiting room. In order to distract her from worrying about the family that was meeting without her, she was invited to trim dead leaves off of some plants that had bothered her when she entered, a task she accepted with delight. When the therapist talked with the adult children, she emphasized the importance of using the assessment information to begin long term planning in several important domains (i.e., legal, financial, and housing planning).

The therapist also began to evaluate the family members' reactions to the diagnostic label (Probable Alzheimer's Disease) as well as the evidence of such serious deficits. Marsha and Jill both cried when their mother left the room. Brian spoke quietly of his concerns about how long Marsha could continue to provide the level of assistance Genevieve would need, given how stressful it had become. Marsha was visibly appreciative of his empathy and readily agreed that she was exhausted and weary of her mother's constant repeated questions and badgering about details. Marsha became quite visibly anxious, however, when she began to consider what it would take to convince their mother to leave her home. She blurted out to Jill a demand that Jill would have to make the decision when it was time to move her mother, and would have to handle the details. The therapist recommended that while no decisions needed to be made today, some longer term planning for how they would handle the future housing transition might be helpful. Marsha noted that Jill knew about that sort of thing, so she suggested that she could bow out and let Jill take over. Because this sounded like a replay of their lifelong roles that always led Marsha to resent Jill's strength, the therapist recommended that the daughters set a time to go visit facilities together, and come back and report on what they saw. The therapist also asked Marsha for permission to talk with her individual therapist about how this pending transition might interact with Marsha's ongoing individual treatment, which Marsha readily granted.

Marsha's individual therapist suggested that one of Marsha's major fears about her mother moving into assisted living was that it would leave her again unsettled. Marsha viewed herself as both a support and a dependent of her aging mother, but worked hard not to acknowledge her fears to Jill. The therapist also reported that Marsha consistently relied on Jill to make decisions because Marsha was terrified of standing up to her mother after years of hearing from Genevieve what an incompetent, inadequate person Marsha was. Apparently, Genevieve and her husband both had shown a strong preference for Jill long before adulthood, and framed their view of Marsha as inadequate and odd from childhood. This information was framed as evidence of Marsha's challenges to accomplish her developmental tasks due to long-standing systemic problems in the family. Thus, facilitating Marsha's development emerged from the assessment as another priority.

At the third family session, the therapist focused on assessing how the daughters worked together as caregivers. The specific task was to arrange a housing transition. First, the therapist asked for a report on their visits to housing options. Marsha was encouraged to offer her evaluation of the sites first because it disrupted their habit of letting Jill lead in ways that undermined Marsha. Marsha showed remarkable observational skill regarding the daily lives of the residents at each facility and how those would relate to Genevieve's preferences. After the daughters came to ready consensus on which facility they preferred, the therapist directed them to talk about how they would know when it was time for placement.

Marsha began to weep as she bemoaned her mother's hatred of the idea of moving and her mother's rages at Marsha in the past few weeks whenever Genevieve believed Marsha was planning to move her. Jill admitted that their mother's temper had become increasingly volatile and that she was often focused on her daughters' "trying to put me away." Both were very uncomfortable with the idea of confronting their mother directly about the move. However, Jill expressed concern that Marsha may be wearing out currently such that placement needed to occur sooner rather than later. Marsha's initial response was defensive anger at being viewed as incompetent. The therapist facilitated careful dialogue between the daughters to clarify that Jill's intention of being supportive was misconstrued by Marsha as critical, a pattern both acknowledged reflected patterns of interaction between their parents. The family rule was that evidence of need for support meant one was inadequate for the job. Throughout her life Marsha had heard offers of support from Jill as critical rather than as a sign of affection and solidarity. Much of the session was spent in a family life review that outlined the sisters' lifelong patterns, and linked them to their parents' communication patterns.

At the close of the session, the therapist revisited the question that precipitated the work on the sibling relationship – how would they know when to move their mother? Jill stated her belief that Marsha be the one to make the decision, because she was the one bearing the greatest burden. Marsha agreed, but expressed a strong burden from that responsibility. She agreed to discuss her distress over that burden with her individual therapist.

A final session, three months later, was called at Marsha's request. She and her psychotherapist had been working on her anxiety about making the decision, and her general pattern of avoiding making decisions. She recently decided that the burden was excessive, and she was ready to ask for Jill's help in arranging the placement. Although she struggled with guilt, anxiety, and obvious sadness about coming to this decision, Marsha spoke clearly and strongly on her own behalf. Jill immediately responded warmly in support of the decision, and complimented Marsha on the caregiving burden she had carried as well as the psychological work she had done to get to the point of making this decision. Both wept as they embraced spontaneously, and they began to explore the pragmatic aspects of making the housing transition.

The therapist facilitated a plan by which the daughters would meet bi-weekly to discuss practical aspects of the move over breakfast with no other family present. The sisters were encouraged to work on maintaining the mutuality they had achieved in the decision-making process thus far, because it would help them maintain solidarity in the face of their mother's anger and resistance, which did in fact surface when the move was actually completed.

Comment on the Case

The case of Genevieve and her daughters demonstrates how long standing family dynamics can be magnified by later life crises that bring family members together in a working relationship for the first time in decades. Genevieve, the "identified patient" was a true patient whose disorder was unnamed and misunderstood. The evaluation required careful assessment of her cognitive, physical, social, and psychological functioning before the family conflict could be addressed. In addition, information about Marsha's individual functioning was obtained in order to determine what kind of decision-making structures would make sense. Marsha's cognitive competence was adequate to share responsibility for decisions, but she was uncomfortable claiming equal authority or responsibility with Jill. The therapist then began to investigate what would make it possible for the daughters to form a strong decision-making subsystem. She identified a need to build a stronger boundary around the sibling relationship by strengthening attachment bonds and to foster a more balanced power relationship. As she shared information about the details of the decisions that must be made, the therapist assessed what kind of support Marsha would need in order to claim a shared role, and what help Jill would need in order to adopt a stance that would not interfere with Marsha's efforts. Each step in the intervention led to another point in the assessment plan until the daughters were able to maintain mutual affection, trust, and power in the planning process.

REFERENCES

Almeida, O. P., Forstl, H., Howard, R., & David, A. S. (1993). Unilateral auditory hallucinations. *British Journal of Psychiatry, 162*, 262-264.

American Psychiatric Association. (1994). *Diagnostic and statistical manual of mental disorders* (4th ed.). Washington, DC: Author.

APA Working Group on the Older Adult. (1998). What practitioners should know about working with older adults. *Professional Psychology: Research and Practice, 29*, 413-427.

Baltes, P. B., Reese, H. W., & Lipsitt, L. P. (1980). Life-span developmental psychology. *Annual Review of Psychology, 31*, 65-110.

Blow, F. C., Brower, K. J., Schulenberg, J. E., Demo-Dananberg, L. M., Young, J. P., & Beresford, T. P. (1992). The Michigan Alcoholism Screening Test - Geriatric Version (MAST-G): A new elderly-specific screening instrument. *Alcoholism, 16*, 372.

Boszormenyi-Nagy, I., & Sparks, G. M. (1984). *Invisible loyalties*. New York: Brunner/Mazel.

Burns, B. J., & Taube, C. A. (1990). Mental health services in general medical care and nursing homes. In B. J. Fogel, A. Furino, & G. L. Gottlieb (Eds.), *Mental health policy for older Americans: Protecting minds at risk* (pp. 63-84). Washington, D.C.: American Psychiatric Press, Inc.

Burns, B. J., Wagner, R., Taube, J. E., Magaziner, J., Purmutt, T., & Landerman, L. R. (1993). Mental health service use by the elderly in nursing homes. *American Journal of Public Health, 83*, 331-337.

Carstensen, L. L. (1991). Socioemotional selectivity theory: Social activity in lifespan context. *Annual Review of Gerontology and Geriatrics, 11*, 195-217.

Cohler, B. J. (1988). The adult daughter-mother relationship: Perspectives from life-course family study and psychoanalysis. *Journal of Geriatric Psychiatry, 21*, 51-72.

DeRyke, S. C., Wieland, D., Wendland, C. J., & Helgeson, D. (1991). Psychologists serving elderly in long-term care facilities. *Clinical Gerontologist, 10*, 35-48.

Fillenbaum, G. & Smyer, M. (1981). The development, validity, and reliability of the OARS multidimensional functional assessment questionnaire. *Journal of Gerontology, 36*, 428-434.

Folstein, M. F., Folstein, S. E., & McHugh, P. R. (1975). Mini Mental State: A practical method for grading the cognitive state of patients for the clinician. *Journal of Psychiatric Research, 12*, 189-198.

Fry, P. S. (1986). Assessment of pessimism and despair in the elderly: A Geriatric Scale of Hopelessness. *Clinical Gerontologist, 5*, 193-201.

Gurland, B. & Wilder, D. (1984). The CARE interview revisited: Development of an efficient, systematic clinical assessment. *Journal of Gerontology, 39*, 129-137.

Hagestad, G. O. (1988). Demographic change and the life course: Some emerging trends in the family realm. *Family Relations, 37*, 405-410.

Herr, J. J., & Weakland, J. H. (1979). *Counseling elders and their families*. New York: Springer.

High, D. M., & Rowles, G. D. (1995). Nursing home residents, families, and decision making: Toward an understanding of progressive surrogacy. *Journal of Aging Studies, 9*, 101-117.

Jeste, D.V., Alexopoulos, G.S., Bartels, S.J., Cummings, J.L., Gallo, J.J., Gottlieb, G.L., Halpain, M.C., Palmer, B.W., Patterson, T.L., Reynolds, C.F., & Lebowitz, B.D. (1999). Consensus statement on the upcoming crisis in geriatric mental health: Research agenda for the next 2 decades. *Archives of General Psychiatry, 56*, 848-853.

Knight, B. G., & Kaskie, B. (1995). Models of mental health service delivery to older adults. In M. Gatz (Ed.), *Emerging issues in mental health and aging* (pp. 231-255). Washington, D.C: American Psychological Association Press.

Lawton, M. P., Moss, M., Fulcomer, M., & Kleban, M. H. (1982). A research and service oriented multilevel assessment instrument. *Journal of Gerontology, 37*, 91-99.

Lezak, M. D. (1995). *Neuropsychological assessment (3rd ed.)*. New York: Oxford

Lindenberger, U., Scherer, H., & Baltes, P. B. (2001). The strong connection between sensory and cognitive performance in old age: Not due to sensory acuity reductions operating during cognitive assessment. *Psychology and Aging, 16*, 196-205.

Manson, S.M., Ackerson, L.M., Wiegman, D. R., Baron, A. E., & Fleming, C. M. (1990). Depressive symptoms among American Indian adolescents: Psychometric characteristics of the Center for Epidemiologic Studies Depression Scales (CES-D). *Psychological Assessment: A Journal of Consulting and Clinical Psychology, 2(3)*, 231-237.

Mattis, S., Jurica, P. J., & Leitten, C. L. (2001). *Dementia Rating Scale-2*. Odessa, FL: Psychological Assessment Resources, Inc.

Mittelman, M. S., Ferris, S. H., Steinberg, G., Shulman, E., Mackell, J., Ambinder, A., & Cohen, J. (1993). An intervention that delays institutionalization of Alzheimer's disease patients: Treatment of spouse-caregivers. *The Gerontologist, 33*, 730-740.

Mitrushina, M. N., Boone, K. B., & D'Elia, L. F. (1999). *Handbook of normative data for neuropsychological assessment*. New York: Oxford.

Pruchno, R. A., Blow, F. D., & Smyer, M. A. (1984). Life events and interdependent lives: Implications for research and intervention. *Human Development, 27*, 31-41.

Qualls, S. H. (1995). Marital therapy with later life couples. *Journal of Geriatric Psychiatry, 28*, 139-163.

Radloff, L. S. (1977). The CES-D Scale: A self-report depression scale for research in the general population. *Applied Psychological Measurement, 1*, 385-401.

Roberts, R., Rhoades, H. M., & Vernon, S. W. (1990). Using the CES-D Scale to screen for depression and anxiety: Effects of language and ethnic status. *Psychiatry Research, 31*, 69-83.

Rook, K. S. (2000). The evolution of social relationships in later adulthood. In S. H. Qualls & N. Abeles (Eds.), *Psychology and the aging revolution* (pp. 173-191). Washington, D.C.: American Psychological Association.

Schulz, R., O'Brien, A. T., Bookwala, J., & Fleissner, K. (1995). Psychiatric and physical morbidity effects of dementia caregiving: Prevalence, correlates, and causes. *The Gerontologist, 35*, 771-791.

Segal, D. L., Coolidge, F. L., & Hersen, M. (1998). Psychological testing of older people. In I. H. Nordhus, G. R. VandenBos, S. Berg, & P. Fromholt (Eds.), *Clinical geropsychology* (pp. 231-257). Washington, DC: American Psychological Association.

Shields, C. G., King, D. A., & Wynne, L. C. (1995). Interventions with later life families. In R. H. Mikesell, D. Lusterman, & S. H. McDaniel (Eds.), *Integration family therapy: Handbook of family psychology and systems theory* (pp. 141-158). Washington, D.C.: American Psychological Association.

Spreen, O., & Strauss, E. (1998). *A compendium of neuropsychological tests: Administration, norms, and commentary* (2nd ed). New York: Oxford.

Stommel, M., Given, B. A., Given, C. W., Kalaian, H. A., Schulz, R., & McCorkle, R. (1993). Gender bias in the measurement properties of the Center for Epidemiologic Studies Depression Scale (CES-D). *Psychiatry Research, 49*, 239-250.

Stone, R., Cafferata, G. L., & Sangl, J. (1987). Caregivers of the frail elderly: A national profile. *The Gerontologist, 27*, 616-627

U.S. Bureau of the Census. (2000). *National population projections.* [On-line]. Available: *http://www.census.gov/population/www/projections/natproj.html.*

Wisocki, P. (1994). The experience of worry among the elderly. In G. Davey & F. Tallis (Eds.), *Worrying: Perspectives on theory, assessment and treatment* (pp. 247-261). New York: Wiley.

Yesavage, J. A., Brink, T. L., Rose, T. L., Lum, O., Huang, V., Adey, M. B., & Leirer, V. O. (1983). Development and validation of a geriatric depression screening scale: A preliminary report. *Journal of Psychiatric Research, 17*, 37-49.

Chapter 7

ASSESSMENT OF INFIDELITY

Tina Pittman Wagers[*]
Private Practice
Boulder, Colorado

INTRODUCTION

Data on the prevalence of infidelity is difficult to obtain, not only because people are often reluctant to report infidelity, especially in interviews and clinical situations, but also because definitions of infidelity vary widely from one person to the next. For example, this chapter includes emotional infidelity in its range of extramarital involvements, but not everyone shares that definition. 85% of respondents in the Sex in America survey expressed disapproval of infidelity (Laumann, Michael and Gagnon, 1994). 21% of men and 11% of women in the National Health and Social Life Survey (NHSLS; Laumann et al, 1994) reported extramarital involvement, though Schwartz and Rutter (1998) point out that underreports were possible with the methodology used. Other studies have found higher rates of extramarital involvement. Glass and Wright (1992), who included emotional infidelity, report that 44% of married men and 25% of married women had at least one extramarital involvement, and some estimates are higher. Far from benign, infidelity has ruinous consequences on marriages, though there is debate about these numbers, too. Janus and Janus (1993) found that 40% of divorced women and 44% of divorced men report extramarital sexual contact during their marriages. Infidelity is the most singularly identified problem that is correlated with divorce (Amato and Roberts, 1997.)

Infidelity is prevalent enough that clinicians may encounter it often, though they may not always accurately identify it. One study estimated that infidelity is the event that brings 25% of couples to couples treatment. In the course of treatment, another 30% of couples will reveal an infidelity (Glass and Wright, 1992). Clearly, couples therapists need to have tools and strategies for identifying, assessing and treating couples affected by infidelity. The present article identifies a model of infidelity and rationale for assessment of infidelity based

---

[*] Tina Pittman Wagers, M.S.W., Ph.D., is a Licensed Clinical Psychologist in Private Practice in Boulder, Colorado.

on data and other literature available on the topic to date. Although I refer to both couples and partners, most of the studies on infidelity have been conducted in heterosexual and married populations, so my conclusions and suggestions are limited to that population. Further, this chapter is written from a western cultural perspective, and it is acknowledged that different cultures may evidence different rates of, and attitudes towards, infidelity. This is not to suggest that infidelity is not problematic elsewhere in the world: one study suggests that infidelity is the most often cited reason for divorce among a number of cultures (Betzig, 1989).

ASSESSMENT OF INFIDELITY – A RARE OCCURRENCE

A problem that may bring over half of couples to treatment certainly deserves routine investigation, not only because of its direct role in treatment, but also because of the far-reaching consequences it can have, such as its role in divorce, effects on children, and involved parties' traumatic responses to infidelity. Yet there is little in the professional literature to suggest that clinicians regularly assess the presence or effects of infidelity. Although therapists regard infidelity as a significant issue in couples' treatment, most report they don't know how to treat in (Whisman et al, 1997). Though notable contributions have been made to the literature on infidelity treatment, (Pittman, 1989; Glass and Wright, 1997; Brown, 1991; Gordon and Baucom, 1999, Lusterman, 1999) one is nevertheless swayed by Neil Jacobson's observation that infidelity is the "dark underbelly" of couples therapy (1998). Like domestic violence and alcoholism, even very skilled couples therapists miss the opportunity to treat infidelity, primarily because they don't ask about it, and don't recognize infidelity as a possible issue.

Infidelity goes unaddressed far too often, lurking like so much rotting food under the bed of couples treatment and likely to cause confusion, wreak havoc, causing an indiscernible stench if it goes unrecognized for too long. Thus, the first recommendation is to ask about infidelity routinely, as you would ask about matters like history of violence, substance abuse, and whether a couple has children or not. Questions such as "Have there been any sexual or emotional infidelities in the relationship?" can convey to individuals and couples that the therapist is equipped to handle such information, thereby easing disclosure.

The inclusion of emotional relationships in the definition of infidelity raises some tricky issues around the definition of infidelity in general. What is infidelity, anyway? Are opposite sex friendships affairs (or same sex friendships for gay and lesbian clients?) How far into another relationship can one partner go before the original couples system is fractured? Glass and Wright's (1997) definition states that in emotional infidelity, there is greater emotional intimacy than in the marriage, there is secrecy and deception of the spouse, and there is sexual chemistry. But the definition of infidelity lies in the couples' perception of its own boundaries. Each couples' system has its own definition of what is infidelity and what is not, but the most commonly identified factor involves secretiveness, whether it is secretiveness around sex, around emotional issues, or around internet communication. It has been suggested that if one partner doesn't know whether something constitutes an affair or not, they should ask their partner (Pittman, 1989).

A DIFFERENT SYSTEMS PERSPECTIVE

How does infidelity occur in the first place? As psychotherapy has tried to understand infidelity through the years, the theoretical pendulum of how infidelity develops has swung widely from individual to systemic explanations, incorporating various degrees of theoretical and personal bias, and seem as diverse as people's experience of it.

One of the most important developments in the discourse on affairs has been the examination of the traumatic responses of the betrayed spouse. Just like domestic violence or alcoholism or the death of a child, once infidelity occurs, it certainly does belong to the couples system as a major problem, potentially lethal to the relationship, but that does not mean that the couples' system caused the infidelity. Infidelity is often a calamitous event which fractures the system. It can be sexual or emotional, but in either case is outside the bounds of most couples' contracts with each other (with a few notable exceptions). The behaviors of an unfaithful partner serve to change the couples' system fundamentally. The emotional and/or sexual secrets disconnect the partners from one another, and bond one partner to his or her affair partner. Research has supported the notion that the more secretive the relationship, the more attractive it becomes (Descoll, Davis and Lipetz, 1972). The impact of this secretiveness and betrayal to the system can be profound. To discover infidelity is to discover a rupture in an individual's most relevant, most intimate, most important system, and the emotional fallout is enormous.

Infidelity occurs in both happy and unhappy marriages, though infidelity undeniably has the potential to make a happy marriage unhappy pretty quickly. The data on the correlation between marital distress and infidelity so far do not support the notion that infidelity is caused by marital distress, although marital distress may be part of the context of infidelity for some, and research suggests that more women than men are likely to report such distress. Glass and Wright (1992) report that only 30% of men who had been involved in infidelity reported marital distress before their affair, while 60% of women were unhappy before their affair. Similar findings are reported by Hunt (1969). One caution in interpreting these findings is that the results reported are retrospective. Asked about their marital satisfaction after they had already had the affair, involved partners may have developed a post-hoc explanation of why the affair occurred to reduce their own cognitive dissonance, resulting in an inflated estimation of pre-marital distress. This phenomenon of making external vs. internal attributions of problems has certainly been observed in people's post-hoc explanations of divorce (Amato and Rogers, 1997; Rasmussen & Ferraro, 1979). Similarly, in cases of infidelity, betrayed spouses tend to blame marital problems on the infidelity, and infidels blame the infidelity on marital distress (Spanier and Margolis, 1983). Many involved partners may not even recognize the presence of distress in their marriage before the infidelity occurs, at which point, they justify their behavior through the identification or magnification of some relational flaw. These involved partners may make statements, uttered or silent, such as "the relationship I had with Bill/Terry/Amanda made me realize how empty my marriage had been" or " I needed more excitement/adoration/attention/sex than I had in my marriage." A tempered clinical expectation with which to approach these cases is that in something less than 60% of cases where the woman was the involved spouse, and in something less than 30% of cases where the husband was, a therapist is likely to discover a history of distress which predates the infidelity. Even given the presence of distress in the relationship that precedes infidelity, the affair cannot be viewed as having been caused by the distress, no more than abusive behavior or alcoholism can be viewed as caused by relationship distress. While pre-existing marital distress can be regarded as one factor that may have pushed the unfaithful spouse closer to a decision point, at which point they entered an affair, other individuals at the same decision point might have chosen to enter counseling, buy a new car, change their behavior, or start exercising. That individual's decision making still needs to be a focus of assessment and treatment.

ASSESSMENT IN GENERAL

Assessment starts at the beginning of treatment, and although the biggest piece of assessment takes place at the beginning of treatment, assessment should be ongoing throughout the therapist's contact with the couple. Assessment should be a fluid process, responsive to the changes that occur as treatment progresses. Some formal assessment instruments may be helpful to the clinician for gathering specific information about symptoms the partners may be experiencing, about aspects of the affair, and also about the relationship in general, and some suggestions along those lines will be discussed below. However, as Nichols and Schwartz (1995) suggest, clinicians are cautioned not to rely so heavily on formalized assessment instruments that an artificial atmosphere is created, possibly quashing natural interaction during the session. The topic of infidelity is delicate, painful and needs to be accomplished with respect, sensitivity and attention to non-verbal cues and the therapeutic relationship. Attending to relevant information is greatly enhanced when it is included in the context of the therapeutic hour.

Assessment is inextricably intertwined with treatment. Decisions the therapist makes about how and when to ask a question, and how to respond to the information gathered, need to guide the treatment plan. This chapter suggests a structure for assessment that incorporates stages of treatment suggested in the literature on infidelity.

THE ROLE OF INDIVIDUAL SESSIONS IN ASSESSMENT OF INFIDELITY

The majority of the current chapter discusses assessment (and treatment) strategies to be used in couples' sessions. Infidelity is not truly resolved until the couples' system copes with the crisis it presents to the system, understands its meaning, and makes a decision about how to move forward. Couples' sessions are certainly the most favored arena in which assessment and treatment tasks can be accomplished. However, there are some circumstances wherein the clinician may have contact with an individual affected by infidelity.

If a client in individual treatment discloses involvement in, or suspects a spouse's involvement in an affair, efforts should be made to engage the couple in treatment as soon as possible, assuming that couples' treatment is not contraindicated for reasons of safety or other urgent matters. The risks of not doing so are that the individual will develop a distorted perception of the infidelity as an individual rather than a systems issue, or become entrenched in his or her own justifications around the causes of the affair, which may rely on distortions of the marital relationship. A more thorough discussion of justification for affairs can be found below.

Of course, sometimes individuals have no interest in salvaging the couples' relationship, in which case the therapist can give the client honest feedback about the situation, but sometimes little else.

> Kim A. presented for only one treatment session, for reasons which will become clear. She joyfully described her affair with a man in another state. They had devised a plan for her to leave her husband and move to this other state to marry him and help run his profitable business. She described her marriage of 12 years as initially strong, but now only adequate, and lacking in sexual excitement and adventure, especially since the adoption of their 5 year old son. Besides, the new relationship presented the possibility of a new professional partnership, since she and the affair partner were in the same field. The question she posed to me was this: when would it be a good time for her son for his parents to divorce, and his mother to move with him to another state? I suggested that maybe when her son was 25 or 30 it would be easier, and that maybe she should reveal her plans to her husband and seek couples treatment before making her decision.
> She didn't come back.

Some debate has existed about the advisability of individual assessment sessions, though Glass and Wright (1997) Lusterman (1999) and Gordon and Baucom (1999) tout their utility. From an assessment standpoint, these sessions can provide a crucial opportunity to gather more information about the infidelity, assess each partner's functioning more accurately, including assessment of individual psychopathology, get individual histories and histories of relationships, clarify more about individual goals, view of the affair and even safety issues than might be possible or comfortable in conjoint sessions. On the other hand, this method of assessment can have a significant effect on the process of treatment. The possibility of adding more secretiveness to the system, when secretiveness around the infidelity has been so damaging, may be anxiety-producing for some partners. If conducting an individual session with each spouse at the beginning of treatment, the clinician would be well-advised to provide a comprehensible rationale to the couple for such sessions, and define the bounds of confidentiality in a manner with which both partners are comfortable.

Clinicians conducting couples' treatment are certainly cautioned about ongoing individual contact with one partner of which the other partner is unaware, but sometimes clients don't follow this rule. I once had one woman corner me in the bathroom where she hurriedly told me a detail about her affair that she had yet to disclose to her husband. One of the most awkward, and potentially damaging, a therapist can do is to harbor a secret about an affair from one partner.

> A therapist acquaintance, relatively new to the field, was treating a couple, and making little progress in treatment. Two months into treatment she got a phone call from the husband of the couple, who asked her if he could reveal something in confidence. She unfortunately agreed, out of her own frustration with the treatment process, and the hope that his revelation would help her be more effective with the couple. He disclosed the presence of an affair, but stated he did not want the affair to be revealed to the wife. The therapist pleaded with the husband to reveal the affair, offered to reveal it herself, and devised a plan where they could reveal it together, but to no avail. In this case, sadly, the therapy was terminated when the husband told his wife he didn't want to work with the therapist, leaving the therapist feeling quite ineffective and awkward.

Other alternatives are available to termination might have included bringing up the affair in couples' sessions as a hypothesis, thereby pushing the unfaithful spouse towards a disclosure (Pittman and Wagers, 1995) or clarifying at the beginning of treatment that secrets from either partner would not be kept by the therapist. Tricky situations may arise in these cases, but the point here is to not let inappropriate secretiveness be a by-product of assessment fervor. Secrets are damaging to couples' progress, and, in some situations, therapists' secrets are no different than anyone else's in their ability to compound the damage wrought by the affair.

Sometimes an individual seen in couples' treatment is also in individual therapy, and their therapist sometimes knows details about the affair which have not yet been revealed to their partner or to the couples' therapist. While it is responsible to get a release of information to talk to the individual therapist, parameters should be set around the information to be shared so as not to put the couples' therapist in the position of keeping secrets from the other partner. Ideally, information to be shared should pertain to that individual's psychological functioning, history, relevant safety issues, such as history of suicide attempts, and the like.

THE REVELATION OF THE AFFAIR AND INITIAL PHASE OF ASSESSMENT

During the first phase of treatment, obtaining information about safety, couples' basic functioning, traumatic and other emotional reactions, and definition of treatment goals takes priority.

In order to assess, and hopefully to treat, effects of infidelity, the affair first has to be revealed. Sometimes, by the first phone call, the affair has been revealed to, or discovered by, the betrayed spouse. In these circumstances, therapists should note who is calling, how they sound on the phone, how urgent their request for an appointment is, how they state the nature of the problem, and what questions they ask of the therapist. Such observations may yield useful information about goals, investment in treatment and current level of distress.

Alternatively, the affair may be revealed in session, and the first steps of assessment may include observations of who tells the therapist, how they relay that information, affect and non-verbal behavior displayed by each partner, and initial descriptions of what happened and how the affair was discovered or revealed. The importance of this last point is illustrated in the following case:

> Mrs. G. discovered her husband's affair after his affair partner had broken off the relationship and the devastated husband had written the affair partner a letter on their home computer, and left a draft of the letter in the trash can, which Mrs. G. emptied the next day. Mrs. G. kept telling Mr. G. how much better she would have felt if he had just confessed the affair to her. Indeed, rebuilding trust in the relationship took a long time, as Mrs. G. kept wondering if Mr. G. would have ever revealed the affair to her directly.

In some cases, the couple is already in treatment, ostensibly working on another agenda, when the affair is revealed by the involved spouse, or discovered by the betrayed spouse (the former is usually better, especially when accompanied by an appropriate expression of remorse). Situations which present more difficulty to the therapist are those in which the affair may be suspected by the therapist and needs to be investigated. Pittman and Wagers (1995) discuss a case in which the couple presented for treatment and the husband complained about his sudden unhappiness with the marriage. His surprised wife dutifully set about losing weight, changing her behavior, and essentially meeting all of the demands that he had said would make him more satisfied. Still, it was not enough. Suspecting an affair, the possibility was raised by the therapist in statements such as: "Your behavior reminds me of someone who's having an affair" and "If I were your spouse I'd wonder what else was going on that's affecting your view of the marriage, like an affair." Indeed, an affair was revealed and treatment of the infidelity could begin.

SAFETY FIRST

Experts in treatment of infidelity generally agree that the first step in treatment involves attending to the impact of the affair, along with the accompanying threats to safety and emotional turmoil (Glass and Wright, 1997; Gordon and Baucom, 1999; Lusterman, 1999; Pittman and Wagers, 1995). Even if the couple presented for treatment with a different agenda, once an infidelity is revealed, the treatment plan changes focus, and the impact of the affair takes precedence.

The first order of business is a safety assessment. Infidelity by a female partner is strongly correlated with domestic violence and spousal homicide (Daly and Wilson, 1988). Assess any suicidal or homicidal ideation, plan or intent. Conduct a suicide lethality assessment by asking about suicidal thoughts, and if an affirmative answer is obtained, follow up by asking about some of the factors that have been associated with increased risk of suicide. Risk factors include a specific plan that is likely to succeed, feeling of hopelessness or depression, a significant object loss associated with the current crisis (certainly relevant here, as the betrayed spouse has lost the relationship they thought they had, and both partners may be considering divorce), past suicide attempts by the client and past completed suicide by family members or friends (France, 1999). Be aware that the partner who has had the affair is sometimes in as much distress as the partner who has just discovered their liaison. During this first step of assessment, the clinician needs to be sensitive to the therapeutic needs of the couple, and be willing to weave assessment and intervention together so that basic therapeutic goals, such as establishing safety, calming things down, giving the couple a framework by which to communicate with each other, can still be accomplished relatively quickly.

Related to this portion of the safety assessment is an assessment of how the couple is communicating with each other, both at home and in the therapists' office. Although it is vital for couples to talk to each other during this phase of treatment, and the intensity of emotion is understandably high, the level of conflict, and any real or perceived risk of physical aggression needs to be assessed. The therapist should ask about the couples' ability to take time outs, or otherwise safely de-escalate their interactions. The therapist should assess the couple's ability to engage in healthy patterns of communication that include listening, empathizing and appropriate expression of affect. Such communication skills play a part in healing from the wounds of infidelity (Glass and Wright, 1997; Gordon and Baucom, 1999) and in the long-term viability of the marriage (Markman, 1997).

Assess level of functioning to determine whether both parties are capable of caring for themselves and any children that may be involved. Even if the couple does not present a threat to themselves or each other, sometimes there exist threats from or towards third parties. In any of these cases, work out a safety plan, contract for safety where needed, and contact appropriate authorities, or help the couple do so, when necessary. It may also be necessary to enact a duty to warn plan. The DSM-IV's Global Assessment of Functioning scores should elucidate when individuals need an increased level of support with basic functioning.

ASSESSING TREATMENT AGENDAS

Once safety has been assured, it is important to ascertain why a couple is seeking treatment in the first place. Each partner may have different ideas about what they want to accomplish in general, and around an infidelity in particular. Goals may range from wanting the affair to stop, wanting to decide whether to leave the marriage, wanting to keep their options open, wanting to drop off their marital partner in a therapists' office on their way off into the sunset with their affair partner, wanting to put the affair behind them, or, as one betrayed partner recently expressed, wanting to use the revelation of the affair to work on long-standing issues in the marriage.

Individual assessment sessions, as mentioned above, can provide an important venue for discussion of partners' treatment goals. It should come as no surprise that sometimes individuals are not particularly forthright about their agendas, even in individual assessment sessions, so the therapist will need to assess agendas from non-verbal cues, compliance with treatment, and follow-through with homework assignments. One communication phenomenon that has been observed in couples experiencing infidelity is that partners who have been unfaithful, but are motivated to maintain the marriage will use concessions and excuses more often. However, when the transgressor is not as motivated to work on the marriage, the clinician will observe the use of more justifications and refusals in embedded in their explanations of the affair (Benoit and Drew, 1997). Although it is often the person involved in the affair who is deceitful about their treatment goals, sometimes a betrayed partner is equally dishonest.

> Mr. K. dutifully attended treatment with his wife after she revealed her 6 month long affair with a co-worker, and though he told the therapist he wanted to work on the marriage, he did so only half-heartedly. After the marriage (not surprisingly) ended, Mr.K. revealed his relief at the discovery of her affair, since it gave him a way to exit the marriage "without looking like the bad guy." It seems that his true agenda in couples' therapy had been to show up for long enough to cement his role as the innocent victim.

For couples who are committed to working on their relationship, contact with the affair partner has to be stopped immediately (Glass and Wright, 1997; Gordon and Baucom, 1999; Pittman and Wagers, 1995). Stopping the affair is an important part of establishing safety, and, to use Glass and Wright's terminology (1997), integral to the goal of erecting a wall between the involved spouse and the affair partner, while re-establishing windows between the involved and betrayed partners. The clinician will have to continually assess the status of the affair, how feasible the involved partners' plan is for ceasing contact, and whether the betrayed spouse feels assured that the affair has indeed ended. If the affair partner is a work colleague, or if there remain opportunities or obligations for continued contact between the involved spouse and the affair partner, the clinician needs to asses if and how any contact with the affair partner is relayed to the spouse, and how the spouse is coping with that information.

Glass and Wright have observed that ongoing disruptions, analogous to the aftershocks following an earthquake, can hinder recovery (1997). In cases of infidelity, aftershocks can take the form of continued contact with the affair partner, or discovery of additional information related to the affair, or even unrelated stressors, such as children's problems and job pressures. It is important to monitor how each partner is coping with ongoing disruptions in the environment, and how the couples system is responding to these disruptions.

TRAUMATIC REACTIONS

Glass and Wright (1997), Gordon and Baucom (1999) and Lusterman (1999), have all elaborated on models of treatment that view infidelity as a trauma in the life of the couple, and the experience of betrayed spouses as similar to other individuals struggling with post-traumatic symptoms. Within this model, treatment is focused on various strategies for helping the couple arrive at a resolution of the trauma.

Assessment needs to include an examination of possible symptoms resembling those associated with Post-Traumatic Stress Disorder. In his discussion of symptoms experienced by individuals confronted with disasters, France points out that common reactions to events such as hurricanes and terrorist attacks include "confusion, disorganization and emotional numbness." (1999, p.) Discoverers of infidelity can experience symptoms such as sleep disturbance, irritability or anger outbursts, difficulty concentrating, hypervigilance, exaggerated startle response, and recurrent intrusive thoughts about the affair. Avoidance of stimuli associated with the affair is also an important symptom for some partners and couples. For example, if the betrayed spouse's emotions during this initial phase of treatment avoided and unexpressed, there is a risk of long-term resentment and hostility, suggest Gordon and Baucom (1999). Assessment in these cases needs to be a more active process of questioning and investigating the possible presence of symptoms, even if one partner is reluctant to open up. DSM-IV criteria for Post-Traumatic Stress Disorder can provide a framework for the clinician interviewing a betrayed spouse for presence of such symptoms.

More severe traumatic reactions should be expected for partners according to the degree to which their assumptions or expectations about their couples' relationship are contradicted by the discovery of infidelity. The spouse of a habitual philanderer who discovers yet another affair may be angry, depressed, insecure or resentful, or perhaps all of these, but will probably not be traumatized to the same extent as the wife who never suspected that her husband would be unfaithful. A lack of emotional responsiveness to the discovery of an infidelity may therefore be an indication to the clinician of the betrayed spouse's pre-discovery assumptions about their spouse, or about the fragility of their connection. However, the clinician may also hypothesize that emotional numbing is operating in these cases. Asking the betrayed spouse about their prior assumptions about the marriage and their partner is a valuable piece of assessment and may help the clinician make a more accurate assessment of symptoms.

Glass and Wright (1997) and Lusterman (1999) both point out that traumatic reactions are normal responses, and need to be explained as such in the course of treatment. Glass and Wright even suggest handing out the criteria to individuals struggling with these symptoms as a reminder that they are not alone, and the symptoms are to be expected. The "normality" of traumatic symptoms in this context does not preclude an ongoing monitoring by the therapist of the severity of these symptoms, as well as their interference in one or both partners' functioning. Therapist and client can devise monitoring sheets to track presence and severity of traumatic symptoms between sessions.

Therapists should be aware that infidelity does not meet the DSM-IV criteria for a life-threatening event, so assigning a diagnosis of PTSD would be inappropriate. Diagnostic alternatives to be considered here include adjustment reactions, or other depression or anxiety disorders.

As in other disastrous, or potentially disastrous events that people face in the course of their lives, a number of factors influence development of symptoms, and recovery from trauma, and these factors also need to be assessed and monitored. It is widely agreed that social support is an important mitigator of traumatic reactions (Barlow and Durand, 2001; Carroll, Ruger, Foy and Donahoe, 1985). Clinicians should assess what kind of support is available to the couple, individuals' skills in accessing support, the extent to which it is accessed, and whether support is accessed inappropriately– for example, if partners are talking to younger children about the crisis. Other factors which render individuals more vulnerable to the effects of trauma, including prior exposure to trauma, early family instability, a family history of anxiety disorders, and effectiveness of coping skills (Brown and Barlow, 1999; Barlow and Durand, 2001) can be screened in individual or couples' sessions. Communication skills and beliefs of self-efficacy can contribute to resilience to the effects of trauma (v and v, 1999) and should also be assessed.

RANGE OF REACTIONS

Clinicians need to be aware of the range of emotional reactions that are possible in couples where infidelity is, or has been, an issue. Besides traumatic reactions, feelings of anger, sadness, helplessness, hopelessness, isolation, shame, confusion and anxiety are not uncommon. Even before its discovery, partners may report intense and often confusing feelings that they can later relate to the infidelity.

> Mr. H. presented for treatment with his wife following his discovery of her affair. He described feeling for several months that something was wrong, that the tension in the relationship was palatable, that he felt frustrated and helpless by changes in the relationship to which he could attribute no cause until his wife's affair was discovered. Upon discovery, Mr. H. first experienced relief that there had been a reason for his confusing feelings. That sense of relief was followed by a cascade of more typical negative reactions, such as anger, resentment and hopelessness about the relationship.

Different infidelity types may yield differential reactions as well – for example, Shackelford, LeBlanc and DeGrass (2000) found that reactions such as repulsion and nausea may more frequently follow sexual infidelity, while undesirable or insecure feelings may follow emotional infidelity.

Data on the experience of the unfaithful spouse is less clear. Clinical observations suggest that many involved partners have convinced themselves that the primary marital relationship is fundamentally flawed, and must confront feelings of guilt, hopelessness about the marriage, fear of their spouse's response and feelings of loss around the breakup of the affair. Buss and Shackelford also observe that anguish, psychological pain, depression, anger and humiliation can be part of the picture (1997). Depending on the type of affair and personality traits of the involved spouse, other reactions can include indifference or even self-righteousness.

There is some evidence for the existence of gender differences in reactions to infidelity. For example, in one study of college students' predicted reactions to a partner's infidelity, homicidal and suicidal feelings were more frequently predicted for men, and feelings of undesirability and insecurity were more likely to be reported by women (Buss and Shackelford). Although some efforts have been made to demonstrate that women are more upset by emotional infidelity, and men by sexual infidelity, at least one study using physiological reactivity measures (Harris, 2000) failed to support this notion. Instead, women with committed sexual relationships showed reactivity to emotional vs. sexual infidelity that was similar to that of men. The negative impact of marital distress on emotional well-being, especially in women, should be well known by now, as it has been demonstrated in a number of sound studies (Whisman and Bruce, 1999; Jacobson, Dobson, Fruzzetti, Schmaling and Salusky, 1991; Christian, O'Leary and Vivian, 1994). But infidelity presents a much more risky context in which depression may develop. Cano and O'Leary's (2000) recent study demonstrated that events such as infidelity and other Humiliating Marital Events, as they are labeled by the authors, render women perhaps 6 times more likely to develop Major Depression compared to women experiencing garden-variety discord.

So what are we to make of all of the possible ways people can react to infidelity? Many variables that converge in couples' reactions to an infidelity, such as the manner of discovery, the degree to which prior assumptions are shattered, gender differences, individual history and social support. Only a thorough interview and careful attention to verbal and non-verbal expression of emotions is likely to result in an accurate assessment of reactions to infidelity.

ASSESSMENT OF COUPLE'S FUNCTIONING

Basic aspects of couples' functioning, such as communication, satisfaction and level of commitment, should be assessed during the first phase of treatment. While both partners are reeling from the impact of the discovery of the affair, it may be difficult to get an accurate picture of the couples' functioning before the current crisis. Information gathered about general aspects of couples' functioning during the initial phase of treatment should be interpreted cautiously, and clinicians should be aware that a more accurate picture may develop as the crisis becomes resolved and the couple is experiencing less acute distress. Nonetheless, this is an area where a formal assessment instrument can be helpful. For example, measures such as the Dyadic Adjustment Scale (Spanier and Cole, 1974) or the Locke-Wallace Marital Adjustment Test (Locke and Wallace, 1959) both measure several aspects of the couples' functioning, and are relatively short, easily administered and non-intimidating paper and pencil tests. The DAD includes subscales measuring dyadic consensus, satisfaction, cohesion and expression of affection. This last subscale is less reliable than the others, so needs to be interpreted cautiously. The Locke-Wallace Marital Adjustment Test measures global happiness, areas of disagreement, conflict resolution, cohesion and communication. Although the Locke-Wallace is the gold standard of marital adjustment assessment measures, the language in the DAS does not assume a marital status, which might be an advantage for some populations (Fredman and Sherman, 1987). Although not designed as a pre-post test measure, it may be clinically helpful to readminister a formal assessment measure in a later phase of treatment as the couple begins to examine other issues in their relationship besides the initial, all-consuming trauma of infidelity.

Although an abundance of pre-existing issues may be presented by the couple (or, even more likely, by the partner who participated in the affair, which can deflect attention away from the initial painful process of working through the consequences of the affair), thorough examination and treatment of the marital issues needs to occur after the crisis of the affair is addressed, and trust is being rebuilt. It is not unlike presenting for a medical appointment with chest pain. While the patient's eczema may have been a problem for quite some time, it is the chest pain that is potentially lethal and needs assessment and treatment right away.

ASSESSING THE CONTEXT OF THE AFFAIR

As treatment proceeds, and the couple moves into later phases of therapy, both partners need to develop a thorough understanding of what has happened (Glass and Wright, 1997; Gordon and Baucom, 1999; Pittman and Wagers, 1995; Lusterman, 1999). Distinct tasks of assessment related to this portion of treatment include assessment of the couple's history, assessment of individualistic issues of the involved partner, and assessment of the type of affair.

HISTORY OF THE RELATIONSHIP

This piece of assessment may be trickiest of all because even asking questions about history and prior difficulties or areas of dissatisfaction can feel to betrayed partners like "blaming the victim." There is also the risk that focusing to histories of difficulties can contribute to the involved partners' inappropriate justifications for the affair. It may be helpful to some couples to preface the exploration of history with an observation that there is a distinction between "contributing to the context of the affair versus being responsible for engaging in the affair" (Gordon and Baucom, 1999).

Descriptions can be gathered about the couple's initial attachment, pre-morbid functioning, stressors (both internal and external) and prior history of treatment. Part of a couple's history includes their descriptions of positive things about relationship, including what first attracted the partners to each other, descriptions of tough times they have navigated before, and what facilitated those efforts, and what in the past has made them feel hopeful about and committed to the relationship. If a couple's communication skills are adequate, the clinician can have spouses question each other about these issues. Alternatively, the clinician can pose the questions to each spouse individually, while the other partner listens (Glass and Wright, 1997).

INDIVIDUALISTIC ISSUES

One crucial issue to understand is how the involved partner came to view infidelity as an acceptable, desirable or even reasonable behavior or solution. Clinicians can look for clues to the involved partner's choice within the couples' system, which may occasionally yield information in some situations and in some types of affairs. More likely, answers will be found in other systems in which the unfaithful spouse has been involved, such as their family of origin, their peer group, or the system which provided the opportunity for the affair. Even the culture in which we live often unwittingly promotes romantic affairs as a solution to many of life's tedious dissatisfactions. Clinicians can explore the involved partner's descriptions of affairs that have occurred in their social and family environment, the consequences for those behaviors, and what their attitudes and beliefs were about those involvements. Ideally, this material can be discussed in conjoint sessions, so the spouse has the opportunity to understand their partners' belief system and individual vulnerabilities around infidelity.

Glass' Extramarital Justification Questionnaire (1980) can be administered at this stage of treatment, or even at the beginning of treatment, in order to assess how an involved partner may justify their extramarital involvement. People who have entered into affairs often have a good deal of trouble coming to terms with the significance of this decision. Indeed, for many, their infidelity signifies such a departure from their own values and self-image that they are desperate to explain it to themselves and to those around them. As they try to explain their infidelity, it is not uncommon for affair participants to come up with rationalizations such as "I was never in love with my husband/wife/partner" or "My marriage was a mistake." It may make sense to remind couples of the truism, proclaimed by the wise Salvador Minuchin (1999) that "Every marriage is a mistake. Some people just cope with their mistakes better than others." At the very least, though, the clinician should take whatever explanation is offered with a grain of salt. It is important to include a large margin of error in people's self-assessments to make room for the wacky ways people contend with cognitive dissonance.

In the interest of the future of the relationship, though, it is always important to explore what other alternatives people see, and have seen, to the affair. What other ways did they try to address their own dissatisfaction? What other ways can they think of to try to feel more excitement in their relationship? How can they participate more effectively in their own lives, and in the lives of their family?

The clinician should also be aware of individual psychopathology issues, and screen for the presence of Narcissistic, Antisocial, Borderline or Histrionic personality traits or disorders, and for substance abuse and signs of psychosis. Another disorder that may be identified includes Bipolar Disorder. Manic episodes may pose a particular vulnerability to sexual acting-out behaviors (Pittman and Wagers, 1995). The presence of individual psychopathology suggests a poor prognosis and presents a greater risk for future infidelities.

The story of the affair must include an understanding of the type of affair, and its relation to, or isolation from, the marriage. Two distinct proposals of types of affairs in the literature (Pittman 1989; Brown, 1991) differ significantly in terms of their view of the couples' role in infidelity. Brown sees infidelity as directly connected to couples' functioning, while Pittman places the responsibility of the affair squarely on the shoulders of the involved partner. As discussed earlier, some affairs seem to have nothing to do with the marriage, while other times affairs do seem more strongly linked to the context of the relationship, even if the involved partners' distorted, desperate, or indifferent decision making is the pivotal factor which begins the infidelity. Almost always, the type of affair identified is reflective of some model of relationships presented in the involved partner's family of origin or social environment. Clinicians are encouraged to assess the type of affair the involved partner has had with a range of possibilities in mind.

Affairs can be **accidental,** and the involved partner may describe it as unexpected, and assert that they did not seek it out. Accidental infidels, prior to the unexpected affair, did not usually think of themselves as being in love with the affair partner, though they may later justify the affair by stating that they were. They usually feel awkward, uncomfortable, and embarrassed about the affair. They know they have done something wrong, but were too curious, too polite, too accommodating, too friendly or too unskilled at maintaining appropriate boundaries to stop it. (Pittman, 1989, Pittman and Wagers, 1995).

Some involved partners are **philanderers,** who require a steady change of partner, and can't commit to just one relationship. Male philanderers are quite concerned with masculinity, which to them means obtaining victories over women. Charming philanderers have polished social skills, and are usually attractive and confident. Friendly philanderers are in awe of women. Hostile philanderers find danger sexually exciting, and seek relationships that are hostile and overtly threatening. Sexual hobbyists have affairs that they keep secret from their wives, and reassure themselves that this is only fair, given the mythic proportions of their sexual needs. In this framework, women philanderers are rare, and can only meet the criteria after they have given up all romantic and idealistic expectations of men and marriage. (Pittman, 1989; Pittman and Wagers, 1995).

Romantic affairs are committed by people experiencing a temporary form of insanity, convinced that falling in love provides a reasonable excuse to become involved with an affair partner. It usually occurs at times of crisis or instability in the marriage, such as when children arrive, when a relationship becomes too settled, when the children leave home, or when other crises in the environment are encountered (Pittman, 1989; Pittman and Wagers, 1995).

Another type of affair which involves unsolved marital problems is the **marital arrangements.** These affairs can be agreed on, overtly or covertly, by partners who wish to stabilize some dynamic of their relationship, much like importing a third leg into a wobbly two-legged stool of a relationship. Marital arrangements can be found in the relationships of spouses who are not quite married, but not quite divorced either. They exist in the marriages of "psychiatric nurses" to their spouse-patients, who choose affairs with affair partners who can provide some caretaking for the nurse. Marital arrangements also crop up in the relationships of individuals who are uninterested in sex, or unable to perform sexually, and whose spouses import sex from elsewhere. (Pittman, 1989; Pittman and Wagers, 1995).

Brown (1991) also posits that some affairs are designed to get the attention of their conflict-avoidant spouses, to avoid developing real intimacy in the marriage, or to spur the marriage towards termination in favor of another more hopeful relationship.

To tease out the type of affair, the clinician can ask the involved partner what happened, what the appeal of the affair was, how it felt to be involved in the affair and what the motivating factors in becoming involved were. Glass and Wright (1997) also suggest asking the partner how they were different in the other relationship, which is extrememely relevant. An understanding of the type of affair can help the clinician, and, most importantly, the spouse, understand more about what happened, what their partner's vulnerabilities are, what issues still need to be addressed by the individual or within the relationship.

ASSESSMENT OF HEALING AND MOVING FORWARD

Assessment of the couple's commitment to the relationship should take place throughout, via observation and direct questioning (such as: "Having heard all of these details about the affair, are you still committed to reconstructing the marriage?"). The couple's skills and ways of handling emotion still needs to progress through the final stages of treatment, when couples are consolidating their understanding of the story of the affair and any relevant contextual issues, and are hopefully moving forward. Clinicians should assess the couple's capacity for understanding the involved partner's vulnerabilities, and the vulnerabilities of the couple. Communication and conflict management skills should be assessed at the beginning of treatment, as discussed, and this assessment should continue until termination. The couple's capacity for mutual empathy and a shared responsibility for changes in the future need to be assessed as well. Trust level needs to be assessed, though it is recognized that rebuilding trust is a long process. Therefore, relevant questions around trust may involve whether the partners can identify steps towards the rebuilding of trust, and how much confidence they have in their ability to execute the steps.

The notion of forgiveness has been included in several recent treatment models (DiBlasio, Gordon and Baucom, 1999; Glass and Wright, 1997;) Some clinicians may include the concept of forgiveness in treatment, which may be appropriate and helpful in some cases, but not until the end of treatment. If so, the clinician needs to carefully assess the couples' understanding of the concept, the betrayed spouse's capacity for forgiveness, and the role of any resistance to forgiveness.

REFERENCES

American Psychiatric Association. (1994). *Diagnostic and statistical manual of mental disorders* (4th ed.). Washington, DC: Author.

Amato, P. & Rogers, S. (1997). A longitudinal study of marital problems and subsequent divorce. *Journal of Marriage and the Family, 59(3)*, 612-624.

Barlow, D.H. & Durand, V.M. (1999). *Abnormal psychology: An integrative approach.* Belmont, CA: Wadsworth Publishing Company.

Betzig, L. (1989). Causes of conjugal dissolution: A cross-cultural study. *Current Anthropology, 30*, 654-676.

Brown, E. (1991). *Patterns of infidelity and their treatment.* New York: Brunner/ Mazel.

Brown, T.A. & Barlow, D.H. (2001). *Casebook in abnormal psychology.* Pacific Grove, CA: Wadsworth Publishing Company.

Buss, D.M. & Shackelford, T. K. (1997). Susceptibility to infidelity in the first year of marriage. *Journal of Research in Personality, 31*, 193-221.

Cano, A. & O'Leary, D. (2000). Infidelity and separations precipitate major depressive episodes and symptoms of nonspecific depression and anxiety. *Journal of Consulting and Clinical Psychology, 68(5)*, 774-781.

Christian, J.L., O'Leary, K.D. & Vivian, D. (1994). Depressive symptomatology in maritally discordant women and men: The role of individual and relationship variables. *Journal of Family Psychology, 8*, 32-42.

France, K. (1998) Crisis Intervention. In G. Koocher, Norcross, J., Hill, S. (Eds.) *Psychologists' Desk Reference* (pp. 294-297). New York: Oxford Press.

Fredman, N. & Sherman, R. (1987). *Handbook of measurements for marriage and family therapy.* New York: Brunner Mazel.

Glass, S.P. (1981). Sex differences in the relationship between satisfaction with various aspects of marriage and types of extramarital involvements (doctoral dissertation, Catholic University, 1980). *Dissertation Abstracts International, 41(10)*, 3889B.

Glass, S.P. & Wright, T. L. (1992). Justifications for extramarital involvement: the association between attitudes, behavior, and gender. *Journal of Sex Research, 29(3)*, 361-387.

Glass, S.P. & Wright, T.L. (1997). Reconstructing marriages after the trauma of infidelity. In W.K. Halford & H.J. Markman (Eds.) *Clinical handbook of marriage and couples interventions* (pp. 471-507). Chichister: Wiley.

Gordon, K.C. & Baucom, D.H. (1999). A multitheoretical intervention for promoting recovery from extramarital affairs. *Clinical psychology: Science and practice 6(4)*, 382-399.

Harris, C. (2000). Psychophysiological responses to imagined infidelity: the specific innate modular view of jealousy reconsidered. *Journal of Personality and Social Psychology*, 78(6), 1082-1091.

Hunt, M. (1969). *The affair*. New York: World Publishing Company.

Jacobson, N., Dobson, K., Fruzzetti, A.E., Schmaling, K.B. & Salusky, S. (1991). Marital therapy as a treatment for depression. *Journal of consulting and clinical psychology, 59*, 547-557.

Janus, S.S. & Janus, C. L. (1993). *The Janus report on sexual behavior.* New York: Wiley.

Lawson, A. (1988). *Adultery.* New York: Basic Books.

Lusterman, D.D. (1998). Treatment of marital infidelity. In G. Koocher, Norcross, J., Hill, S. (Eds.) *Psychologists' Desk Reference*. New York: Oxford Press.

Mongeau, P. & Schulz B. (1997). What he doesn't know won't hurt him (or me): Verbal responses and attributions following sexual infidelity. *Communication Reports 10(2)* 143-152.

Nichols, M. & Schwartz, R. (1995). *Family therapy: Concepts and methods* (3rd ed.) Needham Heights, MA: Allyn and Bacon.

Pittman, F. (1989) *Private Lies: Infidelity and the Betrayal of Intimacy*. New York: Norton.

Pittman, F. & Wagers, T. P. (1995) Crises of infidelity. In N.S. Jacobson & A. Gurman (Eds.) *Clinical Handbook of Couple Therapy* (pp 295-316). New York: Guilford.

Rasmussen, P.K. & Ferraro, K.J. (1979). The divorce process. *Alternative Lifestyles 2*, 443-460.

Schwartz, P. & Rutter, V. (1998). *The gender of sexuality.* Thousand Oaks, CA: Sage Publications.

Shackelford, T.K. & Buss, D.M. (1997). Cues to infidelity. *Personality and Social Psychology Bulletin,* 23(10), 1034-1045.

Shackelford, T., LeBlanc, G. and Drass, E. (2000) Emotional reactions to infidelity. *Cognition and Emotion, 14(5),* 643-659.

Spanier, G. &Margolis, R. (1983). Marital separation and extramarital sexual behavior. *Journal of Sex Research, 19(1),* 23-48.

Treas, J. & Giesen, D. (2000). Sexual infidelity among married and cohabiting Americans. *Journal of Marriage and the Family, 62(1)*, 48-60.

Vernberg, E.M. & Varela, R.E. (1998) Impact of Disasters In G. Koocher, Norcross, J., Hill, S. (Eds.) *Psychologists' Desk Reference*. New York: Oxford Press pp. 298-303?

Wegner, D.. Lane, J. & Dimitri, S. (1994). The allure of secret relationships. *Journal of Personality and Social Psychology, 66(2),* 287-300.

Whisman, M.A., Dixon, A.E. & Johnson, B. (1997). Therapists' perspectives of couple problems and treatment issues in the practice of couple therapy. *Journal of Family Psychology, 11(3),* 361-366.

Chapter 8

DIVORCE ASSESSMENT BECOMES INTERVENTION

Pat Hudson[†]
Private Practice
Dallas-Fort Worth, Texas

Divorce is a unique experience for each family member dealing with the enormous, jolting change of the ending of a nuclear family. Almost everyone, but particularly the spouse who did not want the divorce, will be struggling to pick up the pieces of their lives and create new lives either alone or with new partners. Wallerstein and Blakeleslee (1990) in the book, *Second Chances* point out that, even if a spouse did not want the divorce, they may find the loss leads to a new and sometimes more pleasant life. The authors also point out that this ultimate sense of a fresh start is not true for children. The process of divorce removes a child from the security of the family and can throw her into a destructive, lengthy process of being in the middle, between the two people she loves most. Children aren't thinking. "This is an opportunity to get a new mom or dad." This chapter, therefore, will focus most on assessing the children of divorce, but we will begin where the divorce starts, with the adults.

Divorce assessment has three purposes. First, the age-old purpose of assessment is to understand what the person and the system are experiencing due to the divorce and how everyone is adjusting to it. Questions can be very powerful tools. They can open the mind of the listener in addition to providing the therapist with helpful information for treatment.

The second purpose of assessment is raising the awareness of the couple who is divorcing. The grief and distraction or even sense of relief of the adults involved may lead to a blindness towards the suffering of the children. The adults often have not had time to educate themselves about the children's emotional tasks of in a divorce. Even more powerfully, assessment itself becomes an intervention by focusing the clients on the strengths of the adults and the children, the possibilities of the future, and the issues to address.

The third purpose of assessment is simply to remind the adults involved of all the practical issues that need to be managed in raising children together while living apart. There are so many future opportunities for conflicts that helping them to plan well now can protect

---

[†] Pat Hudson, Ph.D., is in Private Practice in Dallas-Fort Worth, Texas.

the system of the divorced family from future deterioration. For example, if college costs are going to come up, how will they be handled?

Divorce assessment can occur as soon as the announcement of the divorce is made. In fact, the sooner; the better. The goals of assessment are to discover the challenges that are going to be unique to that particularly system making subsequent treatment more efficient and accurate or, in the best case, unnecessary.

THE ADULTS

There are ten areas to be assessed when dealing with a divorcing adult: the client's construction--ideas--around the divorce; the ability of the client to construct a positive narrative around the future; the historic coping strategies; the availability and reliability of the system around the divorcing person, such as friends and family; the client's perception of the expectations of her family of origin; the level of depression; the boundary skills of the client with regards to the former spouse and her own family of origin; parenting skills; social skills; and level of practical self-management skills such as cooking, cleaning, or banking.

All of these issues are important and there will be several suggested questions to cover each of the assessment areas with clients, but the ideas that clients have about the divorce, the future, and their abilities to deal with the changes deserve the most attention because they will so strongly affect recovery.

The first question I ask a client is, "What lead to the divorce?" (Hudson, 1998). Here the client might respond with answers ranging from, "I have no idea," to "I caught her having an affair." While clients who are steeped in self-recrimination would obviously be suffering, the client who was blind-sided and had no idea a divorce was pending can be utterly bewildered. One client described having taken her two daughters to visit her mother who lived in a nearby city for a four-day weekend only to return home to a letter from her husband saying that he did not love her any more and the marriage was over. When I saw her six weeks later neither she nor their daughters had heard one word from him. This woman had no narrative about the causes of the divorce and was in an emotional state of shock. The first step in treatment was to help her construct a narrative about the situation. It helped that two months into treatment his long-term affair came to light. Her story about the divorce then became his ethical issue as the underlying cause.

From my constructivist orientation I do not necessarily believe that the story the client constructs with be true in the absolute sense of truth. My goal in assessment will be to help the client come up with a story that will lead the him to feel empowered in moving forward with his life. In this process he may identify patterns from both families of origin, individual patterns, or judgment errors that may have influenced the outcome of the marriage.

Clients need to construct narratives around the future as well. When couples have been married for several years, all of their future visions tended to involve the other person. Questions such as "How do you imagine you might enjoy Christmas two years from now?" or ""What are your vacation plans with your children during summer break?" will help you as the therapist assess how the client is doing at constructing a helpful narrative around the future. The questions are also an intervention by reminding the client that there is a future of pleasant possibilities.

Along that same assessment-as-intervention theme, asking clients about difficult times they or other members of their family have had and the how they have coped with the challenges accomplishes the same goal. They may need a little coaching to think this way by questions such as, "Was there anyone in your family who had a spouse die?" "What helped her recover?" or "Did you ever loose a job?" "How did you get over that loss?" These questions assess both the strengths of the individual and of the system. The reminder of the strengths is in itself an intervention.

The availability and reliability of the system surrounding the divorcing family will strongly influence the family member's ability to manage the change. The following questions will assess this area: " Do you work outside the home? Do you have friends at work? Do you see them socially outside of work? Do you have family close by? Are they available to help you? Do you have friends in your neighborhood? Do you go to church? Do you have friends there? Do you have any single friends who could do things with you on the weekend? Are you in any clubs or social activity groups?" Profound loneliness is often a problem with divorced parents. Frequently the custodial parent focuses her life around the children. Assessing other options can open up possibilities of a broader life for such clients. This is not just a mother issue. I worked with a man whose Ex had taken his thirteen year old son to another state. Since the child had been the focus of the father's social life, he had plunged into a depression. Questioning about social possibilities and making assignments helped him begin to recover.

Loss of an attachment results in grief, whether the loss is through death, divorce, or a breakup of a long-term relationship. Depression is the usual reaction to a divorce, even if an individual initiated the divorce. If there is no depression at the time of the divorce, it will likely mean one of two things: The client was never attached to the spouse or the grieving over the marriage has occurred some time previous to the divorce. Scaling questions such as, "On a scale of one to ten, with one being so depressed that you can't get out of bed and ten being feeling good, where would you rank yourself now?" are helpful. Asking about previous down times and how the client coped then would be useful both as an assessment and as an intervention. Suicidality needs to be assessed in much the same way one would treat any depressed client.

One of the ways that client's slow down their healing process after divorce is by keeping habits of dependency with the spouse who has left. For example, a client might still mow the former wife's lawn or a former wife still does the laundry for her ex-husband. While staying involved in parenting is important for the children, assessment questions can help the client identify what are co-parenting behaviors versus pretend-we're-not-divorced behaviors. Constance Ahrons' (1995) in her book, *The Good Divorce,* she describes four typical styles in divorcing couples: Perfect Pals (high interactors, high communicators) comprised 12% of initially divorcing couples; Cooperative Colleagues (moderate interactors, high communicators) were the largest group (38%); Angry Associates (moderate interactors, low communicators) made up about 25%; and Fiery Foes (low interactors, low communicators) comprised the other 25% of divorcing couples. These couples were initially assessed upon divorcing and again at two and four years later. The results indicated that in general couple were likely to be at the extremes initially, either being pals or very angry at the initial assessment phase, but a couple of years later most people had moved to the middle ground of being cooperative colleagues. As a therapist you can look at these results in terms of boundaries in shaping the assessment of the couple.

By asking about how often they see the former spouse, the answers to boundary assessment will be revealed. If the answer is, "Four times a week. I cook him dinner," or, "I spend the night over there most weekends," then boundaries have not been well established. This would be the Perfect Pals couple described by Ahrons. While it is presumptuous to impose a standard of "a great divorce", looking at establishing boundaries that will allow the spouses to form new relationships while still efficiently co-parenting may probably leads to the most successful healing for the adults and the children.

The divorcing person's family of origin is often confused about the appropriate role to take when the adult child divorces. Are you supposed to take your adult children back? Are you supposed to help them out financially? Do you jump in and start parenting again? It can be very confusing for the parents of the adult divorcing child, therefore the therapist needs to assess what the expectations are of the parents of the divorcing adult if not directly, at least through the eyes of the divorcing client. Assessment questions might be: "How are your parents reacting to the news of the divorce?" "Have your parents been coming over more since the divorce? Is it helping you?" "Have they offered to help you out financially?" "How are you feeling about their attitude about the divorce?" "Are your parents helping you?" "How do they feel about your dating?" "Do they offer opinions about your parenting now that you're doing it alone?" If the system is fighting the divorce, interfering with the transition, or blaming your client, it will be much harder on the client.

Boundaries can be come a central focus of the adult in a divorce. The system of the in-laws can be an issue too. As divorces have become more common, grandparents have become more sensitive to not alienating their in-laws. Asking similar questions you asked about the client's parents, your client will cover the boundary issues of both systems.

The therapist's goal is to know the boundaries in two areas. Look at the boundaries around the system of the couple's dissolving marriage as it relates to the larger system of the families of origin. Consider to boundaries around the individual as he or she relates to both the systems of a family of origin and the nuclear family that is dissolving.

These boundary issues may all be related to how effective the divorcing person has been at self-care. If an adult is not good at being an adult, someone may take over his or her life. By self-care I mean the issues of cooking for oneself; maintaining one's clothes, car, and home; paying bills in a timely manner; and maintaining one's health habits such as moderate exercise, etc. These issues are important areas of inquiry because the divorcing spouse who has never prepared a meal for himself or paid a bill is going to have some basic self-care skills to master while dealing with grief. Men on the whole take divorce less well than women. Besides the fact that many men do not have a network of friends, the biggest reason for this is that they frequently have not taken care of themselves but have had a wife or mother take care of them. This is changing as more and more couples share maintenance of the home in more egalitarian ways, but particularly with the older divorcing couple, these issues need to be assessed. You won't know a woman has never paid a bill or man has never cooked anything but scrambled eggs, if you don't ask.

Socially divorce is a huge change. One usually looses a substantial number of friends if one had them in the first place. Assessing the client's ability to make friends and to build a social life is important. Divorced people will have to construct a new life without a partner. Assessment questions may include: "Do you have single friends?" "Have you had much experience dating before you married?" "What activities did you have that you did without your spouse?" "Do you have some friend you can call when you're feeling down?" Divorce can be very isolating, particularly for men since our culture discourages same-sex male friendships outside of sports. Asking these questions may provide an intervention in itself by helping the client identify where he will need to put his efforts to recover from the divorce.

Many, in fact perhaps, all, adults need to improve their parenting skills from time to time as the needs of children change through their developmental stages. Never is that more true than when parents divorce. Often the married parenting style was a reaction to the other parent's style. One parent was the tough one; the other parent was the push-over. Another common problem is that one parent was not truly allowed to parent the children during the marriage. More often this is the father. Of course there are fathers who are not blocked from parenting may elect to be uninvolved. On the other had, it is also becoming more common for the father to be the primary parent in two-career families. Whatever the reason for the style in a marriage, moving from parenting with another person to parenting alone is a jolt. The style may have to change to be productive. Assessing how effective the parent is by inquiring about how well the child complies to requests, how patient is the parent, what are the means of enforcing the parents rules, how angry is the parent with noncompliance, and how overwhelmed does she feel about managing the children are all areas to ask about when divorcing people share offspring. The point of assessing this area is that while parenting is hard with two people, it has the potential of being even harder with one. Knowing what challenges need to be met early on will facilitate the changes needed in the divorce.

Occasionally, I have had clients tell me that they found parenting alone easier because there was so great a difference in parental values, but most of the time parents do better when they can tag-team so that one is not always on duty.

THE CHILDREN

If there are children being affected by the divorce then it is crucial for them to be assessed. The world of a child can be shattered by divorce. A parent the children love may be missing. They may have to move out of the only home they have ever known. They may be dealing with an overwhelmed, depressed parent. The child of divorce will reassess the dependability of relationships; the reliability of their future plans such as college; and their responsibility for the divorce. I have talked to many clients who said, "Basically I raised myself after my parent's divorce." One client recently told me that, because her mother was so overwhelmed when her parents divorced, her father paid for an apartment for my client and her younger brother to live in unsupervised when she was sixteen years old. At 34 she is still dealing with this abandonment and resenting having to be a grown-up so prematurely.

There are five areas to assess relative to children. One is what the child might be experiencing in the middle of the crisis of the divorce. The second area has to do with the long-time coping strategy of the child relative to the divorce. The third area is how the child is navigating through the tasks he has as the divorce unfolds. The fourth area to assess is the vulnerabilities and stage-appropriate strengths of the particular child so that the parents can be prepared to manage the child well. The fifth area to assess is what kind of parenting plan is in place and what areas still need to be discussed.

Divorce has a profound impact on children's world-views and self-concepts. In general, I have the bias of working through the parents initially. If the child does not show difficulties in school, problem behaviors such as acting out, eating disorders, or an increase in mood swings,

I hesitate to have them brought in for therapy. I do not want children to start thinking that they have a mental health problem because of the divorce. They are more likely to have problems, but I don't want the questions of therapy to be the cause of the problems. However, if the focus of the treatment is on the children the Children's Beliefs About Parental Divorce Scale (CBAPS) by Kurek and Berg (1987) is available. It's a simple, straightforward list of 36 questions that assesses the areas of parental blame, fear of abandonment, maternal blame, hope of reunification, self-blame, and peer ridicule and avoidance. I imagine that a re-test of this last item would have significantly changed since 1987 given that divorce is now so common. These questions, such as, "I sometimes think that my parents will one day live together," or "My parents would probably still be living together if it weren't for me," are good starting places for direct discussions with children.

My assessment of the children start and, on rare occasions, may end with the adults. The hope is that assessing the children's issues may raise consciousness of the parents by asking questions such as: "Do you think your child feels lonely now that his mother has moved out?" "Has Brian had to take on more duties because of the divorce?" "How is your child dealing with having a new parental figure?" (Usually there is a new person in one of the parent's lives.) "Has your child's academic performance, health, or behavior at school been affected by the divorce?" "How do you think the divorce may have affected how your child feels about herself?" "Do you can share your thoughts about your Ex's behavior?" "How might that be affecting your child's self-concept?" Here again I hesitate to suggest that problems are going to arise for fear of creating the problems, however literature is very clear that children are affected negatively by divorce (Garrity and Baris 1994). All these questions will both help the practitioner assess how the child is doing through the parent's eyes and help the parent be sensitive to the needs of a child. It is hard for an upset parent to focus on the child's needs when the client may feel they are hemorrhaging emotionally. Asking the assessment questions can pull a parent back to the reality of the child's needs.

Figure 1. **Children of Divorce
(compared to children from intact families)**

**Do more poorly in school
Are often bitter, anxious, or depressed
Have more visits to their primary care physician
Resent the person they feel was responsible for the divorce, even ten years later.
Marry later themselves
Are twice as likely to divorce**
Adapted from C. Garrity & M.A. Barris (1994) *Caught in the Middle: Protecting Children in High-Conflict Divorce,* San Francisco: Jossey-Bass

---

Garrity and Baris (1994) in their book *Caught in the Middle: Protecting Children of High-Conflict Divorce* point out that about 50% of divorcing couples have a high degree of conflict in the first year of separation and divorce. Over time, however, about 38% of couples have mild or minimal conflict, 33% have moderate conflict, and 29% have moderately severe or severe conflict. Other research suggests that 14% become physically violent in their mutual antagonism (Camera & Resnick, 1988). Asking questions about the nature of the conflict and how out-of-control it has become will allow the therapist to assess what the child's world is like as the divorce proceeds. Questions might include, "Has your child heard you fighting?" "Have you ever hit each other?" "Has your child ever seen you be violent with the other parent?" "Were the police ever called?"

While it is devastating for the child to see the people she loves trying to destroy each other, the worst case scenario is the child who feels thrown away by the divorce. As Dr. Bill Doughterty, a renowned marriage and family therapist, said, "When I became a counselor thirty years ago, I used to see runaway kids. Now I see throw-away kids." Most likely, a therapist is not going to see the parent who has dropped out of a child's life, but sometimes there is a chance to assess this probability in pre-divorce counseling. By asking questions such as, "Now that you are thinking that you and Jenny might separate, how do you think Ashley might be affected by your being gone?" It is not that the therapist is trying to manipulate the client into feeling guilty, but that decisions of this magnitude need to made with serious consideration of the consequences.

To assess the child's progress one must consider the tasks of the child. There are five tasks relative to divorce. The first is to face the fact that the marriage has ended. Children will often talk about "When Daddy comes home," or "When we move to Daddy's house," as they are talking about the divorce. Before he can face the ending of a marriage the child must know what "divorce" means. Assessment can help the therapist identify where the gaps are in the child's conception of divorce. Questions clarify the child's understanding such as, "Do you know how people get divorced?" "What does it mean to get a divorce?" "Do you expect that your parents will get back together?" Children usually hope for reconciliation, but finding out how realistic the child is about the likelihood of the parent's reuniting is helpful in assessing how well they are dealing with this task.

The second task is to remove themselves from being involved in the parental conflicts. Even the most well-intentioned divorcing couple I have dealt with slips up on this at times and forces the child into the conflict. "Tell your father…" "Who is your mother seeing?" are examples of how children are kept in the conflict. As the therapist you may ask a child, "How do you handle it if Mom asks about Dad's girlfriend?" "What do you say if Dad tells you to take a message to your mother?" to find out how much the child is in the spy or rescue-the-marriage roles. Asking such questions has the treatment value of preparing children for what may happen and helping them come up with ideas for dealing with conflicts. The assessment becomes a rehearsal for conflicts that may arise. Of course, timing is everything. Asking a child who just found out last week about the divorce how he is going to manage his parents' new significant others would be like shoving the kid in a muddy hole. Ask parents corresponding questions such as, "Do you think Bobby has taken on the role of giving you information about your Ex?" Everyone may have to work together to block this destructive pattern.

The third task is to avoid self-blame. Most clients are aware that children may blame themselves for the divorce and go out of their way to tell the children that the divorce is not the children's fault. In spite of being sensitive to this problem, a child tends to have an egocentric worldview and often blame herself. This is not always totally unrealistic as sometimes a stressful child may lead to more conflicts between the parents. In the assessment process it is important not to accidentally implant the suggestion that the divorce is the child's fault, so rather than asking, "Do you think that you caused the divorce?" I would ask, "Why are your parents getting a divorce?" At the beginning of this chapter we discussed that the parents need to develop a narrative around the divorce. The children have to do so too, although sometimes later in their lives. Assessing their construction about the divorce and steering it away from self-blame by the questions you ask is intervention in itself. Questions such as "Did your parents fight a lot?" "What did they fight about?" will hopefully lead away from self-blame.

The fourth task of the child is to let go of anger about the divorce. Wallerstein and Blakeslee (1990) point at that even ten years after the divorce children may still harbor resentment towards the parent whom they believe caused the divorce, so letting go of anger may be a big challenge for many children. A thirty-year-old woman came into my office still angry about her parent's divorcing when she was twelve years old. Her resentment focused on two areas, how her life would have been better had her parents stayed together and how her father had abdicated his role as parent and allowed the step-mother to impose her greater restrictions. Of course the first question is the quintessential therapist question, "How do you feel about the divorce?" If the child indicates that she is angry, assessing by intervention questions such as, "How well do you imagine that you will get over your anger?" or "When will you have you been angry long enough to stop?" will lead in the direction of resolving anger towards the parent she feels is responsible for the divorce.

The fifth task may not be relevant for the child initially. That is to adjust to a new parental figure. If is has been some time since the divorce, a part of the assessment might be to ask about the child's feeling towards a new partner. Questions such as, "How do you get along with Jill?" "Does she ever help you with your homework?" "Do you do fun things with her?" "Does she ever punish you?" All these questions will help you assess how the new evolving system is progressing for the child.

Often the child is in the middle of a battleground. In divorces, particularly those with high-conflict, children develop one of four strategies to cope with the divorce (Garrity & Baris, 1994).

Manipulator

They may become skillful at manipulating the situation for their own gain. If in your assessment you learn of a child reporting, "Daddy let's me have any toy I want," then you might suspect that the child is using the manipulation strategy. Parental assessment questions that would be appropriate if you are thinking the child has this coping style are: "Does your child tend to get his way usually?" "Do you find the child encouraging you to compete with the Ex for his attention?" Here I would be cautious about creating a problem where there might not have been one, so it is better to wait until you hear things that suggest a manipulator strategy before opening up the inquiry.

Diplomat

The second strategy of a child in a high conflict divorce is to become a little diplomat. The child who never says anything bad about anybody in the family, who never carries messages, who hides his own feelings, is one who may have developed the diplomatic strategy. This is somewhat harder to assess because parents rarely complain about the child. If however you hear phrases such as, "She never gave us a day of trouble, not even during the divorce," then the child may have become a diplomat. This is probably a relatively good thing and I would not want to mess it up by questioning it as though it were a pathological problem. Best to be sensitized as the therapist to the possibilities that the upset might show up in other ways such as anorexia.

The Chronically Regressed

A more common problem for both the parents and for the child is the child who becomes chronically stuck in an earlier stage of development. Questions that might open this up are "Does your child have friends his own age?" This would be a question that might reveal someone who is stage-stuck if the answer was he always plays with younger kids. Another area to reveal the regression issue is, "Are there things that Matt did when he was younger that he is doing again, such as wetting the bed?" In order to assess the developmental stage the therapist may need to review what is appropriate for each stage. Table one provides a summary of what is typical of each stage.

Figure 2. **Reactions To Divorce Based Upon The Stage/Age Of The Child**

Toddler
- Resist transitions
- Make up stories about the divorce
- May regress

Five through Eight
- Have concrete questions about the divorce
- May do more poorly in school
- Look for heroes

Nine through Twelve
- Tend to become parent companion or rescuer
- May be curious about sex
- May be resentful about the change

Adolescents
- Escape to other families
- May take extreme stances about contact with a parent
- Tend to bounce back and forth between parents

Assessing the child's development by asking "Does your child....(followed by what the general suggestions are in the Stages/Ages box for that age child)" may help determine if the child is progressing normally. By doing this you can help the parents understand what the child is doing. If the child's reaction was more extreme, for example, if rather than having grades drop a little the child was flunking, then this would be a good opportunity to plan for treatment.

The Shattered Child

In the worst cases, children will become unable to cope and be shattered by the experience. One of the most dramatic cases I had that demonstrated this was a girl, Alison, whose parents had a very high conflict, violent divorce. For thirteen months, Alison did not speak. She would basically be compliant in school and do what she was told at home, but she would only nod her head. Through family therapy, which was challenged by this particular symptom, Alison began to speak after a year. I did not have the opportunity to do assessment during the initial divorce phase, but one can hope that questions asked of the parents might have prevented this extreme response.

While these four strategies of reacting to the high conflict divorce are typical of children dealing with divorce, the individual child's temperament and his ability to be flexible may determine how well he reacts to the divorce. Helping parents identify which of the children will have difficulty will help a therapist and the parents prepare the child for the transition.

THE INDIVIDUAL CHILD

We have considered the strategies that children may adopt and just how pathological a reaction may become. Which child will be shattered versus the child that may become a diplomat will be easier to predict if the therapist look at the child as and individual. The following are questions that make clarify the strengths and support of the system around the child.

Self-soothing

Good questions for dealing with a child's ability to comfort herself are: "As babies, did your daughter have trouble self-soothing (the ability to stop fussing on their own)?" " How long does or did it take to settle your child to sleep?" "What helps?" Assessing such issues helps the parents realize which child may need therapy or just extra care in the divorce process.

Transitions

Transitions happen in any child's life. These usually evolve around school, daycare, and visits to friend's and family members' homes. Assessment questions include, "Describe your child's adjustment to preschool or kindergarten. Was this a child that you couldn't leave without a major crisis?" "Has your child spent nights away from home with grandparents or friends?" "How did the child manage the separation?" If a child has never spent the night elsewhere, then there may be a problem the first time he has to leave his house to visit the other parent.

If the child is still very young, "What, if any, transitional object (blanket, teddy bear, doll) does your child use and how important is that to your child?"

A client of mine was a divorcing father. He wanted to toughen up the four-year-old so the dad would not let the child have the blanket at his house. Through questions I helped him see that transitional objects were not a sign of any abnormal weakness in the child and would be put away over the normal course of time. Helping a parent identify ways to help a child in transition is one of the tasks of divorce therapy. Asking questions about transitions and transitional objects helps raise the parent's awareness.

Some transitions seem more natural than others. In assessing the plans for transitions I ask about natural transitions such as being picked up from school as a natural way of changing the possession of the child for visitation.

Support

Probably all of us could use supportive friends, but in the case of a child whose life is disrupted by divorce, support may be crucial. Assessment questions about support are: "Is there someone other than a parent (an aunt, uncle, grandparent, or older sibling) who has been a stabilizing force in the child's life? If so, will child continue to have easy access to that extra support?" "What are ways you can be sure the child has the extra help available?"

It may be hard for a parent in the middle of a depression to think of many things that could be described as pleasant, therefore you might need to ask specifically about grandparents, aunt, uncles, siblings, and friends.

"Is there a counselor in your child's school?" Calling the school counselor will keep the parent informed about resources which are available to the child as well as alert the school to the fact that the child may be distracted for a while. In my own family it was helpful for one of my children to attend the school's support group. He came home with a perspective on how much worse things could be that what he was experiencing. This resource may not crossed the parent's mind.

"Is there a group for children of divorced parents at your school, church, or synagogue?" The religious community often seems in a bind about divorce. There is a hesitancy to do anything that seems like it might be promoting divorce while at the same time wanting to help those who are suffering. Children, being the innocent by-standers of divorce, are an obvious place to provide services without "encouraging" divorce.

Of course, the most important support for the child is the other parent. Asking questions in your assessment such as, "Have you let your child know that time with the other parent is important?" "Have you been careful to be sure your child is available when the other parent comes to pick him up?" "Have you let you child telephone the other parent when you have him?" will clarify the importance of the other parent in the child's support.

Part of the problem with sharing a child with the another parent may be lack of creativity with the parent's free time. Ask questions such as, "What are some of the things you are now free to do when you child is at his other parent's home that you could not do in the past?" "Have you noticed yet that the only great thing about divorce is that you can have guilty-free, no-cost free time from parenting?" I know this implies a certain bias on my part, but free-time is the only great thing about divorce. I have often had clients who suffered initially at being separated from a child only to find out that unstructured free time was an unexpected compensation. Proper assessment can make this suggestion to the parent whose life has revolved around a child.

Anxiety

"What things scare your child and are there many things he is fearful about?" I think the anxious child is most vulnerable to having difficulties dealing with the transitions of divorce. Most children thrive in predictable environments and the environment of divorce is often dramatically unpredictable for even years following the initial separation.

Forgiveness

"How has your son or daughter handled conflicts with friends, family members, teachers?" If the child already has a style of being unforgiving, the divorce situation is going to present more challenges. As reported earlier, children may still be angry as much as ten years later. Seeing this trend in other relationships helps the therapist and the parent prepare for the challenges of healing.

General Health

"Does the child have any health problems, such as asthma, stomach problems, or headaches?" Children of divorce have more physical problems and go to a primary care physician more often. If the child has a history of health problems, divorce is likely to exacerbate the problem. Being aware of somatic tendencies helps the parents prepare for the best treatment for the child.

CHILDREN'S AGES AND STAGES

What a one-year-old needs is different from a kindergartner or a middle school child. Being aware of the typical reactions children have at each stage can help you in you're assessment process with the family.

Toddler

Toddlers resist transitions. They often don't like going anywhere particularly without mom. Asking a divorcing parent about the predictability of the environment now that the divorce is starting will help the parent to be aware of what is normal for the child. There can be some education in the question, "Knowing that toddlers need predictability, how is Amanda handling going between households?"

Toddlers make up stories about the divorce. Asking the parent if the child has ideas about where mommy has gone or where daddy is now, will help the parent be aware of normal toddler behavior and help identify any inaccurate ideas that the child has about what has happened. One mother discovered that her child thought that the father had taken up permanent residence at the airport since he had traveled so often during the marriage.

Parents often have unrealistic ideas about how a small child will express his upset at the divorce. Since toddles are not articulate about their feelings I would not ask, "How is Matt feeling about the divorce?" Instead, assess any changes in behaviors, particularly acting out. One three year old boy was upset about his dad's moving out. When the father came to pick him up he just walked up to his dad and kicked him in the shins without warning. Unexpected outbursts might be a better focus of assessment than discussions about feelings.

Assessment best assessment of toddlers focuses on regressive behaviors such as bed-wetting, thumb-sucking, or asking for a bottle. Questions around these areas will help you as the therapist identify any problems and help the parent pay attention to the needs of the toddler.

Five through Eight

Young school age children have concrete questions such as, "Are we going to have a place to live?" "When will I see daddy?" "Don't you love him anymore?" "What if you stopped loving me?" Assessing the questions the child has asked by questioning the parent, helps prepare the parent for future questions.

To find out if the child needs treatment, ask the parent if there has been any communication from the school about the child's performance.

At this stage of life children look for heroes. This is the my-dad's-stronger-than-your-dad stage. Assessing what the child admires about the other parent through the parent's eyes raises the parent's awareness of the need to keep these images in spite of parental resentment.

Nine through Twelve

If the child is approaching middle school they are likely to become a parent's companion or rescuer. One child who had an exiting parent who traveled frequently said "It doesn't matter, Mom. He was gone all the time anyway." this would be a typical rescuing statement by a child. Asking the divorcing parent, "Have you noticed your child trying to take care of you?" can be a useful question if the child is at this stage of development. One ten-year-old daughter decided that she wanted to help her lawyer dad by cleaning his apartment while he was at the office. In this process she decided to do the laundry which to her included washing and drying three business suits that were on the floor of his closet. Rescuing can be expensive.

Children this age may be resentful about the divorce. They are sophisticated enough to know that their lives are being altered profoundly. They may be upset and blaming about the lifestyle change imposed upon them. To children ages nine through twelve games are played by the rules or they are not played. To a child this age the rules have been broken by divorce. Assess how the child is managing this by asking if she has complained about the alterations in living. Even asking a parent these questions helps normalize the reaction of the child and informs the therapist about the child's reactions.

Adolescents

In a high conflict divorce an adolescent may informally divorce his family. Often the adolescent will escape to other families when there are problems with the health or mental health of the parent without divorce being an issue. Assess this by asking, "How much time does your child spend at friend's houses?" This can be a wise strategy on the adolescent's part and will help you know how she is functioning.

Adolescents may take extreme stances about contact with a parent they blame for the divorce. I have found teen-aged clients who refuse to speak to a parent particularly if there has been an affair. If your only client is a divorcing partner, then assessing this by asking how the adolescent is taking the divorce will let you know if the treatment needs to include the adolescent.

It is no news flash that adolescents are rebellious and therefore may use the divorce to bounce back and forth between parents when rules are enforced. Asking questions such as, "Are groundings at your Ex's enforced by you and vice versa?" will open up this line of inquiry and avoid the yo-yo child.

Although I do not know of any research to support this, it has been my experience that the only child is likely to be more upset by his parent's marital and divorce problems. The buffer of siblings often protects and distracts the child from parental difficulties. Without the buffer, an only child may be more likely to need treatment in response to a divorce.

There are many practical issues that must be dealt with in a divorce where there are children. Assessing all the practical issues will be a great service to the family because it may avoid future expensive legal costs as well as bitter feelings. The following topics need to be addressed in the parental plan.

THE PARENTING PLAN

Visitation

Visitation is the first topic couples tend to bring up as soon as the impending divorce is announced. The time plan will need to be rigid at first but later this can be more flexible.

"How would you like to divide the child's time with each of you? " "How will the transportation between the households be managed?" "Who will drive?" "How will you phase in overnights, if they are not happening yet?" "Do you wish to be asked to watch the child when it is not your time to have the child?" "Who will take responsibility for the care of the child if your daughter or son is too sick to go to school?" "Can times be traded?" (The child should never arrange Trades. The parents may directly discuss changes or, in more hostile situations, write to each other.) This usually gets easier over time.

"If the other person refuses to see the child, how are you going to handle that?" It is always alarming for a child when a parent abdicates the role of parent, but this is a reality for far too many children. Generally, if a parent drops out of a child's life, then treatment is needed.

Phone Calls

If phone calls have been a problem either by being excessive or by the calls not being responded to, you may wish to agree how long, how often, and when they are to occur.

"Will phone calls be allowed?" "Can either the child or the absent parent initiate the calls?" "Can the child have a phone installed by the absent parent to facilitate the calls?"

Belongings

It is much better for each household to have complete sets of kids' clothes and toys so that there can be fewer disputes over what was left where and why.

"What, if anything, is not to travel, such as expensive sports or electrical equipment?" "If something, such as homework is forgotten, how are you going to handle the extra trip?"

Holidays

Holiday visits are generally negotiated without considering regularly scheduled visits. Asking if the couple has sat down with the child's calendar and talk about specifics will help facilitate the discussions and help avoid conflicts in the future.

Here is a list to consider with the divorcing couple:

Christmas Eve	Halloween
Christmas Day	Thanksgiving
New Year's Eve	School Days off
New Years Day	Birthdays
Spring Break	Rosh Hashanah
Easter or Passover	Yom Kippur
July 4th	Mother and Father's
Memorial Day	Day President's Day
Labor Day	

Extracurricular Activities

Sports and hobbies can be very expensive. Here are some issues you might want to settle early in the divorce process.

"Who is going to pay for the activity, such as music or sports camp?" "Who is going to provide transportation?" "Who attends?

Religious Training

You may wish to specify whether or not you are going to provide religious training or education.

"If you attend a church or synagogue, who will take the child to services and training?" "If there are special transition ceremonies such as confirmation or Bar Mitzvahs, how are these going to be handled in terms of attendance and any costs and preparation for the celebration?"

Medical and Professional Appointments

Naturally, if there is an emergency, either parent can initiate care. Here are some other issues that you might want to discuss in advance:

"Who will schedule dentist and doctor appointments?" "Are non-traditional treatments to be shared financially the same as conventional treatments?" "Who will provide transportation?" "If the child has special medical needs, such as a disability, what extra procedures are required and are those to be traded?"

School

Communication with the school is ultimately the responsibility of each parent. Most schools will send other parent the report card. Working together for the child's education may be one of the most important places for affecting the child's future. The following are issues that you may discuss now that can smooth the road ahead.

"If a change of school is necessitated by the divorce, how will the selection of the school be handled and by whom?" "If a private school is needed for some reason, how will tuition be handled?" "Will you attend school conferences together or schedule separate conferences?" "How will access to report cards be handled?"

"What about attendance of school functions? Will you attend those on alternate occasions or together?" "If the child requires tutoring, who will pay for it?"

Vacations

For many of us our happiest childhood memories were of vacations. Keeping vacations conflict-free by making agreements now can be a great gift for the child. If a vacation is pre-planned, then it should not be included as a visitation-day trade-off. Telephone numbers should be provided in advance, in case of emergency. Here are a couple of discussion items for the assessment:

"Is travel out of the state allowed? What about out of the country?" "How long are trips to be?" "How will phone contact with the other parent be handled?" Phone cards can be a big help for this.

"What will the sleeping arrangements be while on vacation?" This issue can be important particularly if the child is being thrown in with other aged children, etc.

Rules at the Other Household

This can be a big source of conflict. Unfortunately there is no easy solution to this problem. Each parent is responsible for the household rules in his or her home.

As the therapist you can determine if this is going to be an areas of conflict by asking if the couple had difficulty with value differences in the marriage. "Was homework or bathing important to one and not the other spouse?" It may be that you suggest people who are divorcing make requests about bedtime, bathing, food, or homework, but each spouse has the right to set up his or her household as each sees fit. If it is not abusive, seriously neglectful as in a health issue such as childhood diabetes, or life threatening, the client needs to focus on accepting the reality of two different families now raising the child.

Communication Tools

Assessing the method that the couple is going to use in communication back and forth about the child will help start the post-divorce family off on a good foot. It is a useful idea to have a notebook that you pass back and forth particularly if the child is young. Particularly when a child is too young to speak for herself, a notebook will answer question such as "Was the toddler fed? Is he or she on medications? Are there any bowel or bladder issues? How is potty training going?" All this can be well handled with minimal conflict by a written communication. Fax machines and Email are also useful especially if talking leads to more conflicts. Asking if the couple has tried these yet may raise more possibilities for better communication.

One Final Tip

When conflicts seem to drag for years following divorce, the couple may be creating a "negative intimacy." Divorced couples who go back to court over and over again keep a negative passion going and can do damage to their child. When the therapist observes that this is happening, questions such as, "How has this kept you close to your former spouse?" "How has this affected your child?" may raise the awareness of the parents engaged in negative intimacy and help you know if the child may need counseling.

CASE STUDY

The day after Christmas Mark announced to his wife Beth that he was filing for divorce and was moving out before New Year's Day. They had two children, Becca, ages ten, and Chad, age sixteen. Beth called my office in tears and asked for an emergency appointment. Over the holidays I often have cancellations, so I was able to get her in the next day. She said she knew that Mark had been thinking of leaving for some time, but it still caught her off guard. She suspected he was having an affair with a single co-worker and knew that probably contributed to his leaving now. Beth and Mark had already told the children that Dad was moving out. The assessment in my first session consisted of helping Beth construct her story around the divorce, which basically was that Mark was in love with someone else. We dealt with Beth's views about her contribution to the demise of the marriage. We also dealt with her strengths. She had supportive family nearby, was active in a church, and had a job that paid her adequately. She was an attractive woman and more confident than most of my clients. She thought she could attract a man in the future. At the end of the first session I asked if she would invite Mark to come to a session. I promised not to pressure him into staying, but said I wanted to help them set up a plan for the children.

Mark agreed to come and I saw them together eight days later. The atmosphere in the therapy room was strained as the session began, but as I set the agenda firmly on the well-being of the children the tension disappeared. My value system is that Mark should stay and try therapy first, but I did not experience him as in any way open to this possibility. I have a booklet that goes over the many of questions I mentioned in this chapter. During our first joint session we used the booklet as we went through the topics about stages, children's strengths, and about half the topics to be settled. We decided they would each take a booklet and think some of the other topics over the next few days. We scheduled a session again a week later. By that time, using the assessment questions in this chapter, it was clear that Chad was seemingly so involved in his own life that the divorce was not affecting him but that Becca was trying very hard to rescue the parents and had begged her dad to move back home. School had only been back in session for a week when her fifth grade teacher called to ask why Becca was having so much trouble. I scheduled a session that was split between time alone with Becca and time with both Becca and her parents together. In the session I continued with some assessment questions about the future so that Becca could hear what the game plan was going to be. This helped her feel more certain about her future and increased her confidence that she was not going to loose her father in the process. The parents were able to put their anger and differences aside for the sake of Becca. My belief is that Becca's progress would have been hampered without this assessment opportunity. I scheduled a future session a month after this Becca's first session with Becca and her mom, who had primary possession of Becca. The plan was to see the effects of the initial assessment session after some time had passed. I also saw Beth on a weekly basis for that month. Becca's behavior in school improved and she seemed to be managing the transition better by the time I saw her again.

I don't doubt that there may be future difficulties as other people enter the lives of all these people. At this point I have invited Chad to come in, but he has declined. Beth will continue therapy twice a month and Becca will return as needed, but I feel we had a better start than most divorcing families and that tragedies of children lost in the shuffle were avoided by the wisdom of Beth and Mark in seeking help right at that crucial transition.

All of the assessment issues discussed in this chapter assume two functioning adults who have some caring for the safety and well-being of the child. Unfortunately most therapist have to deal with the occasional and seemingly more frequent case of a violent spouse in the divorcing process. No assessment is complete for someone without questions about violence or threats of violence. As I am writing this chapter there have been a string of cases of estranged husbands killing their wife and children. If violence or homicide is at all a possibility then the treatment plan priority is family violence treatment not divorce treatment.

In conclusion, assessment in divorce is a powerful treatment tool. You as the therapist have the opportunity to be a healing force. You can help a divorcing parent or, better yet, a couple manage the transition with as much consideration for avoiding damage to the children as possible. By the power of your questions, you can change the life of a child.

REFERENCE

Ahrons, C. (1994). *The good divorce: Keeping your family together when your mariage falls apart.* New York:Harper Perennial.

Grrity. C.B. & Baris, M.A. (1994). *Caught In the middle: Protecting the children of high-conflict divorce.* San Francisco: Jossey-Bass.

Hudson, P. (1998). *You can get over divorce.* Rocklin, CA: Prima.

Kurdeck, L.A.& Berg, B. (1987). Children's Beliefs About Parental Divorce Scale: Psychometric characteristics and concurrent validity, *Journal of Consulting and Clinical Psychology, 55*, 712-718.

Wallerstein, J.S. & Blakeslee, S. (1990). *Second chance: Men, women, and children a decade after divorce*. New York: Ticknor and Fields.

Chapter 9

ASSESSING PARENTING CAPABILITY

Chelsea T. Wolf[*]
University of Colorado at Denver
John J. Peregoy[‡]
Morehead State University, Morehead Kentucky

INTRODUCTION

At the dawn of the 21st century, there continues to be growing awareness in the mental health fields that there is no prototype for a family. Families do not necessarily consist of a working father, a stay-at-home mother, 2.3 children, and a white picket fence enclosing a yard. This middle class perspective has been replaced with a myriad of families that vary in many ways, including the number of parents and children, ethnicity, sexual orientation of family members, place of residence, and economic status. Indeed, as Sciarra (2001) remarked: "The 1980s saw a dramatic rise in different family structures, among them the single-parent family, grandmother as primary caretaker, and homosexual couples raising children" (p. 141). Given this tremendous diversity in family structure, there is also an incredible variance in parenting values, beliefs, and styles. Parenting styles are influenced by many factors, including culture, society, SES, region were one lives, to name but just a few.

Not only is there a tremendous variation in parenting practices, but parenting in all types of families is a complicated and multifaceted task. Thus, it is very difficult to assess parenting capabilities adequately. Assessment of parenting capacity differs from case to case (Gopfert, Webster, Pollard, & Nelki, 1996), and as Black (1990) noted, "assessment is therefore always a contextual exercise" (p. 47). Cates (1999) has described assessment as an art, where the evaluator's "influence, intuition, and creativity" (p. 631) play an important role.

---

[*] Chelsea T. Wolf, MS received her Master of Arts degree in Marriage and Family Counseling from the University of Colorado at Denver.
[‡] John Joseph Peregoy, Ph.D., is at Morehead State University, Morehead Kentucky. He is CEO of Consulting, Diversity, and Educational Services.

The purpose of this chapter is to examine the use of parenting assessments. In order to do so we will briefly look at the history of child welfare and the evolution of parenting assessments. The next section will explore the use of assessments. Following will be an exploration of pros and cons, as well as ethical issues related to the administration and use of parental assessments. Finally, we will discuss implications of conducting parental assessments in multicultural settings.

The Need for Assessment

Despite, however, the inherent difficulty in assessing parenting capability, it can be vital in order to ensure the well being of children in our society. Appropriate and effective assessment of parenting capacity can help protect children from neglect and abuse. Indeed, often as a result of parenting assessments, thousands of children are taken from their parents' care every year, in order to safeguard their welfare (Campion, 1995). For the purposes of this chapter, we will use Cates' (1999) definition of assessment: "assessment refers to the administration of multiple psychological tests, instruments, or techniques, as well as behavioral observation, to obtain a pool of data" (p. 631).

The fundamental purpose of parenting assessments is to shield children from inapt parenting. However, there is no clear and objective definition of inadequate parenting. This certainly poses a problem when assessing parenting capabilities. However, by investigating reasons why children might be removed from their parents' care, one can begin to understand what, at least in our society, defines inadequate parenting. Campion (1995) described several reasons why children might be taken from their parents, including:

* Abandonment
* Neglect
* Physical abuse
* Failure of attendance at school
* Failure to protect child's health, e.g. by withholding medical treatment to an ill child,
* Inadequate parenting arising from parental illness/disability (p. 17)
* Criminal behavior of child/parent
* Sexual abuse
* Poor home environment

The reasons most often cited for the use of parenting assessments is to investigate a child's environment which may not be conducive to a child's health and well being.

Uses for Parenting Assessments

There are many uses for parenting assessments. One primary use is for the evaluation of current child abuse and neglect. Parenting assessments are also helpful in adoption and fostering cases in order to evaluate prospective parents. Additionally, divorce disputes and custody battles often make use of parenting assessments, when one parent challenges the parenting capacity of the other. Furthermore, the assessment of parenting capability is also very important in the evaluation of the *potential* risk of failure for parents and the prediction of future parenting capacity. Information for assessing parenting capabilities can come form a variety of sources.

Who is Involved in the Therapeutic Process

Given the many facets of families and of parenting, it is advantageous to have the expertise of many different professionals when assessing parenting capability. Various agencies and individuals can each contribute important, unique information about the children, parents, and family. For example, in addition to counselors and psychotherapists, the education system, social services, mental and physical health workers, and the judicial system may have a role in the assessment process (Gopfert et al., 1996).

From a systemic perspective, children and families are integral parts of multiple contexts, including extended families, religious or spiritual organizations, and communities. When approaching parental assessments from this systemic perspective, it is important to evaluate not only the parents and children themselves, but also the contexts of which they are a part. For example, in addition to assessing the family members, Schuff and Asen (1996) recommended evaluating the parents', the children's, and the family's social context, as well as their professional network including educational services, medical doctors, social workers, and counselors.

THE BACKGROUND TO PARENTING ASSESSMENTS

The History of Child Welfare

In order to provide an accurate history of parenting assessments, it is important to begin with a background of the history of child welfare. Throughout history, there have been myriad cases of cruel and abhorrent treatment of children. Not only were children often viewed simply as property to be bought and sold, there are also many historical examples of infanticide, deliberate mutilation, as well as gross physical and sexual abuse.

> The history of childhood is a nightmare from which we have only recently begun to awaken. The further back in history one goes, the lower the level of child care, and the more likely children are to be killed, abandoned, beaten terrorized and sexually abused
> **(DeMause, 1976, as cited in Black, 1990, p. 45).**

During the fourteenth, fifteenth, and sixteenth centuries, a series of laws, summarized in the Elizabethan Poor Laws of 1601 were passed in England. These laws greatly influenced child welfare policy in England for the next 250 years. American colonies, too, adopted the Poor Laws. These laws mandated that the local government assume responsibility for the poor. Additionally, the laws mandated that parents were legally responsible for the livelihood of their children and grandchildren. However, although the family prevailed as the principle caretaker of children, the Poor Laws did allow for the placement of children in apprenticeship positions, primarily when the children were indigent or delinquent. For the apprenticeship, the children were taken from their parents, and made to live in the family home of the apprentice (Trattner, 1999).

In early America, there were a large number of orphaned, as well as illegitimate and poor children. These children were often placed in apprenticeship positions. The practice of placing children in apprenticeships continued due largely to the prevailing belief that everyone should be attached to a family. Apprenticeships were also viewed as an effective method of discipline for children. Additionally, the apprentice system lowered the amount of indolence while increasing the number of trained workers who could contribute to a town (Trattner, 1999).

During the nineteenth century, there was a move away from home-relief, or helping families within a family setting. In 1824, the Yates Report, stated that home relief had contributed to negligence of morals and education in the children, as well as to the cruel treatment that some received. Subsequently this Report recommended that institutional care be established as the fundamental solution for the education, moral instruction, and humane treatment of children. Also in 1824, the first state supported facility for juveniles, the House of Refuge for Juvenile Delinquents, was established in New York City. The middle of the nineteenth century saw a continued increase in facilities for children, and by 1890, there were 600 established juvenile institutions (Trattner, 1999).

Towards the end of the nineteenth century, there was a shift in the American society's view towards children. Fredrick Froebel viewed children not as little adults, rather as special individuals in need of play and recreation, greatly influenced this change. Additionally, the change was affected by Darwin's developmental perspective on human growth and by Freud's theories regarding the importance of nurturance in infancy. Finally, the research of G. Stanley Hall contributed much information on human development, and influenced the shifting perspective to children (Trattner, 1999).

Also towards the second half of the 19th century, family care again became favored over institutional care. In 1853, Reverend Charles Brace and the New York Children's Aid Society embraced a policy of family care, or placing-out. Over the next 25 years, Brace removed over 50,000 poor, vagrant, and delinquent children from their parents in New York City, and placed them in different family homes, often in the Western United States. This removal of children from their homes continued into the late 19th century, despite the growing opposition of the children's biological parents as well as individuals in the Western United States (Trattner, 1999).

With the turn of the century, the understanding of children and family continued to increase and the placing-out of children had largely replaced institutional treatment. Again, the focus was on preserving the home whenever possible. However, if that was not feasible, the National Conference of Charities and Corrections Committee in 1899 urged that children be placed only in homes investigated and approved by a social worker or psychologist. During this time period treatment for the parents and parental visits were encouraged. Moreover, in 1909, the White House Conference on Children recommended in-home services when possible, and stated that children should not be removed from the home simply because of the poor economic conditions of the family. From 1910-1930, the trend to support the nuclear family continued. When it was necessary to remove children from their parents, they tended to be placed in private homes (Trattner, 1999).

Child abuse in the United States began to gain notoriety in 1874. The case of Mary Ellen, an abused child, found no assistance because there was no law to stop child abuse. It was finally the Society for the Prevention of Cruelty to Animals that brought the case of Mary Ellen to court. Although some states did have child abuse laws, the enforcement of these laws seems to have been sporadic. From about 1875 to 1910, family violence received some national attention. However, after 1910, little attention was placed on domestic violence until the 1960's. Then, in 1964, Dr. Henry Kempe described the Battered Child Syndrome. In 1974 congress passed The Child Abuse Prevention and Treatment Act in 1965, and states enacted mandatory reporting laws (Dolgoff & Feldstein, 1984).

Beginning in the 1970's, the government concentrated on reuniting children and parents through child welfare programs (Hartman & Laird, 1983). Today, the emphasis is again on the preservation of the family. However, there remain a great number of children who are removed from their parents' care each year. In 1999, for example, 171,000 victims of child maltreatment were out-placed in foster care settings (U.S. Department of Health and Human Services, 2001). Public concern about the welfare of children continues to be a significant issue in the United States today. Parenting assessments offer one means by which to ensure the humane treatment of our children.

The Evolution of Assessing Parenting Capacity

By examining the history of child welfare, one can see that the assessment of parenting capability, in one form or another, has long been in existence in the United States. Children were removed from their parents' care from the earliest period in American history. For reasons ranging from idleness to poverty, children were placed in apprenticeships, institutions, and foster care.

Little literature exists, however, about the manner in which early parenting assessments were conducted. It seems that children were removed from their parents due to *their* behavior, rather than the assessed skills of their parents. Although we know that parenting capacities were assessed long ago, it is unclear exactly how the decision to remove children from their parents' care was made.

The Current Framework for Assessing Parenting Capacity

Campion (1995) suggested that there are currently three basic frameworks from which to assess parents and their children. These frameworks are the legal, social work and medical paradigms. The first framework that she suggests is the legal framework which,

> ...is governed by the laws of a state and is supposed to provide a general framework applicable to every member of society with equal fairness. It concerns itself with whether parents are breaking any existing laws and how children can be protected by recourse to the courts
> *(Campion, 1995, p. 18).*

The second framework for parenting assessment is the social work framework which is,

> ...based on observation of whether a family is conforming to the minimum standards of legally acceptable behaviour and is concerned with looking at the social and economic context of parenting with a view to alleviating the stresses on families
> *(Campion, 1996, p. 18).*

The social work framework will largely be focused upon in this chapter. The third framework for assessing parenting capacity is the medical framework. This framework is be used by medical professionals such as pediatricians, family practitioners, and psychiatrists.

This framework "concerns itself with clinical appraisal of one or several members of the family in terms of their physical and mental state with a view to seeking out pathology" (Campion, 1996, p. 18). Assessing parenting capacity generally begins when a report from an agency or a person is filed regarding the health and welfare of a child or children in a household.

CONDUCTING ASSESSMENTS OF PARENTING CAPABILITY

Beginning the Process of Parenting Assessments

The process of assessing parenting capacity can be initiated from several sources. Any individual, friends, neighbors, and family members may notify child protective services if he or she suspects child abuse or neglect. This notification to child protective services can be made on an anonymous basis, protecting the informant from potential reprisal. Additionally, teachers, counselors, or medical doctors, upon noticing atypical behavior or appearance in the children and/or parents, may also make the initial report. These individuals in positions of trust are obligated by law to file child abuse reports with appropriate agencies. After being altered to the possible abuse or neglect of a child, child protection services may choose to investigate the family. It is then determined whether the child should be immediately removed from the parents, or whether the child can remain at home pending further evaluation and assessment (Campion, 1995).

Diverse professionals play a role in the assessment of parenting capability, including counselors, psychologists, teachers, pediatricians, and social workers (Campion, 1995). When considering parental assessments, Gopfert et al. (1996) suggested that professionals contemplate the following questions:

1. Why is there a question of whether the current parent-child relationship is adequate?
2. Which decisions need to be made as a result of the assessment and for whose benefit?
3. Who is responsible for making these decisions?
4. Who will be responsible for implementing the decision and if it is a professional or service, has the professional or service concerned been involved in the decision-making process?
5. Is the assessment addressing the needs of the child *and* the parent(s) rather than meeting the 'need' of professionals or institutions for containment of their anxiety? Which needs of the child and parents will be met by this decision? Which will not?
6. What is the ultimate likely balance of benefits? (p. 287)

The foregoing questions serve as anchors for assessing parenting capabilities and out-placement of children.

Assessing Parenting Capabilities

Upon determining that a parenting assessment is necessary or could be beneficial, Gopfert et al. (1996) suggested examining the past, current, and future abilities of the parent to care for the child. Similarly, Schuff and Asen (1996) suggest composing a "four dimensional picture" of parenting ability. These four dimensions include:

1. A 'snapshot' of the current child-parent(s) relationship.
2. A 'photo album' of the family's own history.
3. A 'live sample' of current family interaction.
4. An 'aerial shot' of the family's eco-map (Schuff & Asen, 1996, p. 136)

When evaluating all dimensions of parenting capacity, it is advantageous to see the parents together, separately, and with the children. In this way, the assessor can gain an understanding of how the parents relate to each other, as well as to their child (Black, 1990).

There are many techniques and instruments available to assess parenting capacity. Typically, assessment of current parenting ability is largely descriptive. Assessments can involve asking both parents and children direct questions, both closed an dopen-ended quesitons. Watching parent-child interactions as they undertake a certain task can be useful. The assessor can then directly observe and evaluate the parenting skills and parent-child relationship. Often, assessment tools take the form of checklists or semi-structured questionnaires (Gopfert et al., 1996).

Considerations Regarding Parent-Child Relationships

When conducting a parenting assessment, there are five major aspects of a parent-child relationship that should be taken into consideration (Steinhauer,1991). Each of these aspects of the parent-child relationship can be evaluated throughout the therapeutic process, from intake to termination. These five components of parent-child relationships are:

1. Quality of attachment relationship
2. Ability of parents to perceive and respond to the needs of the child
3. Ability of parents to transmit the values of society
4. Quality of parent-child relationship
5. Continuity of relationship (Steinhauer, 1991).

Three of these aspects of parent-child relationships will be explored further. The. Components for further exploration include the quality of the relationship, the parents ability to perceive and respond to the needs of the child and the ability of the parents to transmit the values of society to the child.

Quality of the Attachment Relationship
Attachment behavior is "any behavior designed to get children into a close, protective relationship with their attachment figures whenever they experience anxiety" (Howe, Brandon, Hinings, & Schofield, 1999, p. 14). There are four identified types of attachment

behaviors in children: 1) insecure-avoidant, 2) secure, 3) insecure-ambivalent, and 4) insecure-disorganized. Typically, these attachment styles form at an early stage of a child's life. Usually, a child's primary attachment figure is his or her mother or main caregiver.

Secure attachment to a primary caretaker is vital for a child's optimum psychosocial development, and allows a child to acquire individuation and autonomy (Gopfert et al., 1996). For example, individuals identified as having secure attachment relationships tend to have a positive outlook on life, are socially competent, and are able to deal effectively with strong emotions, including anxiety, and anger (Howe, et al, 1999).

Parents, or other primary caregivers, largely determine whether a child will form a secure attachment relationship. Howe, et al., (1999) noted:

> Mothers of secure infants are rated at the positive end of 'responsivity.' Most of the time, they are sensitive, accepting, cooperative, available, accessible and dependable. Mother's tend to be good at reading their children's signals. There is synchrony between mothers and their infants, involving well-timed, reciprocal, rewarding interactions. Communication of feelings, needs and wants is accurate. Parents have empathy (p. 47).

The therapist or social worker can assess the quality of the parent-child attachment relationship throughout the therapeutic process. Vera Fahlberg (1985) composed checklists for assessing the parent-child attachment relationship. These checklists are relevant for families with children throughout the developmental and chronological age. By observing the parents and children, and by paying particular attention to the behaviors listed on the checklist, one can gain an understanding and insight into the attachment relationship. Following, is a sample of some of the observations that can be made by the assessor:

Birth to one year
Does the child...?
- appear alert?
- enjoy close physical contact?
- show interest in the human face?
- appear outgoing or is he passive and withdrawn?

Does the parent(s)...?
- respond to the infant's vocalizations?
- exhibit interest in and encourage age-appropriate development?
- show the ability to comfort the child?
- enjoy close physical contact with the child?

One to five years
Does the child...?
- explore the environment in a normal way?
- respond appropriately to separation from parent?
- respond appropriately to parent's return?

Does the parent(s)...?
- use appropriate disciplinary measures?
- accept expressions of autonomy?

Primary school children
Does the child...?
- appear proud of accomplishments?
- react realistically to making a mistake? Does he show fear, anger, or acceptance?
- have the ability to express emotions?
- appear to be developing a conscience?

Does the parent(s)...?
- show interest in the child's school performance?
- accept expression of negative feelings?
- assign age-appropriate responsibilities to the child?

Adolescents
Is the adolescent...?
- engaging in positive peer interactions?
- free from severe problems with the law?
- comfortable with reasonable limits or is he constantly involved in control issues?
- developing interests outside the home?

Does the parent(s)...?
- set appropriate limits
- trust the adolescent?
- have reasonable expectations of chores and/or responsibilities adolescent should assume?
- show affection? (Fahlberg, 1985, p. 91-93)

Ability of Parents to Perceive and Respond to Child's Needs

When assessing parent capability, it is important to determine whether parents are able to accurately respond to their child's needs (Gopfert et. al, 1996). Black (1990) suggested that mental health professionals could gain this information primarily through observing parent-child interactions, as well as parent-parent interactions. When observing the familial interactions, there are many aspects to consider. For example, are the parents able to empathize with their child? Do the parents meet their child's needs before their own? How do the parents cope with their child's behavior such as tantrums, wetting, and crying? Does the child appear well-fed, well-groomed, and rested? Do the parents demonstrate affectionate behavior towards their child, such as holding, hugging, and approval? Do the parents encourage and praise the child? Are the parents promoting physical and cognitive development in their child? Is the child's development age-appropriate or delayed (Black, 1990)?

Additionally, Cooper (1985) describes 11 danger signs and consequences of which to be aware. The 11 D's may occur if children's needs are not met:

- death
- damage
- deprivation
- disturbance in personality development

- delay in language and speech development
- distorted perceptions of people and relationships
- demanding behavior
- dependency
- delinquency
- detachment (Cooper, 1985)

Ability of Parent to Transmit the Values of Society

An important piece of children's development is an understanding of their social and cultural environment. It is very important that parents transmit the fundamental values of the culture to their children. The verbal and physical actions, as well as the explanations of their parents greatly influence children's understanding of many aspects of their culture. For example, parents can transmit to their children concepts of what is 'right' and 'wrong.' Parents can also model appropriate behavior. It is important that parental behavior be congruent with their stated values, given that observable behavior is often more influential than words or instruction (Steinhauer, 1991).

Additionally, "parental values should allow the child to develop a fit with the surrounding culture" (Gopfert et. al, 1996, p. 283). Otherwise, children may have great difficulty in a society in which societal values conflict greatly with those of their family. However, in families of recent immigrants, values and culture may obviously differ from one's original place of origin, and as a result contribute to intergenerational conflict (Gopfert et al., 1996).

Examples of Specific Parenting Assessment Instruments

There are many instruments available to predict and assess parenting capability. While these instruments may indeed have some utility, one must use caution when interpreting the results, and the results should be interpreted only by a qualified professional. Furthermore, when using assessment instruments, it is important for both students and mental health professionals to use them only in conjunction with additional clinical assessments. The instruments should not be used as the sole determinant of parenting capability.

Child Abuse Potential Inventory

One instrument useful in the assessment of parenting capability is the Child Abuse Potential (CAP) Inventory (Milner, 1986). The intent of this 160-item questionnaire is to screen parents who are at a high risk for physically abusing their children. The CAP can be self-administered and was designed at a third-grade reading level. The inventory takes approximately 10-20 minutes to administer. Individuals taking the CAP either "agree" or "disagree" to statements regarding an opinion or a psychological condition.

The CAP has well-established psychometric strengths. A variety of studies has shown internal consistency reliabilities ranging from 0.74 to 0.98. Split-half reliabilities have ranged from 0.84 to 0.98, and test-retest reliabilities from 0.75 to 0.91 (Heinze & Grisso, 1996).

Adult-Adolescent Parenting Inventory

Another instrument which can be used to assess parenting, is the Adolescent-Adult Parenting Inventory (AAPI) (Bavolek, 1984). The AAPI is intended to assess teenagers' parenting and child-rearing attitudes in order to screen for pregnant teens who are at risk for physical child abuse. This inventory consists of 32 statements regarding children's behaviors and abilities, and parenting duties. Individuals respond to these statements on a five point Likert-type scale ranging from strongly agree to strongly disagree. The AAPI is designed at a fifth or sixth grade reading level. Scores on this inventory indicate a level of risk (high, medium, low) for demonstrating physically abusive parenting behaviors. It is important to note that the AAPI is not meant to be a predictor of future physical child abuse, but rather an assessment of current parenting notions (Bavolek, 1989). The AAPI is one of the more well standardized and reliable parenting assessments (Steinhauer, 1991). Additionally, "its construct validity is impressive, and its concurrent and predictive validity are promising" (Steinhauer, 1991, p. 85).

Parenting Stress Index

The Parenting Stress Index (PSI, Abidin, 1990) is intended to be used with parents of children who are 12 years or younger. The purpose of the PSI is to identify stressors experienced by parents that are related to parenting behaviors that may place the child at risk. In addition to identifying at-risk children, the PSI can be useful as a screening tool to identify parents parenting in need of parenting skills and parenting education. The current, third edition of the PSI consists of 101 items to be answered on a five point Likert-type scale. Responses range from strongly agree to strongly disagree. The PSI measures stress in three domains: 1) Child Domain, 2) Parent Domain, and 3) Life Stress. The PSI demonstrates strong validity and satisfactory reliability (Heinze & Grisso, 1996). Once a clinician has triangulated data from several sources, the data needs to be synthesized.

Synthesizing the Assessment Information

Finally, it is important to synthesize the information gathered throughout the assessment process. After synthesizing the data, there are three groups in which cases may fall (Steinhauer, 1991):

1. Group A: The child's development is not currently, and has never been, at risk. The parents sufficiently meet the child's needs. No further intervention is necessary, unless requested by the family.
2. Group B: The child's current adjustment is impaired, although overall developmental progress shows no serious problems. The onset of family problems and parenting impairment is recent with no chronic inability to parent. The parents have a past history of using/seeking help to cope with psychological are familial problems, and are currently willing to use available help. Parents accept some responsibility for their role in their problem, and family has external support system, including friends, extended family, and other professionals. Therapeutic intervention can significantly help parenting capability.
3. Group C: The child's physical, emotional, cognitive, and social development have been chronically and seriously impaired. Parenting impairment has been persistent. The parents have refused psychological or familial help in the past, or else did not benefit from it. Currently, the parents reject psychological help. Parents do not accept

responsibility for their role in the problem. Family has no external supports such as friends, extended family, or professionals. Therapeutic intervention likely may not improve parenting capability. (Steinhauer, 1991)

Other Considerations when Assessing Parenting Capabilities

Another important consideration when conducting a parenting assessment is to gather a careful history of the child's development. For example, did the mother receive prenatal care during pregnancy? Did the mother use cigarettes, alcohol, or drugs during the pregnancy? Has the child experienced any emotional, cognitive, behavioral, or academic problems? If so, when did these problems begin? What is the status of the child's attachment relationships? Has there been any history of parental violence or neglect? Are the parents, or other family members, affected by a psychiatric problem? If so, what is the diagnosis, severity, and duration of the illness (Steinhauer, 1991)?

When assessing parenting capability, it is vital that the assessment process *always* aims to be therapeutic for the children *and* the parents. As Black (1990) states:

> The use of positive statements and genuine empathy for a parent who cares *about* but cannot care *for* a child can help the parent to accept a recommendation which is painful, particularly if help can be given to the parent on how to cope with family or community condemnation if she gives up her child
> *(Black, 1990, p. 48).*

It is important to take the parents' views regarding the situation into account, and to allow them, if possible, to be involved in decisions regarding their child's future. Furthermore, it is of great importance to look at the child's perspectives and wishes when evaluating parenting capacity (Campion, 1995).

PROS AND CONS OF ASSESSMENT USE

Benefits to Parenting Assessments

The assessment of parenting capacity is indeed a challenging task, and there are both advantages and disadvantages. Perhaps the most obvious benefit to conducting a parenting assessment is the protection of the well being of the child. In this society, the safeguarding of those who are unable to protect themselves is valued as an important concept. A significant goal of parenting assessments is the protection of children from neglect and abuse.

According to the U.S. Department of Health and Human Services (2001), in 1999 there were estimated 826,000 child victims of maltreatment, 58.4% of victims suffered from neglect, 21.3% from physical abuse, 11.3% from sexual abuse, and 35.9% from other forms of abuse. Horrifically, an estimated 1,100 children died in 1999 due to abuse and neglect. Nearly 90% of the child victims were maltreated by at least one parent (U.S. Department of Health and Human Services, 2001). Clearly, it is vital to protect children from the neglect and violence that they experience in their homes. Although parenting assessments are not always

100% accurate in the evaluation of risk to the child, they do provide the capability to begin to protect children from this abuse and neglect by evaluating parents and caregivers.

Another benefit to assessing parenting capacity is that the assessment can be therapeutic for the parents and the children. Not only is the child's safety guarded, but also the parents are protected from the consequences that they might face as a result of harming their children (Campion, 1995). For instance, parental assessments can evaluate the *risks* of parenting, thus alleviating potential child abuse or neglect. If an assessor deems a child to be at risk due to insufficient parenting, family therapy and other interventions can be used to ensure that no harm comes to the child and subsequently to the parents. Indeed, assessments can serve as a springboard for intervention techniques, and, when necessary, for the removal of the child from the potentially harmful situation (Black, 1990).

Parenting assessments need not occur only in cases of suspected child abuse or neglect. Assessments can also serve as a tool that can help parents recognize and understand their parenting styles. For example, in families with two or more primary caregivers, it can allow the parents to see where the parenting style of one caregiver differs from that of the other. The understanding of one's parenting style can enable one to change current parenting behavior in order to better meet the family's needs. Furthermore, parenting assessment techniques can be important because they allow the counselor to determine if it may be useful to teach or impart parenting skills within the therapeutic setting.

Finally, parenting assessments can be beneficial when they focus not only on parental weaknesses, but also on parental strengths and resources (Schuff & Asen, 1996). The assessments can be used to identify what the parents are doing well for their children. As a result, parents can capitalize upon these strengths. In this way, parents may feel empowered by their parenting skills. They can recognize the parenting styles, techniques, and values that are benefitting their child, and can continue to use them.

Disadvantages of Parenting Assessments

Despite the many benefits to parenting assessments, there are disadvantages as well. First, one must recognize that the assessment of parenting capacity is a subjective process, based largely upon the views and values of assessor. The professionals assessing the parents influence the actions and responses of the parents and of the children. For example, parents can act differently towards their child because the mental health professional is observing. Similarly, the child or parents may answer questions based on what they believe the assessor is expecting to, or wants to, hear. Certainly, neither the professionals conducting the assessment, the parents, nor the children exist in isolation; the presence of each effects the others (Schuff & Asen, 1996).

Another example of the subjectivity of parenting assessments concerns the checklists used to assess the parent-child relationship. For instance, Fahlberg (1985) provided checklists to assess the attachment relationship between parent and child. These checklists require that the assessor interpret the questions as well as the observations, and it is inevitable that the assessor's values are intertwined with this process. For example, it is the assessor who decides what are "appropriate limits" to set for adolescents, or "appropriate disciplinary measures" for children (Campion, 1995). In this case, the evaluation of the parent-child attachment relationship could differ from assessor to assessor.

Adcock and White (1985) explain the problems with the subjectivity of parenting assessments:

> The criteria that are used are often not explicit. Professionals have their own standards based on a combination of values, knowledge and case law but these standards are not usually shared. The determination of, for example, the appropriateness of the parental behavior is left completely up to the professional who is evaluating the parents and the parent-child relationship standards are not usually shared. They are not clearly described in text books on the law, medicine, or social work. It is uncertain whether there is any consensus of public opinion about a minimum sufficiently good level of parenting. Consequently parents and children who come under professional scrutiny are very much at a disadvantage. Parents do not know how they will be judged or what they can challenge. It is often unclear what changes they have to make for standards of care to be acceptable.
> *(Adcock & White, 1985, as cited in Campion, 1985, p. 29)*

Another disadvantage to the assessment of parenting capability is that the mere suggestion of a parenting assessment can be detrimental to the parents' self-concept. This can have an incredibly negative impact on the parents' sense of their own ability to parent effectively. For, as Gopfert (1996) remarked, "an assessment of parenting implicitly carries the message that the parents are not good enough" (p. 277). Furthermore, a negative experience with the assessment process may deter the parents from seeking psychological help again for themselves, their children, and their families.

Although the protection of the child's welfare is the utmost priority, disruptions in parenting due to the desire to help the child, may be equally, if not more, damaging to the child's development (Gopfert, 1996). Indeed, one of the five important aspects of parent-child relationships is continuity of care (Steinhauer, 1991), and it is certainly important that children experience permanence in their relationships.

There are myriad of ways that assessments can disrupt parenting, and potentially cause the child to experience discontinuity of care and of relationships. For example, disruptions in care can include:

> …a mixture of assessment procedures and arrangements, including assessment in a child's home, a short-term foster placement with access for the parents, reunion with the family, total breakdown of the family situation, or long-term stay in a children's home with high staff turnover
> *(Gopfert, 1996, p. 276).*

Furthermore, legal involvement in parenting assessments, particularly in child custody cases, also has the potential to be harmful to the child, as well as to the entire family. For instance, legal proceedings in child custody cases tend to discourage the involvement of valuable, informal support systems for the child and family (Gopfert, 1996).

There are definitely consequences when a child experiences discontinuity of care. These consequences may include "delinquency, criminality, personality disorder, marital breakdown, child abuse and mental illness" (Black, 1990, p. 45). Thus, it is important for mental health professionals to consider a child's continuity of care and of relationships when assessing parenting capacity, particularly when considering the possible removal of children from their parents. In some cases, it may actually be more beneficial to both the parents and the child, if the mental health professional does not overtly assess parenting capability.

Instead the professional can strive to help and support the family in other ways (Gopfert, 1996).

Finally, although the placement of children in foster care is primarily meant to remove a child from an unsafe situation at home, there is also the potential for abuse and neglect in foster care settings. For instance, according to the U.S. Department of Health and Human Services (2001), in the United States approximately 171,000 victims of child maltreatment were placed in foster care in 1999. Sadly, however, over 2% of total child fatalities due to abuse or neglect occurred while the child was in foster care. Clearly, there can be dire consequences for removing children from parents' homes and placing them in foster care. Even if parents demonstrate on-going problems providing adequate care for their children, removing a child from his or her parents is not always the least detrimental alternative (Gopfert, 1996).

ETHICAL IMPLICATIONS OF PARENTING ASSESSMENTS

Ethical Issues and Interpretation

As discussed in the preceding section, one of the major disadvantages to parenting assessments is the subjectivity that is involved. This inherent subjectivity clearly creates a great ethical compromise. Ryburn (1991) stated:

> ...every statement made in an assessment report by a social worker is as least as much a statement about that particular social worker, in the wider context of her or his role and agency, as it is a statement about those who are being assessed. (p. 21).

However, despite this subjectivity, there is often an underlying belief that there is an objective reality regarding those whom are assessed (Ryburn, 1991).

The belief that the process of parenting assessment is objective rather than subjective is certainly an ethical liability. In order to avoid this ethical trap, students and professionals must remember that the assessment of a parent or family is simply a snapshot in time, only one opinion made at one point in time. This subjective 'reality' discovered through the assessment process can change not only from assessor to assessor, but also from moment to moment. Indeed, we must be cognizant that a decision made by the assessment process, is not a "finite decision" that is necessarily "right for all future time" (Ryburn, 1991, p. 25). For instance, parents who are unable to care for the needs of their children when they are teenagers, may be exemplary parents when they reach 25 or 30 years old (Ryburn, 1991). Similarly, parents may be able to raise one child, but may be unable to provide appropriate care for another. For example, a parent may be unable to care adequately for a child with a chronic illness, or a physical or mental disability, while they provide appropriate care for the child's siblings (Black, 1990).

Furthermore, parenting assessment instruments with a scoring system may create additional ethical compromises. Assessment scores may over-simplify the assessment process. Additionally, they may mask the fact that the assessments continue to depend largely on the subjective interpretations of the individual conducting the assessment. Furthermore, assessment scores may produce less reliable decisions compared to those decisions made by a trained professional (Gopfert, 1996).

Further Ethical Considerations

It is so important to recognize that as mental health professionals, we wield tremendous power in child welfare, custody, and adoption cases. Indeed, as Cates' (1999) stated: "Information is power. Assessment information is life-impacting power" (p. 637). However, though we gather this powerful, life-changing information through parenting assessments, we will never know the objective truth of a parent's capacity to provide care for his or her children. We will never predict with 100% accuracy the outcome of a child's development.

Though it may be challenging, we must recognize that we are not always the experts in evaluating one's ability to parent. Parents and children themselves may indeed have more clarity on the "reality" of a situation. Thus, as students and professionals in the mental health fields, it is crucial that, whenever possible, we strive to include the parents' and the children's opinions throughout the assessment process. In this way, we are not only reminded that we do not necessarily know what is best for our clients, but we also remember that our opinion is one of many. As Ryburn (1991) stated:

> To listen effectively to the consumer voice would require of us a recognition that the values which we hold, the attitudes which we have towards those whom we assess, our use of language, and many other individual characteristics, will all be key determinants of the assessments which we make (p. 22.)

We must remember our humility in this field and maintain openness towards the potential of individuals, families, and systems to change.

USING PARENTAL ASSESSMENTS IN A MULTICULTURAL SETTING

Considerations when Assessing Parents in a Multicultural Setting

When conducting a parenting assessment in *any* environment, including of course in a multicultural setting, it clearly remains paramount to keep the safety and welfare of the child in the foreground. However, when working with clients and families, it is also tremendously important to take into account both the world-views of the clients and of the therapist (Sue & Sue, 1999). Similarly, when assessing parenting capacity, it is very important to view the parents and the family unit within a cultural and ethnic framework, and recognize that a family's world-view will inevitably shape parenting practices (Gopaul-McNicol & Brice-Baker, 1998).

To begin with, it is important to take into consideration culturally determined norms and patterns of parenting when assessing parenting capacity (Schuff & Asen, 1996). Unfortunately, no instruments currently exist which assesses a family's sociocultural background (Meller, Ohr, & Marcus, 2001). However, Gopaul-McNicol and Brice-Baker (1998) offer the following areas to consider when evaluating the role of cultural norms on parenting practices:

1. *Conception, pregnancy, and delivery.* How is pregnancy viewed in the parents' culture? What type of childbirth is typically preferred?
2. *Infant care.* Who primarily cares for the infant? What are the attitudes towards crying, tantrums, etc.?
3. *The older child.* What are the cultural expectations for boys and girls?
4. *Discipline.* What are the beliefs and opinions regarding discipline? What are the limits of permissible behavior in boys and girls? When conflict arises, how does the family handle it?
5. *Nature of relationships.* What are the children's duties towards their parents? What are parents' obligations to their children? Who makes decisions in the family? What networks and support systems do the family have available?
6. *Young adults.* When do the parents expect that the boys and girls should leave home?
7. *Health care.* How do the parents decide to seek health care for their children? What medical services do the parents seek out for their children?

It is truly vital that the professionals conducting the parenting assessment account for the parents' cultural norms. As professionals, we must recognize that parenting practices differ across cultures, and one culture's practices are not necessarily superior to another's.

When contemplating the use of parenting assessments in multicultural settings, there are several additional considerations. It can be very important to consider the impact of immigration on parenting (Gopaul-McNicol and Brice-Baker,1998). For instance, what stresses and losses did the family face when they immigrated? What are the parents' expectations of their children in the new country? When assessing a cross-cultural family, it can be very important for the mental health professional to explore the different levels of acculturation between family members. Additionally, a challenge with recently immigrated families is that the children often gain mastery of the English language before the parents do. Clearly, this can disrupt the family hierarchy as the children serve as translator for the adults (Gopaul-McNicol & Brice-Baker,1998).

When working in a multicultural setting, it can also be particularly important to explore how the parents are helping their children develop their own ethnic identity. Gopaul-McNicol and Brice-Baker (1998) noted that assessing parents' roles in their children's ethnic identity formation should have the following goals:

1. Determining how important ethnic identification is to the parents.
2. Determining how parents might feel thwarted in their efforts to pass on a cultural legacy to their children.
3. Identifying strengths in the parents that could have been overlooked.
(Gopaul-McNicol & Brice-Baker, 1998, p. 47)

The mental health professional can gather information regarding the parents' ability to assist their children in developing an established identity, by clinical interviews and home-visits. Through interviews and observations, the assessor can learn much about the saliency of the culture for the family. For example, what language is spoken in the home? Does the family were ethnic clothes at home? What types of food does the family eat? What are some of the rituals practiced by the family? Do the children have cultural role models? How do the parents discuss ethnic stereotypes and discrimination with their children (Gopaul-McNicol & Brice-Baker, 1998)?

Advantages of Assessing Parenting Capability in a Multicultural Setting

There are several advantages and disadvantages to assessing parenting capacity. Clearly, the primary advantage to conducting a parenting assessment with *any* family system is that it has the potential to protect the safety of the child. Furthermore, the interventions that may arise as a result of the assessment can be helpful to both the parents and the child. Additionally, when using an instrument to assess parenting capacity, the instruments are often self-administered, and can be both completed and scored in a short period of time (Gopaul-McNicol & Brice-Baker,1998).

Disadvantages of Assessing Parenting Capability in a Multicultural Setting

There are, however, several cons to assessing parenting capacity, particularly in a multicultural setting. Particularly instruments used in parenting assessments do not take into account cultural norms and values. In addition, the assessment instruments are likely to have been normed on majority group populations, and thus the results are not necessarily valid for individuals outside of that normative population (Padilla, 2001).

The instruments tend to rely heavily on the parents' ability to read and comprehend the questions on the assessment. This is clearly a disadvantage, especially with parents who speak little or no English. Yet another disadvantage is that the assessment instruments may not deal with issues that are pertinent to certain cultures (Gopaul-McNicol & Brice-Baker, 1998). For example, the instruments typically will not address "how to raise children to maintain their practice of the Jewish faith when the majority of their classmates are Christian" (Gopaul-McNicol & Brice-Baker, 1998, p. 41).

Assessing Parents in a Multicultural Setting

However, there are beneficial ways to assess parenting in a multicultural setting. For example, directly observing the parent-child interactions through structured play or role-plays can be very useful. These techniques can help the professional to understand the parenting styles and to see how the parents handle the child's emotions, wishes, and behaviors. Additionally, the assessor may learn what the parents' culture considers to be good and bad behavior (Gopaul-McNicol & Brice-Baker, 1998). The assessor can then combining the data gained in the naturalistic observations with information regarding the family's cultural norms and practices. Then, the professional conducting the assessment can begin to piece together a picture of family functioning and parenting capacity within a cultural framework.

It is important to recognize the impact of culture on parenting. It is also important to recognize that some parenting behaviors may be contrary to the host country customs and laws. When this situation arises, it is incumbent upon the professional conducting the assessment to identify two things. First, is the parent's behavior cultural or idiosyncratic?

Second, the professional needs to network within agency and community resources to address incongruencies in a positive and empowering fashion for the family.

CONCLUSION

The intent of this chapter was to provide human services students and professionals with an awareness of the multitude of issues involved with the assessment of parenting capability. There exist a variety of parental assessment techniques and instruments, and there are pros and cons to each of these. Students and helping professionals need to be cognizant of the many ethical issues involved with conducting an assessment.

The use of parental assessments is of particular challenge when working across cultures, with indigenous peoples, immigrants, refuges, and with individuals who may be in this country illegally. It is our hope that this chapter has assisted those in the mental health professions in determining the appropriateness of administering a parenting assessment, as well as provided an understanding of the implications involved when doing so.

REFERENCES

Abidin, R. R. (1990). *Parenting Stress Index* (3rd ed.). Odessa, FL: Psychological Assessment Resources.

Bavolek, S. J. (1984). *Adult-Adolescent Parenting Inventory (AAPI)*. Eau Claire, WI: Family Development Resources, Inc.

Bavolek, S. J. (1989). Assessing and treating high-risk parenting attitudes. *Early Child Development and Care, 44*, 99-112.

Black, D. (1990). What do children need from parents? *Adoption and Fostering, 14* (1), 43-51.

Campion, M. J. (1995). *Who's fit to be a parent*. New York: Routledge.

Cates, J. A. (1999). The art of assessment in psychology: Ethics, expertise and validity. *Journal of Clinical Psychology, 55* (5), 631-641.

Cooper, C. (1985). "Good-enough," borderline and "bad-enough" parenting

Dolgoff, R., & Feldstein, D. (1984). *Understanding social welfare* (2nd ed.). New York: Longman Inc.

Gopfert, M., Webster, J., Pollard, J., & Nelki, J. S. (1996). The assessment and prediction of parenting capacity: A community-oriented approach. In M. Gopfert, J. Webster, & M. V. Seeman (Eds.), *Parental psychiatric disorder* (pp. 791-309). Cambridge: Cambridge University Press.

Gopaul-McNicol, S., & Brice-Baker, J. (1998). *Cross-cultural practice: Assessment, treatment, and training*. New York: John Wiley & Sons, Inc.

Fahlberg, V. (1985). Checklists. In *Good-Enough Parenting*. . In M. Adcock and R. White (Eds.) *Good-enough parenting* (pp. 91-93). London: BAAF.

Hartman, A., & Laird, J. (1983). *Family-centered social work practice*. New York: The Free Press.

Heinze, M. C., & Grisso, T. (1996). Review of instruments assessing parenting competencies used in child custody evaluations. *Behavioral Sciences and the Law, 14* (3), 293-313.

Howe, D., Brandon, M., Hinings, D., & Schofield, G. (1999). *Attachment theory, child maltreatment and family support: A practice and assessment model.* Mahwah, New Jersey: Lawrence Erlbaum Associates.

Howell, D., & Ryburn, M. (1987). New Zealand: New ways to choose adopters. *Adoption and Fostering, 11* (4), 38-40.

Meller, P. J., Ohr, P. S., & Marcus, R. A. (2001). Family oriented, culturally sensitive (FOCUS) assessment of young children. In L. A. Suzuki, J. G. Ponterotto, & P. J. Meller (Eds.), *Handbook of multicultural assessment: Clinical, psychological, and educational applications* (2nd ed., pp. 461-496). San Francisco: Jossey-Bass Inc.

Milner, J. S. (1986). *The Child Abuse Potential Inventory: Manual* (2nd ed.). Webster, NC: Psytec Inc.

Padilla, A. M. (2001). *Issues in culturally appropriate assessment.* In L. A. Suzuki, J. G. Ponterotto, & P. J. Meller (Eds.), *Handbook of multicultural assessment: Clinical, psychological, and educational applications* (2nd ed., pp. 5-27). San Francisco: Jossey-Bass Inc.

Ryburn, M. (1991). The myth of assessment. *Adoption and Fostering, 15* (1), 20-27.

Schuff, G. H., & Asen, K. E. (1996). The disturbed parent and the disturbed family. In M. Gopfert, J. Webster, & M. V. Seeman (Eds.), *Parental psychiatric disorder* (pp. 131-151). Cambridge: Cambridge University Press.

Sciarra, D. T. (2001). *Assessment of diverse family systems.* In L. A. Suzuki, J. G. Ponterotto, & P. J. Meller (Eds.), *Handbook of multicultural assessment: Clinical, psychological, and educational applications* (2nd ed., pp. 135-168). San Francisco: Jossey-Bass Inc.

Steinhauer, P. D. (1991). *The least detrimental alternative: A systematic guide to case planning and decision making for children in care.* Toronto: University of Toronto Press.

Stevenson, P. (1991). A model of self-assessment for prospective adopters. *Adoption and Fostering, 15* (3), 30-34.

Sue, D. W., & Sue, D. (1999). *Counseling the culturally different: Theory and practice* (3rd ed.). New York: Wiley.

Trattner, W. I. (1994). *From poor laws to welfare state: A history of social welfare in America.* New York: The Free Press.

U.S. Department of Health & Human Services. (2001). *Child maltreatment 1999: reports from the states to the national child abuse and neglect data system.* Washington, DC: U.S. Government Printing Office.

Chapter 10

PARTNER VIOLENCE ASSESSMENT

Sandra M. Stith, Carrie Penn and David Ward[*]
Virginia Tech, Falls Church, Virginia
Dari Tritt
United States Air Force, Brooks AFB, Texas

Partner violence is a pervasive social problem that has devastating effects on all family members as well as on the larger community. While this chapter focuses on violence in heterosexual relationships, partner violence is also a substantial problem in gay and lesbian relationships (Burke & Follingstad, 1999; Miller, Bobner, & Zarski, 2000). Between 2 and 4 million women are victims of partner violence each year (American Bar Association, 1995; National Clearinghouse for the Defense of Battered Women, 1994). Rates of violence vary based on the sample from which the rates are calculated. The 1995 National Violence Against Women Survey indicated that twenty-two percent of women and seven percent of men report being victimized by an intimate partner at some point in their lifetime. Even higher rates are reported from large-scale random sample studies that ask respondents to report on violence in response to family conflict. These studies find annual rates as high as ten to thirty-five percent while studies that look specifically at violent crimes indicate rates ranging from 0.2 to 1.1 percent (Straus, 1999). Regardless of the context in which violence rates are calculated, it is clear that partner violence is an all too common occurrence in many American families.

Need for Clinical Assessment

Although partner violence is a pervasive problem, it is often hidden from health care practitioners. O'Leary, Vivian, and Malone (1992) found that only six percent of women

---

[*] Sandra M. Stith, Ph.D., is a professor and program director of the Marriage and Family Therapy Program at Virginia Tech's Falls Church Campus; Lt. Col. Dari Tritt Ph.D., is the Director of Research for the United States Air Force Family Advocacy Program, Brooks, AFB, Texas. Carrie Penn and David Ward are Master's Candidates at Virginia Tech, Falls Church, Marriage and Family Therapy Program.

seeking counseling indicated on their intake form that marital violence was a significant problem in their relationship. However, when asked to complete a standardized assessment instrument, fifty-three percent indicated that their husbands had physically assaulted them. In another study, Stith, Rosen, Barasch, and Wilson (1991), found that while only twelve percent of 262 families initially reported partner violence as the presenting problem, partner violence was occurring in at least forty percent of the families.

Clients have various reasons for not reporting the presence of violence in their relationships (Aldarondo & Straus, 1994). Clients may perceive violence as acceptable and/or tolerable and therefore not an important issue to bring up in therapy. They may be unaware of the impact that the violence has on themselves and the relationship. Clients involved in severe forms of violence may be fearful of potential repercussions from telling the therapist. Clients consumed with shame and humiliation are particularly in danger of not telling anyone, including their therapist, about the violence. Every client is different and will have his or her own reasons for not reporting or for underreporting the occurrence of violence, but it is the therapist's responsibility to use appropriate techniques to assess for partner violence.

Unfortunately, therapists often fail to identify abuse even in the context of clear evidence given by their clients. In a study by Hansen, Harway, and Cervantes (1991), family therapists were given vignettes with obvious evidence of severe violence. However, forty percent of the therapists failed to recognize the abuse and therefore would have left the abuse untreated.

Therapists fail to identify the occurrence of physical violence in their clients' relationships for several reasons (Aldarondo & Straus, 1994). First and foremost, many therapists simply do not ask about abuse. Second, even when they do ask, clinicians often use terms such as "violence" and "abuse" that clients may not associate with their relationships. Therapists increase their chances of detecting violent relationships when they ask clients about specific violent behaviors such as "pushing," "biting," and/or "kicking." Finally, sometimes therapists inquire about violence in the presence of both partners and thereby limit the accuracy of the clients' report. Neither the batterer nor the victim may feel comfortable disclosing the abuse in the presence of their partner. Each partner should be asked separately about any violence that might be occurring.

Due to the high potential for abuse to be underreported by clients and undetected by therapists, it is important for therapists to familiarize themselves with both verbal and non-verbal cues that may indicate the occurrence of abuse. Therapist should also be aware of the potential dangers of overlooking evidence of violence. The next section will address the cost of undetected violence in the context of the client's well being, family functioning, and the therapeutic relationship.

Cost of Undetected Violence

A true accounting of the costs of partner violence is difficult to obtain, partly because incidents are thought to be greatly underreported (Bureau of Justice Statistics, 1994). A consideration of the costs must include medical, mental health, police, legal, social services to victims and perpetrators, and loss of productivity on the job. An estimated thirty-five percent of women in hospital emergency rooms go there for treatment of injuries caused by partner violence (American Bar Association, 1995). The American Medical Association estimates that American women are four times more likely to be injured by an intimate partner than in a motor vehicle accident (American Medical Association, 1992). Naturally, abusive relationships are related to significant distress, which decreases individual and family quality of life. Survey findings suggest that wife beating has significant adverse effects on women's mental and physical health. One study indicated that severely assaulted women had twice as many headaches, four times the rate of depression, nearly six times more suicide attempts, and twice as many days in bed due to illness as women who were not abused (Gelles & Straus, 1990).

Undetected violence can also have significant effects for other members of the family not directly involved in abuse. Partner abuse has been linked to profound and long-lasting negative emotional and behavioral effects on children who witness assaultive behavior (Jaffe & Sudermann, 1995). Children who have observed violence between their parents have been found to assault their siblings and their parents, to commit violent crimes outside the family, and to assault their own intimate partners more often than children who have not witnessed violence between their parents (Gelles & Straus, 1990; O'Leary, 1988). Children in families where there is partner abuse are also more likely to be hit themselves (Jaffe, Wolfe, & Wilson, 1990). The American Bar Association Commission on Partner Violence reports that 87% of children who witness partner violence develop psychological symptoms such as aggressive behavior and depression (American Bar Association, 1995).

The occurrence of violence in relationships can also have a significant impact on the therapeutic process. Therapeutic change is often difficult when the system involves intimidation, power, and fear (Aldarondo & Straus, 1994). Clients attempting to change are often faced with change-back messages from those around them. One can only imagine the difficulty faced by clients who are trying to change within relationships where power and intimidation are already well established. Because abuse is often associated with power and control, cessation of physical violence should be addressed before any other therapeutic work proceeds.

Given the prevalence of partner violence in couples that come to family therapists for treatment, the likelihood that violence will continue once initiated, and the resulting negative consequences, family therapists must be competent to assess this significant therapeutic issue (Stith, 2000). All therapists need to assess for the possibility of partner violence with every family they see. Although many family therapists believe they do not treat partner violence, it is unlikely that this is the case. It is more likely that the violence has remained hidden because the therapist has not clearly assessed for it. A recommended assessment procedure is presented in this chapter, but first we will review the theory that guides this process and discuss current tools you may choose to use in your assessment.

Systems Theory and Partner Violence

Systems theory is the over-arching theory that guides the assessment procedure recommended in this chapter. Based on systems theory, partner violence is viewed in the context of relationship dynamics and patterns. Considerable controversy continues to surround the use of a systemic perspective in the treatment of partner abuse (Hare-Mustin, 1978, 1980; Taggart, 1985; Westerlund, 1983). Some professionals have suggested that systems theory blurs the boundaries between the batterer and the battered, and implies that the victim is "co-responsible" for the assault (Stith & Rosen, 1990). Because systems theory views interactions as circular rather than linear, it is often criticized for leading to "victim blaming," and thereby suggesting that the victim did something to deserve the abuse. However, systems theory focuses on *how* individuals are involved in violent relationships rather than identifying blame or fault for the violence (Anderson & Cramer-Benjamin, 1999; Giles-Sims, 1983). Therefore, systems theorists continue to hold individuals responsible for their actions that contribute to abusive interactions (Anderson & Cramer-Benjamin, 1999). Consequently, when assessing violence from a systemic perspective, the individual actions and the responses of both partners should be viewed within the context of the violent episodes (Anderson & Cramer-Benjamin, 1999; Giles-Sims, 1983).

Within this model, the family is viewed as a dynamic organization of interdependent components that continually interact with each other (Cunningham et al., 1998). This model assumes that the couple or family is the unit for assessment and intervention, rather than one family member in isolation. For example, Wileman and Wileman (1995) found that reductions in violence were associated with both the man assuming responsibility for his own violence and with the woman decreasing her vulnerability and taking an active role in balancing power in the relationship.

The holistic approach that results from systems theory emphasizes the importance of examining, not only characteristics of individuals involved in the violent relationship, but the dynamics that occur within the family context. Relationship characteristics appear to mediate the significance and interpretation given to violence both by the aggressor and the victim (Cunningham et al., 1998). Underlying relationship dynamics may impact each partner's decision to remain in the violent relationship despite the violence, or may play a part in maintaining the violence. Marital satisfaction appears to be an example of such a dynamic (Aldarondo & Sugarman, 1996; Straus & Yodanis, 1996). In a study involving the prediction of mild and severe husband-to-wife physical aggression with 11,870 randomly selected military personnel, Pan, Neidig and O'Leary (1994) found that marital discord was the most accurate predictor of physical aggression against a partner. For every 20% increase in marital discord, the odds of mild spouse abuse increased by 102% and the odds of severe spouse abuse increased by 183%. Therefore, when couples come to counseling with relationship problems, risk for domestic violence should always be considered.

There are a variety of other reasons why it is important to conduct an assessment of both members of the couple and the dynamics between them if they intend to remain together. First, male batterers are a heterogeneous group (Gondolf, 1988; Saunders, 1992; Stuart & Holtzworth-Munroe, 1995). Holtzworth-Munroe and Stuart (1994) reviewed the batterer typology literature and reported that three descriptive dimensions (i.e., severity of marital violence, generality of violence [toward the wife or toward others], and presence of psychopathology/personality disorders) have consistently been found to distinguish subtypes of batterers. They suggest that three subtypes of batterers exist (i.e., family only, dysphoric/borderline, and generally violent/antisocial) and that tailoring treatment to each subtype of violent men might improve treatment outcome. Stuart and Holtzworth-Munroe (1995) hypothesize that family-only batterers are likely to be the least violent of the groups and that they are likely to have developed problems such as insecure attachment patterns, mild social skills deficits, and low levels of impulsivity. They further hypothesize that this type of batterer may be the most appropriate for couples treatment:

Family-only batterers tend to have stable marriages characterized by relatively high marital satisfaction and a high level of commitment to the relationship. Thus, couple therapy may be appropriate if the violence is not severe (independently verified by the female partner) and both partners are highly motivated to improve the relationship. (p. 168)

Johnson (1995) has made distinctions between "common couple" and "intimate terrorism" violence between partners. Common couple violence is characterized by a partner's use of violence that erupts during a specific argument. On the other hand, patriarchal terrorism reflects violence that is embedded in an generalized pattern of a partner's desire for control. This typology focuses on the individual's use of violence as it relates to the dyadic context of the relationship and lends an important viewpoint to clinicians' understanding of partner violence. From the growing partner violence typology literature, then, it has become increasingly clear that all batterers do not need the same type of treatment.

In addition to treating subgroups of batterers differently, there is also reason to include female partners in assessment and treatment. Both men and women are often violent in relationships. In fact, most research has found that women initiate and carry out physical assaults on their partners as often as do men (Stith & Straus, 1995). Despite the much lower probability of physical injury resulting from attacks by women, assaults by women are serious, just as it would be serious if men "only" slapped their wives or "only" slapped female fellow employees (Straus, 1993). If reciprocal violence is taking place in relationships, treating men without treating women is not likely to stop the violence. In fact, cessation of partner violence by one partner is highly dependent on whether the other partner also stops hitting (Feld & Straus, 1989; Gelles & Straus, 1988). In addition, when women use violence in relationships, they are at greater risk of being severely assaulted by their partners (Feld & Straus, 1989; Gondolf, 1988). Therefore, it is important that both partners are included in a thorough assessment.

Additionally, it is important to remember that violence does not necessarily mean the demise of the relationship. In fact, 50 to 80% of battered wives remain with their abusive partners or return to them after leaving a woman's shelter or otherwise separating from them (Ferraro & Johnson, 1983). Failing to assess and provide services to both parties in an ongoing relationship may inadvertently disadvantage the female partner who chooses to stay.

Therefore, using this framework, it is imperative for the clinician to interview both partners individually to assess for physical violence. It is also important to recognize that aggression within the couple system is having an impact on witnessing children. A thorough assessment of the impact that violence is having on a family should include an assessment of children in the home. Assessments can guide the clinician in a path toward a better understanding of the situational and interpersonal context in which the violent episodes develop and are vital for determining appropriate treatment procedures.

ASSESSMENT TOOLS

Assessment of partner abuse through the use of assessment instruments is an important step to thorough assessment of abuse. Several tools exist to aid assessment and will be discussed in this section.

The most widely used instrument is the Conflict Tactics Scale (CTS) (See Straus and Gelles, 1990 for actual instrument). The CTS, originally developed by Straus (1979), contains

18 items and asks respondents about their own behavior as well as their partner's behavior. It can be used with offenders and victims. Several items on the scale pertain to psychological abuse and the last 9 items pertain to the use of physical aggression in the marriage. Straus, Hamby, Boney-McCoy, and Sugarman (1996) have developed a revised version of the CTS. This version contains 78 items, and is more comprehensive in its assessment of psychological, physical, and sexual abuse than the original CTS.

Clinicians sometimes want a more thorough assessment of current psychological abuse in a relationship. The Psychological Maltreatment of Women Inventory (PMWI) Short-Version is a 14-item instrument designed to be administered to women in order to evaluate the level of psychological maltreatment they received from their male partners in the last 6 months (see Tolman, 1999 for a copy of the items). The instrument has two sub-scales: Dominance-Isolation (e.g., my partner accused me of having an affair; my partner tried to keep me from doing things to help myself) and Emotional-Verbal (e.g., my partner called me names; my partner tried to make me feel crazy). This short version was developed from the original 58-item PMWI (Tolman, 1989; See Tolman 1999 for a list of items on both the original and short versions). Tolman (1999) suggests that the short version might be used as a quick screening device to help signal to clinicians whether further assessment is needed.

There are several instruments currently being used to aid in predicting future violence (See Roehl & Guertin, 1998 for a review). This chapter will look at two, the Dangerousness Assessment (DA) and the Spousal Assault Risk Assessment (SARA).

The DA was developed by Campbell (1986). The DA is used to assist battered women understand and assess the lethality of their situation. The scale contains two sections. The first section asks the battered women to write on a calendar the days in the past year that she was abused and to rank the severity of the abuse (1=slap, pushing, no injuries and/or lasting pain through 5=use of weapon, wounds from weapon). The second section contains 15 yes/no items that are related to the risk of homicide (i.e., is there a gun in the house, have you ever been beaten by him while you were pregnant). Refer to Campbell (1995) for the actual instrument.

The SARA was developed by Kropp and Hart (1995, 1998). The SARA provides practitioners with "a set of guidelines for the content and process of a thorough risk assessment" (Dutton & Kropp, 2000, p. 175). The SARA contains 20 items to consider while assessing for future risk. The items were selected after an extensive literature review. The SARA is not a psychological test. As Dutton and Kropp (2000) explain, "Its purpose is not to provide absolute or relative measures of risk using cutoff scores or norms but rather to structure and enhance professional judgments about risk" (p. 175). Items are scored on a 0 to 2 scale (0=absent, 1=subthreshold, and 2=present). The SARA also asks clinicians to indicate whether the item is "critical," defined as, "those [items], given the circumstances of the case at hand, are sufficient on their own to compel the evaluator to conclude that the individual poses an imminent risk of harm." The SARA manual can be purchased from the BC Institute of Family Violence, www.bcifv.org.

Of course most clinicians use the DSM-IV-TR for diagnostic purposes. No single diagnosis is a good predictor of being a victim or offender in a violent relationship. DSM-IV-TR diagnostic categories which may be identified in violent couples include Relationship Problems, with a category, "Problems Related to Abuse of Neglect-Physical Abuse of Adult," V61.1. Some individuals in violent relationships have grown up in abusive homes and experience post-traumatic stress disorder (PTSD). PTSD was identified in 33 percent of women in physically abusive marriages presenting for treatment in one study (Cascardi, O'Leary, Lawrence, & Schlee, 1995). Some offenders may be diagnosed with Intermittent Explosive Disorder (IED), but according to DSM-IV-TR, if the violence is purposeful, IED should not be used. Since many violent men use violence to control their partner, this diagnosis may be inappropriate in many cases. In any event, every individual who is in a violent relationship is unique and will need an individualized assessment.

ASSESSMENT PROCEDURE

The first step in assessing partner violence is to determine if any aggression is occurring in the relationship. This assessment should take place with every couple being seen and should include, both an oral interview and a written assessment instrument. It is important that interviews regarding potential interpersonal violence be held separately. When each person is asked privately about their own and their partner's violence, the therapist is able to consider each person's story and the consensus or lack of consensus between stories. Therapists can increase the odds that violence will be detected by the language they use in asking about potential violence. As mentioned earlier, asking a couple about how conflict is handled in their relationship and what happens when they get angry or in a fight, is more likely to result in violence being detected, than is asking about violence or abuse. Also, asking about shoving, pushing, and grabbing is more likely to result in an admission by clients, than is asking about violence.

Each partner should complete assessment instruments in different rooms so that they can feel safe to report accurately on their experiences and so that they will not be endangered by their responses. Many clinicians include a measure of relationship violence (e.g., CTS) in the intake assessment package completed by all clients. Other clinicians include questions in their intake package, such as, "Does anyone in this family have concerns about the way anger is handled? If so, explain." Or, "Are you ever uncomfortable with the way conflict is handled between adults in your family? If so, explain." They follow up with concerns identified on the intake with appropriate assessment tools. For example, if clients indicate some concern about suicide or depression, they might ask clients to complete a depression instrument. When using a tool such as the CTS therapists will generally have their own approach to introducing the tool and then incorporating the client answers into future sessions. When therapists are comfortable with a tool clients will be more likely to ask questions or voice concerns about answering any questions.

Lethality Assessment

If the therapist establishes that violence is occurring in the relationship, he or she should immediately assess the dangerousness and potential lethality of the situation (Holtzworth-Munroe, Beatty, & Anglin, 1995). The therapist should ask about the severity, frequency, and chronicity of the violence, whether it has been escalating, and the victim's belief about the dangerousness of the situation. The victim's prediction of the risk for severe assault is one of the best predictors of dangerousness (Weisz, Tolman, & Saunders, 2000). However, the victim's prediction should be taken with some caution since some victims underestimate the danger they are in.

The therapist should also investigate whether guns or other weapons are available in the home; if they are, the therapist may require that all weapons be removed from the home during therapy. A variety of other factors need to be considered in an initial assessment of a couple where there has been violence or with an individual offender or victim. Substance abuse can get in the way of any treatment effort and can increase the risk for severe violence to occur. Depression and suicidality (on the part of either partner) can co-occur with partner violence, increasing its intensity. If the victim decides to end the relationship, the risk for suicidal behavior on the part of the offender can be especially high.

The therapist should assess for psychological abuse and stalking. While psychological abuse is generally present if physical abuse is occurring, the extent and seriousness of the abuse is an indicator of the safety of the situation. Also, stalking can be an indicator of more serious physical abuse or homicide. Has the abusive partner been violent outside of the home? Have there been any arrests or protection orders in the past due to that person's violent behavior or threats of violence? If restraining or protection orders were in place were they followed? The therapist should also determine each person's history with abuse. Did they witness or experience physical abuse as a child? Do they believe that physical abuse is acceptable? Has there been violence in previous relationships? Knowing about these attitudes and experiences can help guide the therapist in determining appropriate treatment options. Finally, important protective factors should be assessed. Does each partner have a strong social support system? Does the offender appear to take responsibility for his/her actions and be ready to make changes in his/her life? These factors interact with the risk factors described above in determining the acceptability of a conjoint treatment methodology.

The overall assessment should be undertaken in the context of a working alliance (O'Leary & Murphy, 1999). High dropout rates among this group often come from a punitive rather than a supportive approach to assessment and treatment. Both victims and offenders often expect to be blamed. Also, any good assessment should also assess strengths and resources. Any treatment plan that comes out of this assessment should build on pre-existing strengths and coping strategies.

CASE STUDY

Janice has been a family therapist for four years. During that time she has been working with a family services agency. One couple she saw recently caused her to reflect on her skills in assessing for interpersonal violence. The couple, Sara and John, was seeking marital counseling at the encouragement of Sara due to ongoing and increasingly frequent arguments. Their two sons were becoming more aggressive in their play and the 6 year-old son's teacher had expressed concern to the parents about this. The couple has been married for 8 years, and has two children (boys 2 and 6). John is in the Air Force and is 28 years old. Sara is a stay-at-home mom who volunteers at their son's school. Sara called the agency and asked if there was someone who could help them stop fighting so much.

The therapist, Janice, met with John and Sara for a conjoint session. Both partners filled out intake packets individually. In the intake packet and during the first session both denied any occurrence of emotional or physical abuse. The primary concern of both partners was their increasing anger with one another, and that Gabe, their 6-year-old son, had been seen for behavioral problems and diagnosed with Attention-Deficit/Hyperactivity Disorder. Neither Sean, the 2-year-old son, nor John had any significant mental health problems. Sara had seen her family practice physician and told him about her depressed mood but no treatment was provided. Sara avoided eye contact and was tearful several times during the initial session with the therapist. John was angry and quiet. Both shared their thoughts openly, with John blaming Sara for starting most of the arguments. Sara agreed that she does pick at John because he has made her pretty much a single parent since he is always out with his work buddies. There was no present or past history of substance abuse for either partner. Janice was concerned about Sara's untreated depression, although Sara had no suicidal ideation, no history of significant mental health problems, and no previous suicidal thoughts. During the second session, both partners answered agreed that there had been pushing during their arguments and both stated they did not know how to avoid this from happening again. Janice wondered if the whole story was being told about the level of aggression in the home. She was also concerned that if Sara was fearful of John's behavior it might be difficult to discuss with him present. Janice was also interested in asking in more detail about the use of physical aggression or emotional abuse in the home and in assessing if there was any danger to the children.

Since the couple had been told during the intake session that Janice would probably want to see each person individually, after the second session, Janice scheduled the next sessions for each person individually. John initially expressed concern about separate sessions and stated that he was concerned that Janice would take Sara's side and that the counseling would not work. John had questions about why, if they wanted couple counseling, that individual sessions were being scheduled. Janice again explained that some individuals are more comfortable talking about some issues without their partner present. Janice reassured both John and Sara that all of the couple issues would be brought back to the couple sessions. Janice also explained that they would each be filling out assessment instruments before the next sessions.

John was the first partner interviewed individually. Before the session John filled out several instruments, including the CTS (Straus, 1979), the Beck Depression Inventory (Beck, Ward, Mendelson, Mock, & Erbaugh, 1961), the Revised Dyadic Adjustment Scale (Busby, Christensen, Crane & Larson, 1995), and the Michigan Alcohol Screening Test (Selzer, 1971). These tools were used by Janice to enhance her assessment of couple violence, depression, substance abuse, and relationship satisfaction.

John began the session by explaining that their family had been at their current duty location for 16 months. He was happy with his job but Sara was complaining a lot about how much time he spent after hours with his work buddies, leaving her alone with the children most of the time. They argued about this a lot. Recently, over the past two months, they began pushing each other. He would grab Sara to get her to listen. She would push him away. They would both get increasingly angry. On one occasion, about a month ago, he slapped her on the face. That scared both of them and John reported that they no longer let their arguments get so out of control.

John did not observe any physical aggression between his parents growing up. His father was a strict disciplinarian and he was spanked, but not physically abused as a child. Janice asked several more questions about this to understand what John's definition of abuse was. He had been raised to never hit a woman and to fight only in self-defense. He was upset with himself that he had slapped Sara and was embarrassed by this behavior. During this session Janice began to see that John's embarrassment was expressed as hostility and blame towards Sara. He didn't really see violence as a large part of their problems but he also admitted that he never thought he would slap his wife. He also began to see that he was spending more and more time with his friends because he was afraid if he got into a serious argument with Sara that things might get out of control again; things could end up getting physical again.

When John realized that the therapist did not react critically to his reports of aggression, he told her how he had thoughts about leaving Sara because he didn't know if he could be the type of husband he should be, in other words non-violent and supportive. He was beginning to feel hopeless about the marriage and scared. He stated he still loved Sara very much but things were pretty bad. Janice talked about her concern for safety and wanted to offer some suggestions to John as well as cover the same material with Sara during her session. These suggestions included how to take a time-out from an argument until John felt he could manage his emotions so that there was low risk for any violence. He was asked to not "make" Sara abide by the information he was receiving during this session and to focus on his own feelings and behaviors; that Janice would cover this information with Sara later, and then during their next couple session they would go over these techniques together. John agreed and stated he felt relieved that he had admitted to these issues. He was feeling more hopeful then he had in a long time.

After the session, Janice reviewed the assessment tools John completed. She was encouraged to note that John did not report any problems with alcohol or depression. His level of marital satisfaction was low and his level of violence was consistent with his verbal report.

During Sara's session the information John provided was confirmed. Janice asked Sara to fill out the same assessment tools, including the CTS, to improve her overall assessment of this couple and to be sure that other types of violence or substance abuse were not part of the couple's history. The results were consistent with the history both Sara and John provided. No substance abuse problems were noted and, while there was some evidence of depression, it appeared to be low and not primary. Sara also reported low satisfaction with her marriage.

Janice went over the same information on time-outs that she and John had covered. She also explained that when Sara pushed she was responsible for that action and when John pushed he was responsible just as he was when he slapped her. Sara disagreed with this at first explaining to Janice that she, Sara, was so angry with John that she deliberately egged him on. While Janice agreed that this was not beneficial behavior on Sara's part she also emphasized that when either partner chose to use aggression, that was an individual choice and that person had other options available. Sara denied being fearful of John but was concerned that he might hit her again if things got that out of control.

In the next several sessions Janice spent part of each session going over techniques to assist the couple with managing emotions that felt out of control and assisting them with agreeing how they as a couple would adapt these techniques. They also worked part of each session on taking responsibility for their own behavior, especially any behavior that was aggressive or abusive. Janice also asked John and Sara in their individual session about the children during the couple's arguments. They both stated that the children were not in the room when the pushing occurred or the day that John slapped Sara. The children had been in bed or outside playing. John and Sara both felt sure that the children had not heard or seen any of this behavior. Janice worked with John and Sara on their understanding of how children are affected by these altercations between their parents even if they are not in the same room when the violence occurs.

By the time they had their third couple session, and had two individual sessions each, both partners felt more hopeful, had a plan to talk with their six-year-old son about what he was feeling, and could see how much the pushing, verbal abuse, and the slap had affected their ability to connect and to communicate. They came to see how much damage it was doing to their trust and how they went to great lengths to avoid one another because they did not trust themselves to use non-physical approaches to their fights. Sara eventually admitted to having heard her parents have awful fights when she was young, and while she never saw them hit one another and never saw any bruises, she did remember crying in her bed at night when they fought, threw things, and cursed one another. She and her brothers had a lot of physical fights so she found it easy to push John back when he pushed her the first time. She had not realized how much anger was behind her pushing. She had always seen John as the angry person. Sara also began to feel her depressed mood lessen as she expressed this anger more directly.

While the focus of the rest of their sessions was on other marital issues, they touched base each session on how they were managing their conflict, using time-outs and other non-physical approaches to disagreements, and the progress being made in having safe discussions or arguments.

SUMMARY

This case clarifies the importance of completing a thorough assessment of violence with each individual. If the therapist had accepted the clients' denial of any violence during the first session and on the intake form, it would not have been addressed. Also, if a more thorough assessment of the dynamics of the relationship and the level of violence had not been undertaken, conjoint therapy might have endangered Sara. In this case the physical aggression was relatively new and both individual partners motivated to end it. When an individual takes responsibility for the abusive behavior as John did the therapist's job is much easier and conjoint treatment is much more appropriate than when denial is strong and/or abuse is chronic or severe.

Sara and John represent a couple that valued non-violent interactions and who sought help when their arguments began feeling out of control. There was no indication that the aggression was on-going, or that either partner was afraid. The therapist, along with John and Sara, agreed that there was not a primary aggressor and the dynamics of their aggression followed Johnson's (1995) typology of "common couple violence", although both partners felt John had more potential to be physically aggressive.

While being direct about the harmful consequences of using aggression in interpersonal relationships, the therapist was not critical of either partner and was able to connect with each partner. She assisted them with their growing awareness of how they came to use aggression within their marriage and how they could have disagreements in the future without violence being a factor.

Some couples have a significant history of violence, such as injuring the partner, using control tactics to have power over the partner, using money or the children to control the partner's actions, being verbally and emotionally abusive, or raping or stalking their partner.

If these dynamics had been present it is likely the victim would be fearful and a different approach to providing counseling would be necessary to ensure that they stayed safe. If the therapist had found the couple to be involved in more serious violence or with what Johnson (1995) calls patriarchal terrorism, which is almost always male-to-female violence, she would have referred the couple to same-gender treatment to address the violence and ensure safety before continuing with conjoint therapy. The therapist should only continue with conjoint therapy after fully assessing the violence, which can take several sessions with each partner seen individually, and assessing it to be low to moderate, without fear on either partner's part and no significant history of severe aggression or emotional battering. Placing full responsibility on the person using aggression only enhances the couple coming to terms with managing their choices and keeping the home violence free. Without assessing and addressing any abuse occurring within the relationship, the abuse could worsen or at least is not likely to end without intervention. The therapist's work with couples will be compromised if interpersonal violence is not addressed directly. By asking about partner violence and openly discussing the consequences of violence in the relationship, therapists assist couples in confronting the violence and beginning the work to eliminate violence from their relationship.

REFERENCES

Aldarondo, E., & Straus, M. A. (1994). Screening for physical violence in couple therapy: Methodological, practical, and ethical considerations. *Family Process, 33*(4), 425-439.

Aldarondo, E., & Sugarman, D. B. (1996). Risk marker analysis of the cessation and persistence of wife assault. *Journal of Consulting and Clinical Psychology, 64*(5), 1010-1019.

American Bar Association. (1995). *Report from the American Bar Association commission on domestic violence.*

American Medical Association (1992). Violence against women. *Journal of the American Medical Association, 267*(23), 107-112.

Anderson, S. A., & Cramer-Benjamin, D. B. (1999). The impact of couple violence on parenting and children: An overview and clinical implications. *The American Journal of Family Therapy, 27*, 1-19.

Beck, A.T., Ward, C.H., Mendelson, M., Mock, J., & Erbaugh, J. (1961). An inventory for measuring depression. *Archives of General Psychiatry, 4,* 53-63.

Bureau of Justice Statistics. (1994). *Violence between intimates.* (Publication No. NCJ-149259). Washington, D.C.: U.S. Department of Justice.

Busby, D.M., Christensen, C. Crane, D.R., & Larson, J.H. (1995). A revision of the dyadic adjustment scale for the use with distressed and nondistressed couples: Construct hierarchy and multidimensional scales. *Journal of Marital & Family Therapy, 21*(3), 289-308

Campbell, J. C. (1986). Nursing assessment for risk of homicide with battered women. *Advances in Nursing Science, 8*(4), 36-51.

Campbell, J. C. (1995). Prediction of homicide of and by battered women. In J. C. Campbell (Ed.), *Assessing dangerousness: Violence by sexual offenders, batterers, and child abusers. Interpersonal violence: The practice series* (Vol. 8, pp. 96-113). Thousand Oaks, CA, USA: Sage Publications, Inc.

Cascardi, M., O'Leary, K. D., Lawrence, E. E., & Schlee, K. A. (1995). Characteristics of women physically abused by their spouses and who seek treatment regarding marital conflict. Jour*nal of Consulting & Clinical Psychology, 63*(4), 616-623.

Cunningham, A., Jaffe, P. G., Baker, L., Dick, T., Malla, S., Mazaheri, N., & Poisson, S. (1998). *Theory-driven explanations of male violence against female partners: Literature update and related implications for treatment and evaluation* (pp. 70). London, ON.

Dutton, D. G., & Kropp, P. R. (2000). A review of domestic violence risk instruments. *Trauma, Violence & Abuse, 1*(2), 171-181.

Feld, S. L., & Straus, M. A. (1989). Escalation and desistance of wife assault in marriage. *Criminology, 27*, 141-161.

Ferraro, K. J., & Johnson, J. M. (1983). How women experience battering: The process of victimization. *Social Problems, 30*(3), 325-339.

Gelles, R. J., & Straus, M. A. (1988). *Intimate violence.* New York, NY, USA: Simon & Schuster, Inc.

Gelles, R.J., & Straus, M.A. (1990). The medical and psychological costs of family violence. In M.A. Straus and R.J. Gelles (Eds.), *Physical violence in American families* (pp. 425-430). New Brunswick, N.J.: Transaction Publishers.

Giles-Sims, J. (1983). *Wife battering: A systems approach.* New York: Guilford Press.

Gondolf, E. W. (1988). Who are those guys? Toward a behavioral typology of batterers. *Violence and Victims, 3*(3), 187-203.

Hansen, M., Harway, M., & Cervantes, N. (1991). Therapists' perceptions of severity in cases of family violence. *Violence and Victims, 6*(3), 225-235.

Hare-Mustin, R. T. (1978). A feminist approach to family therapy. *Family Process, 17*(2), 181-194.

Hare-Mustin, R. T. (1980). Family therapy may be dangerous for your health. *Professional Psychology, 11*(6), 935-938.

Holtzworth-Munroe, A., Beatty, S. B., & Anglin, K. (1995). The assessment and treatment of marital violence: An introduction for the marital therapist. In N. S. Jacobson & A. S. Gurman (Eds.), *Clinical handbook of couple therapy.* New York: NY: Guilford.

Holtzworth-Munroe, A., & Stuart, G. L. (1994). Typologies of male batterers: Three subtypes and the differences among them. *Psychological Bulletin, 116*(3), 476-497.

Jaffe, P.G., & Sudermann, M. (1995). Child witnesses of woman abuse: research and community responses. In S. Stith and M. Straus (Eds.), *Understanding Partner Violence: Prevalence, Causes, Consequences and Solutions.* National Council of family Relations.

Jaffe, P. G., Wolfe, D., & Wilson, S. (1990). *Children of battered women.* Newbury Park: CA: Sage.

Johnson, M. P. (1995). Patriarchal terrorism and common couple violence: Two forms of violence against women. *Journal of Marriage & the Family, 57*(2), 283-294.

Kropp, P. R., & Hart, S. D. (1995). *The Spousal Assault Risk Assessment Guide* (2nd ed.). Vancouver, Canada: B.C. Institute on Family Violence.

Kropp, P. R., & Hart, S. D. (1998). *Spousal Assault Risk Assessment: User's Guide.* Toronto, Canada: Nult-Health Systems.

National Clearinghouse for the Defense of Battered Women. (1994). *Domestic Violence.* (Statistics Packet, Third Edition). Philadelphia, PA.

O'Leary, K. D. (1988). Physical aggression between spouses: A social learning theory perspective. In V. B. Van Hasselt & R. L. Morrison (Eds.), *Handbook of family violence* (pp. 31-55). New York, NY, USA: Plenum Press.

O'Leary, K. D., & Murphy, C. (1999). Clinical issues in the assessment of partner violence. In R. Ammersman (Ed.), *Assessment of family violence* (pp. 46-94). New York: Wiley.

O'Leary, K. D., Vivian, D., & Malone, J. (1992). Assessment of physical aggression against women in marriage: The need for multimodal assessment. *Behavioral Assessment, 14*(1), 5-14.

Pan, H. S., Neidig, P. H., & O'Leary, K. D. (1994). Male-female and aggressor-victim differences in the factor structure of the Modified Conflict Tactics Scale. *Journal of Interpersonal Violence, 9*(3), 366-382.

Roehl, J., & Guertin, K. (1998). *Current use of dangerousness assessments in sentencing domestic violence offenders*. Pacific Grove, CA: State Justice Institute.

Saunders, D. (1992). Woman battering. In R. Ammersman & M. Hersen (Eds.), *Assessment of family violence: A clinical and legal sourcebook* (pp. 208-235). NY: Wiley.

Selzer, M. (1971). The Michigan Alcoholism Screening Test: The quest for a new diagnostic instrument. *American Journal of Psychiatry, 127*, 1653-1658.

Stith, S. M. (2000). Domestic Violence. Clinical Update: *The American Association for Marriage and Family Therapy, 2*(3).

Stith, S. M., & Rosen, K. (1990). Family therapy for spouse abuse. In S. M. Stith & M. B. Williams & K. Rosen (Eds.), *Violence Hits Home: Comprehensive Treatment Approaches to Domestic Violence* (pp. chapter 5). New York: Springer.

Stith, S. M., Rosen, K. H., Barasch, S. G., & Wilson, S. M. (1991). Clinical research as a training opportunity: Bridging the gap between theory and practice. *Journal of Marital and Family Therapy, 17*(4), 349-353.

Stith, S. M., & Straus, M. A. (1995). Introduction. In S. M. Stith & M. A. Straus (Eds.), *Understanding Partner Violence: Prevalence, Causes, Consequences, and Solutions* (pp. 1-11). Minneapolis: National Council on Family Relations.

Straus, M. A. (1979). Measuring intrafamily conflict and violence: The conflict tactics (CT) scale. *Journal of Marriage and the Family, 41*(1), 75-88.

Straus, M. A. (1990). Measuring intrafamily conflict and violence: The Conflict Tactics (CT) Scales. In M. A. Straus & R. J. Gelles (Eds.), *Physical violence in American families: Risk factors and adaptations to violence in 8,145 families* (pp. 29-47). New Brunswick, NJ: Transaction Publishers.

Straus, M. A. (1993). Physical Assaults by Wives: A Major Social Problem. In R. J. Gelles (Ed.), *Current Controversies on Family Violence* (pp. 67-87). Newbury Park: Sage Publications.

Straus, M. A. (1999). The controversy over domestic violence by women: A methodological, theoretical, and sociology of science analysis. In X. B. Arriaga & S. Oskamp (Eds.), *Violence in intimate relationships* (pp. 17-44). Thousand Oaks, CA, US: Sage Publications, Inc.

Straus, M.A., & Gelles, R.J. (1990). How violent are American families? Estimates from the National Family Violence Resurvey and other studies. In M.A. Straus and R,J, Gelles (Eds.), *Physical violence in American families* (pp.95-112). New Brunswick, N.J.: Transaction Publishers.

Straus, M. A., Hamby, S. L., Boney-McCoy, S., & Sugarman, D. B. (1996). The Revised Conflict Tactics Scales (CTS2): Development and preliminary psychometric data. *Journal of Family Issues, 17*, 283-316.

Straus, M. A., & Yodanis, C. L. (1996). Corporal punishment in adolescence and physical assaults on spouses in later life: What accounts for the link? *Journal of Marriage and the Family, 58*, 825-841.

Stuart, G. L., & Holtzworth-Munroe, A. (1995). *Identifying subtypes of maritally violent men: Descriptive dimensions, correlates and causes of violence, and treatment implications, Understanding partner violence: Prevalence, causes, consequences, and solutions* (pp. 162-172). Minneapolis, MN: NCFR.

Taggart, M. (1985). The feminist critique in epistemological perspective: Questions of context in family therapy. *Journal of Marital & Family Therapy, 11*(2), 113-126.

Tolman, R., M. (1989). The development of a measure of psychological maltreatment of women by their male partners. *Violence and Victims, 4*(3), 173-189.

Tolman, R., M. (1999). The validation of the Psychological Maltreatment of Women Inventory. *Violence and Victims, 14*(1), 25-37.

Weisz, A. N., Tolman, R. M., & Saunders, D. G. (2000). Assessing the risk of severe domestic violence: The importance of survivors' predictions. *Journal of Interpersonal Violence, 15*(1), 75-90.

Westerlund, E. (1983). Counseling women with histories of incest. *Women & Therapy, 2*(4), 17-31.

Wileman, R., & Wileman, B. (1995). Towards balancing power in domestic violence relationships. *Australian & New Zealand Journal of Family Therapy, 16*(4), 165-176.

Chapter 11

CHILD SEXUAL ABUSE ASSESSMENT: THE TRI-MODAL INTERVIEW PROTOCOL

Linda E. Homeyer[*]
Southwest Texas State University
Daniel S. Sweeney[•]
George Fox University

The sexual abuse of children has become an overwhelming phenomenon. According to the U.S. Department of Health and Human Services (2002), there were an estimated 826,000 victims of child maltreatment nationwide in 1999, along with 2,974,000 family-based referrals to child protective agencies. Family-based referrals may include more than one child in the family. This report noted that during this time period, the highest victimization rates were for the zero- to three-year-old age group. Sexual abuse made up 11.3% of the total child maltreatment victims. While there is no agreement on the actual prevalence of child sexual abuse, Gorey and Leslie (1997) published a review of 16 U.S. studies and reported adjusted prevalence rates of between five and eight percent for males and twelve to seventeen for females.

Marriage and family therapists are frequently involved in the treatment process, and are often requested to conduct evaluations and assessment. Since abuse is most definitely a systemic issue, marriage and family therapists have unique training and perspectives to bring to the evaluation process. Family therapists recognize that the process is as important as the outcome. This is true for assessment as well as therapy. Perhaps this is most true when working with children.

Child therapy should be process-oriented, not investigative by nature. The purposes of therapy do not necessarily align well with the purposes of abuse investigations. However, while assessment and evaluation are not therapy, they can be therapeutic. The purpose of the

---

[*] Linda E. Homeyer, Ph.D., is Coordinator of Clinical Training at Regis University, Denver, Colorado.
[•] Daniel S. Sweeney, Ph.D., is Associate Professor and Clinical Director, Graduate Department of Counseling, George Fox University, Portland, Oregon.

Trimodal Interview Protocol (TMIP) is to provide a child-friendly means for obtaining the requisite information in an alleged child sexual abuse situation. Recognizing that children communicate differently than adults, the protocol involves the integration of play therapy theory and techniques. The TMIP is thus titled because it includes three interview phases and the tri-modal acquisition and verification of details.

It is important to distinguish between the following assessment procedure and a complete child sexual abuse investigation. The complete investigation often includes extensive forensic, medical and psychological assessment including investigative interviews of all family members including the alleged perpetrator. There are few standards of practice in the assessment of child sexual abuse. While presented as an interview protocol, the TMIP is essentially a communication modality. It is not designed to be a comprehensive investigation method but a single component within one. The TMIP focuses on the child: What sexual abuse, if any, has this child experienced?

This chapter does not, and indeed cannot, comprehensively address the issue of child sexual abuse assessment. In addition to other approaches, there are structured interview formats and assessment instruments that may be used adjunctive to the TMIP. Professionals dedicated to the area of child sexual abuse assessment should explore the continuum of resources and seek appropriate training.

CHILD SEXUAL ABUSE ASSESSMENT

There is, unfortunately, a continuing need to assess children in the area of sexual abuse. This chapter will not detail symptomatic behavior of children who have been sexually abused. Professionals must be very careful in relating sexual behavior in children with a diagnosis of sexual abuse. While in the past, symptom profiles were used diagnostically; it is simply irresponsible to make these assumptions. Although some sexually abused children do engage in sexualized behavior, there is not a significant correlation in the research (Drach, Wientzen & Ricci, 2001). Additionally, in terms of symptomatic behavior in general, there is no single symptom that characterizes the majority of sexually abused children (Kendall-Tacket, Williams & Finkelhor, 1993).

One goal of assessment and evaluation is to provide an objective picture of a given situation. This is not easily done with the issue of sexual abuse. Friedrich (2002) discussed several challenges to objectively understanding sexual abuse:

> First, sexual trauma is highly variable across victims. Consequently, the assessor is never evaluating a consistent set of circumstances from one child to the next. Second, trauma is rarely an isolated event. Rather it is couched within a number of individual and systemic contexts. Each of these contexts operates to make a child more or less vulnerable to the trauma. In addition, the child is also on a developmental trajectory that predates the victimization and carries the child beyond the moment of trauma. Although this can be protective, it does create the potential for a lifetime of aftereffects (pp. 1-2).

This potential for a "lifetime of afteraffects" underscores the importance of conducting a thorough and appropriate assessment in cases of child sexual abuse. Just as effective therapy should be built upon a solid treatment plan, the sexual abuse evaluation serves as a platform and springboard for psychological, medical, legal and social interventions.

The focus of the TMIP is upon facilitation of children's disclosure and validation of sexual abuse. Recognizing the variability in contexts and child developmental issues, the evaluation seeks to gather accurate and consistent information. Lamb (1994, as cited in Wolfe & Birt, 1997) makes six recommendations for eliciting the most accurate information from children:

1. Interviews should occur as soon after the event as possible.
2. Multiple interviews should be discouraged, particularly if these are conducted by different interviewers.
3. Leading questions should be avoided whenever possible; however, use of leading questions should not be automatically be considered reason to disregard a child's recollection of events.
4. With older children, open-ended questions are the best format for eliciting free narrative accounts.
5. For children age 6 or under, who might have difficulty responding to open-ended questions, direct, developmentally sensitive questions can be used with great care to avoid contamination.
6. Every interview should be videotaped, to avoid multiple interviewing and to create a record of how the interview was conducted (p. 597).

These recommendations fit very well with the objectives and process of the TMIP.

PLAY THERAPY AS PART OF THE ASSESSMENT PROCESS

It is asserted that a play therapy approach to child sexual abuse assessment has considerable evaluatory and therapeutic benefit. As a prelude to the discussion of the TMIP, it is important to define play therapy. Landreth (1991) defines play therapy as a "dynamic interpersonal relationship between a child and a therapist trained in play therapy procedures who provides selected play materials and facilitates the development of a safe relationship for the child to fully express and explore self (feelings, thoughts, experiences, and behavior) through the child's natural medium of communication, play" (p. 14). There are several elements to this definition that are key for the TMIP as well as play therapy.

Sexual abuse evaluations are best conducted within the context of a *dynamic interpersonal relationship*. This creates a sense of safety for the child being interviewed. Sexual abuse evaluators should be *trained in play therapy (and evaluation) procedures*. The evaluation process involves the use of *selected play (and evaluation) materials*. A random collection of play media or assessment instruments is not appropriate. Like play therapy, sexual abuse evaluations should be *facilitated*, but out of necessity will have a directive element. It is only within a *safe relationship* that children are able to *fully express and explore self*, including the difficult issue of sexual abuse. And finally, it is crucial to recognize that children's *natural medium of communication is play*.

Landreth, Homeyer, Glover and Sweeney (1996) emphasized the importance of recognizing the value of play therapy when dealing with traumatized children:

Psychological trauma is an extremely stressful event or happening that is usually atypical in the life experiences of the child and is remarkably distressing to the child to the point of being overwhelming and causing the child to be unable to cope. Young children should not be expected to verbally describe such experiences because they do not have the verbal facility to do so, and such experiences are usually too threatening for the child to consciously describe. The natural reaction of children is to re-enact or play out the traumatic experience in an unconscious effort to comprehend, overcome, develop a sense of control, or assimilate the experience. This repetitive playing out of the experience is the child's natural self-healing process (p. 241).

While this refers to the therapeutic process, the same dynamics apply to the assessment process as well. Compelling children to disclose can be traumatic for them. Without doubt, child sexual abuse interviews should not be retraumatizing. Sgroi (1982) appropriately emphasizes that when conducting the evaluation, the "interview for validation should, on balance, have a therapeutic, rather than traumatic, effect" (p. 54).

Play and projective modalities create safety for the child client, both in therapy and in the assessment process. Another example is the use of art and drawing. Riordan and Verdel (1991) suggest "the use of art in conjunction with behavioral observation enables the counselor to make an assessment without causing the child to retreat further into inner denial of the abuse" (p. 119). Although projective modalities are subjective and open to interpretation, "they are of potential value if they are used judiciously as a means of communicating with children and helping them to impart thoughts, fantasies and feelings" (Anastasi, 1982, as cited in Babiker & Herbert, 1992).

Play therapists have qualities and training that are well suited for being evaluators of sexual abuse. These include having a deep and profound respect for children, having an understanding of child's play, viewing play as a natural form of communication, and being comfortable with play as a means of therapeutic communication. Unfortunately, not all marriage and family therapists fit this description. Many therapists who work with families exclude children from participation in family therapy sessions (Chasin, 1989; Gil, 1994). A study conducted by Korner and Brown (1990) found that family therapists who had received specialized training with children, or who felt that their training with children was adequate, were those most likely to include children in the family therapy process. Too few marriage and family therapists have adequate training in child therapy, which is reflected in the fact that child therapy is not a requirement for COAMFTE (Commission on Accreditation of marriage and Family Therapy Education) accredited graduate programs in marriage and family therapy.

Recognizing that a trusting relationship will be needed for a child victim to disclose, a therapist trained in entering the child's world though play is a valuable asset to the evaluation process. The play therapist is a fully present, attentive and non-demanding adult — interacting with the child through observing, listening and making reflective statements identifies the play therapist to the child as a very different kind of adult. Nonverbal attendance is crucial when assessing sexually abused children. Hynan (1999) notes that the examiner's tone of voice, facial expression and specific word usage might convey to the child critical connotations about another individual. This can encourage incrimination and lead the evaluation process astray.

There are a number of very basic play therapy techniques that are used in the TMIP, and are very utilitarian and effective as part of the sexual abuse assessment process:

1. *Allowing the child to lead*: This gives the child the opportunity to have some level of control during the interview process. Recognizing that the abuse process involves the removal of power and suspension of control, it is imperative that the child is provided a setting to regain some control. This is true both for the therapeutic and evaluation process. Friedrich (1990) states "a pace that is nonpressured and respectful ... can be therapeutic, reminding the child that the intrusiveness of the evaluation process can be manageable and not overwhelming" (p. 67). Allowing the child to lead results in the child feeling more secure in the evaluation setting as well as with the evaluator. Play therapists also are sensitive to play disruptions. Play disruptions are a sudden break in play or a slowly spreading inability to play. This occurs when the play becomes so emotionally overwhelming that the child cannot continue to play. This is not an evasion of, or noncompliance with, answering questions. Returning the lead to the child at this point and allowing child directed play helps the child to understand that the emotions are self-manageable.
2. *Tracking behavior*: Through verbal and nonverbal tracking of the child's behavior, the evaluator communicates to the child that her actions have significance and are worthy of the complete and focused attention of the evaluator. This encourages the child to continue with her disclosure as she becomes aware of the evaluator's nonjudgmental and accepting responses.
3. *Restatement of content*: Assessment can become therapeutic and reparative when the child hears supportive comments while disclosing. The evaluator does not give words of praise, which might subtly direct the child the child's responses. Nor does the evaluator offer criticism, or displeasure with the child's answer, so the child will not feel discouraged or inadequate. Rather, children feel understood, which results in encouragement to express self, which leads to a reduction in defenses and an increased ability to verbalize.
4. *Reflection of feelings*: This basic empathic understanding provides encouragement and validation for the child's world. This is in sharp contrast to the victimization experience, where the abuser does not allow the child to express feelings. Open acknowledgement of the child's feelings adds to the child's sense of safety to disclose.
5. *Limit setting*: If sexual behavior were to occur by the child towards the evaluator during the assessment process, a gently worded therapeutic limit can be used. The limit would include an option for an appropriate way to express self (e.g., using anatomical dolls or other toys). This process allows children to experience the evaluator as one who does not choose to interact through sexualized contact, as do abusers. It also allows the child to feel valued and understood, without feeling judged, punished, or stigmatized.

It is not possible to fully describe the play therapy process. The interested reader is encouraged to engage in further reading and training. Supervised experience in the field is considered imperative.

ANATOMICALLY DETAILED DOLLS

A significant part of the TMIP involves the use of anatomically detailed (AD) dolls. While the use of AD dolls has been controversial, they have been widely used in the child sexual abuse assessment process. Essentially, the use of anatomically detailed dolls in interviews appears to increase the probability of disclosure among children being evaluated for possible sexual abuse (Wolfe & Birt, 1997).

The American Psychological Association adopted a statement on the use of AD dolls. In part, this statement posited: "In general, such dolls may be useful in helping children to communicate when their language skills or emotional concerns preclude direct verbal responses. These dolls may also be useful communication props to help older children who may have difficulty expressing themselves verbally on sexual topics . . . doll-centered assessment of children when used as part of a psychological evaluation and interpreted by experienced and competent examiners, may be the best available practical solution for a pressing and frequent clinical problem (i.e., investigation of the possible presence of sexual abuse of a child)" (American Psychological Association, 2002).

Koocher et al. (1995) reminds that young children's recollections of events are often less complete than older persons, and that cues and reenactments may result in elicitation of more complete information from children. The use of AD dolls facilitates this process. In relation to what is considered convincing in sexual abuse evaluations using AD dolls, Koocher et al. (1995) also note that "the most convincing evidence with AD dolls was ascribed to 6- to 12-year-old children's reports that included verbal description" (p. 204).

A review of the research with AD dolls shows that they are not considered traumatized in and of themselves, nor do they elicit sexual behavior in children who have not been sexually abused (Simkins & Reiner, 1996). Additionally, AD dolls have not been found to increase the number of false abuse reports but rather augment children's abilities to communicate with evaluators (Bartlett-Simpson, Kneeshaw & Schaefer, 1993).

Undressing AD dolls and touching the genitalia cannot distinguish between children who have been sexually abused and those who have not. Thus such behaviors cannot be considered abnormal play or be regarded as evidence of sexual abuse (Bartlett-Simpson et al., 1993).

Everson and Boat (1994, as cited in Wolfe & Birt, 1997) identified seven functional uses of anatomically detailed dolls:

> (1) comforter [child-oriented play material helps relax a child]; (2) icebreaker [dolls help introduce the sexuality topic in a nonleading, nonthreatening manner]; (3) anatomical model [dolls assist in assessing the child's knowledge and terms for sexual parts and function]; (4) demonstration aid [the child can "show" rather than "tell"]; (5) memory stimulus [dolls may stimulate memories and spontaneous disclosures of abuse-related details, such as the offender's clothing or body characteristics]; (6) diagnostic screen [dolls may prompt the child's disclosure of sexual activity]; and (7) diagnostic test [sexual doll play can be interpreted as indicative of abuse; however, no guideline advocates using the dolls in this fashion and most caution against this, although critics of anatomically correct dolls often refer to this issue] (p. 595).

These functional uses correlate well with the process of the TMIP.

Children's memory of events is essentially similar to that of adults. Most researchers conclude that children's recall of both stressful and nonstressful events tends to be accurate but incomplete (Wolfe & Birt, 1997). The use of AD dolls is a method for facilitating recall in the stressful experience of a diagnostic interview.

TRI-MODAL INTERVIEW PROTOCOL

The TMIP recognizes that children communicate differently from adults and that children who have been abused often bring a host of negative affect to the evaluation and therapy process. The advantage of taking a child-centered play therapy approach in the TMIP process reduces the concern that children are manipulated. Oberlander (1995) notes that some examiners question the validity of using play sessions in evaluations because the evaluators are "active, initiating, probing, guiding, directing, and controlling" (p. 480). However, a child's memory does tend to be accurate as long as there are not purposeful or inadvertent actions to distort it (Hynan, 1999). The benefit of the assessment being conducted by those following the child-center play therapy approach is the evaluator knows how to follow, and not lead, the child.

As noted in the discussion on play therapy, children lack the cognitive and verbal skills to participate effectively in a standard forensic interview. Saywitz & Goodman (1996) emphasize that children can easily misunderstand questions posed by interviewers, and the meaning of the child's answers may be misinterpreted. Some basic rules for questions during the TMIP include:

1. Use simple words — one or two syllables are best.
2. Use simple sentences — the shorter the better.
3. Be concrete. If "private parts" are referred to as the body parts under a bathing suit, but the child was molested in the bathtub (where suits aren't worn), disclosure could be thwarted.
4. Discover the child's words & language and use them.
5. Clarify word meanings if necessary (the word "papa" may refer to the child's father, but could also refer to all adult males).
6. Do not label body parts, toys, people, gender, etc., until the child has done so. Then remain consistent.
7. Begin with general, open-ended questions and move to more specificity.
8. Be specific in terms of time (specific day or month, night or day, etc.).
9. Look for the child's nonverbal cues — the frustrated child is unlikely to say so, and the confused child is unlikely to ask for clarification.

The first "tri" in the TMIP recognizes that children, like adults, have different learning and communication styles. These include auditory, visual and kinesthetic modalities. It is important during the first phase of the interview to assess for the child's comfort and use with each modality. It is also helpful to use all three modalities during the interview process, which provides the child the opportunity to fully express self, and is helpful for the validation of details about the abuse experience.

A child who is *auditory* will likely be more verbal, both about the abuse experience and in general. This child may respond to questions more often with verbalizations rather than play behaviors.

The child who is more *visual* will respond to both visual cues from the evaluator and may use drawing as a primary mode for communicating. Drawings may include a floor plan of the house or room in which the abuse occurred, a drawing of the perpetrator, or a drawing of self. It is helpful to have anatomically detailed drawings available for the child's view and use.

A child who is more *kinesthetic* will be the one who is more apt to engage with the AD dolls, as well as other play materials.

The next "tri" involves the three phases of the TMIP. These include: (1) Rapport Building & Developmental Assessment Phase; (2) Information Gathering Phase; and (3) Closure Phase. It is important to remember throughout these phases that children will "test" the evaluator to see if she is genuinely interested, caring and safe. This needs to happen before children will disclose. Since they have so often been repeatedly disappointed in adults, either through victimization or the failure of others to protect them, having a safe place to disclose is crucial. This basic outline fits with the research of Bartlett-Simpson et al (1993) who suggest that the validity of child sexual abuse interviews can be enhanced by: (1) beginning with a free play period in which dressed dolls are readily accessible; (2) asking open-ended questions before more direct ones and avoiding leading questions; and (3) conducting a body parts evaluation and use the child's words when possible. All TMIP interviews are videotaped.

Preparation for the Interview

The interview takes place in a room with carefully selected materials without too many distractions and away from excessive hallway noise. Materials include a set of a family of four anatomically detailed dolls, anatomical drawings (Groth, 1990), paper and crayons/markers, animal hand puppets (some with tongues), child's tape player, and 2 toy telephones. Having both the child and evaluator sitting on pillows on the floor assists in equalizing the power differential between adult and child.

Objectivity is essential. It is preferable that the evaluator not be aware of the details of the alleged abuse. This provides a high level of internal independence on the part of the evaluator. External independence is retained by not allying with any particular person prior to the interview. Only the child and evaluator are in the room during the interview. This is an absolute. The validity of any disclosure would be ruled inadmissible and invalid in most venues including court.

Rapport Building and Developmental Assessment Phase

The essential purpose of this phase is to establish a sense of safety for the child, to establish the "give-and-take" of asking and answering questions, and for the evaluator to focus on this particular child. This phase is the time to obtain a language sample, to determine primary communication modality, and for a general assessment the child's developmental level. Gould (1998, citing Steward et al, 1993) suggested: "The evaluator should listen to the child's narrative report, examining it for two variables: the content and the child's spontaneous use of language. The examiner should then match his or her own sentence length and complexity to that of the child" (p. 103).

This phase begins with free play, in the presence of the evaluator. The evaluator combines child-centered play therapy tracking (as noted above) with initial questions to connect with the child. As the process begins, the evaluator may determine that a child is very reluctant after several attempts to connect. The evaluator might say: "I can see that you don't want me to talk and play with you right now. I'll leave you for a little bit and come back later to see if you want to play." After leaving the child for about five minutes of free playtime, the evaluator can return. If the child is still unable or unwilling to engage, it may be appropriate to terminate the interview.

Questions during this phase and later phases are nonleading. Leading questions are not only inhibiting for children in this process, but can also contaminate the interview process. Morgan (1995) provides a succinct definition of leading questions: "those that direct the child's response by providing information not yet stated or by including the answer within the question itself" (p. 47).

The questions that are initially asked in the TMIP are very simple and generally nonthreatening. These include asking the child for her name and age, asking for the names of all those who "live at your house" (the concept of family may be too abstract for young children). Clarify which are the parents or other "grown-ups" and who are other children. Older children can provide ages other the other children. If not, asking if the other child is "your size," "bigger," or "smaller," will help clarify. Children seem to respond well to questions about pets even if they don't have any.

The global assessment of the child's developmental level occurs in a variety of ways. One is asking the child to count and name all the colors of the crayons or markers with which he is drawing. Spontaneous or directed drawings are also helpful. Human drawings are one of the easiest to assess. Also, asking age appropriate questions regarding if the child knows the alphabet, home address, or can write his or her name, will assist in identifying if the child is generally on track developmentally.

If the child is at ease and able to answer questions effectively, the TMIP continues at this point. If not, it is more effective to end the session here and schedule a second interview. The child must be able to tolerate being in the interview room with the evaluator, feel in enough control to tell the evaluator "no" if necessary, and not need to please the evaluator. If these dynamics have not been attained, then schedule another session.

Introduction of the anatomically detailed (AD) dolls segues to the next phase of the interview. Set aside the toys and other materials to avoid distraction, keeping them in reach for later use. A simple introduction to the AD dolls is helpful: "These dolls are different than the kinds you might have at home. These are special dolls that have body parts like people." Then ask the child to, "Pick the doll that's most like you." Have the child pick up the doll and do all the handling.

The evaluator continues to track and reflect the child's behavior and feelings during this time. Children need to know throughout the interview process that most of their play is not only permissible (with appropriate limits) but acknowledged and understood. It is important for the evaluator to be self-aware during this process, so that the child's affective level is matched and that no overt or covert leading occurs by the evaluator's verbal or non-verbal reactions.

The interview moves to body parts identification and function. Body-part surveys are an integral component of a sexual abuse evaluation, and involve the assessing of a child's knowledge of body-part names and functions (Koocher et al., 1995). The process should begin by discussing nonsexual body parts.

The evaluator points to nonsexual parts and asks: "What is this called?" These parts include hair, eyes, nose, mouth, ears, hands, fingers, toes, etc. The child is then asked to undress the doll with such questions as: "These clothes come off. Please take the shirt off" or "Make the doll look like it's ready to have a bath."

This process allows the child to become comfortable with the dolls, and with being asked questions. The question-asking process automatically distinguishes the evaluation process from routine child-centered play therapy, where questions are avoided. The questions should be asked in the same form whether asking about sexual or nonsexual body parts. It is also important to remember that the perpetrator may also use nonsexual body parts inappropriately during the abuse incidents.

Since children typically begin undressing with the shirt, they should then be asked to identify body parts that are now apparent. These include breasts, nipples, chest hair, bellybutton, etc. The child is then asked to remove the rest of the clothing and identify body parts in the same manner. These include penis, vagina, buttocks, and anus. End the questions with non-sexual body parts, such as legs and feet, assists in placing all body parts in context and not focusing only on sexual areas o the body. This helps to relieve any possible developing anxiety or embarrassment and to normalize the process.

It is important to remember that children do not have verbal skills adequate to discuss and describe sexual abuse. Evaluators must recognize that children have different terms for body parts; for example, a child being interviewed may call a vagina a "front bottom." Evaluators must also not become embarrassed if a child uses slang and calls a vagina a "pussy" or a penis a "cock."

The first doll is set aside and the process repeated with at least three dolls. These include the adult male, adult female and child doll of the same sex as the child being interviewed. The evaluator should not point out any specific doll, but rather have the child do the selections. This provides the evaluator with the child's labels and names for sexual body parts of adult men and women as well as self.

Children are also asked to identify the dolls. The evaluator asks: "Is this a girl or boy doll?" This needs to be asked even if an adult doll is selected. Then the child is asked: "How do you know this is a boy/girl doll?" "Who is this?" "What is this doll's name?" These questions are asked of each doll that the child picks up.

Information Gathering Phase

This is the core of the interview process. The purpose is fundamentally to assess whether abuse has occurred. If this is the case, the goal is to gather enough details to be able to both protect the child and validate the incident. It may be helpful to vary the question type to keep the child engaged as well as not to overwhelm the child. Variations in questions are recommended, as Faller (1996) suggested using a continuum of question types, ranging from open-ended, to focused, to multiple choice, and to yes-no.

Using the AD dolls as props, the following questions may be asked during this phase.

1. Have you been touched on your body?
2. Have you touched anyone else's body?
3. Have you been hurt on your body?
4. Have you hurt anyone's body? [Remember, however, that sexual abuse may not cause physical pain.]
5. Has anyone ever done something you didn't like to your body?
6. Has anyone ever made you do something you didn't want to do to his or her body?
7. Has anyone every seen you with your clothes off? [Obviously need to distinguish between an abuser from a parent helping bathing.]
8. Have you seen anyone without his or her clothes on?
9. Did anyone ever tell you to keep a secret about your body?
10. Did anyone every tell you to keep a secret about their body?
11. Do you have any secrets?
12. Has anyone kissed you? Where did they kiss you? [There are obviously appropriate and inappropriate kissing behaviors.]

The evaluator can ask about specific body parts, but must include nonsexual as well as sexual parts (e.g., eyes, mouth, hands, breasts, belly button, genitalia, legs, feet, etc.). This helps to ensure that the interview is not biased or leading the child in a sexual direction.

If the child reports: "He kissed me there" and points to the AD doll's genitalia, the evaluator responds with: "Show me with the doll(s)." It is also important to ask the child to repeat the doll's name, even if given previously. It would not be appropriate for the evaluator to say: "This is Daddy, right?" This is leading. An appropriate response might be to say: "Now, this is . . .," with the evaluator's voice trailing off so that the child can finish the statement.

The evaluator should be cautioned against asking the child to "make believe," "pretend," "let's play," or "tell me your story." In a court situation, this will be seen as an invitation for the child to fantasize, especially by the defense counsel.

Following the disclosure of the sexual abuse, it is important for the evaluator to identify the offender and gain further incident details. These include:

1. *Who*: What was the person's name? If this is not known or the child is unable/unwilling to name, a description of the person can be asked for.
2. *Where*: The location of the abuse is important. Was it in a specific house or apartment? Indoors or outdoors? In a specific room of the house?
3. *When*: This may be difficult with young children since the concept of time is abstract. It is helpful to attach timing to specific events, such as holidays, birthdays, or during a weekend visit with a parent or grandparents. Further detail might be found out by asking about weather (hot, cold, snowing, etc.) and time of day in terms of night or day. Coupled with information from the parent interview can help in establishing the time.
4. *Frequency*: How many times did the abuse occur? The evaluator might start with: "Did this happen more than that one time?" This may culminate in: "Every time that you visited?"

Following the child is crucial. A child may spontaneously begin relating an abusive incident once the undressing of AD dolls begins. Ask facilitative questions that provide the child with ability to free narrate as much as possible. This holds true if the child begins disclosing at any point in the interview. Remember that this is a semi-structured protocol for just this reason.

If there is a disclosure, use of the three learning and communication modalities come into play at this point. Use the modalities to check the details of the incident. If the child has primarily used the kinesthetic modality, demonstrating, then ask the child to draw while explaining the incident from another perspective. For example, ask the child to draw details onto a floor-plan outline of the place the abuse occurred. If the child was molested in her bedroom, she could begin by drawing where the furniture is (bed, dresser, etc.). She can then draw herself on the bed, tell what she wears, what happens when the molester comes in, what he says, etc. The use of anatomical drawings is particularly useful. The child, using one colored marker can identify on the child drawing where he has been touched. Using the same color marker, he can mark on the adult drawing where he was required to touch the adult. Using a second color he can mark on the child where the adult touched him, then mark on the adult drawing what the adult touched him with (such as mouth, finger, hand, penis). During the drawing activity, previous revealed information can be clarified and additional details obtained. Information that seemed inconsistent can be explored for veracity. This is also when information that seems to be the result of coaching can be checked.

Closure Phase

The purpose of this phase is to provide a bridge for the child back to the child's normal world, and to normalize the interview experience. Just as therapy needs to have a termination phase, so does the sexual abuse assessment process. Free play is a very appropriate way to transition back from the interview process to normalization. The child may have experienced a considerable range of emotions, some close to overwhelming, that can be processed through free play, while the evaluator takes on the more therapeutic stance of responding. There a number of key elements to this closure phase:

1. Affirm the child: This is a process of encouragement, not praise. The child needs to be told: "You worked really hard today." This is not the same as: "You did good today" or "Mommy will be proud of you," which are praise statements. Praise is leading and is only given for adult-pleasing behavior or results. The child has been engaging in a stressful process. Acknowledging that the process of disclosure is hard work is basic encouragement. If the child is exhibiting negative affect, the appropriate response is a reflective statement, such as: "You look sad." Feelings need to be reflected and affirmed. It is not the role of the evaluator to provide comfort and assurance. The evaluator, like a therapist, should reflect feelings in a way that affirms the child, communicates acceptance of the feelings, and sends a message of confidence in the child's ability to move on.
2. Do not make promises that you cannot keep: It is not appropriate for the evaluator to say things like: "We'll keep _____ in jail so he can't hurt you again." This obviously cannot be guaranteed to a child. The evaluator should also avoid making promises to remain in contact with the child. While this time has been emotionally intense and a

connection is often established, it is not possible or appropriate for an evaluator to maintain contact with clients. An important issue to remember here is that abusers lie to children, and professionals should avoid falling into this dynamic even when well intentioned.

3. Allow the child a chance to ask questions: Remember that the abuse situation left the child with no sense of control. When being asked questions about the event, the child still has very little control. By allowing the child the opportunity to ask questions, the evaluator is providing opportunity for the child to another chance to be re-empowered. The evaluation has been a unique experience, and the evaluator is a unique person. The child should be able to ask about these things.

4. Allow & encourage drawing and free play: These are activities that further promote the child's sense of being in control. The sensory and kinesthetic nature of these activities are in contrast to the interview process, and help reduce elevated emotional responses and provide children a sense of mastery.

5. If no abuse has been disclosed: There are many reasons why this may occur. First, and foremost, it may be that no abuse occurred. After all that is the purpose of the interview, to discover what, if anything occurred. If no abuse was found, it is appropriate to provide anti-victimization training. At the same time, if suspicion of abuse remains, the child's family and evaluator must be open to considering another interview. Sorenson and Snow's (1991) research indicates that 72% of children who were sexually abused denied it in their first interview. In this case every effort should be made to maintain safety of the child until a clearer determination can be made. Children's physical and psychological boundaries must be protected until the next interview. Ultimately, children cannot be forced to disclose abuse. There are many reasons why children, who may have been sexually abused, refuse to talk about it or play it out. This ranges from strong threats from the perpetrator to keep the secret to a desire to protect others.

  It is also helpful to ask the child for a drawing. This can be a free drawing or one with specific instructions, such as the Kinetic Family Drawing (Burns & Kaufman, 1980). This promotes normalization and return to routine life discussed above. I also allows for one additional opportunity for children to provide insight into their family relationships.

6. Give the child a business card: While this may seem unusual, providing the child with a business card provides a symbol of the interview/disclosure process. A brochure or flyer may also be considered. This provides not only a symbol of the process, but also a transitional object as the child moves on to home, school, and other areas of life.

SYSTEMIC ISSUES

Obviously, child sexual abuse does not occur in a vacuum. Since the majority of sexually abused children are victimized by someone they know, the family and social system must be examined. Although the TMIP focuses on the child, it is crucial to attain information from significant others in the child's life. This will involve structured interviews with the parent(s). It is important to keep in mind that a few referring parents have ulterior motives. It is crucial that the evaluator probes for such dynamics during the parent interview and assess for coaching when interviewing the child. Assessment instruments filled out by parents are useful and recommended. Instruments such as the *Child Sexual Behavior Inventory* (Friedrich, 1998) check for both developmentally related sexual behavior and sexual abuse specific items. The *Child Behavior Checklist* by Achenbach (1991) provides a measure of a range of behavior.

There are several pieces to the puzzle in child sexual abuse evaluation. The TMIP is one piece of this puzzle. In their discussion of child sexual abuse assessment, Babiker and Herbert (1998) noted "evaluation requires a creative process that weighs up different pieces of information from various sources and places them in a systemic and developmental context" (p. 234). Systemic and developmental issues must not be ignored in the evaluation process.

The complete evaluation process must involve all members of the household, whether or not related to the child victim. There are inter- and intra-personal dynamics that should be explored, as well as inter- and intra-generational issues. Gould (1998) summarized several systemic areas that should be examined, noting that: "The evaluator needs to explore how . . . connects with each member of the family. Each subsystem, such as siblings, triangles, and complementary and symmetrically reciprocal relationships, needs to be assessed along with dimensions of emotional closeness-distance, regulation of intimacy, rigidity-flexibility, authoritarian-permissive, and active-passive, among other relevant factors" (p. 89).

Systemic issues are all the more important to consider in light of intrafamilial abuse. This is particularly underscored by the fact that father-daughter (including stepfather and stepdaughter) incest is estimated to account for approximately 60-80% of sexual abuses cases (Greenfield, 1996). Intrafamilial sexual abuse presents complex systemic dynamics, including those noted in the previous paragraph. Additionally, children who experience intrafamilial abuse are said to present higher rates of symptomology than children who are abused by nonfamily members (Ferrara, 2002). While this does not minimize the trauma experienced by children who experience abuse by nonfamilial perpetrators, the emotional and behavioral distress may be intensified for children and family members in cases of intrafamilial cases.

Recantation in child sexual abuse cases is often systemically based. Rieser (1991) suggests several familial factors related to recantation, including secrecy related to family systemic pressure, rigid boundaries between the family and external world creating an exaggerated sense of family loyalty, lack of family support and possible pressure to recant, family stress related to prolonged and intense interaction with professionals, and related family intervening events. Other systemic issues related to recantation involve the inability of the family in dealing with the child's out of control behavior, general family conflict, and the father's difficulty dealing with the child's disclosure (Gonzales, Waterman, Kelly, McCord & Oliveri, 1993). Sorenson and Snow (1991) discuss recantation as a part of the disclosure process. Recanting occurred in 22% of the cases Sorenson and Snow researched with 92% of those children subsequently reaffirmed their abuse.

Family context is crucial in understanding sexual behavior in children. This is true for all families, whether abuse has been reported or not. Mrazek and Mrazek (1981), for example, discuss a continuum of acceptable expressions and verbalizations of sexuality in families, ranging between the polarizations of complete permissiveness and complete repression. This range will affect the impact of the sexual abuse and the disclosure process.

It may also be pertinent to briefly discuss gender as it relates to both the child and the evaluator. Since girls are more often victims of sexual abuse, and since males are more often perpetrators, it might be argued that females are more appropriate and effective as evaluators. This generalization appears to be true anecdotally, but deserves greater attention in the research literature. Boys may be more reluctant to disclose abuse due to embarrassment and fear of disbelief by others (Hunter, 1990), while girls may experience a greater sense of abandonment from mothers who failed to protect (Ferrara, 2002). The noncoercive and child-directed ethos of play therapy and the TMIP may overcome any gender issues that complicate the evaluation and treatment process.

An overall goal of the TMIP is to empower children who have experienced the disempowering trauma of abuse. As such, the focus is as much on the child's strengths and potential as on the disclosure itself. This fits with post-modern systemic theory, in that it is positive-focused and strengths-based. The evaluation itself, and the gathering of corollary family history should therefore work at identifying functional patterns of coping and communicating as opposed to focusing on dysfunctional patterns and behaviors.

CASE EXAMPLE

Caitlin, three years old, had recently moved from her mother's home to that of her father and stepmother. After the father reported her physical condition to Child Protective Services (CPS), CPS validated physical and medical neglect in the home of her mother. When Caitlin began to ask her four-year-old stepbrother to play with her sexually, and she reported to her father and stepmother she had learned to play sexually with her mother's boyfriend, a report of sexual abuse was made to CPS. CPS closed the case as unable-to-determine when the investigator was unable to get Caitlin to disclose any information about sexual abuse.

Caitlin was already seeing a play therapist in my office when the sexual abuse allegations occurred. I was asked to do a sexual abuse assessment after CPS had finished their investigation.

Caitlin connected with me easily. This was due, in part, to her already feeling safe and comfortable in the office suite. During the first phase, she drew in scribbles, labeled few colors correctly, and was unable to draw any form of human figure. She seemed to be a bit behind developmentally, probably as a result of her earlier neglectful family environment. Verbally, Caitlin chattered easily and spontaneously talked about her "drawings." She cooperated with undressing the anatomically detailed (AD) dolls. She names the dolls as a mommy, daddy, and girl. She labeled breasts as "boobies," vaginal area a "tee-tee," penis as "privates," and buttocks as "butt." While interacting with the AD dolls she spontaneously stated that both her mother and mother's boyfriend had "kissed her tee-tee." When asked to demonstrate with the dolls, she put female child doll's vaginal area to her mouth. (Three-year-old children often interact with their own bodies; either pointing to their own body parts or uses self-and-doll as Caitlin did in this example. That is quite developmentally appropriate.) Caitlin then picked up the adult male doll and put the penis in her mouth, calling it "kissing." When I asked what happened next, she replied, "Blood comes out." Clarifying, I ask, "What color was it?" She responds, "White ... and it tasted yuckie ... like old milk." (Her father later stated that when living with her mother, she often had to use curdled milk on her cereal.) Caitlin had a play disruption at this point.

After allowing Caitlin some free play I introduced the anatomical drawings. I asked her to pick one that looked most like her stepfather. She selected the adult male drawing. Using a marker, she was able to mark on the drawing where she kissed him, "right here on the butt," and in response to my question "anywhere else" she marked on his penis. She spontaneously reached past me and marked on the adult female drawing's breast. On my query she first labeled that drawing as "a sexy girl," then as her mother. As Caitlin continued to mark on that anatomical drawing she talked about "kissing" her mother's "tee-tee" and reported getting hair in her mouth. At this point she was also able to use the adult and child AD dolls to show the sexual activity she had described and marked on drawings. She stated the sexual activity with her mother's boyfriend occurred when she "takes off her clothes in the bathroom" and when all three of them were in her mother's bedroom.

Caitlin again experienced a play disruption. In this case, I assessed I had sufficient consistent and detailed information to believe that sexual abuse had occurred so I shifted into the Closure Phase. I allowed Caitlin free-play and I tracked her as if we were in play therapy. This worked very well for her, calming and reassuring her that she was in a safe environment. She had her regular play therapy session the following day, which also was an important outlet for her dealing with the emotions that were evident in this interview.

Caitlin's father completed the *Child Behavior Checklist* (Achenbach, 1991). She scored in the clinical ranges in the following subscales: Internalizing and Externalizing (both at 98th percentile); Anxious/Depressed (73rd percentile); Withdrawn (71st percentile); Sleep Problems (78th percentile); Aggressive Behavior (78th percentile). The remaining two subscales of Somatic Problems and Destructive Behavior were both in the normal range. On a checklist of behaviors often seen in sexually abused children twenty of the forty-five behaviors were identified as exhibited by Caitlin. This checklist was used to help identify sexual specific behavior.

Based on all of the above information, my opinion was that both her mother and stepfather had sexually abused Caitlin. Her father and stepmother responded appropriately and continued to send her to play therapy. I saw them for three parent support sessions and testified in court on behalf of Caitlin in a custody hearing.

SUMMARY

The TMIP is a sexual abuse assessment interview protocol. It is designed to interview the alleged child-victim of sexual abuse. The TMIP integrates child-centered play therapy techniques to assist the child in feeling safe and encourage disclosure of any abuse. The TMIP utilizes the three learning and communication modalities to access the child's primary method of expression. The TMIP has three phases to provide the evaluator in a clear plan throughout the interview process. This protocol is meant to assess the child's experience, not as a comprehensive investigation.

It is crucial that individuals who conduct sexual abuse evaluations have the appropriate training and supervised experience. It is recommended that graduate level mental health professionals who have additional training in child development, play therapy, the use of anatomically detailed dolls, and forensic interviewing conduct the TMIP.

REFERENCES

Achenbach, T.M. (1991). *Child behavior checklist.* Burlington, VT: University of Vermont.
American Psychological Association (2002). The use of anatomically detailed dolls in forensic evaluations. Washington, DC: American Psychological Association. Retrieved

January 23, 2002, from APA database on *http://www.apa.org/pi/cyf/cyfres.html#anadolls*.

Babiker, G., & Herbert, M. (1998). Critical issues in the assessment of child sexual abuse. *Clinical Child and Family Psychology Review, 1*(4), 231-252.

Bartlett-Simpson, B., Kneeshaw, S., & Schaefer, C. (1993). The use of anatomical dolls to assess child sexual abuse: A critical review. *International Journal of Play Therapy, 2*(2), 35-51.

Burns, R., & Kaufman, S. (1980). *Kinetic family drawings*. New York: Brunner/Mazel.

Chasin, R. (1989). Interviewing families with children: Guidelines and suggestions. *Journal of Psychotherapy and the Family, 5*(3/4), 15-30.

Drach, K., Wientzen, J., & Ricci, L. (2001). The diagnostic utility of sexual behavior problems in diagnosing sexual abuse in a forensic child abuse evaluation clinic. *Child Abuse & Neglect, 25*, 489-503.

Faller, K. (1996). *Evaluating children suspected of having been abused*. Thousand Oaks, CA: Sage Publications.

Ferrara, F. (2002). *Childhood sexual abuse: Developmental effects across the lifespan*. Pacific Grove, CA: Brooks/Cole.

Friedrich, W. (2002). *Psychological assessment of sexually abused children and their families*. Thousand Oaks, CA: Sage Publications.

Friedrich, W. (1998). *Child sexual abuse inventory*. Orlando FL: Psychological Assessment Resources.

Friedrich, W. (1990). *Psychotherapy of sexually abused children and their families*. New York: Norton.

Gil, E. (1994). *Play in family therapy*. New York: Guilford Press.

Gonzales, L., Waterman, J., Kelly, R., McCord, J., & Oliveri, M. (1993). Children's patterns of disclosures and recantations of sexual abuse allegations in psychotherapy. *Child Abuse & Neglect, 17*, 281-289.

Gorey, K., & Leslie, D. (1997). The prevalence of child sexual abuse: Integrative review adjustment for potential response and measurement biases. *Child Abuse & Neglect, 212*, 391-398.

Gould, J. (1998). *Conducting scientifically crafted child custody evaluations*. Thousand Oaks, CA: Sage Publications.

Greenfield, L. (1996). *Child victimizer's: Violent offenders and their victims*. Washington, D.C.: U.S. Department of Justice.

Hunter, M. (1990). *Abused boys: The neglected victims of sexual abuse*. New York: Ballantine Books.

Groth, A.N. (1990). *Anatomical drawings: For use in the investigation and intervention of child sexual abuse*. Orlando, FL: Forensic Mental Health Associates.

Hynan, D. (1999). Interviewing: Forensic psychological interview with children. *The Forensic Examiner*, March/April, 25-28.

Kendall-Tacket, K., Williams, L., & Finkelhor, D. (1993). Impact of sexual abuse on children: A review and synthesis of recent empirical studies. *Psychological Bulletin, 113*(1), 164-180.

Koocher, G., Goodman, G., White, C., Friedrich, W., Sivan, A., & Reynolds, C. (1995). Psychological science and the use of anatomically detailed dolls in child sexual-abuse assessments. *Psychological Bulletin, 118*(2), 199-222.

Korner, S., & Brown, G. (1990). Exclusion of children from family psychotherapy: Family therapists' beliefs and practices. *Journal of Family Psychology, 3*, 420-430.

Landreth, G. (1991). *Play therapy: The art of the relationship.* Philadelphia: Taylor & Francis.

Landreth, G., Homeyer, L., Glover, G., & Sweeney, D. (1996). *Play therapy interventions with children's problems.* Northvale, NJ: Jason Aronson Inc.

Morgan, M. (1995). *How to interview sexual abuse victims: Including the use of anatomical dolls.* Thousand Oaks, CA: Sage Publications.

Oberlander, L. (1995). Psycholegal issues in child sexual abuse evaluations: A survey of mental health professionals. *Child Abuse & Neglect, 19*(4), 475-490.

Rieser, M. (1991). Recantation in child sexual abuse cases. *Child Welfare, 70*(6), 611-612.

Riordan, R., & Verdel, A. (1991). Evidence of sexual abuse in children's art products. *School Counselor, 39*(2), 116-121.

Saywitz, K., & Goodman, G. (1996). Interviewing children in and out of court. In J. Briere, L. Berliner, J. Bulkley, C. Jenny, & P. Reid (Eds.), *Handbook on child maltreatment*, (pp. 298-318). Thousand Oaks, CA: Sage Publications.

Sgroi, S. (1982). *Handbook of clinical intervention in child sexual abuse.* Lexington, MA: Lexington Books.

Simkins, L., & Reiner, A. (1996). An analytical review of the empirical literature on children's play with anatomically detailed dolls. *Journal of Child Sexual Abuse, 5*, 21-45.

Sorenson, T., & Snow, B. (1991). How children tell: The process of disclosure in child sexual abuse. *Child welfare, 60*(1), 3-15.

U.S. Department of Health and Human Services. (2002). The Administration for children and families: Victim reports. Washington DC: U.S. Department of Health and Human Services. Retrieved March 20, 2002, from DHHS database on *http://www.acf.dhhs.gov/programs/cb/publications/cm99/cpt2.htm*

Wolfe, V., & Birt, J. (1997). Child sexual abuse. In E. Mash & L. Terdal (Eds.), *Assessment of childhood disorders* (Third edition). New York: The Guilford Press.

Chapter 12

FAMILY ASSESSMENT OF DRUG AND ALCOHOL PROBLEMS

Linda Chamberlain[†]
Regis University, Denver, Colorado
Cynthia L. Jew[•]
California Lutheran Univesity

SUBSTANCE ABUSE AND FAMILY DYNAMICS

Assessment of drug and alcohol problems is a critical skill for therapists working with families regardless of the setting. Many families that seek counseling are impacted by the effects of substance abuse or dependence on the part of one or more members, or by a history of substance related problems that weave through several generations. The focus of this chapter is on providing a basic level of information and skills to assist family therapists in assessing the existence, intensity and potential impact of substance abuse on the families they serve.

Because the effects of substance abuse are so ubiquitous, family therapists who are not familiar with the signs and symptoms of "the beast" will surely find themselves lost in the maze that a family creates around this problem. It has been estimated that more than 10% of the population in the United States comes from a home where there was an alcoholic parent or caregiver (Ackerman, 1983). For drugs other than alcohol, there is no clear indication of the numbers. For every family member who is drug dependent, there are many close to them who suffer. Although a significant number of families don't identify substance abuse as a primary problem, a careful screening and assessment is vital to helping problematic families determine whether drugs or alcohol are an integral part of the dilemmas they experience.

Substance abuse problems are both "systems-maintaining and systems-maintained" (Kaufman, 1985, p. 37). Treadway (1989) defines substance abuse as "...when an individual

---

[†] Linda Chamberlain, Psy.D., is Coordinator of Clinical Training at Regis University, Denver, Colorado.
[•] Cynthia L. Jew, Ph.D. is Associate Professor at California Lutheran University, Thousand Oaks, California.

has a pattern of being dependent on the use of substances to alter and control mood states, is unable to easily regulate this use, and experiences some form of distress if unexpectedly deprived of access to it" (p. 11). The presence of substance abuse problems in a family plays a critical role in influencing their relationships and dynamics. Substance abuse is a complex and progressive disorder that creates an increasingly disruptive environment as the problems related to addiction increase. Living in an addicted family system "results in progressive and mutifaceted emotional disturbance for all of the members" (Forrest, 1978). Drug or alcohol abuse in a family is so compelling that it generally becomes the primary organizing factor which determines how the family maintains some semblance of structure and stability (Lewis, 1992). In some respects, the substance becomes a ghostly, but powerful member of the family; one that everyone in the household learns to relate to and interact with in order to preserve the family. Most clinicians realize that a chronic pattern of drug or alcohol use impacts the family in ways that devastate normal patterns of life (Margolis & Zwegen, 1998). Not only do addicted individuals change dramatically during the process of addiction, so does everyone in the family. It is truly a family problem; one that radically alters interpersonal dynamics and relationship patterns.

Patterns of Behavior

Substance abusers develop clear patterns over time of focusing their life on activities that afford them opportunities to indulge in using their drug(s) of choice. Especially with illegal substances, the user becomes increasingly involved in socializing with others who also use in order to protect themselves from detection. Users prefer to use with others who use like them. Family members or friends who are "straight" become increasingly excluded from a significant part of the user's life. As a person's "affair" with a substance grows and the barrier of denial is fortified, the chasm in their important relationships with family and friends deepens. Family conflict related to their substance use, a constricted social life, lack of involvement in activities that do not afford an opportunity to use, and general withdrawal from "straight" friends are signals that a family member's problematic relationship with drugs or alcohol is well underway. The more advanced the dependence on the substance, the more alienated the user becomes from others who don't indulge with him/her.

Patterns of behaviors that are found in families of abusers are well established (Todd & Selekman, 1991; Treadway, 1989). The strength of the dependence on the substance is easily evidenced when users fail to make attempts to prevent family breakups or isolation from significant others in order to maintain their substance use. Intimate relationships that endure a user's increasing dependence on a substance become distorted through the denial or "enabling" behaviors exhibited by the user's family. There is a "coevolutionary" process in the family system. "Through an infinite series of small adjustments family members learn to cope with an abusing member. As they adapt to him he adapts to them." (Treadway, 1989, p. 14).

Family members, like the user, progress through different phases in their journey with the addict. Addiction is often classified as a "family illness" because the effects of the addiction on those who are in a close relationship with the abuser also experience symptoms that, while different, are frequently as serious as those suffered by the addict. Serious levels of depression or anxiety are often seen in both partners and children of substance abusers.

Domestic violence and child abuse are fairly common co-occurring patterns in these families. Essentially, every one in the addict's family and social system suffers.

Four Stages in the Family System of the Addict

Stages or phases (Washousky, Levy-Stern & Muchowski, 1993) can delineate the dynamics that are often seen in families with substance dependent members. Although these stages represent common patterns of family interaction with substance users, not all families can be defined or described using this criteria. These are not discrete stages; it is likely that there will be some overlap or that several stages will be in evidence simultaneously. Also, not every family will experience the same intensity or exact set of responses in each stage. Some families may stay in a prolonged state of denial, even to the point of the addict's death. The description of the stages, however, can provide some guidelines for assessing the dynamics in the user's family and provide a basis for treatment planning with both the addict and other family members.

1. Denial

In this stage, family members deny that there is a substance abuse problem. They try to hide the substance abuse both from each other and from those outside the family. Excuses are made, members "cover" and make excuses for the addict's behavior, other explanations are offered, and the family begins to isolate from others who might suspect "something is wrong."

2. Home Treatment

Family members try to get the addict to stop using. Hiding drugs or bottles, nagging, threatening, persuasion, and sympathy are attempted. Home treatment, or the family's effort to stop the addict from using without seeking outside help, may fail because the focus is on controlling the behavior of someone else. The roles in the family often change significantly, usually with deleterious effects. Children may try to care for a parent, coalitions among family members are formed, and family members ignore or minimize their own problems by keeping the focus on the addict.

3. Chaos

The problem becomes so critical that it can no longer be denied or kept secret from those outside the family. Neighbors, extended family and friends become aware of the problem. Conflicts and confrontations in the family escalate without resolution. The consequences for family members become more pronounced and a child or partner of the abuser may experience serious emotional or physical problems. Threats of divorce, separation, or withdrawal of family support are often made but not acted upon.

4. Control

A spouse or family member attempts to take complete control of and responsibility for the abuser. At this point in the process, the pattern of the abusers relationship with the drug(s) is defined as substance dependence or addiction. If still living within the family, the addict becomes an emotional invalid who exists as a type of parasite on the family. Control is often exercised through divorce, separation, or a total emotional alienation from the family. The family, like the addict, exists in a state of suspended animation; trapped in a cycle of helplessness and futile attempts to control the addict's behavior.

Assessing the Social and Family Related Symptoms

As previously noted, it is important to have access to family members, friends, and/or important others in the drug users life in order to adequately assess a substance abuse problem. If a substance abuser has somehow entered the mental health system through a doctor's referral or employer's recommendation, it is highly likely that the situation has become unmanageable enough for significant others in the abuser's life to break the barrier of denial. As with the abuser, it is critically important to undertake the assessment in a supportive, caring, non-judgmental manner. Many family members experience a high degree of guilt or shame about the abuser's behavior and feel that the continuation of the substance use is somehow their fault. They may feel that they have not been a good enough spouse, child, or parent or that they have created so much stress in the abuser's life that they have promoted the user's growing dependence on substances. This sense of responsibility on the part of other family members is often promoted by the substance user as a form of their denial and projection of the problems onto others. "If only my wife would stop nagging me about how much debt we're in, I wouldn't need to drink to relax", "If the damn kids would be quiet when I'm home watching TV, I wouldn't have to smoke a joint to unwind".

In addition to gathering information from others who are familiar with the abuser, counselors must be alert to some of the common social consequences that often appear in an addict's life. Frequent job loss, a driving under the influence (DUI) arrest or other legal problem (particularly domestic violence), the breakup of important relationships, a series of moves (also called "the geographic cure"), a history of psychological or medical problems that are unresolved, and a lack of interest in activities that were once important to the individual are all indicators of an addiction. Several of the assessment devices discussed in the next segment of the chapter will assist the clinician in gathering information related to the social characteristics of substance abuse.

Who, What, When and Where to Assess

Families entering treatment for substance abuse related problems are sometimes the last to understand that the drugs or alcohol are a critical factor in the evolution and maintenance of problematic dynamics between family members. In clinical settings that are devoted to treatment of substance abuse, the existence of a substance related problem may be clear to the therapist from the outset. In more general family therapy settings, the therapist will need to include several evaluative tools and procedures to identify whether or not drugs and alcohol are playing an important role in family dysfunction.

Whenever possible, involving all adult members and school age children in intake interviews can be a useful way to begin an assessment. As is true with other problems that affect family functioning, substance abuse is defined as a family problem, not an individual issue. Although only one or more family members may be abusing alcohol or drugs, the effects on every member of the family are direct and problematic. The belief that family interactions are crucial to the creation and maintenance of substance abuse implies that family involvement will be critical at all stages of assessment and treatment. Every member of the family is impacted by any member's problem with drugs.

In arranging for family assessment sessions, the therapist needs to be aware of some basic concerns. If there is a history of domestic violence or child abuse, safety must be the first consideration. Given the high correlation of violence and sexual abuse with substance abuse, care must be taken to provide a safe setting to engage the family in the assessment process. Individual meetings with the parents or adults in the family may be necessary in order to create an environment in which partners, spouses or adult children can speak freely in response to assessment questions. All parties must, however, be clearly aware that the purpose of the information being gathered is to help the therapist understand and initiate a workable treatment plan for the entire family.

Referrals from physicians, other clinicians, or the legal system may be clearly defined as serving the purpose of assessing a drug or alcohol problem. Frequently, it is a spouse or partner of the abuser who initially contacts a therapist for evaluation and treatment. The partner may describe specific concerns about the user's behavior, or may indicate that another member of the family, often a child, is experiencing some difficulty. If the initial contact indicates that there is someone in the family who is actively using drugs or alcohol, the therapist must be clear that all family members are to come to sessions sober and straight. Most assessments, however, will probably be undertaken as a part of the clinicians normal interviewing procedure.

Resistance and denial are frequently in evidence when requests are made to bring in all family members. Particularly with a substance abuser, other family members may be unclear why they also need to be involved in meetings. Assuring all parties that it will be helpful to you to have a more complete history and understanding of the problem can help with cooperation. As Doweiko (1996) notes, a "fundamental aspect of chemical dependency is deception" (p.319). To minimize inaccuracies and denial regarding a person's substance use, the therapist should use as many different sources of information as possible. Immediate family, extended family, friends, colleagues and neighbors may be important sources of information. It is common for someone abusing alcohol to report that they only drink once or twice a week, and consume "just a few beers". When the spouse is questioned, however, he or she may report that the drinker is highly intoxicated at least three or four times a week and that "a few" refers to 6 packs of beer, not single bottles.

ASSESSMENT TECHNIQUES

The Assessment Interview

The most important aspect of any assessment of substance abuse is the clinical interview. A carefully planned and conducted interview is the cornerstone of the assessment process (Chamberlain & Jew, 2000; Craig, 1993). It is still true that the best assessment tool is a skilled and knowledgeable clinician who asks the necessary questions in a manner that supports honest disclosure. We find it disturbing how many mental health professionals do not include at least some questions about drug and alcohol use in their standard interview format. Clinical training programs often lack course work or opportunities for practical experience that expose medical and mental health professionals to the dynamics and treatment of addictive disorders. As Craig (1993) notes, despite the endemic rates of substance abuse and it's link with other psychological and familial problems, only "about 5%" of graduate students in mental health programs take a course on addictions (p. 182). It is our hope that clinicians or students who are using this text will commit to asking at least some basic questions about both current and historic use of drugs and alcohol as a regular part of their assessment process with all families.

As previously noted, the initial assessment of a substance abuse problem is often complicated by the prevalence of denial on the part of substance abusers and other family members. Unless they are actively committed to establishing abstinence, most users minimize or distort their relationship with drugs and alcohol. Conducting an assessment interview for substance abuse is generally enhanced tremendously by including family members in the process. Certain aspects of a substance abusers pattern of drug/alcohol use are often clarified during interviews with family members. Involvement of the family early in the process of assessment and treatment also encourages a more systemic focus on the part of the family and allows the therapist to assess the needs of partners and children in addition to the needs of the substance abuser

Initially, it is still important to ask the client directly about his or her use of drugs or alcohol. A useful question is: "Do you believe that your use of alcohol or other drugs has caused problems in your life?" Many clinicians find it helpful to assure the client that they are not asking questions about substance use in order to make judgments. Often, people will respond less defensively if they are reassured that "I'm not here to tell you that you are or aren't an addict or alcoholic. I simply need to understand as much about the problem as I can and to help you and your family determine whether your drug or alcohol use may be playing a role in the current situation". Other family members should also be asked whether they consider drug or alcohol use on the part of anyone in the family to be a cause of or contributor to family problems.

An interview format that gathers information specific to substance abuse should be a standard part of the assessment process. An example of a structured interview format is the Substance Use History Questionnaire (Appendix A: Substance Use History Questionnaire). It may be given to the substance user to complete or the questions can be asked during the interview. Adult partners and adolescent of older children may also be asked to fill out the questionnaire as it relates to the substance using family member(s). The information from this procedure will help in determining what additional assessment instruments to use. Information regarding work habits, social and professional relationships, medical history and previous psychiatric history are also necessary for the assessment. Questions related to each of these areas should be included as a part of the standard intake interview.

Most importantly, a thorough family history of any alcohol or drug abuse should be pursued. Genograms (McGoldrick & Gerson, 1985) that indicate members of the family who were likely to have or were identified as having problems with chemical dependency can be very useful in establishing patterns of use in both the current and previous generations. Clearly, there are genetic factors involved with the patterns of addiction that run through families. Through research involving twin studies, adoption studies, animal models and multi-generational, longitudinal studies, there emerges a "powerful demonstration of the influence of genetic factors" on the risk for addiction" (Margolis & Zweben, 1998, p. 45). Construction of a genogram as a part of the assessment process helps both the family and clinician to see patterns of addiction that may have run through generations. Because of the toxic physiological and psychological effects of chronic drug and alcohol use, family histories that indicate a prominent history of heart disease or other cardio-vascular problems (particularly at younger ages), liver disease, depression, suicide, death at young ages, miscarriages, mental retardation or learning disabilities (often linked to fetal alcohol syndrome), and/or legal problems associated with aggressive behavior should alert the clinician to explore more completely the likelihood that alcohol or other drugs have a genetic foothold in the family.

It is important to note that family members and significant others may be unaware of or reluctant to divulge information about substance abuse with a family member. They are often experiencing denial, much like the abuser, or avoiding a confrontation. Common misinformation about substance abuse may divert the focus of the problem to other factors that are then presented as the primary problem. For example, a spouse may describe their partner as using alcohol to relieve feelings of depression rather than identifying the substance use as a causal or maintaining factor in their partner's emotional turmoil. Due to the shame and embarrassment that frequently accompany the admission of substance abuse, the clinician may need to reassure everyone involved in the assessment that appropriate help can only be made available if an understanding of the problem is accurate and complete. It is also important for the therapist to respect the initial defensiveness of the family, rather than immediately confronting them.

The following questionnaire can be given to family members or significant others in order to gain important information about the user's pattern of drug or alcohol use. Information gathered from others can be compared to the responses given by the abuser in order to assess the degree of minimization or denial that may be present. A "yes" response to any of the following questions indicates some possibility of substance abuse; a "yes" response to four or more indicates a substance abuse problem.

Questionnaire: Do You Have a Spouse, Friend or Loved One Who Has a Drinking or Drug Abuse Problem?

1. Do you worry about how much they use drugs or drink?
2. Do you complain about how often the drink or use?
3. Do you criticize them for the amount they spend on drugs or alcohol?
4. Have you ever been hurt or embarrassed by their behavior when they are drinking or using?
5. Are holidays in your home unpleasant because of their drinking or drugging?
6. Do they ever lie about their drinking or drug use?
7. Do they deny that drinking or drugs affect their behavior?
8. Do they say or do things and later deny having said or done them?
9. Do you sometimes feel that drinking or drug use is more important to them than you are?
10. Do they get angry if you criticize their substance use or their drinking or drug using companions?
11. Is drinking or drug use involved in almost all your social activities?
12. Does your family spend almost as much on alcohol or drugs as it does on food or other necessities?

13. Are you having any financial difficulties because of their use?
14. Does their substance use keep them away from home a good deal?
15. Have you ever threatened to end your relationship because of their drinking or drug use?
16. Have you every lied for them because of their drug use or drinking?
17. Do you find yourself urging them to eat instead of drink or use drugs at parties?
18. Have they ever stopped drinking or using drugs completely for a period of time and then started using again?
19. Have you ever thought about calling the police because of their behavior while drunk or high?
20. Do you think that alcohol or drugs creates problems for them?

ASSESSMENT TOOLS

To assist in the diagnosis and assessment of substance abuse, psychometric instruments are often very helpful. There are a variety of specific psychometric instruments that are generally available to counselors. Material from the initial interview with the family should help the clinician select appropriate measures that will enhance their understanding of the exact nature, dynamics, severity, and effects of the client's substance use. For example, several tools are focused on alcohol abuse while others assess abuse of additional or other substances.

Although there are many tests, questionnaires and other materials available to counselors, the items reviewed in this chapter were chosen based on their widespread use and availability, ease of administration and scoring, and reliability and validity. The assessment devices that are included in this segment include the Short Michigan Alcoholism Screening Test (SMAST), the Drug Abuse Screening Test (DAST-20), the CAGE Questionnaire, the Alcohol Use Inventory (AUI), the Substance Abuse Subtle Screening Inventory-3 (SASSI-3), and the Addiction Severity Index (ASI). In addition, those who are trained to use the Millon Clinical Multiaxial Inventory (MCMI-II) and/or the Minnesota Multiphasic Personality Inventory (MMPI-2) may use information from those tests to help with diagnostic and treatment considerations. Some information on using these tests in the assessment of substance abuse will also be reviewed.

Short Michigan Alcoholism Screening Test (SMAST)

The most researched diagnostic instrument is the self-administered Michigan Alcoholism Screening Test (MAST) which was created in 1971 by M. L. Selzer (Selzer, 1971). The 25-item MAST correctly identifies up to 95% of alcoholics, and the SMAST, an even shorter form of the MAST has also been shown to identify over 90% of the alcoholics entering general psychiatric hospitals (Mendelson & Mello, 1985, p. 304). The MAST was originally validated with treatment seeking alcoholics. Numerous studies have used the MAST and the SMAST to assess both adolescent and adult populations in a variety of settings. The SMAST may realistically and effectively be used with virtually any population. The Short Michigan Alcoholism Test (SMAST) can be administered as a True/False questionnaire or it can be given verbally. It consists of the following thirteen of twenty-five questions taken from the MAST.

Short Michigan Alcoholism Screening Test

1. Do you feel you feel you are a normal drinker?
2. Does your wife/husband, a parent, or other near relative ever worry or complain about your drinking?
3. Do you ever feel guilty about your drinking?
4. Do friends or relatives think you are a normal drinker?
5. Are you able to stop drinking when you want?
6. Have you ever attended a meeting of Alcoholics Anonymous?
7. Has drinking ever created problems between you and your wife/husband, a parent or other near relative?
8. Have you ever gotten into trouble at work because of drinking?
9. Have you ever neglected your obligations, your family, or your work for 2 or more days in a row because you were drinking?
10. Have you ever gone to anyone for help about your drinking?
11. Have you ever been in a hospital because of drinking?
12. Have you ever been arrested for drunken driving, driving while intoxicated, or driving under the influence of alcoholic beverages?
13. Have you ever been arrested, even for a few hours, because of other drunken behavior?

The SMAST is very easy to score. One point is given for each of the following answers: NO on Questions #1, 4 and 5; YES on all other questions (# 2, 3, and 6-13). A score of 0-1 indicates a low probability of alcoholism, a score of 2 points indicates the client is possibly alcoholic, and a score of 3 or more point indicates a strong probability of alcoholism.

The Drug Abuse Screening Test (DAST-20)

The DAST-20 (Skinner, 1982) is a 20 item self-report inventory designed to measure aspects of drug use behavior, not including alcohol. It was derived from the Michigan Alcoholism Screening Test (MAST) and reflects similar content. DAST-20 scores are computed by summing all items positively endorsed for drug use. Higher scores indicate a greater likelihood of drug dependency. The DAST-20 is designed for use with adult male and female drug users.

The DAST-20 is a useful tool for helping to differentiate between several categories of drug users. In clinical trials, the DAST-20 scores demonstrated significant differences between the alcohol, drug, and poly-substance abuse groups. DAST-20 scores were also found to correlate highly with other drug use indices.

The CAGE Questionnaire

The CAGE (Ewing, 1984) is a 4-item questionnaire that includes questions related to a history of attempting to cut down on alcohol intake (C), annoyance over criticism about alcohol (A), guilt about drinking behavior (G), and drinking in the morning to relieve withdrawal anxiety, sometimes known as an "eye-opener" (E) (Gallant, 1987, p. 50). Most questionnaires duplicate information by using different phrases or words to detect similar patterns of behavior. The authors of the CAGE found that they could eliminate many questions and still have a powerful tool for assessing alcohol dependency. This is also an extremely useful questionnaire to use with family members or others that are participating in the assessment.

The CAGE was originally developed and used with adult alcoholics presenting for treatment. Like the SMAST, the CAGE may be used to screen for alcoholism in a variety of health care settings. Use of the CAGE questions effectively discriminates alcoholics from non-alcoholics at or above the 90% range.

The CAGE is generally administered verbally as part of the diagnostic interview. Instructions for administering the CAGE include observing the client's attitude in responding to the questions. The counselor should ask them to explain any "Yes" answer and watch for signs of rationalization, denial, projection of blame, and minimization. The first question deals with the alcoholic's common problem of repeatedly trying to get the drinking under control only to lose control again and again once she resumes drinking. The next detects sensitivity to criticism of drinking behavior. The third question taps into the personal sense of guilt, and the fourth looks at the tendency to use morning drinking as a remedy for excessive drinking the night before.

CAGE Questionnaire

To administer the CAGE, the client is asked to answer yes or no to the following questions:

1. Have you ever tried to **C**ut down on your drinking/drug use?
2. Are you **A**nnoyed when people ask you about your drinking/drug use?
3. Do you ever feel **G**uilty about your drinking/srug use?
4. Do you ever take a morning **E**ye-opener or use alcohol/drugs to relieve the effects of alcohol/drug use?

Only "YES" responses are scored on the CAGE. One "yes" response indicates a possibility of alcoholism, two or three "yes" responses indicate a high alcoholism suspicion index, and four "yes" responses indicate an alcoholism diagnosis is highly likely. As with the SMAST, the CAGE questions can be adapted as an assessment tool for other substances. With the CAGE, the questions are simply rephrased to indicate the drug(s) of choice. For example, question #1 becomes "Have you ever tried to cut down on your cocaine use?"

Follow-up inquiries to any "yes" answer can assist the clinician in getting more detailed information. If the drug user answers "yes" to question #2 and admits to being annoyed when others asked him about his drug use, the clinician can ask all members of the family do relate incidents when this occurred. The CAGE questions can be particularly useful for generating discussion about events and problems in the family related to drug or alcohol use.

The Substance Abuse Subtle Screening Inventory-3 (SASSI-3)

The Substance Abuse Subtle Screening Inventory-3 (SASSI-2) (Miller, G., 1985) is a single page, paper and pencil questionnaire. On one side are 52 True-False questions that generally appear unrelated to chemical abuse; on the other side are 26 items that allow clients to self report the negative effects of any alcohol and drug use. Clients can complete the SASSI-3 in approximately 10-15 minutes, it is easily scored, and training is available in interpretation and use of the SASSI-3 as a screening tool for identifying substance abuse. The SASSI is available only to therapists who have met certain criteria and completed some training in its use. Information, training, and materials are available through the SASSI Institute, P.O. Box 5069, Bloomington, IN, 47407

The primary strength of the SASSI-3 is in identifying abuse patterns that are hidden by the more subtle forms of denial common to substance abusers. Items on the SASSI-3 touch on a broad spectrum of topics seemingly unrelated to chemical abuse (e.g. "I think there is something wrong with my memory" and "I am often resentful"). The questions are designed to be non-threatening to abusers to avoid triggering the client's defenses and denial. The SASSI-3 is resistant to faking and defeats efforts to "second-guess" the "right" answer. As a result, the SASSI-3 is effective in identifying clients who are minimizing or in denial about their substance abuse. It is also effective in identifying substance abuse regardless of the drug of choice. There are both an adult and adolescent inventory and both are adapted for either male or female clients.

The data from research with the SASSI-3 indicates approximately a 90% accuracy in identifying substance abuse patterns in clients. Thousands of test items were designed or considered, then given to samples of alcoholics, other drug abusers and controls (non-substance abusing people). The Inventory was tested over a period of 16 years and is still being adapted and updated. Counselors have used the SASSI-3 as a screening tool for court ordered substance abuse programs, employee assistance programs, and in general mental health settings.

The Alcohol Use Inventory (AUI)

The Alcohol Use Inventory (AUI) (Wanberg & Horn, 1983; Horn, Wanberg & Foster, 1986) is a hierarchically organized set of self-report scales that provides a basis for diagnosing different problems associated with the use of alcohol. The AUI is based on the hypothesis that alcoholism should be diagnosed from a multiple-syndrome model and the AUI scales are designed to provide an operational definition of the multiple manifestations of alcohol related problems. It should be used to provide a more thorough diagnostic picture if there are clear indications from the SMAST or CAGE that an alcohol problem is probable. Like the SASSI, the AUI is a protected test and must be ordered through the publisher.

The AUI consists of 228 multiple choice items (expanded from 147 in the original test). The specific areas of assessment that are the focus of the AUI are: motivation for treatment, physical health, anger and aggression management, risk taking behavior, social relationships, employment and/or educational situation, family situation, leisure time activities, religious/spiritual activities, and legal status. The AUI is a very simple test to administer and can generally be given to the client with little additional instruction. The client should be told that it is important he respond as honestly as possible to all questions and not to skip questions or give more than one response per question. Both hand scored and computer scored versions of the AUI are available (Horn, Wanberg, & Foster, 1983).

The Addictions Severity Index (ASI)

The Addiction Severity Index (ASI) (Fureman, Parikh, Bragg, & McLellan, 1990) provides basic information that is useful both for the clinician and the clients. The ASI manual provides clear instructions for administration, scoring, and use of the data in planning treatment strategies. The current ASI is designed for use with adults, but variations for use with adolescents are being developed. A particular strength of the ASI is it's utility with dual diagnosis populations. For treatment planning purposes, the ASI is especially helpful in determining the severity of the client's drug use and the need for additional or extended treatment.

The ASI is administered as a structured interview with specific questions that cover several basic areas of treatment needs, including: medical, employment/support, drug/alcohol use, legal, family/social relationships, and psychiatric. The drug/alcohol subscale includes an extensive history of all drug and alcohol abuse, the longest period of abstinence, and previous drug treatment history. Administration of the ASI relies on fairly basic clinical interviewing skills. Clinicians can adjust questions to use terms that are familiar to the client and fit with his/her level of education and "sophistication". In some treatment settings, the ASI questions can also be given as writing projects for the client's to further examine their history of drug/alcohol use and the impact it has had on their situation.

The client uses a zero to four-point scale to rate how "bothered" he/she has been in the past 30 days by problems in the different areas that relate to their substance abuse. This serves to give a clearer picture from the client's perspective of how they rate the severity of their problem and gives some indication of their desire for treatment. These ratings are then compared with the therapist's ratings on the same scales. The ASI can also be given to family members for purposes of constructing a more complete picture of how the family views the problems with substance abuse. With the influence of denial or minimization on the client's perceptions, it is common for the interviewer and some other family members to perceive a higher severity of problems than the substance user.

The Millon Clinical Multiaxial Inventory (MCMI-II) and Minnesota Multiphasic Personality Inventory (MMPI-2)

Although both the MCMI-II and the MMPI-2 are primarily designed for the assessment of personality and general emotional/psychological functioning, they are often used to assess a full-range of psychopathology, including substance abuse. Both are copyrighted, protected evaluation instruments that require additional training to administer, score and interpret. Both have elaborate computer scoring programs available through the resources that sell the tests. Incorporated into both the MMPI-2 and MCMI-II are validity scales which may help to identify clients who are "attempting to look good" or answering randomly.

The MCMI-II is useful in identifying several aspects of personality functioning: clinical syndromes (e.g. depression, anxiety), changing symptoms and personality styles or disorders. It is certainly a useful addition to any evaluation in which there is a question of dual diagnosis. It is a simple, true/false, 173 question self report regarding the clients behavior and experience. Given the difficulty of hand scoring, it is generally scored by a computer program.

The symptom scales on the MCMI-II are useful in corroborating a clinical impression of the types or patterns of symptoms experienced by the client. The personality scales may help a clinician understand the relationship between the client's substance use and his or her typical pattern of managing their experience and relationships. For example, someone with a score indicating a Narcissistic Personality style may use drugs to establish or maintain a particular image. Understanding a client's basic personality can be very useful in planning treatment to address specific character traits that may either support or undermine there recovery.

Like the MCMI-II, the MMPI-2 is useful in identifying behavioral and personality patterns and clinical symptoms. These tests are generally used as part of a comprehensive personality or behavioral assessment. The MMPI-2 is a self-report questionnaire that consists of 567 true/false questions. There is also a version of the MMPI-2 for adolescent populations, the Minnesota Multiphasic Personality Inventory-Adolescent (MMPI-A).

The MMPI has been used extensively for over 20 years in the evaluation of alcoholics. Gilberstadt and Duker's (1965) research indicated a common pattern in MMPI scores among alcoholics. Elevations on scales 2, 7 and 4 represent a combination of personality characteristics commonly found in male alcoholics. These scores reflect depressive, obsessive-compulsive and sociopathic features. They also reported symptoms of anxiety, marital discord, financial problems, insomnia and tension that were reflected in the MMPI profiles of alcoholics.

In addition to the basic clinical scales, both the MMPI-2 and MMPI-A contain items that indicate the possibility of substance abuse problems. The MacAndrew Alcoholism Scale-Revised (MAC-R), was developed using items from the original MMPI and became widely used as a method of screening for substance abuse problems. The revised MAC (MAC-R) deleted several questions and added others to further refine the content of the scale. The MAC-R has been an effective tool for identifying substance abuse problems in both adults and adolescents (Graham, 1990).

Two other subscales on the MMPI-2 are the Addiction Acknowledgement Scale (AAS) and the Addiction Potential Scale (APS). Persons who obtain a high score on the AAS are usually acknowledging a substance abuse problem and additional assessment of the nature of their substance use would be indicated. The APS may help discriminate between persons who abuse substances and those who do not. Both the APS and AAS are still in the process of being validated and evaluated for their reliability in assessing substance abuse problems. Particularly with the APS, high scores on this scale should be corroborated with other data and information.

Assessment of Family Functioning

In addition to determining whether or not a member of the family is dependent on drugs or alcohol, it is vital for family therapists to be aware of problematic behavior patterns that may be exhibited by others in the family. Addictive family systems are often described by children who grew up in them as more conflictual, less communicative, more isolated, more achievement-oriented, less clearly organized and less consistent (Jarmas & Kazak, 1992). Research has demonstrated that alcoholic parents are less likely to display positive affect when relating to their children (Fitzgerald, Zucker, & Yang, 1995). Evidence is also building for a correlation between hyperactivity, attention span-distractibility, and higher levels of aggression in boys raised in families with an alcoholic parent (Ham, Fitzgerald, & Zucker, 1993).

When a parent is assessed as having a drug or alcohol problem, it is imperative that the therapist assess the possibility of behavioral or psychological problems in all family members. Spouse and partners often present with moderate to severe symptoms of depression or anxiety. The higher potential for domestic violence and sexual abuse must also be considered when working with these families. Any indications of these types of problems should provide a "red flag" for the clinician to complete a thorough evaluation of drug and alcohol use in the family.

Diagnosis

Professionals who have to make decisions about the presence or absence of substance abuse or dependence for their clients must make a series of complex judgments. An adequate conceptualization of substance abuse and addiction emphasizes the interaction between the individual user, the physiological effects, and the social context in which the user functions. Establishing a standard set of rigid diagnostic criteria for addiction is not only improbable but is not likely to be beneficial to clients. The simple diagnostic definition that "addiction exists when drug or alcohol use is associated with impairment of health and social functioning" is a useful general thesis (Mendelson and Mello, 1985, p. 18).

Inconsistent attitudes and imprecise standards for what constitutes an "addiction" have always complicated the diagnosis of substance abuse. Inadequate definitions of chemical dependence have often been cited as the primary reason for a lack of success in developing adequate epidemiological, diagnostic, and prognostic assessment tools. As Gallant (1987) notes, "With many medical illnesses...the etiology or pathologic abnormality, prognosis, and treatment are known, and no preexisting public or medical concepts interfere with the scientific identification of the illness" (p. 1). This is certainly not the case with the diagnosis of substance abuse. Here, much of the information needed to establish a diagnosis is based on self-reports from an often unreliable population given the preponderance of denial and minimization. Long-standing prejudices and moral attitudes further complicate making an adequate diagnosis. While the DSM-IV offers seemingly clear, behavioral descriptions of symptoms that constitute abuse and dependence, exceptions to the rule are always a possibility.

Case

The Simmons family has arrived for a first session. Father, Brad, is tall and pleasant looking; mother, Angie is petite and obviously nervous as she fidgets in the waiting room; son, Sean, age 14, looks every inch the hostile, provocative, disenfranchised adolescent he was described to be by his mother during the intake call. Becky, the older daughter, is home for spring break. She is in her second year of college at a campus several hundred miles away from home. Becky looks acutely uncomfortable and irritated that she was asked to attend the family meeting.

Angie seated herself in between husband Brad and Sean as they arranged themselves around the consultation room. Becky sat somewhat apart from the family, leafing through a magazine that she brought in from the waiting area. Angie began by describing concerns about Sean's recent expulsion from school for possession of marijuana. Father nodded agreement but remained silent throughout most of the history taking. Sean appeared disinterested and answered questions with as much brevity as possible. Becky added details periodically but stated that she has not been as involved with the family since leaving for college.

When asked about any history of drug or alcohol use in the family, Sean suddenly looked intently at his mother and sighed resignedly when she claimed that no one else in the family had problems associated with substance abuse. "Yeah, right", he muttered. Both mother and father quickly reasserted that their concern was the recent problem with Sean using marijuana. Becky turned her attention back to the magazine and remained silent.

After the initial session, in which basic information about the family was gathered, meetings were scheduled for each member to come in independently and complete the Substance Use History Questionnaire (Appendix A), the CAGE, the ASI and an MCMI-II. Separate interviews were conducted with information from the assessment tools with a focus on concerns about drug and alcohol use in the family. As Angie and the children expressed concerns about Brad's alcohol use, family sessions were resumed to develop a treatment plan for all family members.

APPENDIX A

Substance Use History Questionnaire

1. What substances do you currently use?
(Check all that apply)

_____ alcohol   _____ amphetamines (uppers)
_____ cocaine   _____ barbiturates (downers)
_____ marijuana   _____ nicotine (cigarettes)
_____ other (specify)_____

2. What are your present substance use habits?
_____ daily use _____ social use (with friends or at parties) _____ weekend use
_____ occasional heavy use (to point of intoxication)
_____ occasional light use (not to point of intoxication)

3. How many days ago did you last take a drug or drink? _____ days

4. Have you used daily in the past two months? _____ yes _____ no

5. Do you find it almost impossible to live without your drugs or alcohol?
_____ yes _____ no

6. Are you always able to stop using when you want to?
_____ yes _____ no

7. Where do you do most of your drinking or drug use?
(check all that apply)
_____ home
_____ friends
_____ bars, restaurants, or other public places
_____ parties or social gatherings
_____ other

8. Do you drink or use during your work day? _____ yes _____ no

9. Do most of your friends use like you do? _____ yes _____ no

10. With whom do you use or drink? (check all that apply)
_____ alone _____ neighbors
_____ family _____ co-workers
_____ friends _____ strangers

11. Do you consider yourself to be a
_____ very light user _____ fairly heavy user
_____ moderate user _____ heavy user
_____ non-user

12. Do friends or family think you use more than other people?
_____ yes _____ no

13. Have any family or friends complained to you about your drug or alcohol use?
_____ yes _____ no

14. Do you feel you use more or less than other people who use?
_____ yes _____ no

15. Were your drug use or drinking habits ever different from what they are now?
_____ yes _____ no
If "yes", please explain why the habits changed

16. Has your drinking or drug use ever caused you to (check all that apply):
　　_____ lose a job or have job problems
　　_____ have legal problems (DUI, arrest for possession)
　　_____ have medical problems related to your use
　　_____ have family problems or relationship problems
　　_____ be aggressive or violent

17. Have you ever neglected your obligations, family, or work for two or more days in a row because you were drinking or using drugs?
　　_____ yes　_____ no

18. Because of your alcohol or drug use, have you felt
(check all that apply):

	OFTEN	SOMETIMES	SELDOM	NEVER
Tense or nervous	____	____	____	____
Suspicious or jealous	____	____	____	____
Worried	____	____	____	____
Lonely	____	____	____	____
Angry or violent	____	____	____	____
Depressed	____	____	____	____
Suicidal	____	____	____	____

19. Do you ever feel bad about things you have done while using?
　　____yes ___ no
If yes, please specify:

20. People use alcohol and/or drugs for different reasons. How important would you say that each of the following is to you?

	Very	Somewhat	Not important
it helps me to relax	____	____	____
helps me be more sociable	____	____	____
I like the effect	____	____	____
people I know use drugs or drink	____	____	____
I use when I get upset of angry	____	____	____
I want to forget or escape	____	____	____
it helps to cheer me up	____	____	____
makes me less tense of nervous	____	____	____
makes me less sad or depressed	____	____	____
helps me function better	____	____	____
to celebrate special occasions	____	____	____
other (please specify):			

21. Have you tried to stop using drugs or alcohol in the last two months?
_____ yes _____ no
If yes, did you experience any medical or physical problems when you stopped? (please explain)

22. Have you ever gone to anyone for help about your drinking or drug use?
_____ yes _____ no
If yes, please explain:

23. Have you ever attended a meeting of Alcoholics Anonymous (AA), or any other self help group because of your drug or alcohol use?
_____ yes _____ no

24. Do you feel that you have an addiction to alcohol or drugs?
_____ yes _____ no

25. Do you want help with a drug or alcohol problem at this time?
_____ yes _____ no

REFERENCES

Ackerman, R.J. (1983). *Children of alcoholics: A guidebook for educators, therapists, and parents*. Holmes Beach, FL: Learning Publications, Inc.

Chamberlain, L. & Jew, C. (2000). Assessment and diagnosis. In Stevens, P. & Smith, R. (Eds.), *Substance abuse counseling: Theory and practice, 2nd Edition*. Columbus, OH: Merrill/Prentice Hall.

Craig, R. J. (1993). Contemporary trends in substance abuse. *Professional Psychology: Research and Practice*. 24(2), 182-189.

Fitzgerald, H.E., Zucker, R.A., & Yang, H. (1995, March). Developmental systems theory and alcoholism: Analyzing patterns of variation in high-risk families. *Psychology of Addictive Behaviors*, 9 (1), 8-22.

Forrest, G. (1978). *The diagnosis and treatment of alcoholism, 2nd Edition*. Northvale, NJ: Jason Aronson, Inc.

Gallant, D. (1987). *Alcoholism: A guide to diagnosis, intervention, and treatment*. New York: W.W. Norton & Company.

Gilberstadt, H., and Druker, J. (1965). *A handbook for clinical and actuarial MMPI interpretation*. Philadelphia: Saunders.

Graham, J.R. (1990). *MMPI-2: Assessing personality and psychopathology*. New York: Oxford

Ham, H.P., Fitzgerald, H.E., & Zucker, R.A. (1993, June). *Recent evidence of behavior disregulation in sons of male alcoholics*. Paper presented at the annual meeting of the Research Society on Alcoholism, San Antonio, TX.

Horn, J. L., Wanberg, K. W., & Foster, F. M. (1983). *The alcohol use inventory (AUI): computerized and paper-pencil forms*. Baltimore, MD: PsychSystems.

Horn, J. L., Wanberg, K. W., & Foster, F. M. (1986). *The alcohol use inventory: test booklet.* Minneapolis, MN: National Computer Systems, Inc.

Jarmas, A.L. & Kazak, A.E. (1992, April). Young adult children of alcoholic fathers: Depressive experiences, coping styles, and family systems. *Journal of Consulting and Clinical Psychology*, 60(2), 244-251.

Kaufman, E. (1985). *Substance abuse and family therapy.* Orlando, FL: Grune & Stratton.

Lewis, J. (1992). Treating the alcohol affected family. In L'Abate, L., Farrar, J., & Serritella, D. (Eds.), *Handbook of differential treatments for addictions.* Needham Heights, MA: Allyn & Bacon.

Margolis, R. & Zweben, J. (1998). *Treating patients with alcohol and other drug problems: An integrated approach.* Washington, D.C.: American Psychological Association.

McGoldrick, M. & Gerson, R. (1985). *Genograms in family assessment.* New York: W.W. Norton.

Mendelson, J. & Mello, N. (Eds.). (1985). *The diagnosis and treatment of alcoholism.* New York: McGraw-Hill.

Miller, G. (1985). *The substance abuse subtle screening inventory.* Bloomington, IN: The SASSI Institute.

Selzer, M. L. (1971). The Michigan alcoholism screening test: The quest for a new diagnostic instrument. *American Journal of Psychiatry*, 127, 1653-1658.

Skinner, H. A. (1982). Statistical approaches to the classification of alcohol and drug addiction. *Alcoholism: Clinical and Experimental Research*, 77, 259-273.

Todd, T. & Selekman, M. (Eds.) (1991). *Family therapy approaches with substance abusers.* Needham Heights, MA: Allyn & Bacon.

Treadway, D. (1989). *Before it's too late: Working with substance abuse in the family.* New York: W.W. Norton & Company.

Wanberg, K. W. & Horn, J. L. (1983). Assessment of alcohol use with multidimensional concepts and measures. *American Psychologist*, 38 (10), 1055-1069.

Washousky, R., Levy-Stern, D., & Muchowski, P. (1993, January/February). The stages of family alcoholism. *EAP Digest*, 38-42.

Chapter 13

MULTICULTURALLY SENSITIVE AND AWARE COUPLE AND FAMILY ASSESSMENT AND TESTING

Karin Jordan[‡]
George Fox University, Portland, Oregon
Jesse Brinson[*]
University of Nevada, Las Vegas

We live in a complex and increasingly varied society, a pluralistic one with diverse value systems and beliefs, languages, and behaviors, sexual orientations, family structures and function, attributing varied meanings and importance to education, work and society. Today one in every four Americans is a person of color (Homma-True, Greene, Lopez, & Trimble, 1993). The marked increase of many Europeans immigrating to the United States around the turn of the century resulted in many different cultures and ethnicities coming to this country. The expectation at that time was, according to Atkinson, Morten & Sue (1989), that America was a "melting pot" where all people blend together. However, with the civil rights movement came a rejection of cultural assimilation and an emerging belief in cultural pluralism. This means that the unique characteristics, beliefs, values, behaviors, etc. of different cultural and ethnic groups are retained while at the same time sharing some common elements generally held by the dominant Caucasian culture. Atkinson, Morton & Sue (1989) wrote "various ingredients are mixed together, but rather than melting into a single mass, the components remain intact and distinguishable while contributing to a whole that is richer than its parts alone" (p. 7).

The relevance of this for mental health practitioners is that they must be culturally and ethnically sensitive when doing assessment, and particularly when they use standardized assessment instruments. Assessment is an ongoing process that starts with the first contact between the client(s) and the therapist, and continues throughout the process of therapy.

[‡] Karin Jordan, Ph.D., Associate Professor and Chair, Graduate Department of Counseling, George Fox University, Portland, Oregon.
[*] Jesse Brinson, Ph.D., is Associate Professor, Department of Counseling at the University of Nevada, Las Vegas.

Assessment can be conducted by observing the members of the couple or family system interact with one another as a whole and with the therapist, but also through a more formalized process and such things as structured interview, using such techniques as a multicultural genogram, or using standardized couple and family assessment instruments. Standardized assessment instruments are believed to be objective instruments that assess individual couple or family members function and/or perceived couple/family system function. Couple and family assessment instruments are like assessment instruments in any other science, insofar as they are generally standardized on a primary middle class Caucasian population. In this respect, it could mean that a couple and/or family assessment instrument might not accurately assess the function of ethnically or culturally diverse individuals, couple/family members, or the system as a whole. In the face of such diversity in couples and/or families where instruments are administered, mental health practitioners need to be aware of the importance of doing culturally and ethnically sensitive assessment and testing.

MULTICULTURAL CONSIDERATIONS

Goldenberg and Goldenberg (1993) wrote that it is important for mental health practitioners as they work with culturally and ethnic diverse clients, to assess the family development and current function by exploring issues such as cultural groups, kinship networks, socialization experiences, communication styles, typical male/female interaction styles, and the role of the extended family. Mental health practitioners, as they work with culturally and ethnically diverse clients, need to be aware of how these clients have experienced living as an ethnic minority individual, couple, or family by asking questions addressing issues of language barriers, cultural shock, prejudice and discrimination, feelings of powerlessness, suspicions of institutions, hopelessness, and rage (Goldenberg & Goldenberg, 1996). There will also need to be considerations made based on whether the client (individual, couple or family) was born and raised in the United States, if they are a recently arrived immigrant family, immigrant American family (foreign-born parents, American-born or American educated children), or immigrant-descendent family (Ho, 1987). When mental health practitioners work with any of these immigrant individuals, couples, or families it is important that adaptation difficulties should be assessed for, by asking questions about language, education, economics affective and emotional well being. Issues that need to be considered are when they arrived in the United States, why they came to this country (by choice or force, or to escape oppression, terrorism, etc.), if they have found a support system and if they feel like they are accepted into this country, their community, their job, their school. All of these things might impact how multicultural clients (individuals, couples, families) function in this culture.

THINGS TO CONSIDER

Ethnic background is believed to be the fundamental determinant of how individuals, couples, and families establish and maintain values, beliefs, and norms, as well as behaviors and emotions. Ethnic pattern are generally passed on from one generation to another within a family and are generally reinforced by the community they live in. Many of these values and beliefs are learned and reinforced not overtly, but covertly. It is not surprising that these messages play a strong role in the development of individuals, couples, and families as they move through different stages, and are likely to be retained for generations (Goldenberg & Goldenberg, 1994). Therefore it is important that mental health practitioners assess such things as what the term "family" means. When exploring the meaning of this term, it would also be helpful to assess the meaning of family loyalty, honor, unity, obligation, and responsibility. Family life cycle issues need to be assessed, because they might differ from the dominant White Anglo-Saxon Protestant (WASP) life cycle stages, into which immigrant families and other ethnic minority families are more or less assimilated. This should not however negate the need to explore such issues as how and who selects the partner for marriage, or childrearing practices, etc. Additionally, mental health practitioners who want to provide culturally sensitive and aware therapy should be take note of:

- The history and current experience of the client/client system
- The cultural and personal values of the client/client system and how they influence the present problem
- The spiritual value system of the client/client system
- Verbal and non-verbal communication of the client/client system's culture and any variations in language use from non-standard American English
- The client/client system's problem in the context of their family, and at times the larger system
- The client/client system's racial identity with their own race and each client as a unique individual (Atkinson, Morten & Sue, 1993).

Finally, issues of poverty, racism, stereotyping, and powerlessness and the possible scars from them should be assessed for. It is important that mental health practitioners explore these important topics, in order to avoid generalizations and stereotyping, and even worse add to existing scars (Ho, 1987).

CONDUCTING CULTURALLY SENSITIVE ASSESSMENT

Culturally sensitive assessment issues are important considerations for mental health practitioners working with families from ethnically and racially diverse backgrounds, as is their awareness of their own biases. Assessment is made culturally sensitive through a continuing and open-ended series of substantive and methodological insertions and adaptations designed to mesh the process of assessment with the cultural characteristics of the group being studied (Padillo & Medina, 1996). Family systems therapists have underscored the importance of knowing culturally specific aspects of conducting assessments, with racially diverse clients in particular. Boyd-Franklin (1987) provides a multi-systems approach to the assessment process with black families drawing from general systems theory and her own clinical experiences. Ho (1987) describes an ecological systemic approach for therapy with ethnically diverse families. McGill (1992) describes the concept of the cultural story for working with ethnic minority families. On the basis of the literature, as well as our own clinical experience, it is clear that culturally sensitive assessment requires changes from the traditional methods and procedures that are implemented when working with families from the dominant society.

Given that assessment affects the lives of individuals as well as the family unit, it is critically important that practitioners have a working paradigm for interacting with, and engaging in, the practice of culturally sensitive assessment with ethnically diverse clients. In this chapter, we will discuss culturally sensitive family assessment from a developmental stage perspective, within the context of a systemic point of view. Specifically, we will address culturally sensitive assessment issues that should be considered during the following topics: setting the stage, pre-assessment stage, assessment techniques, assessment instruments, and guides and things to remember during the assessment process. Finally, a case study will demonstrate how to do a culturally sensitive assessment, and the benefits of doing one. Throughout the chapter we will speak of family assessment as it pertains to racial minorities, yet we are aware of many variations of culturally sensitive assessment. We hasten to add that the clinical issues associated with culturally sensitive family assessment continue to evolve. Thus, the practitioner should not view the areas discussed in this chapter as all-inclusive. As more and more clinical and research evidence becomes available, practitioners should continue to incorporate the new information into their clinical repertoire.

Setting The Stage

The initial encounter represents the first meeting between the practitioner and the family in which the focus is on joining with the family. Building the interpersonal relationship is considered important by traditional family systems standards because it is believed that a deeper level of interpersonal intimacy will foster deeper levels of trust, thereby creating a condition for greater information sharing. Fostering trust with racially diverse families for the purposes of assessment can be a difficult proposition at best. The problem is made difficult in many instances because racial minorities struggle for their daily survival in an environment that many view as discriminatory and oppressive. Thus, many families will view relationship building as a manipulative process designed to make families believe that the practitioner is really interested in their concerns. Racially diverse families could be hesitant and suspicious about the motives of the practitioner, particularly if the assessor is from the dominant society. This is particularly evident in families dominated by male heads of household. That is to say, most men of color encounter racial profiling on a regular basis. As a result of this practice, they have come to view males and females of the dominant culture as someone who cannot be trusted. It is a kind of reverse stereotyping. Given that building a working relationship is critically important in the process of culturally sensitive assessment, we will offer a fairly extensive set of recommendations for your consideration. It is important to keep in mind that each client (individuals, couples, and families) should be viewed as a unique system. Ethnic stereotyping should be avoided.

1. Beware of your attitude. A significant issue regarding the interactions between practitioners and culturally diverse families is the concern that practitioners' attitudes toward racial minority families do not display any hint of bias. Perceived arrogance on the part of the practitioner will influence the assessment results adversely, as will biases held by practitioners. If a white practitioner is evaluating the family, the

attitude of the assessor becomes even more important. Many families will make an assessment of the practitioner on the basis of nonverbal behaviors. For example, families will evaluate the practitioner on the basis of whether or not the individual displays a "quick smile". Many people of color believe the quick smile reveals a condescending attitude on the part of many white people. It is important that the practitioner display a warm, inviting smile that does not hint of insincerity.

2. When greeting the family in the waiting area, it might be helpful to shake hands with each member and do so in a relaxed, inviting manner. Greet each individual by his or her surname, including the children. Frequently it is a sign of the family's comfort level when they initiate a more informal greeting.

3. Don't worry about being politically correct. Don't seem overly anxious to meet the family or act as if you've got something to prove by telling them how many culturally different families you have worked with in your professional career. In fact, some families might even expect you to be a bit anxious, awkward even. Just remember that the family is concerned about your transparency.

4. Acknowledge friends and associates. Friends often accompany racially diverse families to treatment. This is certainly the case in African American and Latin families. If this is the case, ask the family if they would like their friends to be a part of the initial contact. While this goes against the concept of confidentiality, Boyd-Franklin (1989) points out that therapists often walk out into a clinic waiting area and invite the "family" for a session and leave the friend or neighbor they brought along outside. She adds that with all families, but particularly with black families, it is necessary to find out who those people are and their contribution to the presenting problems. We have found that oftentimes, the friend or neighbor is an extended family member, although not necessarily by birth. These individuals may even carry familial titles (aunt, uncle, etc), and will often provide valuable feedback to the family about whether the practitioner is really concerned with the well being of the family. In other words, these individuals might be considered the "lookout" for the family, looking out for cues that the practitioner is really interested in the family or whether the family is viewed as just another number. In addition, it is helpful to ask if all the people present represent the entire family. There may be other people living in the home that should be invited to session.

5. Ask the clients how they feel about working with a culturally different (or similar) practitioner. From the family's perspective, this shows that the practitioner is really concerned about the family's best interest. A top priority for many culturally different families is finding a practitioner that is a member of their racial or ethnic group. Many families believe that a culturally similar practitioner would better understand some of the developmental and systemic issues that are currently impacting family functioning. For example, if a racially diverse family is having disagreement regarding whether to send a child to private school, a culturally similar practitioner might interpret this as a family that is struggling with whether they are becoming more like a mainstream family. While every family wants the best education for their children, it often presents a family dilemma when some members of the family believe that sending children to a private school is trying to be more like members of the dominant group. Some families may even refer to this as selling out, which is becoming more mainstream in thought and behavior. In the meantime,

if a racially similar practitioner is not available, the family will likely view the current therapist as culturally sensitive, given that he or she acknowledges that possible consideration.
6. Often, interacting with the children first is helpful. Although families of African American Hispanic, and Native American origin tend to be hierarchical in nature, we have found that making small talk with the children prior to interacting with the parents helps foster rapport building with families. Perhaps there is a universal acceptance that practitioners who like children can't be all bad. When interacting with the children, particularly children over age thirteen, there are two questions the practitioner should ask: "First, are you feeling comfortable at this moment?" Even if the children respond with a definitive, yes, the second question should be "Is there anything I can do to help you feel more comfortable?" As compared with mainstream youth, most minority youth face much more severe psychological stresses at the prospect of having to be evaluated, because for them, the evaluation represents an alien cultural setting (Pai, 1990). In most instances, if the children leave the session indicating they really like the practitioner, the odds are great that the interpersonal attraction between the practitioner and the children will enhance the family's willingness to participate in the assessment process.
7. Assessing the family's attitude toward assessment instruments is important, because some families have experienced testing that is not culturally or racially sensitive. Therefore, given the objective information that families may have about testing, the practitioner must give the family a strong degree of reassurance that the assessment process will not unduly harm the members of the family.
8. Respect each family's uniqueness. To assess culturally diverse families, practitioners must understand that culturally diverse families do not represent a monolithic group. That is to say, there are within group differences as well as between group differences. For example, a Haitian family is different from a Jamaican family, as a Swede is from a German. Appreciating this uniqueness can be useful in working with racially diverse families after initial trust has been established.
9. Be collaborative. The family must be informed, active participants throughout the assessment process, and should be asked to comment on any area, at any time, that makes any member of the family feel uncomfortable. If the family believes that a question is too invasive psychologically, it could be a good idea for the family to skip that particular question. The practitioner would then make the necessary adjustments accordingly.
10. Beware of cultural differences. In order to have an effective assessment with racially diverse families; it's necessary to understand something about culture. The many areas where cultures are quite different will give practitioners opportunities to show caring as they help.

Pre-Assessment Stage

When working in a helping relationship with culturally different families, a major objective during the pre-assessment stage is to determine the family's current level of family identity development (FID). FID as we use it here refers to gaining an understanding of the attitudes and behaviors that exist within each member of the family, as well as within the family unit. From a family systems perspective, this implies that the practitioner should get a good understanding of the political, social, economic, and cultural factors that are instrumental in shaping the attitudes, beliefs and behaviors of individuals within the family unit. Gaining an understanding of these attitudes and beliefs assists the practitioner in gaining insight into why people think, do, and feel as they do.

Typically, racially diverse families form their identity development based on a three-tier model. The beginning stage of FID could be called *primary identity*, which suggests the family's beliefs, values, and norms are strongly influenced by the ties they maintain with their ethnic community. *Secondary identity* is permeated by the beliefs that assimilation to the majority culture and the denunciation of one's own group values and ideals are the only way to function as a family. In this stage, favor of more mainstream family traditions and values are given consideration over traditional views. *Tertiary identity* indicates that family members allow for divergent points of view within individual members, and continually think of ways to resolve any unnecessary family conflicts. Needless to say, the family is most ready to receive culturally sensitive assessment during *the tertiary identity* stage. During this stage, members typically have a heightened sense of awareness that the family is in need of third party assistance, and therefore become more open to providing and sharing information.

In addition to recognizing FID, Ramirez and Price-Williams (1974) pointed out that assessment with respect to the family's cultural styles (FCS) is important during the preassessment stage. In their model, families can be conceptualized along three dimensions: traditional lifestyles, modern orientations, or a combination of traditional and modern. The extent to which practitioners can identify the cultural style, and potentially match the cultural style with the practitioner's own cultural style, allows practitioners to be flexible in a supportive and accepting manner. Ramirez (1999) provides a comparison and contrast of thirteen domains within the traditionalism–modernism dimension. We have added five additional dimensions for your consideration. Keep in mind the views within each category will be affected by the political, social, and family context in which they are reared.

1. Gender-role definition. Traditional environments tend to emphasize strict distinctions between gender roles, whereas modern environments encourage more flexible boundaries between these roles.
2. Family identity. Family loyalty and identification are emphasized in traditional communities while individual identities are more valued in modern societies.
3. Sense of community. Traditional cultural styles encourage a strong sense of community while modern environments emphasize individualism.
4. Time orientation. People reared in traditional communities have a stronger past-and present-time orientation while people who are more modernistic are oriented toward the future.
5. Age status. Traditional societies associate increasing age with increasing wisdom, whereas modern societies value the vitality of youth.
6. Importance of tradition. Traditional environments value traditional ceremonies as a reinforcement of history, whereas modern value orientations tend to view tradition as a potential barrier to progress.

7. Subservience to convention and authority. In traditional societies, people are socialized to follow norms and conventions and to respect authority; in modern societies people are encouraged to question authority.
8. Spirituality and religion. Traditional societies emphasize the importance of spirituality and religion in life events; modern societies are characterized by an emphasis on science and secularism.
9. Sexual orientation. Traditional societies generally accept a more literal interpretation of their scriptures concerning sexual orientation and family; modern societies are more likely to view decisions about sexual orientation as part of the individual's right to choose his/her own lifestyle, and definitions of what constitutes a family are less conventional than in traditional societies.
10. Death Penalty. Traditional values usually uphold the belief of "an eye for an eye" when it comes to meting out punishment for major crimes. The view is that the person who is believed to have committed the crime is completely responsible for his actions. For most crimes, another view is that circumstances such as reduced mental capacity, the influence of addictive substances, limited opportunity in society, and abuse in childhood, need to be taken into consideration when decisions about punishment are made. Rehabilitation is emphasized over payment of a debt to society.
11. Role of the federal government in education. Traditional belief systems usually emphasize the importance of meeting national standards in educational opportunities.
12. Benefits to single mothers and non-citizens. A traditional belief system emphasizes that single mothers, particularly those who are not U.S. citizens, and their children should not be eligible for economic aid because this is likely to encourage sexual behavior outside of marriage. Modern belief systems view some single mothers as likely victims of sexual abuse and rape and see payment of benefits as a way to prevent criminal behavior and addiction.
13. Money orientation. Traditional belief systems emphasize saving today for a rainy tomorrow, while modern belief systems emphasizes spending now and tomorrow will take care of itself.
14. Sexual practices. Traditional belief systems primarily emphasize the missionary position, while modern belief systems incorporate a variety of sexual acts to enhance personal pleasure.
15. Physical Beauty. A traditional view is based upon the belief that the robustness of gluteus muscles and the thickness of thighs and legs determine a woman's beauty. Whereas, a modern view emphasizes that a woman's beauty is based upon having a slim figure and appearing to be a person who engages in a moderate amount of fitness training.
16. Male attractiveness. One traditional view is the belief that a man must have the ability to attract members of the opposite sex for indiscriminate sexual liaisons. Today, there is a concept of fidelity as the virtue that makes a man physically and emotionally attractive.
17. Skin Color. A traditional view is based on the belief that skin color that has a darker pigmentation is highly valued, whereas a modern view emphasizes lighter or "whiter" skin color as more aesthetically pleasing to the eye.

While we will provide a brief discussion of culturally sensitive assessment tools later in the chapter, there are two methods for assessing identity, the Family Identity Development (FID) and the Family Attitude Scale (FAS) that we will discuss at this point. In the case of FID, the practitioner could explore issues of oppression and discrimination and its role in shaping more traditional family values and beliefs. Focusing on messages received from the family of origin regarding cross-cultural relationships with people from culturally diverse groups is also helpful. Brinson & Morris (In Press) point out that minorities often hold suspicious views of culturally different groups, especially individuals from the dominant culture. The impact of religious/spiritual values should be discussed. Traditionally, racial minorities have used God as a primary resource of motivation for enduring the social injustices of our society. Modernistic families often place religion as a low priority in family orientation. Using the Family Attitude Scale (FAS), the practitioner could determine whether the family views itself as traditional, modern, or a combination of traditional and modernistic. This information tells practitioners what attitudes and behaviors might exist within a particular family unit, as well as what might be going on with individual members. Moreover, it provides a systemic framework to view how those specific views and behaviors might be causing a degree of family conflict.

Assessment Techniques

Assessment techniques should be chosen based on their being culture and ethnicity sensitive. They should be designed so that the couple or family assessed is being assessed on the basis of their own culture and ethnicity.

1. Assessment questionnaires are to be completed either by the couple or family and then reviewed by the mental health professional with the couple or family, or the mental health professional completes the questionnaire together with the couple or family. These assessment questionnaires should include questions such as their ethnocultural identity and qualities, the role and structure of the family, and gender roles. Linguistic considerations are also important, as are questions about how life problems are viewed and generally dealt with. Relevance and perception of seeking mental health services, versus seeking help within the larger family. Information about the natural support system, coping strategies, and traditional values should be assessed.
2. Multicultural genograms (originally described by Hardy and Laszlaffy in 1995) are used to accomplish several goals, one of which is to clarify patterns of relationships and events within and across generations. Through symbols, lines and dates multicultural genograms show how family members and couples or families as a system interrelate. Another goal is to clarify the influence culture has on the couple or family system, their cultural and racial identity values, beliefs, and unique characteristics of both individual members and the system as a whole. It can also serve as an opportunity to get a better understanding of the historical perspectives on the experience of the couple or family, including racism, oppression, and discrimination, and the spiritual importance and influence on the individual and the couple or family system.

Questions about family power, using the Olson and Cromwell (1975) model should be used, focusing on family power, family power process, and family power outcome. The following questions might be asked (Olson & Cromwell, 1975):

- Is power the actual ability to influence another person's behavior, or is it just the potential ability to do so?
- Is power an intentional or an unintentional process?
- Is power both overt and covert?
- Is power who decides, or is it who decides who decides?
- Is power a process or an outcome?
- Does the power struggle mean there is a winner or loser, or is it possible for both individuals to win or lose? (p. 5):

3. Timelines are represented by a vertical axis for the placement of people and events and can show relationships between them. Timelines are a valuable assessment tool that can display lifecycle changes of the couple or family. Topics such as cultural identity, values, beliefs, and norms can be assessed at various times throughout the life cycle.
4. The Multicultural Time-Line Genogram (Jordan, 2001) is based upon the Friedman, et al (1988) time-line genogram. It is a standard multicultural genogram with the timeline in a vertical axis to show individuals and events in the proper temporal relationships with culture and ethnicity as a foundation that influences relationships, self-identity, values, beliefs, and wants. Additional topics of discussion should include time together, how appreciation and affection is shown, commitment, positive communication, ability to cope with stress and crisis and spiritual well being. Finally, topics of freedom, justice, peacefulness, and economic adequacy should be explored. These are just some of the questions that should be addressed, however it is important to understand that these questions are in no way exhaustive.
5. The Culturegram can serve to assess immigrant families by asking questions as to when, why and how they immigrated to the United States. Additional important questions should focus on the ages of family and/or couple members when they entered this country and on what education they had then and what they have today. Related to this are questions about career goals and values. For example, is one's identity based on what they do in their work, or is it based on the family and community they live in, because community is more important than any career or job could be. Another important question to be asked should focus on what language is spoken at home, in the neighborhood, and with friends. The question of clients having potential legal issues relating to their immigration statues should be asked, since these can impact the family's, couple's, or individual's overall functioning. Other important questions to ask relate to the immigrant family's or couple's customs regarding holidays
6. The Family Assessment Wheel is a recently developed, very promising assessment tool which has been well described by Mallick and Vigilante (1997). This tool is designed to give family members an opportunity to talk about their experiences. The center of the wheel focuses on the family situation and what meaning it has to the

family. The five spokes of the wheel focus on the individual's, family's, and/or couple's experience in the areas of: (a) relevant family events, (b) institutional resource assessment, (c) communication, (d) family organization and (e) culture and value aspects (Mallick & Vigilante, 1997). The additional five concentric circles around the wheel focus on the family's and/or couples perceived experience in the areas of: a) culture, (b) risk factors, (c) cohort experience, (d) developmental needs and (e) family/couple situation(s) and resulting needs. This tool is designed to encourage a collaborative effort between the mental health professional and the family and/or couple.
7. The Eco-Map is another tool that is particularly helpful with diverse clients, since it focuses on the external environmental impact on the family (Hartman, 1995). More specifically, it looks at what resources and support the family and/or couple have outside themselves. It also assesses how external stressors such as racism and other factors are dealt with by families and/or couples.

These are just a few examples of culturally and ethnically sensitive assessment tools. As couples and/or families tell their stories, adequate time should be provided to talk in response to the client's statements. These tools will assist both the culturally and ethnically diverse couple or family as well as the mental health practitioner to get to know each other, and determine whether they should work together.

Assessment Instruments and Guides

There are many family and couple instruments, such as the Dyadic Adjustment Scale (DAS) (Spanier, 1976), or the Family Adaptability and Cohesion Evaluation Scale III (FACES III, Olson, 1986), that are widely used by mental health professionals to assess couple and family function. Many of the established couple and family assessment instruments have good psychometric properties. However, many of the existing couple and family assessment tools misinterpret ethnically and culturally healthy couple and/or family functioning, since many of them have been normed on one ethnic group. These should be used cautiously (Fine, 1993). Samuda (1993) points out that most of these assessment tools have been normed on Euro-white, middle-class standards, values, attitudes, beliefs, experiences, and knowledge, creating norms that are most likely not fitting for minority groups. This would most likely result in a score that is not truly representative of the couple or family. Additionally, a match or mismatch of treatment approach/treatment direction and the couple's and/or family's cultural/ethnic norms calls in to question both the predictor and criterion variables. It is therefore important to remember that if a couple and/or family assessment tool has been designed for and standardized for one ethnic/culture group and then administered to another, the assessment tool favors the culture/ethnicity for which the assessment tool was designed. Additionally it needs to be considered that when administering couple and family assessment tools to limited English speaking or otherwise un-acculturated people, it might not accurately reflect the couple's and/or family's function nor guide the process of therapy. Sommers (1989) reported that language barriers influence both the reliability and validity of an assessment tool, since the understanding of test items requires not just understanding the language, but also the meaning of the language. For example, individuals who speak the same language but are from different regions might use very different terms to express the same situation or phenomenon (Santos de Barona & Barona, 1991). English speaking countries such as the United States, Great Britain, and Australia use some terms and phrases differently. This shows that cultural influences need to be considered so as to not create confusing and inaccurate results on couple and/or family assessment tools.

In contrast to individual assessment, culturally sensitive family assessment instruments are not as well developed (Conoley & Bryant, 1996). However, selecting assessment instruments is a key part of culturally sensitive family assessment. There is a need for the development of more culturally and ethnically sensitive couple and family assessment tools that have been designed and normed for a variety of ethnically and culturally diverse couples and families. At this point, we will briefly identify and describe several tools that practitioners should consider during culturally sensitive family assessment.

1. The *Bicognitive Orientation to Life Scale* (BOLS) (Ramirez & Castaneda, 1974) is a personality inventory that assesses the persons "field sensitivity " and "field independent cognitive style of different life domains", for example a person is ambitious in a job setting where ambition is required (field sensitive [FS]), but in the rest of his/her life appropriately motivated (field independent [FI]) (Ramirez, 1999, p.27). Life domains include, but are not limited to: family, education, world of work, etc. This instrument is designed with a likert scale (from Strongly Disagree to Strongly Agree). Each of the questions of the BOLS ask the client to identify their preferences to field sensitive and field independent cognitive style. An example of BOLS questions is:

1. An individual's primary responsibility is to himself or herself. (FI)
2. I learn best by working on a problem with others. (FS)

Reliability of this assessment instrument was tested using Cronbach alphas .85 and .82 for FS and FI items representative. Whereas the correlation coefficients where established with mixed ethnic groups and ranged from .65 to .77.

2. The *Traditionalism-Modernism Inventory* (TMI) (Ramirez & Doell, 1982), was designed to assess to what level a person identifies to traditional (T) or certain modern (M) values and believes at different life domains. Life domains include, but are not limited to: family, education, world of work, etc. This assessment instrument helps identify to which degree a person is flexible and achieved a balance between both the traditional and modern values in different life domains. A positive score on the TMI means that the person is more traditional oriented, whereas a negative score indicates that the person is modern oriented. Whereas a negative score on this assessment instrument means that the person has achieved balanced between traditional and modern values This test is a personality instrument. The questions are designed so that person needs to identify if they do or do not agree with each item. Sample items are:

1. Husbands and wives should share equally in housework. (M)
2. Women with children at home should not have a full-time career or job outside of the home. (T)

There are no validity and reliability data available at this time on this instrument

3. The *Multicultural Experience Inventory* (MEI) (Ramirez, 1983) assesses a personals cultural flex meaning that a person has been exposed to a variety of different languages, values and participation and interaction with people of different cultures in their environment. This assessment instrument was originally designed to assess a person's historical development and present multicultural identity. This assessment instrument was originally designed for "people of color" but has been adjusted to also use with "white" person (Ramirez, 1999, p.167). There is a version for people of "color" and one for "whites". Sample Items are:

1. My childhood friends who visited my home and related well to my parents were of....(People of color Type A item)
2. I attend functions that are predominantly white in nature. (People of color Type B item)
3. My childhood friends who visited my home and related well to my parents were of....(Modified for whites Type A item)
4. I attend functions which are predominantly of minority groups in nature. (Modified for whites Type B item)

This assessment instrument was revised in 1996. Reliability was established by administrating the instrument to 115 Mexican American, white, Asian American (Vietnamese and Korean), and African American male and female college students. Split half reliability for Type A items was r = .87. It was not possible to establish the split half reliability on the Type B items. The correlation coefficients for Type A items ranged from .65 to .71 and for Type B items ranged from .69 to .73 (Ramirez, 1999, p.167). Additional assessment instruments to consider are the Traditionalism-Modernism Inventory-Revised (TMI-R) and the Family Attitude Scale-Revised (FAS-R).

These are just a few examples of culturally and/or ethnically sensitive assessment tools. When using these assessment tools, it is important to remember that instruments for couples and/or families are chosen based on the individual members of the couple and/or family system's level of acculturation, and linguistic, psychological, and socio-cultural factors, since each of these things impact the assessment results (Bernal, 1990). Finally, mental health professionals should remember that when they assess couples and families, the use of standardized tests is only one source of information gathering regarding the couple's and/or family's function. This should be communicated to the couple and or family

THINGS TO REMEMBER DURING THE ASSESSMENT PROCESS

Whether the primary method of assessment is the use of standardized assessment instrument or clinical interviewing, practitioners should be aware of the basic issues involved during the assessment process. Selecting from a systemic framework, we will offer four interrelated principles as guidelines for culturally sensitive assessment during the process.

1. Awareness of attitudes and emotions is important. As they prepare for and take the instrument, practitioners should determine what is causing the family some degree of concern. A family's emotional state could be reflective of issues that are going on within the family environment or general apprehension about the possible use of the test data. In each case, however, the practitioner should share with the family his or her observations of the perceived mood state.
2. Practitioners should administer the test. Turning-off is the operative term if someone who is not familiar with the family is placed in a position of obtaining personal information about the family. If one member of the family has concerns about someone else administering the test, then the results will likely be skewed in a negative direction.
3. Recognize communication characteristics. It is particularly important for practitioners to notice whether the family places greater emphasis on verbal or nonverbal communication, and whether the family prefers English or another native language. In cases in which English is the family's second language, it might be more appropriate for a standardize instrument to be translated into the native tongue. Family members could also assist one another in instrument taking or the assessor could make a translator available for assistance. In addition, practitioners must be aware of nonverbal cues. Some culturally diverse families communicate in nonverbal ways. For example, in many Asian groups, certain gestures, postures, facial expressions, and lack of eye contact may indicate discomfort with the processor or the assessor. In other words, some may use nonverbal cues rather than forthrightness in expressing disagreement or confusion. For more information on doing culturally sensitive and aware couple and family assessment see Geissler (1994).
4. Psychological jargon should be avoided. If verbal communication is important in conveying one's thoughts and feelings, then practitioners should refrain from using abstract psychological terms. Many racially diverse groups prefer more simple, direct forms of communication. The use of psychological terms may say to the family that the practitioner is placing them in a "one down" position without even realizing it.

These key points should be realized as you work with couples and/or families during the course of assessment. While there are other considerations, We are convinced that the aforementioned provide a good foundation and create an environment where culturally and ethnically diverse clients feel that the mental health practitioner is culturally sensitive and aware. This will allow the couple or family to feel more comfortable with the process of therapy and particularly the assessment phase. It therefore will provide a more accurate picture of the couple or family being assessed, since they will most likely behave more naturally.

CASE STUDY

The initial contact was with John and Tina, an African American account executive and schoolteacher, respectively, who were self-referred for marital counseling. John and his wife Tina had been having marital problems surrounding John's affair with a woman from a different racial group. Tina felt that their marital difficulties stemmed from the fact that John had become too self absorbed with his status as an executive with a fortune 500 company, and he had lost his identity as an African American male. She maintained that John was no longer attending church, and rarely associated with other African Americans. John believed that Tina was a southern girl with old-fashioned values. Indeed, she provided little excitement in the area of sexual intimacy. John suggested that the other woman was especially adept at pleasing a man, and said that Tina could take some lessons from the other woman. Tina said that some of the things John described to her were totally disgusting. She said that John should have sex with an animal if he expected her to do some of those things.

The practitioner started the session by looking at the couple's family identity development. The assessment consisted of obtaining their views about their cultural heritages through the use of a structured interview and the MEI (for people of color). Tina said that her family taught her that people should not date outside of their race. She indicated that her church taught her that a good man should be faithful to his wife, and a wife to her husband. She further said that people who date outside of their race could be considered "sellouts". The schools Tina attended from secondary onward were predominately black institutions of learning. She rarely encountered people from other groups during her secondary education. On the MEI, her score indicated a low degree of multiculturalism. John said that he, too, was raised with old-fashioned southern values, but he had since matured and understood the importance of changing with the times. He also said that he had been told that dating outside of his race was no big deal; other men have dated women from his group for hundreds of years. His score on the MEI indicated a high degree of multiculturalism. On the basis of this information and the completion of a thorough intake interview, the practitioner determined that Tina was functioning at the Primary identity stage; whereas John was in the Secondary identity stage of develop. Wanting more information about their family's cultural styles, the practitioner introduced the idea of doing a multicultural genogram, and the couple was open to this assessment tool. Several sessions were spent on gathering information from each of the couple members. They quickly identified that they both were functioning with different cultural styles. They further identified that John had become more modernistic in his orientation to life. The goals of the session then focused on identifying how John developed his modernistic views of the woman's role - and how and why Tina was inclined to maintain her traditional views. The multicultural genogram served as an ongoing assessment tool providing insight and understanding into the couple's beliefs and values.This was only the beginning of therapy and served as a springboard for more discussion, exploration, understanding, and decision-making for this couple.

SUMMARY

In this chapter culturally sensitive family assessment for use with minority families has been presented, recognizing that the United States supports pluralism, and no longer expects ethnic and racial minority groups to be part of the melting pot. Having embraced the concept of pluralism requires that today's mental health practitioners are culturally sensitive from the first contact and throughout the assessment process, which is generally an ongoing process and serves as a guide to the therapist. Additionally, it is important to remember that assessment techniques, as well as assessment instruments, are culturally and ethnic sensitive. There are some limited culturally and ethnically sensitive assessment instruments that have been normed using culturally and ethnically diverse samples. Mental health professionals who are culturally and ethnically sensitive and aware not only get a more accurate perception of the family's function, challenges, support system, etc, but also contribute to joining and ultimately encourage successful treatment outcome when working with an ethnically and culturally diverse clientele.

REFERENCES

Atkinson, D.R., Morton, G., & Sue, D.W. (1989). *Counseling American minorities: A cross-cultural perspective* (3rd ed) Dubuque, IA: Wm. C. Brown

Atkinson, D.R., Morton, G., & Sue, D.W. (1993). *Counseling American minorities: A cross-cultural perspective* (4th ed) Dubuque, IA: Wm. C. Brown

Bernal, E.M. (1990). Increasing the interpretive validity and diagnostic utility of Hispanic children's scores on tests of achievement and intelligence. In E.C. Serfica, A Schwebel, R.K. Russell, P.D. Isaac & L.B. Myers (Eds.), *Mental health of ethnic minorities*, 108-138. New York: Praeger.

Boyd-Franklin, N. (1987). *The contribution of family therapy models to the treatment of Black families. Psychotherapy, 24*, 621-629.

Brinson, J. A., & Morris, J. R. (In Press). Blacks' and whites' perceptions of real-life scenarios. *Journal of Humanistic Counseling and Development*.

Conoley, J.C., & Bryant, L. E. (1996). In Suzuki, L.A., Mueller, P.J., & Ponterotto, J. G. (Ed.) *Handbook of multicultural assessment*. San Francisco, Ca: Jossey-Bass.

Cromwell, R.E. & Olsen, D.H. (1975). *Power in Families*, Beverly Hills, CA: Sage.

Fine, M.A. (1993). Current approaches to understanding family diversity: An overview of the special issue. *Family Relations, 42*, 235-237.

Friedman, H., Rohrbaugh, M. & Krakauer, S. (1988). The time-line genogram: Highlighting temporal aspects of family relationships. *Family Process, 25* (Sep.), 293-303.

Geissler, E. M. (1994). *Pocket guide to cultural assessment*. St. Louis, Mo. Mosby.

Goldenberg, I., & Goldenberg H. (1994). *Family therapy: An overview* (2nd ed). Pacific Grove, CA: Brooks/Cole Publishing Company.

Goldenberg, I., & Goldenberg H. (1996). *Family therapy: An overview* (4th ed). Pacific Grove, CA: Brooks/Cole Publishing Company.

Goldenberg, I., & Goldenberg, H. (1993). Multiculturalism and family systems. *Progress: Family Systems Research and Therapy, 2*, 7-12.

Hardy, K. & Laszloff, T.A., (1995). The cultural genogram: Key to training culturally competent family therapists. *Journal of Marital and Family Therapy, 21*(3), 227-237.

Hartman, A. (1995). Diagrammatic assessment of family relationships. *Families in Society, 76*, 111-122.

Ho, M.K. (1987). *Family therapy with ethnic minorities*. Newbury Park, CA: Sage.

Homma-True, R., Greene, B., Lopez, S.R. & Trimble, J.E. (1993). Ethnocultural diversity in clinical psychology. *The Clinical Psychologist, 46*, 50-63.

Jordan, K. (2001). The multicultural time-line genogram. Unpublished manuscript.

Mallick, M.D. & Vigilante, F.W. (1997). The family assessment wheel: A social constructivist perspective. *Families in Society, 78*, 361-369.

McGill, D.W. (1992). The cultural story in multicultural family therapy. Families in Society: *The Journal of Contemporary Human Services, 6*, 339-349.

Olsen, D.H. (1986). Cicumplex model VII: Validation studies and FACES III. *Family Process, 26*, 337-351.

Padillo, A.M. & Medina, A. (1996). Cross-cultural sensitivity in assessment: Using tests in culturally appropriate ways. In Suzuki, L. A., Meller, P.J & Ponterotto, J.G. (Ed.). *Handbook of Multicultural Assessment.* San Francisco, CA: Jossey-Bass.

Pai. Y. (1990). *Cultural foundations of education.* Columbus, OH: Merrill.

Ramirez, M. & Castaneda, A. (1974). *Cultural democracy, bicognitive development and education.* New York, NY: Academic Press.

Ramirez, M. & Doell, S.R. (1982). *The traditionalism-modernism inventory.* Unpublished manuscript. Austin, TX.

Ramirez, M. & Price-Williams, D. (1974). Cognitive styles of children of three ethnic groups in the United States. *Journal of Cross-Cultural Psychology, 5*, 212-219.

Ramirez, M. (1983). *Psychology of the Americas: Mestizo perspective on personality and mental health.* Elmsford, NY: Pergamon Press.

Ramirez, M. (1999). *Multicultural Psychotherapy,* (2nd ed). Needham Heights, MA: Allyn & Bacon.

Ramirez, M. (1999). *Multicultural psychotherapy: An approach to individual and cultural differences* (2nd ed). Needham Heights, MA: Allyn & Bacon.

Samuda, R.J. (Ed.) (1998). *Psychological testing of American minorities: Issues and consequences* (2nd ed.). Thousand Oaks, CA: Sage Publications.

Santos de Barona, S.M. & Barona, A. (1991). The assessment of culturally and linguistically different preschoolers. *Early Childhood Quarterly, 6*, 363-376.

Sommers, R.K. (1989). Language assessment: Issues in the use and interpretation of tests and measures. *School Psychology Review, 18*, 452-462.

Spanier, G.B. (1976). Measuring dyadic adjustment: New scales for assessing the quality of marriage and similar dyads. *Journal of Marriage and the Family, 38*, 15-28.

Chapter 14

MULTIPLE FAMILY GROUP INTERVENTION AND ASSESSMENT: ISSUES AND STRATEGIES

William H. Quinn[*]
The University of Georgia

Under the magnetism of friendship the modest man becomes bold; the shy, confident; the lazy, active; or the impetuous, prudent and peaceful
~ **William Thackeray (1811-1863), Writer**

Multiple family group intervention is an approach integrating family processes and group dynamics in a manner that provides a learning context to promote behavior change. In effect, the group is a learning laboratory that functions to facilitate goal attainment. *Outcome goals* in group intervention include: symptom alleviation such as curbing delinquent behavior (Quinn, 1999), resolution of interpersonal conflict, information dissemination fostering behavior change (psychoeducation) such as divorce education, and healthy emotional expression such as family group support for schizophrenia patients (McFarlane, et.al., 1995).

While these goals serve as the purpose for group formation, there are *process goals* necessary to attain working relationships which facilitate overall goals of the group. Process goals are those that provide for productive social interactions between and among the group participants, including the group leader, which foster the attainment of outcome goals that are primary to individual and group success.

---

[*] William H. Quinn is Professor, Department of Child and Family Development, University of Georgia, Athens, GA, and Adjunct Clinical Associate Professor, Department of Psychiatry and Health Behavior, Medical College of Georgia, Augusta, GA.

ORIGINS OF (AND RATIONALE FOR) GROUP INTERVENTION

During the early part of the last century social scientists began studying natural groups in society. Social scientists were hoping to resolve political problems using some of the contentions made by those arguing on behalf of the philosophers Rousseau and Diderot. These two philosophers depicted the debate by social scientists who tried to establish whether groups and families were products of the individual or the larger system, the community or institution. In 1920, William McDougall, a social psychologist, published *The Group Mind*. In this text he outlined how a group's continuity depends in part on the group being an important idea in the minds of its members. To be a group there is the presence of boundaries and structures in which specialization of function could be defined. The group emphasizes the importance of customary behaviors that provide a sense of stability for persons through the prediction of certain actions.

Later Kurt Lewin gave us field theory in which he proposed that the group is different from, and more than, the sum or its parts (Lewin, 1951). In the social realm, this meant that persons comprising the group became more than the sum of their individual personalities. An important idea generated from this theory was that group discussions became superior to didactic presentations for changing ideas and behavior. This idea of the group being more than the sum of its parts has prominence in our current social mileau. The prevalence of group formation is evident in program intervention pertaining to medical problems of family members, parent education programs, grief counseling, and early intervention for at-risk youth problems. Lewis offered the notion of 'quasi-stationary social equilibrium', demonstrating that change in group behavior requires an 'unfreezing' and 'refreezing' of members beliefs' and behaviors.

In family therapy, multiple groups were initiated by Peter Laquer in 1950 in which four to six families would meet weekly for ninety minutes (Nichols and Schwartz, 1995). Laquer and his co-therapist would conduct treatment using group therapy principles such as structured exercises to increase the level of interaction and intensity of feeling. Families were used as 'co-therapists' to help confront members of other families from more personal positions than therapists thought they should take. It was thought that families could not do as much reality-testing as groups because the stakes were higher. Family members have to return to the same place together and carry on with their existence in context with each other. Therefore, groups comprised of different families can invoke some level of confrontation or debate that may not be possible in family treatment.

There are many kinds of social groups that originate in different ways and serve multiple purposes. The family group has a 'species-survival purpose' (Becvar, Canfield, and Becvar, 1997). There is a goal to remain a family, in the face of change that is forced upon it by developmental and cultural influences. Other groups are formed consciously for specific purposes, some as an evolving experience in which participants share life-space such as a common event (i.e., illness, loss). Some members come together to perform tasks that are more easily managed by a collective. Still other groups form to attempt to more effectively manage stress or survival challenges.

Each member brings a story to the group (Becvar, et.al., 1997), a particular account of how and why one joins and participates in the group. These stories may have similarities and differences across members. For instance, a similarity in a group of families with youth offenders or drug users is that they share a common characteristic, a group of youth who are all offenders or drug users. At the same time, members may differ in their view of that identity. Someone may believe that the youth is really not an offender because a youth may have been with another youth who offended and was 'in the wrong place at the wrong time'. Or, the other youth 'got off' and the youth in the program may have simply 'got caught', but doesn't deserve to be there. A drug user may claim that others, like parents or school officials, are over-reacting Drug users may minimize their use and therefore their need to be there. One parent may be upset or angry about being implicated in the child's misdeed ('I didn't do the crime so why do I have to do the time?'), while another might be secretly pleased knowing that the opportunity to resolve a chronic family problem is available. Another scenario played out in group formation is one in which a family member accompanies other family members by order or mandate, such as a husband who feels compelled to attend because his wife demands it.

These examples of stories, or parts of stories, about group participants serve to remind us that few assumptions can be made initially about the mind set or emotional state of group members. And, group members can travel different courses to get there; that is, how they got there varies from person to person. In a 'remedial' group, participants unite because of a perceived shared deficit or problem. However, we cannot even assume necessarily that the group agrees it shares the problem This is particularly true of a group of mandated participants, families ordered by the court, agency, or school, or required for hospital admission.

The extent to which a group shares a belief that a problem exists determines the nature of group cohesion as well as problem-resolution tactics. Some parents may believe they should not be in the group, while other parents believe they should be in the group. This condition affects the pace at which a group becomes cohesive and accomplishes its goals.

RECRUITMENT AND RETENTION OF GROUP PARTICIPANTS

One of the challenges in providing group intervention is recruitment. In families it is often true that not everyone is present in treatment to be changed in some way. Some people attend, sometimes begrudgingly, to solidify the notion that one person must change. For family members with a self-perception of innocence or blamelessness, the mind set and communication strategy is one that implicates another family member, such a an acting-out adolescent or neglectful marital partner. These family members may be anxious or worried about the person who has been defined as the problem. However, they often do not make the connection that the person's behavior has anything to do with them. This is quite a remarkable notion to some, that one person's behavior or emotional system isn't connected to anyone else. Nonetheless, it is somewhat common in these families to possess the notion that 'if you would just change everything would be fine.' Or to the interventionist, 'let me know when he is fixed and I will.... (come get him, feel better).' The challenges, then, to form and solidify a group with common aims are clear.

An additional challenge in family group formation is the reluctance held by family members to share their lives with other families. This is particularly true with families who have been identified by an agency or institution such as a juvenile court, school, or medical facility. If a family has been defined as having a problem, they may be self-conscious and desire a more private way to adequately respond to the agency or institution. Families may prefer to resolve difficulties without such a public revelation. This phenomenon can make recruitment challenges for group leaders and program administrators formidable. Group leader skills are essential in successful recruitment and retention of families in group intervention. The assessment of these skills is essential in training group leaders, and in informing group leaders who conduct groups whether group cohesion and trust is forming. A group leader who can measure the group dynamics related to group bonds and positive attitudes about the group experience can then know whether current group leader behaviors are effective. If current group dynamics are determined to be effective, group leader behaviors can be continued. If group dynamics are assessed and found to be insufficient for reaching process and outcome goals the group leader can make adjustments to foster more appropriate group dynamics that meet process goals (i.e., trust, honesty, humor, structure, involvement) which will have a greater likelihood of attaining outcome goals.

The challenge for a group leader to recruit families successfully and attain group cohesion are fromidable. A group role play of a recent first session of a family group meeting illustrates this challenge. A group leader initiated the planned activity of role playing a youth and a parent and planned to ask the group to guess which one she was role playing. The youth and families in this group were required to come due to a juvenile court mandate. The group leader, in the middle of the circle, crossed her arms and looked down at the floor, saying, 'I can't believe I gotta come here, well, I ain't gonna say nothin; I could be home watchin' my favorite TV show'. The group leader was making an attempt to role play a youth. When the group leader asked the group to guess who she was role playing a youth or parent (the youth was the intended family member), one of the parents barked, 'that's me!' I don't wanna be here'. The group laughed because they were surprised at the parent's candor. This serves to illustrate the challenge which group leaders have in forming a cohesive group that shares a positive tone and a willingness to accomplish goals.

The extent to which these stories of different families overlap initially, or as the group process unfolds, contributes to the extent of salience in group formation. The perception develops by its members that the group has a reason to come and remain together. This does not mean that the group members must agree, only that they hear accounts of other members that are persuasive in remaining included in the group. Therefore, a goal set by a group leader may be to establish this validity, a connectedness that fosters further group meetings and, potentially, goal attainment. Some of these group properties are: common experience, belief that something can be learned from someone else that will help a person, obligation to participate, commitment to group well-being, observations that group members have skills (or attitudes) to learn, and belief in the goals of the group existence and shared by other members.

These challenges, which a group leader must accept, require a set of competencies to form, solidify, and successfully terminate a group experience for families. These competencies include attaining a group structure, goal setting, attaining cohesion, building and protecting group norms (level of disclosure, rules of group conversation such as interruptions), and permitting and clarifying group roles (information giver, emotional stabilizer, harmonizer, instigator, etc.) (Gazda, Horne, and , 1999). The factors that contribute to change are the instillation of hope, universality, imparting of information, altruism, the corrective recapitulation of the primary family group, the development of socialization techniques, imitative behavior, interpersonal learning, group cohesiveness, catharsis, and experiential factors (Yalom, 1985). The helping profession, in general, and the group leader, in particular, are interested in the phenomenon of group dynamics because of its relation to client change. Research based on over 300 articles on group work revealed that positive change attributed to group counseling is due to well over 100 reasons cited by authors. These were reduced to nine therapeutic or curative ingredients that were further reduced to one of three categories; cognition, behavior, and emotion (Long, 1988). The nine key aspects are:

* observational learning of healthy behaviors
* universality of concerns caused a therapeutic reframing of each participant's concerns
* opportunities to understand the inner nature of things that leads to meaningful insight
* experiencing 'acceptance' by others
* basking in and reciprocally providing unselfish concern
* experiencing the 'we-ness' atmosphere which buffers alienation
* opportunities to test the validity of both self-defeating thoughts and untapped inherent strengths
* opportunities to ventilate and release what has blocked health change, and
* exposure to an environment of social nurturing that fulfils a basic human need that only is satisfied by interacting with others.

While any specific group may not privilege all of the above dimensions possible within the group context, it is clear that a group leader faces a challenge in promoting a meaningful experience for individual participants and families such that all four group stages can be attained: exploratory, transition, action, and termination. There are at least two sources of influence pertaining to successful completion: (1) the presence of particular characteristics of group members, and (2) the group leader competencies which contribute to this meaningful experience. Both of these influences can be assessed to determine the relative potency of the group experience for reaching outcome goals.

CHARACTERISTICS OF GROUP MEMBERS

It is vital that group members possess characteristics that are conducive to group processes that allow for outcome goals to be met. Appropriateness for group participation can be assessed on several dimensions. First, the target goals for the group existence must be congruent with the goals of the participants. The responsibility for this congruence lies with the group leader who must frame the purpose of the group in a manner that matches the participant's interest or need. Another part of the task of congruence lies with the family members who must accept the rules of group experience. These rules can include civility, common courtesy in the conversational domain (e.g. not interrupting, not cajoling or ridiculing others), participation, and attendance. These aspects cannot be easily ascertained prior to a group's formation and may require a skilled leader to identify, as well as alter inappropriate behaviors or expectations in a manner that builds congruence.

The nature of the group purpose should be clearly articulated so that the group membership can be appropriately ascertained. For instance, if a multiple family group is formed for resolving truancy in school, the operational definition of what truancy is should be established. Some examples might be: being absent 5 or more days without a legitimate excused absence, or, truancy is whatever a school determines it to me (i.e., Mrs. Johnson, I can see that you have a disagreement with the school about whether your daughter is truant but the school is taking the position that Angela is truant and therefore we must help Angela change her school attendance pattern so that the school will consider her to be in compliance and reach an acceptable status'). If a family group member continues to reject the school's criteria, the group member might be helped with exposure to group discussions in which other families accept the school's criteria so that they might become more valid to the objecting parent and, thus, the parent can become more intent on helping the child change instead of being consumed with an agenda of forcing school policy to change. The latter is not the objective of the group experience.

Personal characteristics may interfere with attaining group process that can threaten effective working relationships and impede positive change. Some widely accepted examples might be: a group member who attends under the influence of drugs or alcohol, the presence of psychopathology that disturbs group process goals in significant ways (thought disorder, behavioral abnormalities that distract the group or make them consistently uneasy, emotional outbursts which distract a group from its task or focus). Some of these characteristics can be determined prior to the inception of the group's first meeting by administering screening items in a risk assessment (e.g., Michigan Alcohol Screening Test, dimensions of the MMPI, or self/family reports of drug/alcohol or family violence).

It is important not to automatically screen family group participants out of group participation based on too narrow a set of criteria. For instance, in a recent family and youth offenders group experience, a juvenile court staff member referred a young boy who was autistic. The family group was not oriented toward autistic children. The referral of the autistic child was not known to the group leader until the family arrived, a few minutes before the first scheduled session. As the session unfolded, the presence of emotion (e.g. laughter, loud voices) in the group interaction caused the child to erupt with shrieking sounds and body twitches. This distracted the group from its focus whenever it occurred. The mother of the autistic child began to cry and show frustration. She clearly did not know what to do. After a few incidents, the group leader leaned over to the mother of the autistic child and said, 'you know your son best, you have our permission to do what you feel is best; you can step out of the room with your son, go home now, or try any method here you think might help console him'. The mother appreciated this guidance for it gave her options. After the mother tried to calm her son, and he erupted two more times, mother decided to go outside with him. The remaining group participants felt bad and wanted to help the family. The group uniformly said they wanted the mother and her son to feel like they could stay of they wanted. This was discussed with the mother and son after the group session ended. Mother said she would try one more time and come back next week. The boy smiled. The next week the boy came with this mother to try the group again, and he became slightly more relaxed as the group learned how to relate to each other and to the boy to help calm him. As it turned out, the boy and his mother came each week and completed the program. At the last session, the mother expressed her thanks to the group for sticking with her and her son, and giving them a chance to belong. In this case the juvenile court staff worker did not know about the importance of group cohesion and elements of group process that culminate in desired outcomes. Thus, the group leader was saddled with a predicament that required adept responses. In fact, the court worker primarily wanted the family to try the program because there were few options in services and no intervention available for the boy's problem. This is a common problem in the delivery of human services. This example serves an important purpose. It reminds us that assessment is ongoing, not simply an exercise that precedes intervention. And, group leaders may encounter situations in which the ideal characteristics of group members are not present, yet must meld participants in a manner that forms a 'pseudo-family'. An artifact of this family's vulnerability is that the group bonded via the experience of helping this frustrated and concerned parent and her autistic child.

Diagnosis and assessment *is* intervention. Often there is insufficient information that can be attained prior to the first group session to determine the appropriateness of a referral to a group intervention. Written assessments and interviews by a professional prior to intervention that contribute to a referral decision can be helpful. However, they are often incomplete in determining the appropriateness of a group experience for a family. A group can help individual participants manage their limitations more effectively, and provide a sense of community for a family that labels itself unworthy. Thus, a group leader must be cautious regarding decisions pertaining to assessment that might exclude families who can be helped by their inclusion. And, the other families in the group may be benefitted by having the opportunity to help others, such as in the case of the group with the mother with an autistic child.

While there is a need for the goals of the group to be congruent with the members of the group, sometimes this congruence is not established immediately. For instance, some group members may be more enthusiastic than others. A mother may be excited and committed to utilizing the group experience to improve family functioning or child behavior on some dimension (e.g. school behavior, drug use), but her husband may be ambivalent or recalcitrant. Of course, if the family is most interested in group involvement because of concerns about an individual family member (e.g., child's behavior), the child may be even less interested in the enterprise of family group experience due to the anticipated blame being levied against the child. In addition, children have fewer opportunities to speak without reprisal, as well as having more limited verbal skills. Therefore, they may lack the confidence that a family group experience will be beneficial. It is incumbent upon a group leader to assess this possibility and not use assessment as a screening device to eliminate certain families with 'problematic' characteristics.

GROUP INTERVENTION OUTCOMES

Outcomes of group intervention can be assessed in much the same way as treatment outcomes are measured for individual or family treatment. Assessment is defined as an equation in which assessment equals measurement plus evaluation (Payne, 2002). This formula provides a framework for determining the relative value of an intervention and the specific conditions necessary to attain the goal of the intervention. The selection of measures is dependent on the theoretical lens of the program developers and group leaders of the intervention. These choices can encompass a wide array of dimensions. Davidson, Quinn, and Josephsen (2001) outlined some suggested dimensions of family assessment to consider: (1) *structural* components such as boundaries, subsystems of the family, cohesion, and adaptability; (2) *historical* considerations of the family such as parental development and functioning, intergenerational functioning, and marital history; (3) *developmental* factors such as individual development, family life cycle challenges and adaptations, and contextual factors such as socioeconomic status, and family transitional forces such as divorce and remarriage; and (4) *process* dimensions such as the clarity of family rules and emotional expressiveness, problem-solving abilities, communication, and patterns of family behavior such as rigidity, triangles, and conflict-resolution. Decisions regarding assessment should be congruent with the theory undergirding the group intervention. In the current treatment climate, measuring the outcome of intervention requires an examination of the rsoluton of the presenting problem, such as behavioral problems of children, grief resolution, management of chronic illness, or violence and abuse is essential. The group leaders and program administrators must select criteria to assess changes and improvements in these presenting problems.

Program developers and group leaders can define goals from this framework essential to evaluating intervention effectiveness. The goal to be attained can be measured using standard measures with acceptable psychometric properties of validity and reliability. For instance, symptom alleviation could be measured for child behavior problems using the Child Behavior Checklist (CBC)(Achenbach, 1991), the Behavioral Assessment of School Children (BASC) (Reynolds and Kamphaus, 1992), or the Outcome Questionnaire (OQ 45) (Lambert and Burlingame, 1996) at pre- and post- intervention, and follow-up. Family groups for children with ADHD, autism, or developmental disabilities could be measured using behavioral instruments that tap the goal established by the program and intervention leaders. For example, with a child diagnosed with ADHD, are there changes in a child's classroom behavior or effective responses to parental management that can be observed and recorded? Or, self-report instruments can be utilized to assess change as perceived by the participants. For instance, multiple family group intervention for youth offenders (Quinn, VanDyke, and Kurth, 2002) could establish targeted change to be improvement or enhancement of family functioning, and utilize the Family APGAR (Smilkstein, 1978), parent-adolescent communication scale (Barnes and Olson, 1982), or FACES (Olson, Bell, and Portner, 1985). Standardized instruments provide the vehicle for establishing credibility of an intervention program in the professional community.

Several intended outcomes of family group intervention could be assessed simultaneously. For instance , in the Family Solutions Program for juvenile first offenders (Quinn, 1998), family functioning (Smilkstein, 1978; Smilkstein, Ashworth, and Montano, 1982)), parental attitudes of childrearing (Schaefer, 1965; Schluderman and Schluderman, 1970; Margolies and Weintraub, 1977; Burger, Armentrout, and Rapfogel, 1973), and parent-adolescent communication (Barnes and Olson, 1982) are self-report instruments intended to elicit the perspectives of parents and youth both before (part of the risk assessment prior to the inception of intervention) and subsequent (last session of intervention) to the multiple family group program. It is recommended that the same instruments be administered at a follow-up of at least three months to determine if possible changes stabilize over time and do not return to baseline. It is well known that some interventions have immediate positive effects but over time such changes wash out. Financial support for a program and a wider use of intervention are highly questionable if immediate positive effects at post-intervention wash out over time. At least 3 measurement points (pre-intervention, post-intervention, and follow-up) provide a more reliable protocol of assessment to help determine the validity of an intervention and its lasting impact.

In addition to family environment variables measured using self-report to assess group intervention for youth offenders, a judge, program officer of juvenile justice, or community task force might want to know whether a group intervention program with families is reducing offending behavior that diminishes the disruptions in community life or threatens the safety of its citizens. More unobtrusive measures can be gathered, such as recidivism as reported by the juvenile courts who refer the youth to the program (Quinn, Bell and Ward, 1997; Quinn and Van Dyke 2001). These measures provide the opportunity to evaluate intervention effects that reflect improvements not only in family functioning but the lives of the targeted population participating in the intervention. A judge might hold the notion, 'it is great that families enjoy the family program and get along better, but it is keeping the youth in those families from returning to my court?' Tracking recidivism, especially if these rates are compared to similar youth who do not receive the multiple family group intervention but instead receive probation, is an example of language that builds a bridge between human service professionals on one side, and politicians, community leaders, and law enforcement personnel on the other.

More global effects can be assessed as well. For instance, measures of recidivism for juvenile offenders who complete intervention can serve as a proxy for improvements in community safety or court effectiveness. In turn, successful interventions such as significant change scores between pre- and post-intervention in family functioning, parental attitudes, or family communication, or reductions in recidivism, provide accountability measures which increase the confidence of funding organizations and referral sources in a multiple family group program. For example, the Family Solutions Program as a non-profit organization has secured funding from the United Way and Department of Juvenile Justice partly based on the evaluation of the program demonstrating its effectiveness. Court records are tracked to determine the frequency of repeat offenders and offenses of those youth referred to the program. Comparisons are made between youth offenders who complete the program, those who fail to attend, and a comparison group of youth placed on probation and not referred to the multiple family group program. This evaluation method has led to the determination that multiple family group intervention is effective. For example, using logistical regression methods, a youth who is referred to the Family Solutions Program and completes the program is 6.6 TIMES less likely to repeat offend as a youth referred to probation, and 3.7 TIMES less likely to re-offend compared to youth from the same court who fail to attend or complete the Family Solutions Program (VanDyke and Quinn, in review).

There are several other family approaches which have demonstrated effects using self-report and unobtrusive measures. Webster-Stratton and colleagues have implemented interventions with parents of preschool children and primary school children with the objective of reducing opposition defiant disorder and conduct disorder (Webster-Stratton, Kolpacoff, & Holinsworth, 1988). They showed reductions in rates of these disorders, positive long-term effects, and cost-effectiveness. In a different target population, both Campbell and Peterson (1995) and Goldstein, & Miklowitz (1995) showed that interventions with family groups reduced pathogenic family processes which modified symptom stress. Currently there is more attention to family-focused health care delivery or psychoeducation and family support which may be valuable as a preventive approach to reducing rates of symptomatology or severity of acute episodes of chronic disorders. For example, Sanders, Shepherd, Cleghorn, and Woolford (1994) demonstrated that a behavioral intervention for families of children with abdominal pain prevented relapses, increased the length of time between relapses, and reduced pain levels in patients. Multiple family group intervention has been enhanced by assessment and evaluation of its application to different populations in need. Any interventionist or researcher who develops such an approach to working with targeted populations in need would be benefitted by ongoing assessment using symptom reduction or behavior change goals as variables under study. In this way, not only would further support for such methods be considered, the likelihood of benefitting more patients, families, and at-risk populations would be enhanced.

In current family and multiple family intervention practice there is an under-emphasis on assessment and evaluation. At present there has been less emphasis on the scientific development of construct assessment of family and family group intervention than there has been for individual -focused intervention (Tolan, 2001). Some guidelines for the assessment of family groups for prevention are: defining clearly the population to which the intervention is targeted; gathering base rates to determine the appropriate intervention as well as a base line for assessing change following intervention; examining proximal vs. distal outcomes of intervention (e.g. presence of halo effects at post-intervention that wash out over time); clarification of service-delivery issues such as the targeted variables under study (e.g., risk factors vs. risk-outcome links vs. prevention benefits); and the focus of the intervention (individual vs. family) to determine whether tracking of symptomatology in a family member is sufficient vs. expected change in family processes such as conflict or communication. The development of assessment methods to determine family intervention program effectiveness is increasing but not prolific. If it is viewed that families are powerful forces which substantially influence the trajectory of child development, illness, or individual functioning, then methods must be considered which examine the variables which reflect the goals of intervention. The researcher and interventionist must carefully consider what the intended changes are in the intervention program such that an assessment can adequately answer questions about the viability of an intervention. These outcomes have the power to influence budgetary decisions about which programs will be implemented, expanded, or deleted. In the end, results of evaluation will determine the number of families receiving an intervention which is found to be effective.

CHARACTERISTICS OF GROUP LEADERS

Sometimes it is helpful for multiple family group program developers and leaders to elicit feedback from group participants about their experience. This provides for an opportunity to learn more about the strengths and limitations of the group design and format and whether the group leader has effectively fostered certain group dynamics known to influence positive outcomes. This feedback can be used to protect the elements of the program that are most useful as viewed by the participants, and to modify elements in which the participants report were not helpful. In addition, family participants might reflect experiences that pertain to the group program that were outside the awareness of the group leader and therefore these ideas may not be within the framework established by the program.

This aspect of assessment utilizing the feedback of group participants can actually contribute to a stronger intervention. For example, in the Family Solutions Program, participants are routinely invited to share their perspectives on what they are experiencing in the program, and are even expected to offer suggestions for topics that they think are important to address and discuss. Sometimes these suggestions or requests were not initially within the awareness of the program developers. In a group in which several youth were shoplifters, the parents expressed their hope that the merchants would be available so that their children had an opportunity to negotiate restitution. This would add closure for the youth and allow them to experience the necessity of accepting responsibility for their actions. The group leader considered this to be a useful piece of feedback and tried to comply; but most shop owners were not interested in coming, saying they were too busy, did not have enough help to get away from the shop, or believe their attendance would not accomplish anything and that these youth would be back in the store trying to shoplift again. As a result, the group leader solicited the involvement of a major department store chain who came as a representative of all store owners or clerks. This representative talked about how shoplifters are caught, what the consequences are, and how they predict who will try it again. The parents developed a sense of ownership in the group knowing that their suggestions were taken seriously by the program developers. Group leaders who take time to request feedback from participants convey that they are interested in assuring relevance to the group experience in a world in which each person has so many life choices and obligations. Without relevance, group participation declines and the 'learning laboratory' is in jeopardy of dissolution.

Group participants can be asked about how useful certain activities or assignments were, such as handouts or homework, to identify aspects of the program sessions that enhanced or disrupted their experience. Finally, parents can be asked whether they would recommend the program to others, and whether the financial cost was too much, too little, or about right (Horne, 19). These accountability questions take on greater salience as funding becomes more competitive or as foundations consider their choices and priorities.

Group Process Assessment

While the ultimate importance of family intervention is determined by the established likelihood of positive change or reduced symptomatology of a targeted population, it is a widely accepted notion that there are certain necessary pre-conditions or requirements that must be present in the intervention that are more likely to lead to these desired outcomes for families. Group dynamics are instrumental in the success of failure of a group intervention experience for families. Group assessment is necessary to determine whether families participating in the intervention will benefit and whether the experience of group participants in the intervention is congruent with what is known about group processes that is more likely to produce these outcomes. It is incumbent on group leaders to track these processes such that adjustments can be made in the group process if these known conditions are not visible. If known elements of successful group process are observed, then the group leader can continue with similar group leader behaviors to foster successful group experience.

There are generally two dimensions to the assessment of group intervention process: (1) assessment of group dynamics, and (2) fidelity - the extent to which the intervention was implemented as planned or designed. These two dimensions overlap in that the fidelity of an intervention can be measured by whether particular group dynamics that are prescribed are in fact attained.

Group dynamics and fidelity. The essential elements of the working relationships of the group have been identified. An empirical study by Cassanso (1989) delineated the practice skills necessary to conduct groups. These include: (1) building rapport with each participant, (2) facilitating family interaction, (3) facilitating cross-family interaction, (4) facilitating group cohesion, and (5) accepting and exhibiting dimensions of family roles as needed.

Family therapy training is needed and highly specific treatment manuals are recommended (Carlson, 1998).

The assessment and evaluation of any intervention is valid partly to the extent to which the interventionist, program developer, and/or evaluator can establish that the intervention under evaluation was in fact delivered as specified. In this way it can be assured that what is evaluated is actually the program that was implemented and not something different. For instance, a manual or program guide can be written for group leaders but if one or more group leaders do not adhere to the guide then what is evaluated is not what is written, but instead what the group leader did which may or may not be specified. Thus, the results of the evaluation are not about the program as written but rather about something else which is somewhat unknown. How can this happen that the program (goals, content, and structure) could be different that what is planned? A group leader my not have allegiances to the particular theory that underlies the program guide. Or, the group leader may be easily swayed by group participants who prefer to focus on unrelated topics or content, or desire a group structure not designed by the program developer. Another possibility in which fidelity is sacrificed is if the group leader is unprepared and has a poor understanding of the program as planned. Topics, activities, and homework assignments may be neglected or under-emphasized due to lack of awareness or appreciation for their inclusion in the intervention.

There are both process and content dimensions which circumscribe fidelity. Dumas, et.al., (2001) delineated two ways of examining of fidelity: (1) *content* fidelity which refers to the delivery of specified tasks or activities in an intervention, and (2*) process* fidelity which refers to the manner in which the content is intended to be delivered. These strategies are employed to instill confidence in their Early Alliance program, an intervention to promote competence and reduce risk for conduct disorder, substance abuse, and school failure. A focus on fidelity helps protect a program's integrity and diminishes the chances that the effectiveness of a group is dependent on a particularly skilled or charismatic group leader. While group leaders that are exceptionally skilled or charismatic are valuable to group success, generalizability may be compromised if the transferability of the program is dependent on such qualities that cannot be sustained in other communities or contexts.

To determine whether a group program was implemented as planned so as to assess the congruence between the design and implementation of the program, group participants can be asked to complete a self-report measure to ascertain such congruence. Some examples of questions which might reflect this assessment are:

1. We completed the _____(activity-exercise) in this session.
completely   somewhat   not at all
2. We had a discussion about.........(e.g., communication, discipline, monitoring)
completely   somewhat   not at all
3. We were given a homework assignment.
completely   somewhat   not at all
4. We practiced the steps of effective (e.g., communication, discipline, monitoring).
completely   somewhat   not at all
5. We developed a plan for effective (e.g., communication, discipline, monitoring).
completely   somewhat   not at all

Certain group dynamics are known to provide a context for group interaction that enhance learning, problem-solving, emotional resolution, or family strengths. Some examples of these questions are:

1. The session (e.g., held my interest, was boring, was fun)
completely   somewhat   not at all
2. The group leader was (e.g., enthusiastic, knowledgeable, apathetic).
completely   somewhat   not at all
3. All members of the group participated in the... (activity, discussion).
completely   somewhat   not at all
4. The group leader demonstrated that he/she cared about us.
completely   somewhat   not at all
5. The group leader gave us guidance or good suggestions.
completely   somewhat   not at all
6. The group leader encouraged us to help other families
completely   somewhat   not at all
7. The group leader was respectful and accepted our opinions and ideas.
completely   somewhat   not at all
8. The group leader encouraged us to respect other families.
completely   somewhat   not at all

Responses can be categorized by family age (children vs. adolescents) or role (parent or child) to assess the relative value for a wide range of participants. The benefit of this procedure is to determine whether the group leader (and maybe the program) may be more effective for certain age children, or whether the leader is more effective with parents than for children. Of course, the overall effectiveness of a multiple family group program is best assessed by addressing the question of whether the goals of the group were met. For instance, did the program deter youth offending behavior, truancy, or behavior problems? Did the program increase the parenting skills of the parents? Did the program alter attitudes that are more positive or hopeful? Thus, the assessment of a multiple family group program should include two sets of goals: (1) goals that assess group properties such as group dynamics and fidelity which are known to be vital in the attainment of intervention goals, and (2) the overall intervention goals or the attainment of desired change in behaviors and attitudes.

There are rating systems and procedures that have been developed to compile and summarize data generated from these questions and instruments to modify and strengthen an intervention program. In addition to strengthening the intervention, an additional value in codifying such data is to create a systematic procedure for standardizing intervention. For instance, there are family intervention programs for serious chronic offenders (Henggeler, 2002), behavioral problems including delinquency (Alexander, et.al., 1998) and at-risk youth - juvenile offenders, truant students, and behavior problems (Quinn, 1998, 1999, 2001) which have created web sites to promote standardization of family interventions using these models of intervention in different geographic areas. Just as restaurant chains provide some consistency in menus to provide the consumer with predictable and options and expected results, standardization of intervention using measures of implementation consistency promotes quality-assurance that intervention programs found to be effective are in fact delivered in the manner that they were evaluated and found to be effective.

CONCLUSION

Multiple family group assessment has similarities to single family and individual therapy assessment. This includes an assessment of process dimensions such as therapeutic strategies and behaviors and the level of standardization reached in an intervention program.. Outcome dimensions are similar such as therapeutic goal attainment related to the reduction in symptomatology or presenting problems, and interpersonal relationship improvement. In addition, assessment can be used to determine the appropriateness of the intervention for a particular person or family related to the therapeutic goal and the likelihood of responsiveness to the intervention.

A unique aspect of assessment in multiple family group intervention is the presence of inter-family relationships embedded in group process which is central to the group's purpose and identity. This intervention context is a microcosm of the larger social and cultural context because it represents multiple age and generational participants, and different phases of psychosocial and biological development. This context is purposefully created to provide a sense of community to engender validation and hope, enhance learning, and provide experiences to practice and implement skills applicable to the larger social ecology. Multiple family group assessment is necessary to insure that this microcosm is comprised of individuals and families who can provide the context to attain these goals.

REFERENCES

Achenbach, T.M. (1991). *Integrative guide for the 1991 CBCL/4-18 YSR,TRF profiles.* Burlington: University of Vermont, Department of Psychiatry.

Alexander, J., Pugh, C., Parsons, B., Barton, C., Gordon, D., Grotpeter, J., Hansson, K., Harrison, R., Mears, S., Mihalic, S., Schulman, S., Waldron, H., & Sexton. T. (1998). Functional family therapy. In D.S. Elliott (Series Ed.), *Blueprints for violence prevention.* Boulder, CO: Center for the study and Prevention of Violence, Institute of Behavioral Science, University of Colorado at Boulder.

Barnes, H. & Olson, D.H. (1982). *The parent-adolescent communication scale.* Family Assessment Inventory. University of Minnesota.

Burger, G.K., Armentrout, J.A., & Rapfogel, R.G. (1973). *The Journal of Genetic Psychology*, 123, 107-113.

Campbell. T.L. & Peterson, (1995). The effectiveness of family interventions in the treatment of physical illness. *Journal of Marital and Family Therapy*, 21, 545-584.

Carlson, C. (1998).Multiple family group therapy. In K.C. Stoiber and T.R. Kratochwill (Eds.) *Handbook of group intervention for children and families.* Boston, MA: Allyn and Bacon.

Cassanso, D.R. (1989) Research on patterns of interaction: II. *Social Work with Groups.* 12, 1, 15-39.

Davidson, B., Quinn, W.H., & Josephsen, A.M (2001). Assessment of the family: Systemic and developmental perspectives. In A. Josephsen (Ed.). *Child and Adolescent Psychiatric Clinics of North America.*, 10, 3, 415-429.

Dumas, J., Lynch, A.M., Laughlin, KJ.E., Smith, E.P., Prinz, R.J. (2001). Promoting intervention fidelity: Conceptual issues, methods and preliminary results from the Early Alliance Prevention Trial. *American Journal of Preventive Medicine*, 20, 38-47.

Dumas, J.E., Lynch, A.M., Laughlin,J.E., Smith, E.P. & Prinz, R.J. (2001) Promoting intervention fidelity: Conceptual issues, methods, and preliminary results from the Early Alliance prevention trial. *American Journal of Preventive Medicine*, 20, 38-47.

Gazda, Horne, and Group dynamics: *Prevailing group forces*.

Goldstein, M. J.and Miklowitz, D. J. (1995). The effectiveness of psychoeducational family therapy in the treatment of schizophrenic disorders. *Journal of Marital and Family Therapy*, 21, 361-377.

Henggeler, S. (2002). *www.MSTInstitute.org*.

Henggeler, S.W., Melton, G.B., & Smith, L.A. (1992). Family preservation using multisystemic therapy: An effective alternative to incarcerating serious juvenile offenders. *Journal of Consulting and Clinical Psychology*, 60, 953-961.

Lambert, M.J., & Blasingame, G.M. (1996) *Outcome Questionnaire* (OQ – 45.2). American Professional Credentialing Services LLC.

Lewin, K. (1951). *Field theory in social science*. New York: Harper.

Margolies, P.J., & Weintraub, S. (1977). the revised 56-item CRPBI as a research instrument:

McFarlane, W.A.., Link, B., Dushay, R., Marchal, J., & Crilly, J. (1995). Psychoeducational multiple family groups: Four-year relapse outcome in schizophrenia. *Family Process*, 34 (2), 127-144.

Nichols, M.P. & Schwartz, R. C. (1995). *Family therapy: Concepts and methods*, 3rd Ed Boston, MA: Allyn and Bacon.

Olson, D. H., Bell, R. and Portner, J. (1985) *Faces III Manual*. Department of Family and Social Science, University of Minnesota..

Payne, D.A. (2002). *Applied Educational Assessment*, 2nd Ed. Belmont, CA: Wadsworth.

Quinn, W. H. & VanDyke, D.J. (2001). At-risk youth in the United States: Current status, family influences, and the family Solutions Program (pgs. 66-85). In I. Pervova (Ed.), *People, Time and society*. St. Petersburg University Press: St. Petersburg, Russia.

Quinn, W.H. (1998). *The Family Solutions Program Manual*. Athens, GA: University of Georgia.

Quinn, W.H. (1999). The Family Solutions Program: A Collaboration of The University of Georgia and the Athens/Clarke County Juvenile Court (pp. 89-100). In R. Lerner and T. Chibucos (Eds.), *Serving children and families through community-university partnerships: Success stores*. Boston: Kluwer.

Quinn, W.H., Bell, K., and Ward, J. (1997). The Family Solutions Program. *The Prevention Researcher*, 4, 10-12.

Reliability and factor structure. *Journal of Clinical Psychology*, 33, 472-476.

Reynolds, C. R., & Kamphaus, R. (1992) *Behavior Assessment System for Children*. Circle Pines, MN: American Guidance Service.

Sanders, M.R., Shepherd, R. W., Cleghorn, G. & Woolford, H. (1994). The treatment of recurrent abdominal pain in children: A controlled comparison of cognitive-behavioral family intervention and standard pediatric care. *Journal of Consulting and Clinical Psychology*, 62, 306-314.

Schludermann, S. & Schludermann, E. (1970). Replicability of factors in children's report of parent behavior (CRPBI). *The Journal of Psychology*, 76, 239-249.

Smilkstein, G., Ashworth, C., & Montano, D. (1982). Validity and reliability of the family APGAR as a test of family function. *Journal of Family Practice*, 15, 303-311.

Smilkstein, Ga. (1978). The family APGAR: A proposal for a family function test and its use by physicians. *The Journal of Family Practice*, 6, 1231-1239.

Tolan, P.H. (2001). Family-focused prevention research: "Tough but tender" family intervention research. In H. Liddle, J. Bray, D. Santisteban, & R. Levant (Eds.), *Family psychology intervention science*. Washington, DC: American Psychological Association.

VanDyke, D.J. & Quinn, W.H. Early Intervention for youth offenders: Comparisons of three interventions for juvenile first offenders: Multiple family group completers, drop-outs, and probation. Manuscript in review.

Webster- Stratton, C. Kolpacoff, M.& Hollinsworth, T. (1988). Self-administered videotape therapy for familoies ith conduct-problem chldren: Comparison with two cost-effective treatments an a control group. *Journal of Consulting and Clinical Psychology*, 56, 558-566.

Yalom, I. (1985). *The theory and practice of group psychotherapy*, 3rd ed. New York: Basic Books.

Chapter 15

ETHICAL AND LEGAL ISSUES IN MARITAL AND FAMILY ASSESSMENT

Michael J. Strazi[*]
University of Colorado at Denver
Patricia W. Stevens[*]
Morehead State University

INTRODUCTION

This final chapter will focus on the myriad of ethical and legal issues faced daily by marital and family counselors in the assessment of their clients. Ethical standards and the law in relation to the practice of mental health have continually evolved over the past half-century, forcing cautious practitioners to be ever vigilant in their pursuit of the important details related to the acceptable standards of professional practice. But why are these issues important? For what reason do various professional organizations such as the International Association of Marriage and Family Counselors (IAMFC), American Counseling Association (ACA), and American Psychological Association (APA) publish the expected ethical standards for their members?

On the most basic of levels, the primary purpose for professional codes of ethics is the safety and well being of those served by the helping professions. Equally as important, ethical codes provide professionals with legitimate foundations in their pursuit of licensure and certification from state governments. Ethics also provide professionals with a higher aspirational standard than the simple reactionary guidelines established by lawmakers. According to Remley (1996), "*Law* defines the minimum standards society will tolerate; these standards are enforced by government. *Ethics* represents aspirational goals, or the maximum or ideal standards set by the profession, and they are enforced by professional associations, national certification boards, and government boards that regulate professions (pp. 285-292)."

---

[*] Michael J. Strazi, MA received his Master of Arts degree in Counseling from the University of Colorado at Denver.
[*] Patricia W. Stevens, Ph.D., is Professor and Chair at Morehead State University, Morehead, Kentucky.

Thus, it is the responsibility of the ethical practitioner to know the ethical standards set by his or her professional organization and to aspire to the highest ethical conduct.

It is also important for marital and family counselors to be aware of laws regulating the assessment of clients. Many states have such regulations. However, the specific requirements vary from state to state. For example, the State of Colorado has established educational requirements for the use of psychological tests, depending upon whether the practitioner intends the test to be used for general, technical, or advanced purposes (CRS 12-43-228). For general use, no specific educational requirements are mandated. For technical use, or for those tests that require the application of scientific and psychophysiological knowledge (such as intelligence, aptitude, temperament, personality or interest inventories), one is required to possess a master's degree in a human services field. The practitioner must also have completed at least one graduate level course each in statistics, psychometric measurement, theories of personality, individual and group test administration and interpretation, and psychopathology.

The requirements are more stringent for advanced use, or any battery of three or more tests used to determine diagnostic or causative information, or to make predictions of a client's psychological response to medical, surgical and behavioral interventions. Tests falling in this category include projective tests and neuropsychological tests, among others, depending on the intended use of the instrument. Those practitioners wishing to utilize psychological tests to provide this kind of advanced information must meet all the requirements for technical use, in addition to the completion of at least one graduate level course each in the following areas: Cognition, emotion, attention, sensory-perceptual function, psychopathology, learning, encephalopathy, neuropsychology, psychophysiology, personality, growth and development, projective testing, and neuropsychological testing. They must also have completed at least one year of experience in advanced use practice under the supervision of a person fully qualified under the law.

As mentioned above, laws and regulations regarding testing and assessment in counseling or psychological practice, vary from state to state. It is important for practitioners interested in maintaining an ethical and legal practice to familiarize themselves with their local and state regulations, if any exist, and to adhere to those rules when engaging in the assessment of their clients.

In relation to the assessment of couples and families, there are many specific ethical issues faced by practitioners. First, counselors must determine what type of assessment is most appropriate for a particular client or situation. Keep in mind, as well, that it is difficult if not impossible to divorce assessment from treatment when working with couples and families. That is, the process of assessment is ongoing throughout the course of counseling through the use of informal assessment techniques such as observation, as opposed to the more time-limited and formal assessment techniques such as the use of tests and structured diagnostic interviews. While testing is a common practice for many professionals, there are a variety of other assessment methods available. Perhaps the most common form of assessment is the clinical interview, consisting of a face to face discussion between counselor and client. Another common informal assessment technique is observation, which typically continues throughout the course of treatment. Marital and family counselors can potentially learn a wealth of information about their clients by observing them interact in session. In fact, this is an ideal way to experience the family dynamic as it occurs. Counselors can also gather information on families (particularly children) from other sources in the community, such as teachers, coaches, and ministers. In gathering and using such reports, the counselor must take every step to ensure they maintain their client's confidentiality, and to obtain informed consent prior to soliciting the outside information.

Practitioners choosing to use formal tests to assess a client must be competent and qualified to administer the their tests of choice. Practitioners must be mindful of issues such as identifying exactly *who* will be the client—one identified individual, or the entire family unit, or particular subsets of the family unit, such as the children? In some instances, the client may in fact be the educational or legal system, in which case the counselor must pay special attention to the possible uses of their assessment results. In assessing couples or families from cultures other than that of the practitioner, an ethical assessor must familiarize himself or herself with that culture in order to make a valid assessment. In some cases, a counselor who is not familiar with a client's native language may not be able to produce valid assessment results. Technology also presents a variety of new ethical issues that must be examined such as the question of whether or how much to rely on computers for the testing or assessment of clients. The widespread use of managed mental health care has also forced the helping professions to adjust their previously held ethical beliefs around such issues as client confidentiality and diagnosis when using systemic theory. All of these and other issues are examined in further detail in this chapter. Where appropriate, case conceptualizations are included to help professionals-in-training better understand the application of ethical standards to professional life.

COMPETENCY IN TEST ADMINISTRATION

One vitally important area of ethical concern in testing and assessment is practitioner competence and training. Principle A of the *Ethical Principles of Psychologists and Code of Conduct* (APA, 1995) focuses on practitioner competence. According to this Principle:

> Psychologists strive to maintain high standards of competence in their work. They recognize the boundaries of their particular competencies and the limitations of their expertise. They provide only those services and use only those techniques for which they are qualified by education, training, or experience...They maintain knowledge of the relevant scientific and professional information related to the services they render, and they recognize the need for ongoing education.

This principle is especially important in the assessment or testing of clients. There are a multitude of psychological tests that have been developed over the course of the past century, all of which require specialized training in their administration and scoring. The American Counseling Association (1995) also focuses on testing and assessment competence in its *Codes of Ethics and Standards of Practice:* "Counselors recognize the limits of their competence and perform only those testing and assessment services for which they have been trained."

Both the APA and the ACA maintain formal enforcement mechanisms in their respective codes of ethics that provide for consequences of ethical violations up to and including member suspension or expulsion (Camara, 1997). Organizations dedicated specifically to systemic practice, such as the IAMFC (2000), also include detailed ethical guidelines related to competence in assessment, stating that their members have the responsibility of acquiring and maintaining skills related to assessment procedures and assessment instruments, and to use assessment methods that are within the scope of their qualifications and training. IAMFC members using tests or inventories must have a thorough understanding of measurements concepts, and be familiar with the testing manual, the purpose of the instrument, and any relevant psychometric and normative data related to the test or instrument (Section IV).

Another professional organization that focuses on systemic work is the American Association for Marriage and Family Therapy (1991). The AAMFT's *Code of Ethics* includes a section on professional competence and integrity that outlines expectations of its members, including the possibility of expulsion from their organization should guidelines be violated (Section 3).

While most professional organizations in the helping fields address assessment and testing in their particular ethical codes, psychological testing has historically been seen primarily as a function of psychologists. However, in recognizing the fact that other helping professionals such as counselors and social workers also use a variety of assessment and measurement instruments, the APA has collaborated with both the American Educational Research Association (AERA) and the National Council on Measurement (NCME) on a set of multi-organizational ethical standards focused specifically on psychological testing. This is the *Standards for Educational and Psychological Testing* (AERA, APA & NCME, 1999). The guidelines outlined in these standards have now been in widespread use for several years, and are addressed in the ethical codes of other organizations including the IAMFC (2000), that states that its members strive to maintain those standards in assessing clients.

Why are these professional organizations so determined to ensure that practitioners are competent to administer, score and interpret the psychological tests they employ? One important facet of assessment is that the results can have very important positive or negative consequences for the client being assessed. On the positive side, it is often necessary in marital and family counseling as well as individual counseling to formulate a diagnosis. Counselors use assessment to arrive at the diagnosis and to collaborate with clients on their goals and treatment options. Without a thorough assessment, many viable treatment options might never be considered.

However, counselors must not forget that tests and assessments may also have negative implications, even when administered properly, depending on a variety of factors including the intended use of the assessment, along with its reliability and validity. Consider the aspiring student taking a test for college admissions. The results of this test will be instrumental in determining if the student is admitted to the college of their choice, or even if they are admitted to college at all. Therefore, it is important that the test actually measures the student's prospects for success in college, and whether or not the person scoring the test (or interpreting the computer-scored results) is competent to do so. In the case of an industrial psychologist working for a large corporation, psychological tests are sometimes used to determine employment or retention decisions. In the clinical arena, couples or families taking the Premarital Personal and Relationship Evaluation (PREPARE) or the Family Adaptability and Cohesion Evaluation Scales (FACES III) would not treated as appropriately as possible unless the interpretations of their answers are made by competent professionals qualified to administer, score and interpret those tests.

Although test developers and publishers stand to make immense profits from their tests, most publishers recognize the importance of tester competence as well. According to Hood and Johnson (1997), "a number of publishers will sell tests only to those who are qualified and require a statement of qualification from purchasers of psychological tests" (p.329). They go on to state that most publishers also require the test purchaser to have at minimum a master's degree and a course in psychological assessment as the minimum qualification for purchasing their tests. Even with these safeguards in place, it is ultimately up to the particular professional to ensure that they receive adequate training for any tests they utilize in their practice.

AREAS OF COMPETENCE

What are the particular competencies that determine whether or not a practitioner is competent to administer a particular psychological test? First, practitioners must know *when and why* to administer a test. They must *be familiar* with the tests and assessment tools at their disposal. They must know how to *choose the right test*. Finally, they must know how to *score* the test and *report* the results to the client.

When and Why

In clinical practice, in dealing with both individuals and couples or families, there is not always the necessity that psychological testing be performed. Other ways to assess couples and families include observation, peer reports, and the clinical interview. This is particularly true for the practitioner working from a systemic perspective in the treatment of a couple or family. However, according to Goldenberg & Goldenberg (1998), some counselors prefer to use planned interventions with couples and families that involve the precounseling use of standardized tests and measurements. These practitioners typically believe that the use of psychological tests provide an important supplement to their observational assessments in the area of obtaining an "insider's view" from the perspective of a member of the couple or family. However, such testing can be impractical, and may not generate sufficient data if used alone. One popular test frequently used in conjunction with interview and observational techniques in the assessment of couples and families is the Family Adaptability and Cohesion Evaluation Scales (FACES III) (Olson, 1986). This test was designed specifically for marital and family assessment. This test uses self-report measures completed by each family member that gauge both their perception of the family's current level of functioning and their ideal level of functioning. Discrepancies in scores reflect the degree of satisfaction and dissatisfaction each family member experiences in their daily family interactions.

Regardless of the chosen test, practitioners must be sure that they have identified their own reason for the administration of the test in order to remain ethical. Some considerations in making the choice include whether or not the test results will have any influence on the treatment plan, or whether the clinical questions covered by the test are truly in doubt and in need of clarification. If the answers to these questions are "no", the practitioner should question the necessity of performing time-consuming (and often expensive) psychological testing.

Familiarity and Choice of Test or Assessment

For those practitioners who choose to use psychological tests as part of their professional repertoire, it is important to be familiar with the variety of assessment tools available. This is a particular concern for practitioners who believe that testing is a useful supplement for all assessments. As mentioned above, psychological tests have been in development and use for decades. As family counseling is a more recent development, most of these tests have been geared toward individual assessment. However, there have been quite a few developed specifically with couples and families in mind. One valuable resource, as noted by Goldenberg & Goldenberg (1998), is a handbook entitled *Handbook of Family Measurement Techniques* by Touliatos, Perlmutter, and Straus (1990). This handbook reviews close to 1000 instruments currently in use for appraisal of marital and family functioning.

In becoming familiar with and choosing a particular instrument, the practitioner must keep in mind the questions that are to be answered by the instrument. The practitioner is also responsible for becoming familiar with the reliability and validity of the assessment method or test they choose to use. According to Section E.2. of the ACA Code of Ethics and Standards of Practice (ACA, 1995)

> Counselors recognize the limits of their competence and perform only those testing and assessment services for which they have been trained. They are familiar with reliability, validity, related standardization, error of measurement, and proper application of any technique utilized.

It is clear from this ethical standard that counselors must not conduct an assessment or administer a test until they have become familiar with the scientific research used to validate the test's usefulness in the assessment of a particular disorder or population. According to Camara (1997), "Validity is the overarching technical requirement for assessments..." (p.142). However, that report goes on to note that there are some other identified areas that are important for the practitioner to recognize. Those criteria are: how useful the test is overall, how fair the test is overall, and how well the test meets practical constraints (Cole & Willingham, 1997).

A test's usefulness is generally determined by its application to a particular purpose. For instance, a test that is designed to assist in diagnosis would not be very useful in determining a family's relational satisfaction. Similarly, a test of a couple's cohesion would not be useful in determining the presence of personality disorders.

Fairness in testing and assessment refers to the applicability of the assessment technique to the particular client's culture and background, in addition to how and in what conditions the test or assessment is administered. Another issue of fairness rests with the ultimate test user. Many employers and educational administrators who use test results to determine matters of practical concern such as admissions, employment, and retention, do not themselves understand the principles of validity and reliability, and often make unwarranted assumptions regarding the meaning of test results or assessment findings (Camara, 1997).

Finally, assessment (except in the most ideal research situations) must meet financial and time constraints in order to be of any practical use. In addition, assessment and testing techniques must not be unnecessarily intrusive to the client being assessed.

Once the counselor has become familiar with the variety of assessment techniques at their disposal, it is important that the counselor know how to choose the appropriate technique for their particular purpose. One important factor (to be discussed in more detail in a later section) is the client's culture or ethnic background. Unfortunately, the vast majority of psychological tests were designed and researched using a homogenous population, which brings into question their validity for use with those of differing cultural backgrounds.

Aside from this factor, other considerations in choosing an appropriate instrument involve determining the particular clinical questions to be answered. For instance, one would not choose an IQ test to determine the presence of a mood disorder. This, of course, is an obvious example, but many clinical questions are not so straightforward. Suppose that one is asked to perform a forensic evaluation to diagnose a defendant and determine fitness for trial. There are a variety of tests that could be employed in this situation, depending entirely upon the clinical presentation of the client. In many cases, the choice of test will be dependent upon the theoretical orientation of the particular practitioner. The important ethical factor is to make every effort to match the test to the client and the goal of the assessment.

Scoring and Reporting Results

The final area of counselor competence in the use of assessment techniques (particularly psychological tests) involves scoring tests and reporting test results. Many tests may now be scored by computer, which may be a more reliable scoring method than hand-scoring. However, it is up to the practitioner to ensure that whatever the scoring method, the test results are accurate for the particular test-taker. There are many factors that may skew test results, such as the temperature in the room at the time of the test, the time of day the test was taken, or the mood of the test taker. Other concerns include the question of cultural applicability. What population was the test normed on, and if it was different from the culture of the test taker, how valid can the results be? Competent test users recognize these confounding variables and consider them in interpreting test results.

Perhaps a more frequently occurring ethical concern involves the reporting of test results. There are also a variety of legal requirements focusing on this aspect of assessment. One primary concern of practitioners and clients is confidentiality. Each professional organization for the helping professions focuses on confidentiality as an important tenet of their ethical codes. According to Hood and Johnson (1997) clients have a right to know their test results. However, this can present ethical dilemmas in the area of client confidentiality, particularly in the course of couples or family therapy, where there is likely to be more than one individual present when assessment results are communicated. Confidentiality as a general ethical concern in the treatment of couples and families is addressed in more detail later in the chapter.

Confidentiality issues aside, the counselor is faced with ensuring that the client truly understands their assessment results. "They must be interpreted to clients in such a way that clients understand what the tests mean and also what they do not mean" (Hood and Johnson, p.331). They go on to report that results should be presented descriptively whenever possible, and that the use of stigmatizing labels should be avoided. In other words, the ethical counselor should consider when reporting their findings that the average person has not attended graduate school in counseling or psychology. One cannot expect clients to understand results that are reported in numbers and technical jargon. The counselor must make every effort synthesize their test and assessment results into a clear and easily understandable report that, while giving the client a clear picture of the results, does not leave room for overgeneralization or misinterpretation.

In general, counselors have the responsibility to make every effort to ensure that clients do not come to unwarranted conclusions based on their assessment results. As part of this requirement, the counselor is also responsible for educating others who may view the results, such as other practitioners, school administrators, or employers, in order that the results not be misused. This requirement is outlined in Section 2.02 b of the APA's *Ethical Principles* (APA, 1995). According to that guideline:

> Psychologists refrain from misuse of assessment techniques, interventions, results, and interpretations and take reasonable steps to prevent others from misusing the information these techniques provide. This includes refraining from releasing raw test results or raw data to persons, other than to patients or clients as appropriate, who are not qualified to use such information.

In addition to this requirement, it is the responsibility of the practitioner to make sure that obsolete test results are not used as the basis for decision-making (APA, 1995). The ACA (1995) also addresses this issue in section E.4 of their code of ethics:

> Counselors do not misuse assessment results, including test results, and interpretations, and take reasonable steps to prevent the misuse of such by others...Counselors ordinarily release data (e.g., protocols, counseling or interview notes, or questionnaires) in which the client is identified only with the consent of the client or the client's legal representative. Such data are usually released only to persons recognized by counselors as competent to interpret the data.

Considering the multi-faceted area of counselor competence in choosing and administering tests and assessment techniques, it is clear why the various professional organizations such as the ACA, APA, and IAMFC place such high importance on this requirement. However, the ultimate responsibility for ethical testing and assessment, as with any other area of ethical concern, lies with individual counselors and professional training programs.

ETHICAL CONCERNS SPECIFIC TO COUPLES AND FAMILY ASSESSMENT

The guidelines exemplified in the formal codes established by the various professional organizations may be applied to almost all areas of psychotherapy and assessment. However, there are some areas of particular concern to those practitioners engaging in treatment and assessment of couples and families. Some frequent concerns in this arena include client confidentiality, multiple loyalties, conflicts between therapist values and client values, and coercion in treatment. These areas are examined in detail in this section of the chapter.

Confidentiality Issues

Professional organizations such as the ACA, IAMFC, and AAMFT recognize special confidentiality concerns when working with couples or families. There are a multitude of ethical dilemmas specific to the practice of family counseling that may not be of issue when treating individuals. What does the practitioner do in the case of the spouse who wants to be seen individually as well? What is the expectation for the presence of secrets in therapy? At what point must a therapist draw the line on disclosure in session? Of course, one may argue that while using informal assessment techniques such as observation of a couple's interactions (a particularly frequent technique for marital and family counseling) or joint clinical interviewing, all assessment results are open to be used in session and discussed with all clients present. However, when considering more formal assessment techniques such as tests, the counselor must consider the confidentiality rights of the client being assessed, even if the counselor believes the treatment process would benefit from full disclosure.

Another question in assessing members of a family revolves around how information will ultimately be used. Will one partner use the other's diagnosis or assessment results against them in custody battles or other court proceedings? According to Biggs & Blocher (1987), "the ethical counselor can never divorce himself or herself from the context in which the assessment information will ultimately be used. Typically, assessment information is used to make decisions that impact on the lives of individual human beings" (p.91). These are all questions with which practitioners who work with couples and families struggle. The ACA's *Codes of Ethics and Standards of Practice* (ACA, 1995) addresses the issue of client confidentiality in couples and family work with very clear-cut language. "In family counseling, information about one family member cannot be disclosed to another member without permission. Counselors protect the privacy rights of each family member" (Standard B.2.b.). This code is intended to assist professional counselors in avoiding ethical misconduct in the area of confidentiality.

However, the counselor is still presented with a dilemma. Suppose that one spouse informs the counselor in private or on the telephone that they are having an extramarital affair. This presents the counselor with an ethical conundrum. Should the counselor bring up this issue in conjoint session? The ACA guidelines make it clear that this would be an ethical violation. Should the counselor refuse to see the couple unless the spouse agrees to disclose to the other? This presents other ethical issues, such as client abandonment.

According to Margolin (1998), the guiding principle in dealing with client confidentiality in couples or family therapy is that the therapist must clearly define his/her policy and communicate that policy to the clients at the outset of therapy. In order for the professional counselor to remain ethical per ACA guidelines, they must avoid the above situation by making it clear to the clients prior to the start of counseling what their policy is on secrets. If no secrets are to be allowed in counseling, the counselor must obtain consent from all involved parties authorizing that all information disclosed may be shared with all parties involved in the counseling. As discussed by Corey, Corey and Callahan (1998):

> Family therapists have different perspectives on maintaining confidentiality. Some treat all information they receive from a family member just as if the person were in individual therapy. Others refuse to see any member of the family separately, claiming that doing so fosters unproductive alliances and promotes the keeping of secrets. And others tell family

members that they will exercise their own judgement about what to disclose from and individual session in a marital or family session.

It is clear that there is no absolute ethical answer to this question. In light of the complex issue of confidentiality in this context, one might wonder why a therapist might choose to maintain secrets at all. According to Margolin (1998), a policy that maintains individual secrets has the benefit of obtaining information that might help the therapist better understand the family or couple dynamic. For instance, a therapist may encounter a couple where the female seems particularly reluctant to speak in front of her partner. The therapist may decide to see that spouse privately to determine if there are issues of abuse or other issues that are causing the limited involvement in therapy. If the therapist has stated a policy at the outset that eliminates the possibility of keeping secrets, that spouse would likely be more reluctant to reveal any information to the therapist, further stalling progress.

There are multiple other possible examples where the question of keeping secrets in couples and family counseling plays an important role in therapeutic outcomes. Individual practitioners must be mindful of this issue, and determine for themselves the best possible policy for their practice, or their particular clients.

Multiple Loyalties

The issue of multiple loyalties in couples and family therapy is at first glance linked primarily to the issue of confidentiality. However, there are other concerns involved in treating more than one person in a family unit besides confidentiality. Consider the family that comes to the initial session with their two small children in tow. The parents spend the entire session complaining about the behavior of the children, and demand that the practitioner "fix" the children or eliminate the behavior. In this case, the parents consider the children to be the primary clients in the therapeutic process.

In the course of the session, however, the practitioner may learn that the parents have been arguing frequently, have been distant with one another, or have what seems to be a volatile interactive style. They may be contemplating a separation or divorce. The practitioner may determine that this family would be best served by seeing the parents in couples' treatment rather than seeing the children. In this case, the clients and the provider have conflicting ideas about who is the primary focus of treatment.

How does the practitioner ethically reconcile this issue? His or her assessment of the situation is that the system will be changed through couples' therapy, resulting in a quicker and more efficient change in the children's behavior, but the parents are insisting that the problem lies in the children, and therefore, the children should be the ones in therapy. In most likely scenarios, the counselor will provide the clients with the best treatment possible within the realm of competent practice. Typically, a counselor faced with the above situation may choose to see the entire family, or start out seeing the children alone, then gradually shift the focus of treatment to the parents. In any case, the counselor must base the treatment methods on the assessment, and provide the best possible care under the presenting conditions.

ISSUES OF DIVERSITY

Since the early 1970's, the counseling profession has begun to examine the issues involved in counseling those from diverse backgrounds. In terms of history, this focus on multiculturalism is a relatively recent, although important development (Quinn, 1993). Prior to this, the issues raised by advocates of a more culturally sensitive counseling were paid little attention. Now, however, a course in multicultural counseling is required of accredited graduate counseling programs. Why the emphasis? This new multicultural awareness stems in large part from the previously mentioned concept of "fairness" in assessment. According to Sedlacek and Kim (1995), many widely used measures have established reliability and validity only within White racial samples. However, these measures often are used inappropriately and unethically with populations from different cultures. This exemplifies the problems inherent in using assessment instruments without being fully trained on the methods used to arrive at the normative data. As recently as the early to mid-ninties, researchers such as Pope and Vasquez (1991) and Keitel, Kopala, and Adamson (1996) emphasized the need for education and training in cultural issues, and predicted that this need would increase steadily into the twenty-first century, as the cultural demographics continue to trend toward the United States becoming a nation with no real ethnic majority.

Both the ACA and IAMFC, among others, now include sections on diversity in assessment in their respective ethical codes. According to Section E.8 of the ACA's Code of Ethics and Standards of Practice (1995):

> Counselors are cautious in using assessment techniques, making evaluations, and interpreting the performance of populations not represented in the norm group on which an instrument was standardized. They recognize the effects of age, color, culture, disability, ethnic group, gender, race, religion, sexual orientation, and socioeconomic status on test administration and interpretation and place test results in proper perspective with other relevant factors.

The IAMFC's (2000) ethical codes also address issues of cultural diversity, noting that its members have the responsibility to become educated about issues of cultural diversity and those populations and culture with which they are not naturally familiar.

> Members are committed to gaining cultural competency, including awareness, knowledge, and skills to work with a diverse clientele. Members are aware of their own biases, values, and assumptions about human behavior. They employ techniques/assessment strategies that are appropriate for dealing with diverse cultural groups.

While the issues of cultural awareness are necessary for individual counseling as well as educational testing, they are also important for counselors engaged in marital and family counseling. Counselors trained in western tradition are necessarily taught the theories and practices developed over the last century of psychological treatment research. Unfortunately for the culturally minded counselor, those theories are predominately euro-centric.

Marital and family counselors must recognize the importance of understanding the cultural context of their client families. These families not only have their own dynamic unique to that family and based on its history, but also a dynamic that is highly influenced by a worldview that may be vastly different from the counselor's. According to the Hood and Johnson (1997):

An understanding of the client's worldview is important, because the initial step in the counseling process is to understand the client and his or her issues and problems. Worldview includes the individual's perceptions of human nature (good or evil); focus on the past, present, or future; the emphasis given to individual or group goals; and locus of responsibility (internal or external)...

The "worldview" referred to above is in reference to the manner in which those from different cultural backgrounds view the world from different "lenses." The western ideal of individualism and self-determinism is in sharp contrast to several other cultures throughout the world that tend more to emphasize the collective good as the primary life and family focus. Counselors must be careful not to impose their values on client families that are approaching their presenting issues from that viewpoint. Additionally, counselors must understand that their idea of "healthy family functioning" may not be the ideal functioning style for their clients. In assessing these clients, counselors must be aware that what they might see as "symptomatology" may be part of the family's healthy interactional style.

WORKING WITH MANAGED CARE

Over the past two decades, one major adjustment many counselors have had to make is in learning to work with managed behavioral healthcare. While marital and family counselors have all been taught the theories and practices to provide care to couples and families, few have had any educational experience in how to work within the constraints of managed care oversight. The issues can seem daunting at times and many counselors simply choose not to work with managed behavioral healthcare organizations (MBHO's). However, as more people and employers choose to enroll in these organizations, marital and family counselors must as a practical concern learn to work with them. In fact, counselors who are managed-care savvy can and do learn to grow their practices and prosper under this oversight.

Ethical concerns, however, do come up, especially in the realm of assessment. Many counselors, depending upon their theoretical orientation, take objection to the idea of identifying one particular family member as the identified patient (IP). However, this is a requirement of most MBHO's. This requirement is based on the fact that the MBHO will not cover treatment that is not "medically necessary." The concept of medical necessity is an important one to understand, and is primarily related to the diagnosis. While there are diagnoses specifically related to interactional problems between couples and family members (called "v-codes" and found in the DSM IV), these diagnoses are not typically accepted by managed care companies, as they do not represent a psychiatric or psychological disorder. Therefore, in order to work with managed care, the martial or family counselor must be ready to identify a family member as the IP and assign that person a diagnosis.

In order to remain ethical when assessing couples and families, counselors must pay close attention to the symptoms and patterns between members, and explain to the couple or family about MBHO rules, and the fact that one of them must be identified as the patient. Some families or couples may object to this, especially the family member who is the IP! If they do object, the counselor must be prepared to let them know that they can choose the self-pay option, which will allow them to proceed with counseling without a diagnosis. Another ethical option at this point is to offer them a referral to another counselor.

Marital and family counselors working within MBHO's will find, however, that most families and family members understand (even if they may not agree with) the terms of their managed-care contracts, and are willing to have one member be identified as a patient. Counselors may find that in many cases, the family would rather this be the case, as most wish to avoid the stigma of having their family system labeled as dysfunctional! In these cases, counselors should use their judgment to determine which member is manifesting symptoms, and proceed to work in a systemic way with as many family members as necessary to provide the treatment required.

Counselors can use a variety of assessment techniques, both informal and formal, to determine diagnosis and course of treatment. However, they must be prepared to endure additional oversight if they wish to employ many formal assessment techniques, and be reimbursed for the process. While MBHO's do require a diagnosis and treatment plan, most will not give blanket approval for psychological tests, especially if those tests are expensive, and they have other counselors within their system who have shown expertise in treating couples or families without using tests. In cases where the counselor feels formal testing is required to determine diagnosis or treatment course, the counselor should contact the MBHO for approval (if they wish to be reimbursed specifically for the testing). This request may be denied, in which case, the counselor must choose whether to provide the testing at no additional charge, or offer the clients a referral. The counselor typically may also choose to allow the client to self-pay for non-covered services, if this is allowed under their MBHO contract.

Below is a listing of pointers for marital and family counselors who wish to work with MBHO's. These are restrictions that may be placed by managed care, and may present the counselor with ethical dilemmas. However, most managed care companies recognize the value of treating the system, and many even require it as the most desirable modality of care for specific populations. Treatment of the marital dyad is also supported by most managed care companies, but there are some simple rules to remember when treating your clients who belong to MBHO's:

- **V-Codes are "Free-Codes."** While managed care recognizes that relationship and communication issues are important for family and marital stability, all treatment must be based on medical need.
- **Specific Procedures are not covered.** Do not expect to receive additional reimbursement from the MBHO for performing any particular techniques. Members and providers are frequently disappointed to learn that they will not be offered additional compensation for formal assessment techniques such as psychological testing, or treatment techniques such as Eye Movement Desensitization and Restructuring (EMDR) and biofeedback. Most HMO contracts do not pay for this sort of treatment, but counselors will usually still be paid for the therapy hour.
- **Co-Therapy is not a covered benefit.** It will be the rare case in which the MBHO will pay for couples or families to be seen by two therapists. The primary rationale for this is that the same benefit can usually be achieved through treatment with one skilled therapist.
- **Treatment of multiple family members.** While most MBHO's do not prohibit this practice outright, it is frowned upon. If the counselor is truly doing family therapy, there need be only one identified patient. Goals of treatment should be based on

finding solutions to that client's problems, and if counselors are practicing from a systemic framework, the other family members will continue to be a focus of treatment, even if the counselor is not being reimbursed separately for them.

These are just a few of the common requests that most likely will not be covered by MBHO's. However, there are certain types of managed-care contracts that allow the counselor the freedom to operate in whatever manner they please. If counselors operate under a capitated or "case-rate" system, they can usually employ most any assessment procedure. This is also the case for those counselors working on inpatient units. Typically, the MBHO in those cases pays a flat rate, and the responsibility for fiscal management resides with the counselor or the counselor's employer.

IN CONCLUSION

Considering all the important nuances of assessment in systemic work, it is incumbent upon the ethical practitioner to learn the legal requirements of their locality, and to become cognizant of the ethical guidelines of their specific professional organization. In this era of heightened legal awareness, the possibility of becoming involved in a lawsuit is not only real, but also to be expected. Given this, counselors must make every effort to consider questions of multiple loyalties, confidentiality, and competence to complete certain formal assessments. Newer challenges such as those arising from increased cultural diversity among the United States population and the rise of managed care only add to the possible ethical dilemmas one might face.

In order to maintain the highest ethical standards, marital and family counselors must remember to consult with colleagues and supervisors when faced with an ethical question, and to continually educate themselves on the current legal environment and latest new techniques. One way to be sure and stay up to date is to become actively involved in your professional organization's local chapter. However one chooses to maintain their level of competence, the key to maintaining the highest level of ethics is to always keep ethics in mind when assessing, treating, and interacting with clients.

REFERENCES

American Association for Marriage and Family Therapy (1991). *AAMFT code of ethics.* Washington, DC: Author.

American Counseling Association (1995). *Code of ethics and standards of practice.* Alexandria, VA: Author.

American Educational Research Association, American Psychological Association, and National Council on Measurement in Education. (March, 1999). *Standards for educational and psychological testing* (Rev.). Washington, DC: American Educational Research Association.

American Psychological Association (1995). *Ethical principles of psychologists and code of conduct.* Washington, DC: Author.

Biggs, D. & Blocher, D (1987). *Foundations of ethical counseling.* New York: Springer Publishing Company.

Camera, W.J. (1997). Use and consequences of assessments in the USA: Professional, ethical, and legal issues. *European Journal of Psychological Assessment, 13,* 140-152.

Cole, N. & Willingham, W. (1997). *Gender and fair assessment.* Hillsdale, NJ: Erlbaum.

Goldenberg, H. & Goldenberg, I. (1998). *Counseling Today's Families* (3rd ed.). Pacific Grove, CA: Brooks/Cole Publishing Company.

Hood, A. & Johnson, R. (1997). *Assessment in counseling: A guide to the use of psychological assessment procedures (2nd ed.).* Alexandria, VA: American Counseling Association.

International Association of Marriage and Family Counselors (2000). *Ethical guidelines.* [On line]. Available: *www.iamfc.org*

Keitel, M.A., Kopala, M., & Adamson, W.S. (1996). Ethical issues in multicultural assessment. In L.A. Suzuki, P.J. Meller, & J.G. Ponterotto (Eds.), *Handbook of multicultural assessment: Clinical, psychological, and educational applications* (pp. 29-48). San Francisco: Jossey-Bass.

Margolin, G. (1998). Ethical issues in marital therapy. In R. Anderson, T. Needles, & H. Hall (Eds.), *Avoiding ethical misconduct in psychology specialty areas.* Springfield, IL: Charles C. Thomas: Publisher.

Olson, D.H. (1986). Circumplex model VII: Validation studies and FACES III. *Family Process, 26,* 337-351.

Pope, K.S., & Vasquez, M.J.T. (1991). *Ethics in psychotherapy and counseling: A practical guide for psychologists.* San Francisco: Jossey-Bass.

Quinn, J.R. (1993). Evaluation and Asessment for Transcultural Counseling. In J. McFadden, (Ed.), *Transcultural counseling:.Bilateral and an international perspectives* (1st ed.). Alexandria, VA: American Counseling Association.

Remley, T.P. (1996). The relationship between law and ethics. In B. Herlihy & G. Corey, (Eds.), *ACA ethical standards casebook* (5th ed.) (pp. 285-292). Alexandria, VA: American Counseling Association.

Sedlacek, W.E. & Kim, S.H. (1995). *Multicultural assessment.* ERIC Digest. [online]. Greensboro, NC: ERIC Clearinghouse on Counseling and Student Services.

Touliatos, J., Perlmutter, B.F., & Straus, M.A. (Eds.). (1990). *Handbook of family measurement techniques.* Newbury Park, CA: Sage Publications.

INDEX

A

abuse investigations, 203
abusing alcohol or drugs, 224
academic and family functioning, 74
accidental infidels, 142
Achenbach System of Empirically Based Assessment (ASEBA), 99, 103
Activities of Daily Living, 112
additional assessment targets, 9
adolescent and family developmental issues, 103
adolescent assessment, 69, 73
adolescent developmental period, 67, 68
adolescent psychology, 68
Adolescent Psychopathology Scale, 74, 106
Adolescent socio-emotional functioning, 73
Adolescent-Adult Parenting Inventory (AAPI), 176
Adolescents in family therapy, 103
adverse drug effects, 113
affair partner, 131, 133, 134, 136, 137, 142
age-related problem, 116
aggressive behavior, 79, 81, 82, 189, 227
aging family system, 109, 112
alcohol or drug abuse, 226
American Association for Marriage and Family Therapy, 15, 200, 278, 288
American Counseling Association (ACA), 275, 277, 280, 282, 283, 285, 288, 289
American Educational Research Association (AERA), 278
American Psychological Association (APA), 23, 45, 47, 74, 103, 104, 106, 107, 113, 116, 125, 126, 208, 218, 219, 239, 274, 275, 277, 278, 282, 288
anatomically detailed (AD) dolls, 208, 210, 211, 217-220
anxious child, 158

apprenticeship positions, 169
assessing couples and families, 286
assessing couples, 22, 49, 51, 70, 277
assessing parenting capabilities, 168, 172
assessing parenting capability, 168, 169, 178
assessment instruments, 7-9, 16, 18, 25, 38, 41, 132, 176, 181, 184, 191, 193, 195, 204, 205, 226, 241, 244, 246, 252, 253, 255, 278, 285
assessment of abuse, 191
assessment of couples and families, 9, 276, 279, 282
assessment of individual psychopathology, 133
assessment of infidelity, 129
assessment of parenting capability, 168, 171, 172, 176, 180, 185
assessment of substance abuse, 225
assessment of the couple, 49, 140, 149
assessment questionnaires, 249
assessment skills, 67
assessment strategies, 9, 23, 24, 285
assessment techniques, 5, 9, 179, 244, 255, 276, 281-283, 285, 287
assessment tools and techniques, 4, 9, 11, 49
assessment tools, 4, 7-10, 16, 18, 19, 40, 49, 113, 173, 193, 196, 234, 235, 249, 251-253, 279, 280

B

BASC-Parent Rating Scale (BASC-PRS), 85, 100
BASC-Teacher Rating Scale (BASC-TRS), 85, 100
Beavers Interactional Competence Scale, 28, 33
Beavers Interactional Style Scale, 28
Beavers Systems Model (BSM), 37-39, 45
Beavers Systems Model of Family Functioning, 38, 39, 45
Beck Depression Inventory-II (BDI-II), 86, 97

Beck Hopelessness Scale (BHS), 86-88, 97, 103
Behavior Assessment System for Children (BASC), 80, 83-85, 100, 105, 106, 266, 273
Behavior Assessment System for Children-Self-Report of Personality (BASC-SRP), 80, 85, 100
behavior checklist measures, 85
behavior problems, 12, 112, 117, 219, 266, 271
behavior rating forms, 9
behavioral observations, 21, 42
behavioral-systems assessment, 69
betrayed partners, 136, 140
Bicognitive Orientation to Life Scale (BOLS), 252

C

child abuse laws, 170
Child Abuse Potential (CAP) Inventory, 39, 40, 176
Child Behavior Checklist (CBCL), 79, 81-83, 85, 99, 101, 102, 216, 218, 266, 272
Child Depression Inventory, 86, 97
Child Directed Interaction (CDI), 43, 86-89, 97
child maltreatment victims, 203
child protection services, 172
child protective agencies, 203
child sexual abuse assessment, 204, 208
child sexual abuse evaluation, 216
child sexual abuse interviews, 210
child sexual abuse, 203, 204, 215, 216
child welfare policy, 169
child welfare programs, 171
child's environment, 168
child-centered play therapy techniques, 218
child-centered play therapy, 209, 211, 212
children dealing with divorce, 156
children of divorce, 147
chronic drug and alcohol use, 227
Circumplex Assessment Package
Circumplex Model of family functioning, 29
Circumplex Model of Marital and Family Systems, 39, 40, 46
Circumplex Model, 9, 28, 29, 39, 40, 46
client confidentiality, 277, 281, 282, 283
clinical checkpoint(s), 15, 17-19
clinical interview(ing), 9, 21, 22, 24, 25, 28, 42, 44, 114, 225, 232, 253, 276, 279, 283
clinical interviews, 21, 44, 183
clinical outliers, 16, 18
Clinical Rating Scale (CRS), 28, 30, 39-41, 276
Clinician Rating Scales, 27
clinician rating scales, 38

Codes of Ethics and Standards of Practice, 277, 283
coding systems, 27, 28, 38, 58
cognitive development, 68, 69, 175
cognitive functioning, 111, 112, 116
cognitive impairment, 111, 113, 115, 116, 119, 122
Commitment Inventory (CI), 9
comprehensive conceptual model, 22, 23, 42, 70, 74, 100
concept of forgiveness in treatment, 143
conceptual egocentrism, 68
conducting parental assessments, 168
confidentiality ISSUEs, 283
confidentiality, 72, 281
Conflict Behavior Questionnaire (CBQ), 96, 99
conflict management skills, 143
Conflict Tactics Scale (CTS), 191
context of infidelity, 131
Coopersmith Self-Esteem Inventories, 92, 98
cost effective therapy, 1
couple and family system(s), 3, 9-11
couple relationship, 2, 3, 52, 56, 62
couple systems, 2
couple therapy, 49, 51-53, 60, 145, 191, 198, 199
couple's history, 59, 140, 196
couples affected by infidelity, 129
couples and family counseling, 284
couples therapy, 130
couples treatment, 129, 130, 133, 190
couples' functioning, 139, 141
cultural pluralism, 241
culturally and ethnically sensitive assessment instruments, 255
culturally different families, 245, 246
culturally sensitive assessment, 8, 243, 244, 247, 249, 253
culturally sensitive family assessment, 244, 252, 255
culturegram, 250

D

Dangerousness Assessment (DA), 192
Darlington Family Assessment System (DFAS), 29, 39-41, 47
definitions of infidelity, 129
delirium, 116
dementia, 116, 121, 126
developmental factors, 265
developmental life-cycle transition, 4
developmental stages, 2-4, 9, 24, 70, 151
developmental transitions, 3, 44

diagnosable mental disorder, 110
diagnosis and assessment of substance abuse, 228
Diagnostic and Statistical Manual of Mental Disorders (DSM), 49, 54, 77, 79, 81, 82, 86, 106, 113, 136-138, 192, 234, 286
diagnostic interview(s), 71, 209, 230, 276
diplomatic strategy, 155
distressed families, 27, 30, 32, 95, 96
distressed relationships, 27
divorce assessment, 147, 148
divorced parents, 149, 157
divorced people, 150
divorcing couple, 150, 153, 161
divorcing family, 149
divorcing person, 148, 150
divorcing spouse, 150
domestic violence, 52, 130, 131, 135, 170, 190, 198-201, 224, 225, 234
drug or alcohol use, 222
DSM diagnoses, 49, 79, 81, 82
DSM-IV guidelines, 86, 97
DSM-IV, 74, 77, 97, 113, 116, 192
Dyadic Adjustment Scale (DAS), 9, 30, 32, 58, 60, 62, 64, 65, 95, 139, 195, 251
Dyadic Perspective Taking Scale, 57
dynamic interpersonal relationship, 205
dynamics of family interaction, 11, 27
dysfunctional family systems, 4

E

ecobehavioral assessment, 69
effects of infidelity, 130, 134
effects of trauma, 138
emotional and behavioral adjustment in adolescents, 74
emotional infidelity, 129, 130, 138, 139
emotional intimacy, 130
emotional issues, 130
emotional relationships, 130
emotional structures, 35
emotional well-being, 112, 139
ethical and legal issues, 71, 275
Ethical Principles of Psychologists and Code of Conduct, 277
ethical standards, 275-278, 288, 289
ethnic minority families, 243
evaluating parenting capacity, 178
evaluation process, 24, 45, 72, 120, 203, 205-207, 212, 216
evaluators of sexual abuse, 206
experiential therapist, 50
extended clinical interview, 26

extramarital involvement(s), 129, 141, 144
extramarital sexual contact, 129

F

Family Adaptability and Cohesion Evaluation Scale, 29, 99, 251
Family Adaptability and Cohesion Evaluation Scale-IV (FACES-IV), 29, 96, 99
Family Adaptability and Cohesion Evaluation Scales (FACES III), 278, 279
family and couples therapy, 15
Family APGAR (FAPGAR), 30, 35, 37, 47, 266
Family Assessment Device (FAD), 30-35, 39, 41, 42, 45, 46, 95
Family Assessment Measure (FAM), 31, 35, 39, 42, 47
Family Assessment Measure-III (FAM-III), 31, 35, 47
Family Assessment Methods, 39
family assessment models, 22
family assessment sessions, 225
Family Assessment Wheel, 250
family assessment, 2, 6-8, 10, 11, 21, 25, 29, 40, 45-47, 70-72, 104, 107, 116, 118, 121, 239, 242, 244, 251, 252, 254, 256, 265
Family Concept Assessment Method (FCAM), 35
Family Concept Inventory (FCI), 31, 35, 47
Family Concept Q-Sort (FCQS), 36
family conflict, 36, 96, 111, 124, 187, 249
Family Crisis Oriented Personal Evaluation Scales (F-COPES), 36
Family Crisis Oriented Personal Evaluation Scales, 31, 36
Family Distress Index (FDI), 32, 36, 46
Family Environment Scale (FES), 31-34, 36, 46, 95, 99, 106
Family Evaluation Form (FEF), 32, 36, 45
family evaluator, 24
Family Functioning Index (FFI), 30, 33, 37
Family Functioning Questionnaire (FFQ), 37
Family Functioning Scale (FFS), 33, 37
family genogram, 26, 42, 44
family group formation, 261
family group participants, 264
family group support, 259
Family Health Scales (FHS), 29
family identity development (FID), 246
family interactions, 22, 24, 27, 28, 102, 225, 279
Family of Origin Scale, 56
family processes and group dynamics, 259
Family Solutions Program, 266-268, 273
family structures, 26, 32, 45, 112, 167, 241

family systems, 2, 26, 38, 39, 67, 69, 103, 107, 112, 186, 234, 239, 244, 247, 256
family therapist(s), 15, 24, 50, 67, 153, 194, 203, 221, 234
family therapy, 1, 2, 11-13, 22, 39, 47, 50, 51, 52, 53, 56, 59, 65, 70, 95, 99, 100, 104, 105, 107, 126, 144, 156, 179, 199, 201, 206, 219, 224, 239, 256, 257, 260, 272, 273, 281, 283, 284, 287
family treatment, 41, 260, 265
family violence, 52, 164, 170, 199, 200, 264
forgiveness, 158
formal assessment techniques, 287
foster care settings, 171, 181

G

general family conflict, 216
genetic regression therapy, 16
genograms, 9, 65
geriatric assessment, 116
Glass' Extramarital Justification Questionnaire, 141
global measures, 85
global self-report measures, 74
global self-report, 74
Goal Attainment Scaling (GAS), 2
group assessment, 269
group dynamics, 262, 263, 268, 269, 271, 273
group intervention process, 269
group leader behaviors, 262, 269
group leader(s), 259, 262-266, 268-271
group members, 261-263, 265
group membership, 263
group processes, 263, 269

H

Harter's Self-Perception Profile for Adolescents, 98
health problems, 77, 110, 158
high conflict divorce, 154, 156, 159
high-conflict, 154, 164
historical considerations, 265
histories of difficulties, 140
history of parenting assessments, 169
history of treatment, 140
Home Observation Assessment Method (HOAM), 28
Humiliating Marital Events, 139

I

immigrant families, 243, 250
impaired concentration, 116
inadequate parenting, 168
individual assessment sessions, 136
individual assessment, 7, 10, 50, 72, 133, 136, 252, 280
individual characteristics, 61, 182
individual child's temperament, 156
individual psychopathology, 22, 141
individual therapy assessment, 272
individual therapy, 2, 70, 134, 283
infidelity treatment, 130
infidelity types, 138
informal assessment techniques, 9, 276, 283
information-gathering process, 21
institutional treatment, 170
institutionalization, 111, 126
Instrumental Activities of Daily Living, 112
integrative models for family assessment, 38
International Association of Marriage and Family Counselors (IAMFC), 275, 277, 278, 282, 283, 285, 289
internet communication, 130
interpersonal contexts, 69
interpersonal relationship improvement, 272
intimate relationships, 51, 54, 55-57, 200
intrafamilial abuse, 216
Intrafamilial sexual abuse, 216
Issues Checklist, 94, 98, 101, 102

L

later life family, 118
level of standardization, 272
Locke-Wallace Marital Adjustment Test, 139

M

Major Depression, 77, 139
managed behavioral health care, 15, 16, 18, 19
managed behavioral health organization(s) (MBHO(s)), 15, 16, 18, 19, 286-288
managed behavioral healthcare, 286
managed care companies, 286, 287
managed care environment, 1, 5
managed care organization, 18
managed care providers, 2
managed care requirements, 4
managed care service delivery system, 17
managed care systems, 17
managed care treatment model, 18

managed care, 1, 15, 16, 19, 286-288
manipulation strategy, 154
marital and family assessment, 279
marital and family counseling, 278, 283, 285
marital and family counselors, 275, 276, 286-288
marital arrangements, 142
Marital Communication Inventory (MCI), 58
marital distress and infidelity, 131
Marital Problem-Solving Scale (MPSS), 58, 65
marital resume', 62, 63, 64
marital satisfaction, 131, 191, 196
marital violence, 188, 190, 199
McMaster Clinical Rating Scale (MCRS), 28, 41, 43
McMaster Model of Family Competence, 9
McMaster Model of Family Coping Skills, 9
McMaster Model of Family Functioning, 28, 39, 41, 42
McMaster Structured Interview of Family Functioning (MCSIFF), 30, 39, 41
Mealtime Interaction Coding System (MICS), 39, 41
measure of relationship violence, 193
medical framework, 171
mental disorder, 110
mental health fields, 167, 182
mental health practitioners, 241-243, 255
mental health problems, 195
mental health professionals, 72, 73, 107, 175, 176, 180, 182, 218, 220, 225, 251, 253
mental health services, 71, 82, 105, 110, 115, 249
mental health system, 224
mental health treatment, 16, 111
Millon Adolescent Personality Inventory, 74, 76, 105
Minnesota Multiphasic Personality Inventory-Adolescent (MMPI-A), 75, 78, 85, 103, 104, 233
model of infidelity, 129
Multicultural Experience Inventory (MEI), 253
multicultural genograms, 249
multicultural setting(s), 168, 182-184
Multicultural Time-Line Genogram, 250
Multidimensional Anxiety Scale for Children (MASC), 89, 97, 102, 105
multidimensional assessment tools, 115
multidimensional assessment, 109
multidimensional evaluations, 112
multidimensional, multidisciplinary approach, 112
multilevel assessment model, 21
multi-method assessment, 9, 10, 11
multiple assessment, 9, 10, 23

multiple family group intervention, 259, 267
multiple family group program, 266
multiple family group, 263, 266-268, 271, 272
multiple loyalties, 282, 284, 288
multi-system, multi-method assessment process, 9
multi-system, multi-method process, 10

N

narrative therapist, 50
National Council on Measurement (NCME), 278
neuropsychological tests, 113, 127, 276
nondistressed families, 27

O

observational coding system, 28
observational techniques, 22, 23, 27, 64, 279
Offer Self-Image Questionnaire for Adolescents-Revised (OSIQ-R), 91, 98
outcome assessment, 1, 2, 31
outpatient mental health services, 110
over the counter (OTC), 113

P

Parent Directed Interaction (PDI), 43
Parent-Adolescent Interaction Coding System (PAIC), 98
parent-adolescent interactions, 98
Parent-Adolescent Relationship Questionnaire, 96, 98
parental assessment techniques, 185
parental assessments, 168, 169, 172, 179, 185
parental conflicts, 153
parent-child attachment relationship, 174, 179
parenting assessments, 168, 171, 177, 178-184
parenting practices, 167, 182, 183
Parenting Stress Index, 177, 185
parenting styles, 167
patriarchal terrorism, 191, 198
Personality Inventory for Youth, 74, 75, 105
philanderers, 142
physical abuse, 178, 194
physical and mental health assessments of older adults, 111
physical and mental health, 111, 122
physical disorders, 112
physical health problems, 117
physical therapy, 17
physiological reactivity measures, 139
Piers-Harris Self-Concept Scale, 86, 90, 91, 97

Play therapists, 206
play therapy, 204-207, 209, 217, 218
post-modern systemic theory, 217
Post-Traumatic Stress Disorder, 137
practitioner competence and training, 277
practitioner competence, 277
Premarital Personal and Relationship Evaluation (PREPARE), 278
prevalence of infidelity, 129
primary identity, 247
Problem Centered Systems Therapy of the Family (PCSFT), 41
Problem-Solving, Communication, Roles, Affective Responsiveness, Affective Involvement, and Behavioral Control, 28
process dimensions, 266, 272
Process Model of Family Functioning, 35, 39, 41, 47
process of the family evaluation, 121
process of therapy, 1, 4, 10, 241, 251, 254
professional codes of ethics, 275
projective tests, 9, 276
psychiatric hospitals, 16, 228
psychological abuse, 192, 194
Psychological Assessment, 12, 46, 106, 107, 113, 126, 185, 219, 289
psychological assessments with older adults, 113
Psychological Maltreatment of Women Inventory (PMWI), 192
psychological services, 71, 72, 73, 111
psychological symptoms, 113, 189
psychological tests, 19, 107, 113, 168, 276-281, 287
psychometric instruments, 6, 228
psychosocial development, 68, 174

R

range of emotional reactions, 138
reconciliation, 153
rejection of cultural assimilation, 241
Relationship Belief Inventory, 55, 65
relationship history, 55, 57
report of sexual abuse, 217
Revised Children's Manifest Anxiety Scale (RCMAS), 88, 89, 97, 106
Reynolds Adolescent Adjustment Screening Inventory (RAASI), 74, 106
Reynolds Adolescent Depression Scale (RADS), 75, 77, 87, 88, 97, 101, 102, 106
romantic affairs, 142

S

safety assessment, 135
Secondary identity, 247, 255
secondary stages, 2
Self-Description Questionnaire II (SDQ-II), 93, 98, 101, 102
Self-Esteem Inventories (SEI), 92, 98
Self-Perception Profile for Adolescents (SPPA), 92, 98
self-report assessment measures, 97
Self-Report Family Inventory (SFI), 33, 37, 38, 39
self-report instruments, 9, 29, 266
self-report techniques, 38
self-reports, 5, 21, 36, 104, 234
self-soothing, 156
Semistructured Interview for Children and Adolescents (SICA), 99
sex friendships affairs, 130
sexual abuse assessment interview protocol, 218
sexual abuse assessment process, 214
sexual abuse assessment, 217
sexual abuse evaluation(s), 204, 208, 212, 218
sexual abuse investigation, 204
sexual abuse, 169, 178, 192, 203-206, 208, 212, 213, 216-220, 225, 234, 248
sexual behavior in children, 204, 208, 216
sexual infidelity, 138, 139, 144
sexually abused children, 204, 206, 215, 218, 219
sibling interaction, 28
situational context, 64
skills and accomplishments, 59, 64
Social Climate Scales, 36
social work framework, 171
socially divorce, 150
socio-emotional problems of adolescents, 70
specialized assessment tool(s), 15, 16, 18
specific assessment techniques, 21
specific measures, 70, 85
Spousal Assault Risk Assessment (SARA), 192
spousal homicide, 135
standardization, 8, 77, 87, 271, 280
standardized assessment instrument, 188, 253
standardized assessment tools, 10
standardized conditions, 7
standardized instructions, 7
standardized instrument, 8, 56
standardized tests, 9, 253, 279
Standards for Educational and Psychological Test(s)ing, 71, 278
State-Trait Anxiety Inventory (STAI), 75, 89, 97, 107

State-Trait Anxiety Inventory for Children (STAIC), 88, 89, 97, 107
structural components, 265
Structural Family Interaction Scale - Revised (SFIS-R), 34, 37
Structural Family Interaction Scale - Revised, 37
structured activity, 50
Structured Developmental History (SDH), 100
structured interaction tasks, 27, 38
structured interactions, 28
structured interviews, 9, 215
Student Observation System (SOS), 100
studies on infidelity, 130
substance abuse problem, 223, 224
substance abuse, 10, 16, 52, 53, 72, 104, 113, 116, 130, 141, 195, 196, 221, 224-229, 231-235, 238, 239, 270
Substance Use History Questionnaire, 226, 235
Suicide Ideation Questionnaire (SIQ), 88, 97
system, standardized instruments, 10
systemic framework, 249, 253, 288
systemic perspective, 22, 50, 51, 111, 169, 189, 279
Systems theory, 189

T

Teacher Report Form (TRF), 79, 81, 82, 84, 85, 99, 101, 102, 272
tertiary identity, 247
The Child Abuse Prevention and Treatment Act, 171
theoretically driven process, 50
therapeutic assessment process, 44, 71
therapeutic family assessment, 21, 22, 25
therapeutic process, 173, 174, 189, 206, 284
therapists, 1, 7, 8, 10, 16, 24, 27, 52, 54, 70, 71, 129, 130, 134-136, 188, 189, 193, 198, 203, 207, 220, 221, 231, 238, 245, 256, 287

timelines, 9
toddlers, 158
Traditionalism-Modernism Inventory (TMI), 252
transitions, 156
traumatic experience, 206
traumatic reactions, 137, 138
traumatic symptoms, 137
traumatized children, 205
treatment model, 1
treatment of infidelity, 135
treatment of partner abuse, 189
treatment processes, 1
Trimodal Interview Protocol (TMIP), 204
typical referral categories, 117

U

U.S. Department of Health and Human Services, 171, 178, 181, 203, 220
unstructured activity, 50
unstructured clinical interviews, 9

V

victims of child maltreatment, 171, 181, 203
victims of partner violence, 187
violence rates, 187
violent crimes, 187, 189

W

welfare of children, 171
White Anglo-Saxon Protestant (WASP), 243

Y

Youth Self Report Form (YSR), 79-82, 85, 99, 101, 102, 272